MRS.

Mrs. R

THE LIFE OF ELEANOR ROOSEVELT

Mrs. R

THE LIFE OF
Eleanor Roosevelt

ALFRED STEINBERG

G. P. PUTNAM'S SONS, NEW YORK

© 1958 by Alfred Steinberg

Published simultaneously in the Dominion of Canada by Longmans, Green & Company, Toronto.

Library of Congress Catalog Card Number: 58-10758

MANUFACTURED IN THE UNITED STATES OF AMERICA

To Florence

16 pages of illustrations
will be found following page *160*.

Mrs. R

THE LIFE OF ELEANOR ROOSEVELT

Chapter One

It was a typical weekend at Sagamore Hill in Oyster Bay during the Gay Nineties. The shy, gawky orphan girl had come to spend a few days with Uncle Ted and Aunt Edith's family. Only thirty-six magical hours and she would have to return again to Grandmother Hall's dull place at Tivoli on the Hudson.

The morning was warm but a gentle breeze was stirring as Eleanor Roosevelt's carriage moved onto the stone driveway. Above the crunching jarring noise she could hear her Cousin Alice laughing and ordering the assembled dozen or more Roosevelt cousins to do her bidding in the spacious yard. The half-brick, half-frame house high on the Long Island hilltop sprang into view. Nervously, Eleanor patted her sailor hat, plucked at the balloon sleeves and made a vain effort to stretch her too-short dress below her knees.

"Hello! Dear Eleanor!" Uncle Ted called from the porch, and with a spring he was down the stairs and helping her out of the carriage. Not yet Assistant Secretary of the Navy, or the dashing leader of the Rough Riders, let alone Governor of New York or President of the United States, he was nevertheless renowned even then as an author, U. S. Civil Service Commissioner and the crime-fighting Commissioner of the New York City Police.

"Eleanor, my darling Eleanor." He hugged her to his burly chest. "*Dee*-lighted you came."

"He was a bear," his wife Edith later described the scene. He was so excited at seeing the daughter of his beloved dead brother Elliott "that he tore all the gathers out of Eleanor's frock and both buttonholes out of her petticoat."

From the time she alit from the carriage into Uncle Ted's arms until she waved a sad good-by, young Eleanor's shyness vanished. Her uncle's gargantuan enthusiasm and love for her made the hours fly by like minutes. For more than a day she was able to cast aside her personal burdens. Her blue eyes sparkled and her sandy hair felt radiantly blond as she joined her wildly excited cousins in breathless madcap games led by Uncle Ted.

And these were without end until the children fell exhausted upon the lawn and Aunt Edith cast a reproving stare at her boy-husband. "You must always remember," Sir Cecil Spring-Rice, British diplomat and a friend of his, wrote seven years later when he presided at the White House, "that the President is about six." His idea, for instance, of teaching children to swim was to toss them off the dock into deep water. Rather than suffer this fate, ten-year-old Eleanor, garbed in pantalettes to her ankles and wearing a heavy skirt over them, had jumped in before he could nab her and came up coughing and hacking from all the water she swallowed.

They ran through the hayloft with Uncle Ted in menacing pursuit. He spun yarns with the straw still in their hair. He showed them his game room with the animal heads on the walls. And before they were rested he led them in a game called "Handicap Race" down Cooper's Bluff, the dizzily steep sandbank that ended in cold Long Island Sound. With Uncle Ted in front, Eleanor and the others lined up behind him and went racing down holding hands, rolling, spinning or shoving along until they flopped into the water. "Bully!" he shouted between his clenched, prominent teeth, as they stumbled ashore scratched, bruised and out of breath.

But it was all over too soon: the games, the bumps, the Wild West stories. She would remember for a long while his saddened face, his tear-filled eyes and the helpless way he held out his muscular arm as he told her how much like his brother Elliott she looked. "We'll see you soon, dear Eleanor," he told her as she started away.

"Yes, Uncle Ted," she called back in her high shrill voice. "Soon!"

When her horse had gone clattering down the road, Uncle Ted's wife wiped a tear from her eyes, too, and sat down to write a letter to Auntie Bye, the older sister of her husband and of little Eleanor's father. Auntie Bye was in London where she was running the household of Cousin James "Rosy" Roosevelt Roosevelt, who was First Secretary of the American Embassy. Rosy's young half brother was a thirteen-year-old boy named Franklin Delano Roosevelt.

Edith dipped her pen in the inkwell and thought about Eleanor and what the future might hold in store for her. "Poor little soul," she finally wrote, "she is very plain. Her mouth and teeth seem to have no future. But the ugly duckling may turn out to be a swan."

Chapter Two

WHEN A DAUGHTER WAS BORN in New York City to Elliott and Anna Hall Roosevelt on October 11, 1884, New York social register nabobs hailed the event as a milestone in the uniting of two elite American families. Snob-eyed Peter Marie, whose nod, smile or invitation to dinner automatically raised one to social peerage level in gaslit New York, gave his penultimate honor to the new mother. She was no longer the princess of New York, he announced. She was, instead, the queen. *The New York Times* cautiously referred to her as "one of the most beautiful and popular women in New York society."

On her side, the beauteous Anna Roosevelt gave to her squalling baby, Anna Eleanor, the proud right to claim direct descent from Robert Livingston, one of the largest landholders in Colonial America. Her maternal grandmother had been a Miss Livingston, and in the twenty-one-year-old mind of Anna Roosevelt, a glittering ancestry was the best insurance for providing the proper credentials for the all-important world of High Society. It was a world that she adored and lived for; and one, she felt certain, her new daughter would also. What could be grander than a continual round of fancy balls and formal dinners? This was the ultimate that life had to offer, and they were luckily included by birth in such exciting joy. Her daughter must lead a religious life as she did, too, Anna pondered as she thought of the parties she was missing, for regular churchgoing and daily prayers were also vital factors in the good life.

It is doubtful whether Robert Livingston would have approved of her philosophy. The son of John Livingston, a fire-eating preacher in Scotland, Robert fled with his father to Holland in 1663 following the Stuart Restoration. After a decade as a refugee in an alien land, and following his father's demise, he sailed for America in 1673 with what seemed to many of his compatriots the wild idea of becoming an Indian trader in the tiny frontier village of Albany.

He had no interest in the arts and science. He was unlearned and rather coarse. But there was one thing he understood. That was to bet-

[13]

ter his economic status by whatever means he could. In this endeavor he succeeded beyond his wildest hopes. He proved a shrewd trader with the French and Indians, married cleverly into the patroonish Schuyler clan and only thirteen years after his arrival played on his friendship with the provincial governor to win a land patent grant and establish himself as First Lord of the Manor of Livingston, New York. The manor consisted of a whopping 163,000 precious acres in what is now Dutchess and Columbia counties of New York State. Another provincial governor by the name of Fletcher later charged him with having "screwed himself into one of the most considerable estates in the province by pinching the estate out of poor soldiers' bellies." But Livingston's tart reply as reported by Fletcher was: "I would rather be called knave Livingston than poor Livingston."

Only one recorded mistake was ever noted in Livingston's moneyed career and that occurred when the Crown accepted his word that Capt. William Kidd was the best available man to fight the busy pirates attacking British commerce on the high seas. When Kidd ran up his true colors, Livingston's property was threatened by an outraged monarch. However, after two frantic trips to England to soft-soap his detractors, he died peacefully in his Livingston four-poster with his land still intact.

If original fortune makers show a ruthless nature in attaining their goal, succeeding generations basking in the security of their founder's handiwork often are highly public-spirited. The Livingstons were no exception. For instance, three generations later, Chancellor Robert R. Livingston involved himself headlong in the revolutionary efforts of his country in the war against Mother England. He served on the committee with Jefferson, Adams and Franklin, which was charged with writing a declaration of independence. Later, during Jefferson's first term as President, it was he who opened negotiations with Napoleon to purchase the Louisiana Territory, an event noted by historian Henry Adams as "the greatest diplomatic success recorded in American history." After the deal was closed, Napoleon nudged him and winked at his co-worker, the dour James Monroe, and howled gleefully, "I have given to England a maritime rival that will sooner or later humble her pride."

There were two other activities of his that made his name a byword among Anna Roosevelt's relatives. One was that he was the farsighted partner of Robert Fulton in the early nineteenth-century effort to replace sailing vessels with steamboats. The pioneering steamboat *Clermont,* named after his sprawling estate 110 miles up the Hudson from New

[14]

York City, made history when it maneuvered that distance in just 22 hours, or at the astonishing rate of five miles an hour. His other achievement was that as Chancellor of New York, he swore President George Washington into office on April 6, 1789.

As the nurse carried her baby away, Anna had plenty of time to think about her marriage to Elliott Roosevelt. Theirs had been a whirlwind romance. She had seen him for the first time early in 1883 when he returned from a hunting trip around the world. He had sped across the Pacific to be present at the wedding of his younger sister Corinne to his good friend Douglas Robinson.

Anna had found him exciting from the start. He was tall, aristocratic in demeanor, and his bronzed skin lent him an aura of great mystery that fascinated her. His tight, immaculate, white suit served as a foil for his rippling muscles, his sandy hair and wide mustache. She was not yet twenty, while he was an old twenty-three, and he seemed slightly irresponsible but overwhelmingly dashing as he told her how he had spent part of his $200,000 inheritance to hunt savage tigers in India. She was spellbound as he described to her Oriental castles covering a half mile in area, of a trip he took "over the Ooty cannurd in the Milgerri Hills," of strangely named friends such as Mookiar-Ool-Moolk, Sir Salar Jung and Sadut Alli, and the "Paradise" breakfast he had once eaten— "Rose water and milk left in the dew all night and beaten up with silver leaf in the morning just before breakfast."

Everyone admired him and when she would mention his name, there resulted fond oh's and ah's and stories about his enormous generosity and kindness. His mother, Martha Bulloch Roosevelt, was a gracious Southern woman with a deep Georgian accent, and after Elliott had brought Anna to meet his family at their summer residence at Oyster Bay, Martha regaled Anna with tales of Elliott's early years. One time at age seven, he went out on a blustery winter's day for a walk in his new overcoat. When he returned a few hours later, he was coatless. Upon being questioned, Elliott replied, "I saw this thin little shivering poor boy who didn't have a coat. So I gave him mine."

Her late departed husband, Theodore Roosevelt, Sr., was a bug on physical fitness. After a daughter, Anna, came into the world a cripple and young Theodore an asthmatic with spindly legs, concave chest and poor eyesight, he had spent a great deal of time in a man-made effort to improve their bodies. Elliott, a fine specimen, also goaded his brother Theodore on to develop muscles and outdoor interests. Later when young Teddie went west for his health, he and Elliott took several

[15]

hunting trips together, with Teddie constantly admitting that he was the pupil and his younger brother Ellie the master. He wrote home of one trip when they wore "rough dirty clothes" and carried along "a yellow fool of a setter under the back seat, which is always getting walked on and howling dismally."

Theodore Roosevelt, Sr., died suddenly when he was only forty-six. One result was that Elliott, then three weeks away from his eighteenth birthday, lost the only tempering force his family had to offer. He rebelled at the suggestion of brother Ted that he try to get into Harvard. He had no interest in work. What he craved was adventure, adventures in foreign lands with sultans, sheiks and ferocious animals. Hadn't her own brothers been great adventurers? he asked his mother.

Martha Roosevelt, an unreconstructed rebel to her last breath despite her husband's close friendship with President Lincoln, had spun tale after tale about Uncle Jimmie and Uncle Irvine to her spellbound boys. Uncle Jimmie, James Dunwoody Bulloch, was a daring naval blockade runner during the Civil War and, in his own words, "I was the agent selected by the Confederate Government to manage and direct the general naval operations in Europe." While he handled the construction of the terrorizing warship, the *Alabama,* in England, her younger brother Irvine later served on the vessel in its attacks on Northern shipping.

When the family traveled to England on its many overseas voyages, the greatest attraction of all to Elliott was Uncle Jimmie, an enormous man who looked like a buccaneer. Neither he nor Uncle Irvine could return to the United States after the war and they had taken up residence in Liverpool. Nevertheless, they still had adventure in their souls and turned up mysteriously in New York from time to time under assumed names. The extreme lengths they went to in order to shroud themselves in high mystery always thrilled Elliott. What nicer letter than one that read: "Come to Central Park up the Mall at 3 o'clock on Thursday afternoon of this week and notice a young man standing under the third tree on the left with a red handkerchief tied around his throat"? On this occasion it turned out to be Uncle Irvine.

When Elliott had implored her for permission to use part of his inheritance for an adventure-filled trip around the world, Martha Roosevelt told Anna Hall, she had indulged his whim and dropped her plea that he join his brother Ted at Harvard. And now he was home again, tanned and recovered from a bad siege of Indian fever and still filled with wanderlust.

Anna was sure that Elliott was the only man in the world for her. "All my life and ambition are now centered in you and my objects in life are to keep and be worthy of your love," she had written to Elliott after they announced their engagement at a festive party at Algonac, the stately Newburgh, New York residence of the Warren Delanos, friends of both families.

A snowfall of enthusiastic letters greeted their announcement. Teddy sent a heartwarming note to "Dearest Brother." There was also a letter from James Roosevelt, the Victorian squire of Hyde Park, a distant cousin of Elliott's who took a fatherly interest in the young man's welfare. James was himself a recent bridegroom. Only a few years earlier he had married for the second time, taking for his bride the lovely Sara, one of Warren Delano's eleven children. The marriage had caused some stir because James, with his wrinkled face and gray muttonchop whiskers, was at fifty-two twice the age of his tall bride. Besides, she was much richer than he. When the two were in England on their honeymoon in 1880, Elliott, who was then an immature twenty, had utilized their hotel suite as his temporary headquarters before embarking for India with his hunting equipment. Both Sara and James Roosevelt were so impressed with his dashing manner and gentle spirit at that time that when their son, Franklin Delano Roosevelt, came into the world in January 1882, they insisted he become the baby's godfather. Elliott had quickly consented.

And now came James Roosevelt's letter to Elliott. "We received your letter this morning announcing your engagement to Miss Hall," he scratched his pen across the paper, "and we both send you our warmest congratulations in your happiness. We are so fond of you that we are confident you have made the most happy choice. Your Godson thrives and grows. I have been teaching him how to climb a ladder in a cherry tree."

Shortly after their ultra-stylish marriage in December 1883, Anna had grown aware that despite her love for Elliott, they were incompatible in several important respects. He still had an itching wanderlust that appalled her. Marriage meant settling down and not an oft-repeated desire to roam in the wilds of jungles. Certainly travel was an essential at their social level, but it must be made to the spas and the exclusive haunts on the continent and always with a full retinue of liveried servants.

However, this was not his only failing. Elliott also shared little of her enthusiasm for high society and found it difficult to content himself within the confines of this limited social area. If he couldn't spend his time hunting and shooting, he wanted to work in order to occupy himself. But she thought this silly because they could live fairly well on their inheritances. Besides, if he worked he would be too tired to participate actively in the festive balls and formal dinner parties that swamped the members of her elite set.

Elliott was also given to moods of despondence. Hardly had she begun carrying his child when he acted as though the whole world were coming to an end. Three months after his own marriage, Ted's wife, Alice Lee, was expecting her first child. Elliott, in a happy mood, paid a call at his mother's house in the city to see how his sister-in-law was coming along. What he found there was incredible.

The baby had already been born. Ted, who was out of town, had been notified that he was a proud father and was on his way home. But Elliott found his sister-in-law dying of childbirth complications and on another floor his mother lay in a fatal coma. He went to pieces at these stark realities. When his sister Corinne came calling, unaware of the tragedies, he pulled open the front door and screamed, "There is a curse on this house."

Brother and sister were inconsolable, and when Ted arrived, the three were in utter misery. At the end of a long vigil, the two women died on the same day, February 14, 1884.

For months afterward, Elliott fell into a heavy mood. He drank too much and in general displeased Anna, who was going through the discomfortures of pregnancy. His bronzed skin turned pale and he grew listless. There seemed no end to the depth of his despair.

But then on Saturday, October 11, his baby, Anna Eleanor, was born and the cloud lifted. Elliott was immediately joyous. So far as he was concerned she was "a miracle from Heaven." He was determined that the blue-eyed infant with the wisps of golden hair was to have the best in life and he felt closer to Anna than he ever had before.

Chapter Three

U NFORTUNATELY, the birth of her baby had an unpleasant effect on Anna Roosevelt. As the baby grew into a toddler, she took it as a personal affront that Eleanor was not a ravishing beauty in her family's tradition. The child looked like Elliott—thank goodness, not like his homely brother Ted—and though Anna considered her husband a handsome man, to her youthful mind his features transplanted on a female face just weren't good enough for her.

When Eleanor was able to walk, ritualistically she scampered to her father's dressing room upon arising. Amidst kisses and hugs, she chattered constantly as he dressed. She often danced for him, she recalled later, "intoxicated by the pure joy of motion, twirling round and round until he would pick me up and throw me into the air and tell me I made him dizzy!"

"I remember," her father told her jokingly when she was eight, "when you were a little bit of a girl and you used to call yourself Father's little 'Golden Hair'—and how you used to come into my dressing room and dress me in the morning and frighten me by saying I'd be late for breakfast."

Little Eleanor had a habit of shaking a finger in front of her face when she talked to her father. He was so delighted by her gesture that when she had her picture taken with her finger held aloft, he captioned the shot "Scolding Father."

This joyous relationship was absent in the case of Eleanor and her mother. Anna nagged her daughter because in her presence Eleanor was tense and never smiled. She told several friends while Eleanor was in the room that her daughter reminded her of an old woman without any semblance of spontaneous fun in her. "She is such a funny child, so old-fashioned," Anna complained. While her father called Eleanor "Little Nell" after the little girl heroine in Dickens' *Old Curiosity Shop,* her mother nicknamed her "Granny."

There was the occasion when Eleanor was two years old and her parents took her to visit the James Roosevelts at Hyde Park. The ostensible reason for the visit was that Elliott wished to present a heavy, valuable watch fob to his four-year-old godson, Franklin. "I am told," Eleanor Roosevelt said years later, "that Franklin, probably under protest, crawled around the nursery bearing me on his back." The husky handsome boy, whom she was one day to marry, said of that introductory experience, "I was just full of tacks."

After she had played awhile in the nursery with Franklin, little Eleanor was sent down the stairs, two feet to a step, in her starched white dress to the library at teatime. She "stood bashfully by the door till my mother saw me and called 'Come in, Granny.'"

To little Eleanor, her father was the complete hero. Not only did his masculinity thrill her, but there was also a time when he rescued her from a terrifying fate. It was among her earliest memories how when she was less than three she had started for Europe with her parents and Tissie, one of her mother's three sisters. Just one day from shore in the heavy fog an incoming steamer rammed their boat. Terrified passengers had to be transferred quickly to another boat. Eleanor could remember being dropped from the deck into the outstretched arms of her urging father, who stood in a big rowboat which seemed miles below.

When Eleanor was three, Elliott Roosevelt purchased a large house, which he quaintly called a "cottage," on ten acres at Hempstead, Long Island. Here the gay sporting set of rich idlers who whiled away their time riding and playing tennis had made this area fashionable in the mid-eighties. Good hunting was available as well as hectic polo matches, both sports at which Elliott excelled. His only problem was that he had taken a job in the city in the varied Roosevelt family business interests and he was finding it an increasing strain on his health dashing home to participate in the heavy social schedule Anna mapped out for them. "Anna is wonderfully well," he wrote his sister Bye, in an effort to entice her to come live with him, "enjoys everything, even the moving, and looks the beautiful girl she is. Little Eleanor is as happy as the day is long, plays with her kitten, the puppy and the chickens all the time, and is very dirty as a general rule."

Even the birth of her son, Elliott Roosevelt, Jr., in 1889 did not slow Anna's pace. The children were shunted off to nurses while she found a new interest in the drama. Theatrical greasepaint filled closets and bureau tops when she organized the Amateur Comedy Club, in which she, her brother Valentine, Miss Elsie de Wolfe, her friends the Lawrence sisters and several well-known amateurs put on a series of plays which *The New York Times'* critics labeled "histrionic successes."

[20]

Throughout this period little Eleanor drew even closer to her father. Some of her best memories were of the times she spent sitting on his lap while he told her stories. He told her a great deal about Hiawatha and read Longfellow's story so often to her that she memorized part of it and pleased him immensely by her feat.

He also told her about the Roosevelt family in America. Claes Martenszen of Rosenvelt was the first of the family to arrive in the New World. He came to New Amsterdam in the late 1640's. "A very common ancestor," Eleanor later referred to him with pride. An outsize man, who suffered a lifelong nickname of the "Little Fellow," he soon tired of city life with its company stores and the few hundred motley houses set carefully about the popular tavern. Upstate he wandered during the fifties to work as a farm hand and peddler. Death took him and his wife early, a characteristic of many later Roosevelts, Elliott noted. As a clerk recorded their sad fate, "Janetje Thomas, widow of Claes, the Little Fellow, commonly so called, has lately died, leaving, besides some property, five minor children."

Claes's son Nicholas, who founded the two chief branches of the Roosevelt family, was as determined to get ahead in the world as Robert Livingston. While he was not as successful, he did set the stage for the flowering of his clan. Moving back to the city in 1690—now renamed New York by the conquering British—Nick became a cloth bolter and eventually a prosperous merchant. Family stories were that after Nick became a "Freeman" in 1698 and served as a city alderman, he developed a gnawing desire for a more aristocratic ancestral heritage. First he dropped his Dutch family name of Martenszen and adopted the name Rosenvelt (Rose-Field), and shortly afterward anglicized it to Roosevelt. Next he fabricated a royal Roosevelt crest consisting of three ostrich feathers and a coat of arms depicting a rose bush with three roses. Then to top off his handiwork he adopted a family motto, *Qui plantavit curabit,* quaintly translated as "The one who planted it will take care of it."

It was Nicholas's fourth and sixth sons among his brood of ten children who founded the two important branches of the ensuing American Roosevelts. Johannes fathered the branch that led in five generations to Theodore and Elliott and in six to Eleanor. His younger brother, Jacobus, was followed four generations later by James Roosevelt of Hyde Park and in five by Franklin. Both branches had done exceedingly well in business, not as well as the Astors or Vanderbilts, but enough to be considered among the landed gentry of the nation. Family tradition was that Jacobus's branch consisted of greasy grinds, while

Johannes's brood was more boisterous, and endowed with limitless energy. Elliott told how his grandmother, Mrs. Cornelius Roosevelt, whose husband was reputed to be the fifth richest man in New York, reported gleefully that other society matrons referred to her as "that lovely Mrs. Roosevelt with those five *horrid* boys."

Elliott was especially pleased with the political progress of his brother Ted. The family had expected him to spend his life in pleasant idleness, but he had already served in the New York State legislature and now after his second marriage, to Edith Carew, he was spurting ahead as a civil service commissioner in Washington. The family's only other claim to political fame was Elliott's father who for some obscure reason had served as companion to Mrs. Abraham Lincoln in hat-shopping expeditions to Washington stores. He had also been nominated as Collector of the Port of New York by President Hayes, but Senator Roscoe Conkling of New York had blocked his confirmation.

And so Eleanor Roosevelt's early years progressed in a father-and-daughter intimacy and a troublesome relationship with her mother. At five she was tall for her age and already possessed of the enormous energy and stamina that would characterize her as a woman. The seeds of impatience with sham were already implanted in her mind.

Life might have continued in this trivial fashion for her if an event had not occurred in 1890 to alter the course of her existence. The sporting set at Hempstead was putting on an amateur circus and her father agreed to perform in a riding exhibition. The circus was held on the estate of James M. Waterbury in Westchester County and her father's act was to be one of its highlights. But an accident occurred to his horse in the ring. Elliott was thrown and his leg was broken.

The leg did not heal properly and had to be rebroken and reset. The pain involved "completely broke his nerves," Eleanor remembered his ordeal, and loving him as she did she was "dissolved in tears and sobbed my heart out for hours." He started drinking heavily and steadily. In a month his deterioration was noticeable to all callers. Ted and Corinne came, agreed that a change of scenery might help, and Anna took the suggestion that a trip to Europe might bring him around.

Corinne recalled a prophetic letter from Ted when he and Elliott were away in their late teens while on a hunting trip. Ted wrote her, "We have gone back here after a week's hunting in Iowa. Elliott revels in the change to civilization—and epicurean pleasures. As soon as we got here he took some ale to get the dust out of his throat; then a milk punch because he was thirsty; a mint julep because it was hot; a brandy mash 'to keep the cold out his stomach'; and then sherry and bitters to give him an appetite."

In Europe, Elliott Roosevelt appeared to have recovered from his desire for liquor. He took Eleanor to Venice and matched voices with the gondoliers on the canals. They went to Vesuvius to throw pennies into the lava. Then they traveled through the mountains to Germany. One incident seemed to confirm his reformation. They had gone to a German café and Eleanor spied several children drinking foaming steins of beer. When she insisted on trying one, her father told her flatly she couldn't. But when she persisted, he said he would teach her a lesson. "If you have it," he said, "you have to drink it all." To her father's smug joy, she promptly sickened herself.

It was too good to last. Her father started drinking again and as a last resort, Anna had him put away in a sanatorium. Pregnant again and left alone with Eleanor and little Elliott, Anna decided also to put Eleanor into a convent while she sat out her husband's recovery in a rented house at Neuilly, just beyond Paris. "You have no looks," she told her daughter at their departure, "so see to it that you have manners."

Separated from her family and being thrust among girls who spoke a language unknown to her, it was little wonder that Eleanor found herself in a nightmare. Months passed without companionship. To a six-year-old it was as though her whole world had collapsed. Then one day one of the other children swallowed a penny and became the center of great excitement. Viewing the nuns clasping their hands in concern and pouring out torrential French prayers, Eleanor followed suit a few days afterward and told a sister that she, too, had swallowed a penny.

The results were both worse and better than she had expected. The nuns who recognized an obvious falsehood when they heard one sent for her mother and demanded that Eleanor be removed from the convent. All the way home and even to the time when her younger brother, Gracie Hall, was born in 1891 her mother kept up a running fire of harsh rebukes. Her father, who had come from the sanatorium for the arrival of the new baby, "was the only person who did not treat me as a criminal!" Eleanor later wrote.

But she saw little of him because his drinking caused so great a stir in the house that he was taken back to the sanatorium. Nor did she see him again for a long time because her mother left him in Europe while she returned to New York with her three children.

Eleanor was never to live with her father again. This puzzled her immensely, for a child of her age couldn't understand what was

[23]

the matter with him. Late in 1891, her mother told her that her father had returned to the United States but because he was sick he was going to live in Abingdon, Virginia, where the climate was better for his health. People who came to see her mother whispered about her father and sometimes Eleanor stood furtively in hallways and eavesdropped. But she was too young to make any sense of the low-toned conversations.

The story behind his return was that he had gone from bad to worse in the German sanatorium and had gone to a French sanatorium for more advanced treatment. But even here he had made no improvement and his worried sister Corinne, fearful that he would spend the rest of his life in such unpleasant surroundings, sent a hurried S.O.S. call to her brother Ted to save him. Busy as he was in Washington denouncing the spoils system from his seat as Civil Service Commissioner, Ted rushed to Europe and brought him home.

Elliott was delivered to Abingdon, Virginia, where Douglas Robinson, sister Corinne's husband, owned a coal and real estate development company. Here Corinne could keep close watch on him and give him the love he needed in his condition. She installed him, Eleanor later learned, with the widow of a circuit riding judge, Mrs. John Campbell, in whose house he rented the top floor for himself and his faithful Negro servant, John Smith. No one in town ever saw him drunk, for he religiously stayed in his rooms when in that condition. Excuses were found for long stays in his quarters. Once when he didn't venture out for eight weeks, John Smith spread word that he had been injured by an exploding lamp.

Between binges he was his old charming self. Often the life of the party, an Abingdon resident reported to his daughter years later, "The girls and young ladies were in the height of glory when invited to drive with him behind his fast-stepping trotters in his two-seated yellow jersey, or his high-seated trap." People in Abingdon who were unacquainted with his weakness found him a man of great warmth. He was considered a member of several family circles. When the area was deluged with high snows in the winter of 1892, he organized the entire town into coasting parties. Later people remembered the handsome picture he made standing before open fires and munching apples.

He seemed to take on an individuality unrelated to his wife Anna and little Eleanor. He had his own dogs, horses and local friends to keep him busy when he was not under alcoholic influence. His hunting eye was still sharp and his riding was of such an order that he enjoyed showing off by riding across railroad trestles. When sport palled, he checked into the current status of his brother-in-law's mountain properties. On his own, he invested $30,000 in the Exchange and Deposit Bank of Abingdon. And when the panic of '93 wiped out the bank, he offered to put up enough money to make it solvent. To the poor among the 1,500 local residents of the staid little village, he established himself as a one-man charitable organization. At Christmas, the train from New York brought him 100 turkeys which he parceled out to the most wretched.

For his daughter, Eleanor, who did not share any of his private Abingdon existence, life had turned into a monstrously lonely endless array of days without him. There were dark clouds of worry and self-pity and doubts, all of which could be erased if only he came home.

Life went on after a fashion. Eleanor spent her winters in the house her mother bought at 52 East Sixty-first Street in the city. Impending doom hung in the air. Though her mother attempted to maintain a heavy social schedule to take her mind off her wayward husband, her personal misery shone through her surface gaiety. She suddenly developed severe headaches, and a daily ritual for Eleanor was to stroke her mother's head sometimes for two or three hours at a time.

Troubled as she was, Anna Roosevelt gave no thought to her daughter's education. When the winter social season ended, she took her family to Grandmother Hall's brick mansion at Tivoli-on-Hudson, a few hours' train ride from town. During one summer stay at Tivoli, Eleanor's great aunt, Mrs. Ludlow, who lived nearby, was shocked to discover that little Eleanor could neither recognize the letters of the alphabet nor sew. All the rest of that summer a tutor and a housekeeper kept Eleanor busy learning to read and stitch thread and yarn. Back in the city in the fall, Eleanor slept in her mother's room and each morning upon awakening, her mother made her recite from memory still another Biblical verse that she had spent the previous day learning.

Anna tried to be both mother and father to her three children. But try as Eleanor might to be a part of this program, the spark her mother emitted to her boys failed to reach Eleanor. "I felt a curious barrier between myself and these three," she has admitted. One of the continuing struggles between the two Roosevelt females occurred over Anna's edict that Eleanor could have no sugar. On innumerable occasions little Eleanor was caught with her hand in the cookie jar or with candy secreted inside her dress, and unpleasant scenes developed as a result. Her mother was also convinced that she was not too bright. When Anna hired a teaching service and organized a school in her home, she continually berated Eleanor because of reports of her poor spelling.

The atmosphere held an unpleasant aura of impending doom. Shortly

[25]

after Eleanor became eight, a diphtheria epidemic hit New York. The number of cases mounted astronomically that fall. Her mother, who worried a great deal about her children's catching it, finally came down with it herself at the beginning of December. Doctors faced with limited tools worked round the clock to save her life. When her condition worsened, a wire went out to Elliott in Virginia to come posthaste.

An anxious family waited for him to come. But he did not arrive in time. On December 8, 1892, *The New York Times* carried the following obituary notice: "On Wednesday, December 7, Anna Roosevelt, eldest daughter of the late Valentine G. and Mary Ludlow Hall in the twenty-ninth year of her age."

Her mother's death made no impression on Eleanor at the time. But her father was disconsolate. The fact that he had not come in time left him with bitter self-recrimination. The truth was that he had been at a party when word reached him about Anna. Few trains passed through Abingdon. Pacing back and forth at the terminal as the hours went by, he finally flagged a night train to New York to a halt. By now it was too late.

His sadness was further compounded by his discovery that Anna had made her mother, Mrs. Hall, the guardian of their three children. She specifically excluded him from any overseeing of their upbringing. All rights of a father were denied him.

Eleanor did her best to console him. An aunt told her several years later, "Just after your mother's death when he was in such sorrow, he wrote of 'his little Nell being the greatest help and comfort to him with her loving sympathy,' and again, that same period, he wrote of going to church with you and of your 'nestling close to Father,' and looking over the same prayer book with him." Eleanor's memory of that period of mourning was of a ride in a high dogcart down Madison Avenue with her father—and then he was gone back to Abingdon.

He came again when the children were already moved into Grandmother Hall's city residence. Dressed in black mourning clothes, he talked to Eleanor about a vague future when he and she would live together. He came occasionally after that visit, always without notice, but there was a telepathy between him and his daughter. "Never was I in the house, even in my room two long flights of stairs above the entrance door," Eleanor admitted, that she didn't hear him the instant he walked through the front doorway. And when she did, she would fly out of her room, race down the slippery banister and leap into his arms.

Sometimes he came to take her riding or for a day on the town, proposals that brought frowns to the face of her grandmother who had a strong distaste for him. Riding with his daughter, he was a fearless and bold man of adventure again. Once he took her for a ride through Central Park, where he warned Eleanor that his horse Mohawk would jump over all the carts in the road ahead if he shouted, "Hoopla!" "Oh, Papa," she said to him, her heart pounding, "I hope you won't say it!" He looked at her with flashing eyes while he smoothed his mustache. "I won't," he assured her, understandingly.

On occasion, he took her from Grandmother Hall's house with the best intentions, only to succumb to his thirst. "I remember that my father had several fox terriers that he seemed to carry everywhere with him," Eleanor said. "One day he took me and three of his fox terriers and left us with the doorman at the Knickerbocker Club. When he failed to return after six hours, the doorman took me home."

She remembered that he called at the house in the spring of 1893, some months after her mother's death. He came almost on tiptoe and hat in hand, for her little brothers were deathly ill with scarlet fever. Handsome four-year-old Elliott and little Brudie, as her father called blond Hall, her two-year-old brother, fought for their lives. Hall recovered, but Elliott contracted diphtheria. Doctors worked round the clock to save poor Elliott but, weakened badly by the earlier onslaught of scarlet fever, Elliott died in May.

A great sense of loss hit Eleanor now and she felt even closer to her father. They started a long and often pathetic correspondence. As often happens to sinners, he became a stringent moralizer. "Character begins in infancy and continues until death," he warned her in one letter. Hers needed much improvement. "He suggested that I go out and watch a house being built of bricks—and he called the bricks good habits, cleanliness, truth, thought of others, self-control and generosity. He went on to say the mortar is constant repetition which binds these habits to us; the masons are parents and teachers, guiding and helping; the finished house is your finished character, which, well built, will be ready to stand rain or shine, good fortune or ill fortune."

Back in Abingdon he sought substitutes for his daughter. He wrote Eleanor that he had befriended several little Abingdon girls and talked to them by the hour about his own little Nell. When he gave them dolls, he wrote Eleanor, invariably they named them Eleanor, a fact that pleased him a great deal. This was confirmed when one Abingdon girl sent Eleanor a letter in which she said, "Won't you come down and play with my pretty doll? I named my pretty doll Eleanor Roosevelt Lloyd."

[27]

By 1894 almost every letter from Elliott said, "I miss you terribly." He came less frequently to New York now. But he held out a repetitive hope that somehow and somewhere they would one day live together. It was a dream she found inspiring. Nothing else mattered but that one day she would live with her father and care for him. "Oh, my pretty companionable little Daughter, you will come to Father and what jolly games we will have together to be sure." She clapped her hands and cried, "But when?" Soon, he wrote her, soon. But it could never happen because of her mother's interdiction.

As the year 1894 moved along, he closed one letter to her with a sad: "Goodnight, my Darling Little Daughter, my Little Nell." She thought nothing of it, but on the first day of August when he was out riding, the intrepid horseman was thrown from his carriage.

He seemed all right when he brushed off the dust and waved off bystanders who thought he needed aid. He made it back to the Knickerbocker Club under his own power. However, he realized that the shock had irritated his heart, weakened by his dissipation. For on August tenth, he felt such biting pain that he couldn't get out of bed. And on the fourteenth, at the early age of thirty-four, the short and unhappy life of Elliott Roosevelt came to an end.

When the sad news was finally broken to Eleanor she refused to believe it. He couldn't be gone. He was her life. Nothing else mattered except him.

A copy of the *Virginian,* the Abingdon paper, came to Eleanor with the following editorial: "His name was a byword among the needy and his charities were always as abundant as they were unostentatious." But he was still alive, she told herself, and her great sense of loss did not come until long afterward when she finally accepted the fact that he would not come by to drive her through Central Park or write about their future life together. When it came, it hit her hard. Sixteen years later Aunt Corinne, who had devoted so many years to her ailing brother, wrote her from India, "We carry the same pain in our hearts. This is your father's birthday."

On August 12, 1933, when she was First Lady of the nation, Eleanor Roosevelt passed through Abingdon. An affair had been planned in her honor. But she spent that day roaming through town to find persons who had known her father and to talk over memories with them.

Chapter Four

H AVING LOST HER MOTHER, brother and beloved father within an eighteen-month period, it was no wonder that ten-year-old Eleanor was a sad and bewildered child. Life with Grandmother Hall did little to bring her around. In order to bring Eleanor out of her desolation, Mrs. Hall employed successive French and German governesses to take her on daily walks. However, for months Eleanor was little responsive to their existence. She purposely walked so fast that she left them far behind her. Later on her return she would find her governess sitting in the shade close to home and they would tread the last few yards together. In her mind, Eleanor lived in a dream world that consisted solely of herself and her father. From the time she arose in the morning, all through the day, and at night when she slept, she manufactured adventures with him. This state of unreality was to last most of her first year as an orphan.

In many respects life with Grandmother Hall was little improvement over her previous insecure existence, for her grandmother was ill-prepared to cope with her needs. Until his death in 1880, Valentine Gill Hall had treated his beautiful wife as though she were a baby. Having no occupation except to spend his inheritance, he had run the household, bought furniture, food, his wife's clothing and even overseen the servants. The rearing of their several children was entirely in his jurisdiction, a severe control because he was a religious fanatic.

At his death, the cloistered Dresden doll thankfully turned over the family's affairs to seventeen-year-old Anna, who managed things until her marriage at twenty to Elliott Roosevelt. After that, Mary Livingston Ludlow Hall awakened to the fact that she could in no way control her four remaining children. Maude, Pussie, Vallie and Eddie did as they pleased, went where they wanted to and politely ignored their mother. Grandmother Hall even feared her own mother, the aged Elizabeth Livingston Ludlow. Until the end, Mrs. Ludlow insisted that her daughter visit her every Sunday after church. When Eleanor told the old lady one Sunday that her grandmother couldn't come because she was ill, her great-grandmother rose with fury and ordered her home to send her daughter to her immediately. Grandmother Hall dutifully crawled out of bed and tottered weakly to pay her respects.

But if she were unable to handle her own children, Mrs. Hall did not consider this a serious handicap in dealing with her grandchildren. In fact, her mind was quite set on holding them in check as she had failed to do with her own family. Strictness became her byword and "No" served as her reply to requests Eleanor made.

The old lady developed a penchant for cleanliness, so far as Eleanor and Hall were concerned. She required Eleanor to take two hot baths a week and a cold bath upon arising each morning. Fortunately, Madeleine, the maid carrying out her order, found it a hardship to climb the stairs and test the water and Eleanor cheated by pouring in large quantities of warm water.

She also feared that the children would die of cold. The result was that Eleanor wore long heavy flannels from fall until mid-spring regardless of the weather. On top her flannels she was required to wear a flannel petticoat, then her dress, while her legs were swathed in long heavy stockings set into high-laced shoes.

Grandmother Hall was especially concerned about Eleanor's posture. Eleanor once pointed to the driveway leading to her grandmother's country place while being interviewed and said grimly, "It's about three-fourths of a mile long and when I was a girl I used to have to walk it twice a day with my arms over a walking stick to keep me from getting round-shouldered." During one period when her grandmother was concerned that she might be suffering from curvature of the spine, Eleanor had to wear a heavy steel brace.

Grandmother Hall also considered herself chief censor when it came to Eleanor's reading. This took a strange form. Eleanor was not allowed to read the same book on Sunday that she had begun on another day. If she began a book on a Sunday she was not permitted to finish it until the following Sunday.

Perhaps this was a tribute to Grandfather Hall, to whom Sunday had mystical meaning. "Sunday was indeed a day set apart from other days," Eleanor Roosevelt recalled later, "and some of the things decreed by my grandmother I personally very much resented. I could not play games on Sunday. I had to sit on the uncomfortable little seat in my grandmother's large victoria and drive five miles to and from church." Most times she was sick with nausea before the victoria came to a halt back home. However, she was required to go from there to teaching Biblical verses to the coachman's daughter.

[30]

Even during the week when she was alone with her grandmother an air of strictness hung all about. In a diary she kept when she was twelve, Eleanor noted, "There is a tinner doing the roof over the new porch Pussie is having built; there is a painter on a rickety scaffolding. . . . There is continuous bang, bang, bang, and Vallie has gone to the woods to get away." She was alone with her grandmother in the parlor and she noted the conversation. "Are you tired, Grandma?" "Oh, no." "Will the carpenter be done soon?" "I hope so." ("Prolonged silence during which time I wonder whether it would be rude to begin to read.")

In winter, Eleanor lived with Grandmother Hall in a large brownstone house on West Thirty-seventh Street in the city. A typical upperclass Victorian showcase, it had high ceilings, gilt pieces in the drawing room and in several other rooms overstuffed horsehair chairs that scratched sitters unmercifully. In addition to its inhabitants, the house fairly bulged with the butler, cook, laundress, maids and governesses. With the exception of an occasional summer stay at Bar Harbor, Maine, summers for the Halls passed at Oak Terrace, the large estate with the brick mansion, five miles north of the village of Tivoli and on part of Chancellor Livingston's original estate. The big house contained a total of fourteen bedrooms, the five for the servants being of an order to bed comfortably nine servants. A typical eighteenth-century country squire's residence, its chandeliers held candles, it was cold and drafty except during the hot summers, and its furniture was the heavy somber sort usually associated with permanence.

Grandmother Hall did not believe in formal education for women, and Eleanor was to be no exception to the rule. For her daughter Anna, Mrs. Hall had helped organize "dancing classes," or what were commonly considered pre-debutante schools of a sort, and it was at a Mrs. Parson's class that Anna made her debut into society. From old but vigorous Mlle. Le Clerq, whose pupils came to her house for lessons, Eleanor learned to recite the New Testament in French. She also got a smattering of grammar and arithmetic, but because her teacher did not understand them, these were presented her with such vagueness that she absorbed little. She was also given a piano to pound and spent an hour a day at the keyboard under the watchful eye of Grandma. When a little house was erected in the woods at Oak Terrace, Eleanor learned from Mrs. Hall that it was to be for her. However, it was not meant as a playhouse but instead was an industry center where Madeleine, the maid, was to teach her cooking and sewing.

While the house in a sense gave her some freedom, Eleanor found it had many drawbacks. When Madeleine scowled at the way she darned

[31]

a sock, Eleanor knew she would next proceed to cut an enormous hole in the sock and ask her to fill it with more darning. In addition, when her aunts and uncles discovered the little house, they used it for parties. If they agreed on one subject it was that dishes, glasses, pots and the stove should be left dirty so Eleanor could get some practice the next day. For this Eleanor sometimes had her hair pulled by Madeleine.

Since dancing was a key word in her grandmother's lexicon of what every young woman should know, Eleanor also found this an integral part of her "education." Early in her teens, she went to a school in New York run by a Mr. and Mrs. Dodsworth. Here she learned a graceful waltz and also a polka, two dances that stood her in good stead years later when she entertained in the White House. To make her less awkward, her grandmother also sent her to a ballet school on Broadway so she could learn to dance on her toes. Many of the girls, she found, were training for careers as chorus girls and Eleanor was rather jealous of them. She did appear in one tableau as a willow tree and the audience proclaimed her as being graceful and lithe.

Despite the absence of any real education, Eleanor evinced a deep desire for learning. She used to hide books under her mattress and waken at five A.M. to read them, despite Grandmother's edict to Madeleine that she was not to read before breakfast. When she would ask Mrs. Hall several questions about a book she was reading, that book mysteriously vanished never to be found again. But nothing halted her inquiring mind. She wrote in her diary, "I am always questioning and questioning because I cannot understand and never succeed in doing what I mean to do never, never. I suppose I don't really try. I can feel it in me sometimes that I can do much more than I am doing and I mean to try till *I do succeed.*"

Knowledge came from books, she knew, yet her reading was wildly hit-and-miss. Her grandfather's library was crammed with theological books, which her grandmother considered an enormous education for anyone who would read them. "I never wanted to read these books," Eleanor said, "though I remember shedding tears over the illustrations in the Doré Bible." In fact, the illustrations gave her nightmares. Instead of spending much time in her grandfather's library, she sometimes eluded her grandmother's close watch and passed time "sitting up in an old cherry tree or lying flat on my stomach in the grass reading Dickens or Scott and sometimes a forbidden modern novel which I would steal from my young aunts, purely because I heard it whispered that the contents were not for young eyes."

Uncle Ted, whom she saw now rarely at Oyster Bay, also whetted her appetite for literature. "When the food was cleared away," she once noted, "a book would come out of his pocket and he would read aloud. Or on a rainy day we would go to the gun room at the top of the house at Sagamore Hill and there we would sit and listen to tales or readings or recitations such as delight the heart of a child."

A clear indication of Eleanor's troubled mind at this time was her list of favorite books. One was titled *Misunderstood;* a second was a French book, *Sans Famille;* and another, Hale's *Man Without a Country.* Over all these books she "cried and cried," which led her aunts to joke, "What's the matter, Totty?" Totty was a nickname Eleanor especially detested.

The sadness in these books which, of course, she identified with her own existence was that of unloved people. During this period, she said, "I was more afraid of not being loved than of anything else and therefore I could stand sharp punishment better than a scolding."

Despite her unhappiness and her sheltered existence, Eleanor's interest in underdogs, which was to become her trademark as an adult, received real impetus during this time. Actually, her concern for the hapless and the downtrodden was originally prompted by her father. Before his troubles began, he took her along each Thanksgiving to help serve dinner at the Newsboy Clubhouses, a recreational program for street urchins begun by his father in New York. On those occasions, little as she was, Elliott Roosevelt talked to her as though she were an adult and told her what a wretched business it was that these boys in their tattered clothes were without homes for the most part and many slept in doorways and vacant lots the year round.

His lectures had a profound effect on her. When they were in Italy prior to his entrance into a sanatorium, he hired a donkey and donkey boy to show her the impressive sights about Sorrento. Eleanor, donkey and donkey boy were gone for hours. When they finally returned, the boy in obvious embarrassment rode on top the donkey. Disheveled and worn, little Eleanor ran along the road beside them. "I couldn't let him walk while I rode, Papa," she cried when her father sat her on his shoulder. "His feet were bleeding too much."

Now that she was living with Grandmother Hall, Eleanor was permitted to visit the Orthopedic Hospital in New York to cheer the crippled children. But she wasn't to stand too close to the beds because she might pick up some dreaded disease. The hospital was begun by Grandfather Roosevelt because of his interest in finding a way to treat spinal and hip diseases following the birth of his crippled daughter, Anna. One time during the period when her grandmother was concerned that she had curvature of the spine, Eleanor went so far as to show her own steel brace to the children in one ward of the hospital, in an effort to cheer them.

Grandmother Hall's children also added to her interest and concern with unfortunates by taking her with them on their charity activities. Aunts Maude and Pussie assuaged their own high-spending ways by singing occasionally in the Bowery Mission. Eleanor stood between them clutching her hymnbook and feeling sorry for the human derelicts who probably looked even sadder at the sound of their voices. Uncle Vallie, a sporting gentleman whose interests ran in the channels of tennis and high society, surprised his family by acquiring an interest in dressing Christmas trees in New York's Hell's Kitchen for the poor children. He took Eleanor along and she discovered his secret. A pretty girl he was pursuing at the time also dressed Christmas trees in that bad slum and it was his way to impress her.

Despite these excursions into the outside world, Eleanor's existence under Grandmother Hall's thumb was highly prescribed. She had no playmates her own age except for one girl, Carola de Peyster, whom her grandmother permitted to visit with Eleanor one day each summer. When Eleanor was twelve a family friend, Henry Sloane, asked Grandmother's permission to take her along out west as company for his daughter. Mrs. Hall gave him a sharp and loud "No" to Eleanor's great disappointment.

While her father was alive, Eleanor was permitted to spend much time with Auntie Gracie, her Grandmother Roosevelt's half sister, and with Theodore Roosevelt's family at Oyster Bay. Saturday was her usual day to go to Auntie Gracie's. Often Uncle Ted's oldest daughter, Alice, later the wife of Nicholas Longworth, was there and the two would play and listen to Auntie's stories about her Bulloch family and life on the Georgia plantation before the Civil War. Eleanor was much in awe of Alice, who seemed older than her eight months' advantage and was already saturated with sophistication in dress and manner.

After Elliott Roosevelt was buried, Grandmother Hall forbade Eleanor to visit Auntie Gracie and only rarely did she permit her to visit Uncle Ted. Her bitingly expressed opinion was that Elliott Roosevelt's side of the family was not the least bit serious and she held an active dislike for them. Not even Uncle Ted's charge up San Juan Hill with his Rough Riders in the Spanish-American War in 1898 could alter her opinion one whit. With her close kinship with Uncle Ted, this limitation on their association was painful to Eleanor. When she took part in his roughhouse horseplay, her shyness left her. Besides, he was the only person who took her on overnight camping trips and he had some books her father had inscribed as a boy. One flyleaf that he gave her had her father's signature and several boyish drawings of snakes, including a snake biting a man.

Her only other contact with the Roosevelts was during the Christmas holidays when she was permitted to visit her father's younger sister, Corinne. This was her occasion for meeting teen-age boys. But even here she felt like a rank outsider. All the boys knew each other and the girls who came to Aunt Corinne's parties for teen-agers. She stood apart. But even worse, her grandmother dressed her in clothes that came above her knees during a period when the mode was for dresses that almost reached the floor. Because of Eleanor's height the ridiculousness of her attire turned her face blank when, at the age of fourteen, she went to Aunt Corinne's junior party. On this night about four dozen couples were dancing a polka and she stood on the side lines with her face about ready to burst into a flood of tears.

Suddenly she spied the particularly handsome boy dancing with Cousin Alice. Through the intricate steps he led Alice, all the while with a look of pure joy on his face. It was Franklin, her distant cousin Franklin from Hyde Park. She had seen him the year before at Cousin Susie Parish's cotillion at Orange, New Jersey. But he wouldn't know her now. How could he remember? And why should he?

When the dance ended and the couples clapped and retired from the floor, Eleanor felt even more conspicuous and more unhappy than ever. She tugged at her dress and stared at the ceiling and then at the wall across the way. Franklin was standing with Alice. She watched them laughing and talking and caught his eye when he turned by accident in her direction. He was leaving Alice now and coming across the dance floor. She hugged the wall to make herself as unobtrusive as possible, but he stopped directly facing her.

"Eleanor," he asked with a friendly grin, "may I have the next dance with you?"

"Oh, Franklin," she fairly shouted. "I'd love to."

Around the floor they whirled. She danced with him and he acted as though he enjoyed it, which her frightened mind found hard to believe. When they finished dancing he talked to her for a while, laughed and joked, thanked her and was gone. Her holiday was a success.

Another important event happened to her the following year when she was fifteen. Life with Grandmother Hall turned grim. Uncle Vallie, one of her sons, had developed an excessive taste for alcohol. Eleanor liked him a great deal for he had earlier taught her to ride and jump.

[35]

Uncle Eddie, the younger son of Grandmother Hall, was coming and going from Tivoli with such frequency that no one knew where he would end up. Actually he went to Africa on one unexplained visit without telling his family and he frightened his mother with his pointless wanderlust. But there was Aunt Pussie, too, who was also ripping family stability apart at the seams. Unbound by any maternal controls, she was rushing from one involved love affair to another and was uncontrollably moody between romances. For days on end when she locked herself in her room, she frightened Eleanor and gave pause to Grandmother whether she was still alive or had taken her life, as she sometimes threatened.

At this horrid turn of events within her home, Grandmother Hall grew seriously concerned with Eleanor's future upbringing. A few more years under the home influence would prove catastrophic to her granddaughter.

One day she called Eleanor into her room for a private talk. "Your mother," she told Eleanor, "wanted you to go to boarding school in Europe. And I have decided to send you, child."

Thus ended Grandmother Hall's close control over Eleanor. Many years later, in 1919, when Mrs. Hall died, Eleanor wrote in her journal: "It is only after all these years that I have realized what it meant for her to take Hall, Ellie and me into her home as she did."

Chapter Five

I T WAS AUNTIE BYE, her father's older sister, who made the decision
where Eleanor was to study abroad. Auntie Bye had attended a
Mlle. Souvestre's school at Les Ruches close to Paris in the years between the Civil War and the Franco-Prussian War of 1870. Despite her
crippled state, Auntie Bye had been pushed into most of the school's
activities and she had come away with an assuredness that she could
manage her own affairs in the outside world. In fact, she had gone on
to manage the household of widower James "Rosy" Roosevelt Roosevelt,
the squat, bearded and insufferably snobbish son of James Roosevelt of
Hyde Park through his first marriage to Rebecca Howland. When
Rosy was First Secretary to the American Legation at London in 1893,
Auntie Bye had made a brilliant marriage to a dashing naval officer,
Captain William Sheffield Cowles, who served as naval attaché to the
Legation; and she was acknowledged to be Uncle Ted's chief political
adviser in his meteoric rise to the Presidency at the young age of forty-
two.

When Mlle. Souvestre was found to be still alive, still thriving and
teaching in 1898, there was no question that Eleanor would also attend
her school. So arrangements were quickly made and Eleanor dispatched
to her school, called Allenswood, at South Fields, close to Wimbledon
Common and connected to London by subway.

Eleanor found Marie Souvestre a motherly woman who was fond of
Americans. Short and heavy, with snowy white hair and patrician features, Mlle. Souvestre quickly made Eleanor her special charge because
of her fond memories of Auntie Bye. *"Ma chère petite,"* she called the
fifteen-year-old girl, and worked hard to dispel her shyness and ingrained belief that she was homely.

As a result, the headmistress was often torn between her heart and
her mind. On one occasion Eleanor roomed with a girl with a violent
temper to whom she was much attached. When the girl threw an inkwell at a teacher, who demanded that she be thrown out of Allenswood,
Eleanor ran to Mlle. Souvestre and pleaded amid wild sobbing that the

[37]

girl be retained and given another chance. The wise headmistress recognized Eleanor's unabashed concern with an underdog, but at the same time she recognized that the school's disciplinary system was at stake. In the end, after many sleepless nights, she decided that Eleanor would be finding underdogs to champion her entire life and that the continuing proprieties of Allenswood were more immediately important. The girl was sent home.

Mlle. Souvestre was concerned about Eleanor's horrible lack of previous education. But she recognized her quick, eager mind and poured subjects on her willy-nilly. Eleanor's report card for the term September–December, 1901, showed her taking French, German and Italian at the same time, as well as English literature and history, piano, violin and "danse." Under the stern order of Miss Strachey, who belonged to the renowned British literary Strachey family, she worked up detailed and meticulous notebooks on English and French literature. She was also active in sports and despite her thin long figure made the bruising first hockey team. Mlle. Souvestre methodically wrote on her report cards, *"Excellente élève."*

One reward for her hard work was that she became a member of the small group Mlle. Souvestre invited to her study in the evenings for poetry recitation. It was here that Eleanor discovered she had a phenomenal memory and could repeat flawlessly poems she heard for the first time. Mlle. Souvestre also placed Eleanor close to her dinner seat when grownups came to Allenswood. Days afterward when Eleanor would pass back to the headmistress the gist of those dinner conversations, Mlle. Souvestre would beam as though all the ideas were Eleanor's original thoughts. This art of retaining the best of other people's thinking and picking other people's minds were to become prime tools to Eleanor in later life.

One thing that Mlle. Souvestre discovered was that Eleanor had an old head on her young body. Once when asked to write an essay on Loyalty, Eleanor wrote: "Loyalty is one of the few virtues which most women lack; that is why there are so few real friendships among women for no friendship can exist without loyalty. With a man it is a point of honor to be loyal to his friend but a woman will kiss her best friend one moment and when she is gone will sit down with another best friend and pick the other's character to pieces." Then, obviously with herself in mind, Eleanor went on prophetically: "It may seem strange but no matter how plain a woman may be if truth and loyalty are stamped upon her face, all will be attracted to her and she will do good to all who come near her; and those who know her will always

[38]

love her for they will feel her loyal spirit and have confidence in her, while another woman far more beautiful and attractive will never gain anybody's confidence simply because those around her feel her lack of loyalty."

Mlle. Souvestre considered herself a liberal with the duty to teach her young charges that a gracious life of idleness was a shallow existence. One of the points she continually stressed was service to others and an interest in what was going on in the world. She carried on mightily with the girls against the French Government over the Dreyfus Case. The Boer War then in progress she labeled an abomination; a rather daring position, considering that British fever on this issue was at a high pitch. A result of her condemnation of the fighting was that Eleanor became an early pacifist. The headmistress was also an atheist, an attitude that shocked Eleanor. An early-day feminist, Mlle. Souvestre talked frequently on the importance of ambition. In one essay Eleanor wrote, to her satisfaction: "Some people consider ambition a sin, but it seems to me to be a great good for it leads one to do and to be things which without it one could never have been. Look at Caesar. It was because he was ambitious that they killed him. But would his name ever have come down to us if he had not had enough ambition to conquer the world?" Mlle. Souvestre applauded.

Outside of her studies and her warm friendship with Mlle. Souvestre, Allenswood offered Eleanor still another advantage. For the first time in her life she was on her own. Although her allowance was pitiful compared with what her schoolmates got, she went into London occasionally and spent money as she desired. A little black record book that she kept at the time showed a frequent expenditure for "hansoms," and also handouts to beggars. One notation read, "Poor woman—$1." One time in London she had her fortune read. Uncle Ted was now President of the United States following his Rough Riders' days against Spain in 1898, his term as governor of New York State, then Vice President and finally President after William McKinley was assassinated in 1901. After hearing Eleanor's name, the soothsayer informed Eleanor that she would one day live in the White House as a President's wife. One time Eleanor traveled to Liverpool to visit her father's aunt, Mrs. James Bulloch. It was a tearful session, with the older woman talking about "Ellie Boy" and her great love for him. She had some gold saltcellars Elliott had brought her from India and she later gave them to Eleanor.

There was also a marked change in her appearance. When Mlle. Souvestre ordered her to stop wearing the ridiculously short and unattractive hand-me-down dresses from her aunts, Eleanor was glad to comply, though it produced a strain on her already limited means. One of her great thrills was having a dress made to order in a stylish shop. Mlle. Souvestre was also greatly perturbed by Eleanor's incessant nail biting. She made no headway until one day Eleanor reread one of the many letters from her father that she had brought to England with her. One reading of a paragraph stressing the importance of personal appearance and she swore off nail biting. While the headmistress rejoiced, Eleanor picked up a new habit of pulling a strand of her hair with her fingers.

At Eastertime in 1901, Eleanor accompanied Mlle. Souvestre on a trip to France and Italy. This was another test of her growing independence. Eleanor had to do the packing and unpacking for both as well as make the travel arrangements and buy tickets. In several cities on the Continent, her teacher made her go sight-seeing by herself. "Take your Baedeker and go see it," she would order the sixteen-year-old girl. "For days I would be turned loose in Florence, Rome, Paris, finding my way about, seeing what interested me," said Eleanor, "and then going home and talking it over with Mademoiselle." Mlle. Souvestre always claimed that she was tired and had seen the sights many times before, but Eleanor rationalized her action with— "Perhaps she realized that I had not the beauty which appealed to foreign men and that I would be safe from their advances." In Paris one day when Eleanor roamed the city alone, she bumped into family friends who expressed great shock at finding the timid waif unchaperoned. From their great anxiety to depart, she guessed correctly that they couldn't wait to inform Grandmother Hall of Eleanor's disgrace.

Whether this so-called misadventure had anything to do with it or not, when summer came Eleanor was ordered to come home. The order saddened her because it meant that her stay at Allenswood was to be curtailed to the two years she had already spent there. She didn't know then that an unhappy summer was to bring her back to Mlle. Souvestre.

Pretty Aunt Pussie had come to London to fetch her. She was to be the reason for Eleanor's third year at Allenswood. Hardly had they closed their cabin door and with the echo of the boat's farewell toot still in the air, when Aunt Pussie commenced sobbing, screaming and threatening suicide. Between salty wet handkerchiefs, she mumbled and groaned about a sad love affair. Terrorized by her show, Eleanor counted the hours until they were back in New York.

But the worst was yet to come. Eleanor was to spend the summer together with Pussie at the homes of relatives at fashionable Northeast Harbor. Now past all memory of her last sad romance but enormously

[40]

embarrassed that her niece had witnessed her carryings-on, the mere sight of Eleanor enraged Pussie. The bubbling animosity erupted one July day when the two were alone. "You're so homely," she shrieked at Eleanor, "that no man will ever want to marry you." She tore into the young girl with a passion, angered even more in her taunting account of Eleanor's looks by the fact that Eleanor had become pretty.

When Eleanor maintained her silence, Pussie wildly burst forth with a torrent about her father, Elliott. "You're so innocent, you don't know anything about him," she jeered. She then proceeded to tell Eleanor about Elliott's last years and the shame he had brought on them all. "That's the kind of father you had," Pussie laughed hysterically at the close of her recital.

Eleanor was inconsolable once she learned that Pussie had told her the truth about her father. She ran to her grandmother and pleaded with her to say that it wasn't so. "But it is the truth," her grandmother told her coldly. "It ruined your mother's life."

Her world had come crashing down about her. Her only thought was to hurry back to Mlle. Souvestre's protective arms. "I want to go back to school," she cried to her grandmother. She begged and pleaded with Grandmother Hall at such length that the old lady finally agreed to her return to Allenswood. "But you can stay only one more year and no longer," Grandmother ruled, "because you must 'come out' when you are eighteen."

Her third year at boarding school passed quickly. There were other trips to the Continent with Mlle. Souvestre. There was more galloping reading and writing of innumerable essays without any semblance of punctuation rules. Over and over again she scribbled a strange story in her school notebooks. It was symbolic of something, though she never determined what. It was a vague dream of what might be. "I sat all alone on the beach," she wrote in one version, "waiting for the sunset and watching the waves as they rolled in and broke at my feet. Suddenly I looked up. The fiery red ball was getting lower and lower and just before it touched the sea I saw a beautiful woman rise out of the water to meet it and she held out her arms to it as though begging it to come nearer. Then she shook out her golden hair till the whole sky became golden and as she drew nearer the red light grew softer and softer and blended itself with her hair and as she sank lower and lower it sank with her and just as they kissed the water, her mass of golden hair fell over her and hid her from my sight and all that was left of my beautiful vision was a faint, faint ripple of gold on the water and soon even that disappeared."

[41]

In the summer of 1902, Eleanor left Allenswood following a tearful parting with her wise old teacher. She returned to the United States in time to find that Mlle. Souvestre had written to her relatives: "Elinor has had the most admirable influence on the school and gained the affection of many, the respect of all. To me personally I feel I lose a dear friend in her."

Late in 1902, Eleanor had her "coming out," as Grandmother Hall had insisted. She had vainly tried to convince Grandmother that she be permitted to go to college. But the old lady "humphed" at the strange notion. "All you need, child," she said adamantly, "are a few of the social graces to see you through life."

Her coming out was not a splashy formal business, primarily because of her grandmother's personal troubles. When Eleanor had returned that previous summer to Oak Terrace at Tivoli, it had soon become obvious that she couldn't stay there for long. Uncle Vallie was drinking now with a vengeance and so was Uncle Eddie, although the latter had married and seldom showed up at Oak Terrace. When visitors came to her home, Grandmother Hall met them frozen-faced in fear that Vallie would come down the stairs and cause a scene. One time Uncle Vallie came downstairs wielding a big shotgun and fired through the living-room windows.

Grandmother Hall, who had a great love for Vallie, decided that it would be best for all concerned if she lived in isolation with her weak but charming son. In the fall she and Eleanor took Eleanor's little brother Hall to enroll at Groton in order to get him out of the house. After Reverend Endicott Peabody, Groton's headmaster, led Hall away, Grandmother informed Eleanor that her duty toward the lad was fulfilled. Every term Eleanor was to go to Groton for a weekend and check on her brother's progress and problems as the other pupils' parents did.

As for Eleanor herself, she was sent to live with Aunt Pussie in the old brownstone family home on West Thirty-seventh Street in the city. Pussie's attitude toward Eleanor had softened since her outburst the preceding year, but she was still head over heels in romances. She was always in love with someone, "not always wisely, but deeply," Eleanor observed.

For her "coming out" Eleanor's name was put on almost all Social Register lists for debutante parties. The first one was an assembly ball to which she was escorted by her cousins, Mr. and Mrs. Henry Parish, Jr., with whom she was to live the following year when Grandmother Hall closed her Thirty-seventh Street house. Cousin Susie Parish was also her godmother and so formally concerned with the social proprieties as derived from well-to-do ancestors that Eleanor labeled her as "up-to-date in ancient affairs."

Again Eleanor was the stranger in the ballroom filled with young people who all knew each other. Again the old feeling of despair came over her. But luckily Robert Ferguson, a handsome young Englishman who worked for Aunt Corinne's husband except for the period when he was one of Uncle Ted's Rough Riders, and who helped nurse Anna Hall Roosevelt before her death, strode into the ballroom and discovered Eleanor's plight. After dancing with Eleanor, he made strenuous efforts to dragoon other available young manhood to her side and succeeded admirably. Afterward he escorted her home and did so in following months from other debutante parties.

In her fancy Parisian clothes, Eleanor was treated by an aunt to a large theater party in her honor and to a dance at Sherry's in New York. After this, as the party circuit pace stepped up, she began to feel more at home in the social festivities.

However, one year of social whirling was all she could take. At the end of that period she found herself both exhausted and bored. Besides, two things were taking place that cast a pall over continuing her "coming out."

The first distraction was her interest in social work. She had joined the newly organized Junior League and she and her friend Jean Reid, daughter of Whitelaw Reid, the editor of the New York *Tribune,* taught calisthenics and dancing at the Rivington Street Settlement House. To get to Rivington, she had to walk through filthy, crowded Bowery. The sight of that seamy existence made a mockery of her evening festivities. She had also joined the Consumer League and had begun timidly to go with various members to investigate working conditions in the sweatshops of New York. The word "muckraking" was in the air. Society matrons were eagerly trying to join the movement by crying "Shame, shame" at the animal-like existence of the lower economic levels, an endeavor that appealed to Eleanor.

Her second distraction was far more serious. His name was Franklin Delano Roosevelt.

Chapter Six

ONE WARM AUGUST AFTERNOON in 1902, shortly after her return from England, Eleanor was traveling up to Tivoli from Grandmother Hall's West Thirty-seventh Street home for the weekend. Her mind was still filled with her adventures at Allenswood with Mlle. Souvestre, and she sat staring out the train window. On her lap was the history book she had brought along, but which remained unread because of the bumping and jerking motions of the old New York Central coach car.

Suddenly she heard her name called and she turned her head. "Hello, Eleanor," the young man in the aisle was saying. It was Franklin Roosevelt of Hyde Park.

"Hello, Franklin," she replied with a warm smile.

"So you remember me," he laughed, jutting his chin out.

"Certainly," she said, though it was four years or more since she had last seen him. He was tall and thin, but quite handsome, and looked every bit the Harvard man that he soon told her he was. "How are your parents?" she asked, as he slid into the vacant seat next to her.

His face turned glum momentarily. "Father has been dead almost two years." She commiserated with him. "Mother is in the Pullman car," he added brightly. "Won't you come and meet her?"

Mrs. James Roosevelt knew her at once, though Eleanor did not recognize her. A *grande dame,* expensively clothed and with her head held high over her straight back, Franklin's pretty mother took her hand and asked her to sit with them until their stop at Hyde Park. She talked about Eleanor's parents and told her how fond she and her late husband had been of them. She also mentioned Mr. Dodsworth's dancing classes and remarked that she had seen Eleanor there several times. "You must come and visit us," she told Eleanor when the train stopped at Hyde Park.

She next saw Franklin that fall at a "coming out" party. With Bob Ferguson hovering in the background, he asked her for a dance. After that he began popping up at other debutante dances. Finally he asked her to a house party at Hyde Park. There were several pretty girls present, but Franklin spent most of his time at her side. His mother was also attentive to Eleanor. "I am going to hold a theater party," his mother told her, "and I want you to come." Eleanor went, though she considered the invitation one made in pity for her, rather than on a friendship basis.

As 1903 came in, Franklin began coming to New York with great frequency to take her to plays, or to restaurants, or just for long walks and talks. She began looking forward to his visits and to Aunt Pussie's call to her, "That handsome boy is here again."

As they talked he told her much about his life. He had had a perfectly happy childhood even though his father was twenty-six years older than his mother. When he was born he weighed ten pounds and both he and his mother had been given an overdose of chloroform which had almost killed them. He had been a very mischievous boy, his father applauding his antics and his mother disapproving what she called the "spoiling" of Franklin.

Franklin's father had been the director of several large railroads and corporations, but he spent most of his last decades at the spacious Hyde Park house set atop the steep wooded acres with the magnificent view of the Hudson. He was a real "gentleman of the old school," as his obituary read, and presented an aristocratic appearance with his carefully trimmed muttonchop sideburns and his courtly yet somewhat austere manner.

Franklin's mother, a glittering beauty in her day, was the seventh child and fifth daughter of Warren and Catherine Delano. Her ancestry was a proud long line of China traders and she brought to her marriage an inheritance of a million dollars. She had first met her husband-to-be at the home of Eleanor's Grandmother Roosevelt, where he was taken with her looks as well as her profound interest in music and literature.

As a boy, Franklin was rarely out of her sight. Friends viewed them as a "loving" couple. In the winter when the snow was heavy at Hyde Park she went tobogganing with him and on her frequent trips abroad, they toured museums and galleries hand-in-hand. With the exception of a neighbor boy, only infrequently did he play with children his own age. Sally Roosevelt rationalized his resultant shyness with— "No one knew better than I what a time Franklin had in hiding the self-consciousness he felt when he spoke to any other than the members of the immediate family."

She waited until he was fourteen before sending him off to school. And even then her frequent appearances at Groton were soon consid-

[45]

ered a source of annoyance by the school authorities. Once when Franklin contracted scarlet fever at Groton, she climbed a rickety ladder and stared at him through the window for hours. When her husband died in December 1900, while Franklin was a freshman at Harvard, she rented a house close by the campus so she could be near him.

Most boys would have succumbed to spinelessness under such motherly smothering. But Franklin, while he loved his mother dearly, had an independent streak plus a highly developed sense of humor to save him from envelopment. Years later he jocularly told the story of one of their "crises" when World War II broke out. One of her sisters, then almost ninety, was in France when Hitler started his rampage. Wielding her cane, his mother strode into his office. "Dora is stuck over in France," she charged, "and I want you to send a battleship over for her right away, Franklin."

"But I can't, Mother," he answered smiling. "She'll get home all right. But I can't send a battleship for her."

"Why?"

"I can't, Mother. I just can't."

"Well, Franklin," she said disgustedly, "I don't see why not. What are you President for?"

Franklin was a junior at Harvard when he began squiring Eleanor. Though she enjoyed his company, she didn't take him seriously. He asked her to Harvard for the football games and proms besides making frequent trips to New York for dates, but, in her self-effacing state, she considered all this not a courtship. One time when he came to the Rivington Street Settlement House to pick her up after her dancing class, her little pupils excitedly surrounded her and asked, "Is *he* your feller?" She didn't even blush as she shook her head. "Feller," she admitted, was "an expression which meant nothing to me at that time."

Nor did Sally Roosevelt consider his attentiveness to Eleanor a threat to her close relationship with her son. There were several other girls whom he knew and saw frequently, such as his cousin "Moo," Muriel Delano Robbins, his niece Helen Roosevelt, Mary Newbald and Frances Pell. At Harvard, she was also aware that he saw Dorothy Quincy, a lovely Dedham girl, from time to time, but he was no more serious about her than he was about the others. His mother later recounted, "He had never been in any sense a lady's man. I don't believe I remember ever hearing him talk about girls or even a girl except on that memorable occasion when he had taken a young lady driving in a dogcart on Long Island and found to his consternation that she had fainted." On that occasion when the girl fainted, his mother said with pleasure, he had been so horrified that he dropped the reins and the horse ran wild until stopped by an obstruction. The girl fainted again when she saw their predicament.

While Franklin's intentions toward her were early serious, Eleanor's regard for him developed slowly. In the summer of 1903, he went to Europe at vacation time, but when he returned he rushed to tell her that he had had no fun because he thought of her constantly. After this she considered him her beau, though she was still in doubt about its meaning. When he asked to meet her family, she took him to Tivoli. She warned him about Uncle Vallie, but still she feared a scene. Fortunately, the afternoon passed without incident. Afterward Franklin crowed self-satisfiedly, "Vallie has been exemplary—I seem to have a good effect on him."

She felt he was so untouched by life. Once when one of the little girls at the Rivington Settlement House took ill, she asked Franklin to help carry her home. When he saw the wretched slum where the child lived, he paled and gasped to Eleanor, "My gosh, I didn't know anyone lived like that!" Franklin had a tinge of arrogance in his make-up that bothered Eleanor, but he lost this when Harvard's most exclusive club, the Porcellians, would not accept him as a member, during his senior year. Eleanor noticed the happy change immediately. "It made him more democratic and gave him humility," she said.

The courtship reached a climax in the fall of 1903 when Eleanor went to Groton to visit her brother Hall and Franklin met her there. There was no going on as they were, he told her. When he proposed marriage, Eleanor accepted.

But the road ahead was not smooth for the young lovers. When Eleanor told her grandmother, Mrs. Hall chided her as being too young to marry. "Are you sure you are really in love?" The nineteen-year-old girl uttered a solemn "Yes," which brought a quick smile to Grandmother Hall.

It was much worse at Franklin's end. He waited until Thanksgiving vacation to break the news to his mother. They were at his uncle's house at Fairhaven and after dinner he took her aside. "I am going to marry Eleanor," he told her bluntly.

She was stunned. "Did you ask her? Did she accept you?" He answered "Yes" to both questions.

She appeared to be in a state of shock. That night she wrote in her diary, "Franklin gave me quite a startling announcement." Later on she admitted, "Franklin, unknown to any of us, had become engaged to his distant cousin, a delightful child of nineteen whom I had known and loved since babyhood."

Upon his return to Harvard, Franklin wrote her: "Dearest Mama, I know what pain I must have caused you and you know I wouldn't do it if I really could have helped it! . . . Only now you have two children to love and to love you—and Eleanor as you know will always be a daughter to you in every true way."

When Eleanor heard of Mrs. Roosevelt's distaste of their future marriage, she also wrote her a letter. "I know just how you feel and how hard it must be," she wrote the unhappy woman, "but I do so want you to learn to love me a little. You must know that I will always try to do what you wish for I have grown to love you very dearly during the past summer."

It was not that Sally Roosevelt disliked Eleanor. It was just that she had determined in her own mind that Franklin would live with her for several years after he graduated from Harvard. She had no intention of letting the "child," as she referred to Eleanor, spoil her well-laid plans.

She wrote quickly to Franklin that she had thought over what he had told her on Thanksgiving Day and her conclusion was that he was not in any position to marry. Her father, Warren Delano, she pointed out rather baldly, had married at thirty-three when he was already "a man who had made a name and a place for himself, who had something to offer a woman."

By fast talking, Franklin's mother convinced the two that they should not make any announcement just yet. Franklin was tied up with his work as editor of the Harvard *Crimson,* she said benignly, while Eleanor was enjoying herself in her social work activities, an avocation Franklin's mother found revolting. Why not continue in that fashion for a while and learn a bit more about life?

With their acceptance of her wish, she now busied herself devising a program for saving precious Franklin. First, she must somehow break up their weekends together in New York, when he came down to her town residence and squired Eleanor about the city. Once when she tried to get him to come to Hyde Park for the weekend instead of going to New York, he wrote her in anguish, "I think that E. will be terribly disappointed, as I will, if we can't have one of our first Sundays together— It seems a little hard and unnecessary on us both."

There was no possible way to keep them apart when they were separated only by the Boston train. So in February of 1904, Sally Roosevelt took dire steps and concocted a cruise for herself, Franklin and Lathrop Brown, her son's roommate at Harvard. They were to spend six weeks in the Caribbean, during which time, she hoped anxiously, he would forget all about Eleanor. Off to the West Indies Franklin dutifully accompanied his anxious mother and "Jake" Brown.

When Franklin went on his Caribbean cruise with his mother, Eleanor had accepted an invitation from Auntie Bye to visit her in Washington. And here she had no time to feel blue. Uncle Ted came over from the White House to invite her to stay with his family, but she turned him down with the excuse that the White House overawed her. However, she did see much of Uncle Ted for he was always dropping in at Auntie Bye's. He would sit in the parlor with the two and discuss the current problems facing him. Eleanor sat listening while Auntie Bye offered advice to her brother. They talked about the crisis between Russia and Japan, his decision to run that year for four more years in the White House, the problems involved in lowering the boom on the growing corporate structure of American industry, and a host of other matters. Uncle Ted certainly showed, thought Eleanor, "that he considered her advice was well worth having."

Auntie Bye also pushed Eleanor into the gay social life of Washington. As the President's sister and the wife of Admiral William Sheffield Cowles, she had a full round of teas, luncheons and dinner engagements, to which she took Eleanor. She also introduced her to the younger social set of the capital, including a girl named Cissie Patterson, who was to be her bitter opponent years later as editor of the Washington *Times-Herald*. There was also a long line of young men to squire Eleanor about town. Among the young men who crowded her date calendar were a dashing young Italian named Gherardesca, Major Leonard who had lost an arm in the Boxer Rebellion, and John Lodge.

Following the cruise, Sara Roosevelt took her son up to Washington, ostensibly to see the sights. In reality, however, she hoped to find an overseas job for him. Joseph Choate, an old family friend who was then American ambassador to Great Britain, was in Washington for consultation. Perhaps Mr. Choate would employ Franklin in the London Embassy.

She made an appointment with Ambassador Choate and took Franklin to meet him. She made her pitch with finesse and gentility. Wouldn't the ambassador take Franklin with him to London as his secretary? Choate listened to what she had to say while he watched the fidgety young man alongside her. He was very, very sorry, he replied diplomatically when she concluded. He already had a secretary.

It was in Washington that Franklin found Eleanor, and when he

[49]

did he rushed to Auntie Bye's by carriage as swiftly as he could. Eleanor was overjoyed to see him and glad that his feelings toward her had not changed. She confessed how much she had resented his mother's taking him off on their cruise.

Sally Roosevelt realized that her ruse had failed when she discovered they were spending all their time in Washington together. Uncle Ted invited them to dinner at the White House and Franklin and Eleanor talked to him throughout the meal. Young Franklin sat staring when Uncle Ted rose at one point and began pacing the room. He told Eleanor later what a pleasure and thrill it had been to watch history in the making. By the time they left Washington, Sally Roosevelt told the young couple that they had her blessing. If she couldn't prevent their marriage, she would attempt to control it. Eleanor seemed docile enough and should present no real problem.

The months passed rapidly now. In June Franklin graduated from Harvard. Eleanor came with his mother to Cambridge. They also went to Groton for Prize Day and had a chance to hear Uncle Ted, for he was the chief speaker that day. During the summer, Sally Roosevelt held a number of parties at Hyde Park and had Eleanor as her guest. Later in the summer, Franklin came to Islesboro, Maine, where Eleanor was visiting with Aunt Corinne, and took her back to Campobello, a small island a few miles off the coast of Maine in the Bay of Fundy, which separated New Brunswick from Nova Scotia, and where his mother had her summer place. Aunt Corinne forced her to take a maid along because it would harm her reputation if the two traveled without a chaperone. But once they got to Campobello, they went off alone on long walks and on Franklin's small schooner, *Half Moon*.

Sally Roosevelt argued that Franklin should return to Harvard in the fall and begin law school there. But Eleanor would be too far off in New York City and he refused. When he enrolled at Columbia for his law courses, his mother quickly took a house on Madison Avenue not far off. He spent so much time seeing Eleanor and shopping at Tiffany's trying to decide which engagement ring to buy her that he had little time to study. Nothing interested him except Eleanor. "He will not find himself altogether happy with the law he is studying," Eleanor said, "unless he is able to get a broad human contact through it." He admitted to her that he found law boring.

Eleanor's influence on Franklin was also apparent that fall of 1904 when he voted for Uncle Ted and not for his Democratic opponent, Judge Alton B. Parker. A Democrat, his vote puzzled many of his

[50]

friends. Franklin later gave as an excuse, "I thought he was a better Democrat than the Democratic candidate."

The last remaining requirement before their engagement was to be announced was the Delano clan inspection of Eleanor at their museum-like place at Fairhaven, Mass. But even before this Thanksgiving Day gathering of the clan all her friends knew that she and Franklin would marry. Cousin Teddy Roosevelt, Jr., wrote her a letter from the White House early in November, 1904, and on the envelope he wrote for all the world to see: "Remember me to Franklin. I guess he's not far off."

When they announced their engagement on December 1, Franklin gave Eleanor a silver locket which carried the Roosevelt crest of three ostrich feathers on one side and their initials on the other. This was to be one of her life's treasures. All of her children were to cut their teeth on the locket and, teeth marks and all, she wore it thereafter slipped inside whatever dress she wore.

When the question came up who was to give Eleanor away at the wedding planned sometime the following spring, Uncle Ted insisted that he be given the honor. But Franklin and Eleanor must first be his guests at his inauguration on March 4th, he told them. Of course they were delighted, especially Franklin who considered Uncle Ted the greatest man he knew. They came down to Washington by private railroad car with Roosevelt relatives, sat behind Uncle Ted on the Capitol stairs where they watched him so intently in their great excitement that they didn't listen to a single word of his inaugural address, ate lunch with him at the White House and sat in the special box to watch the inaugural parade, which included 1,000 marching Rough Riders and Geronimo, the captured Apache Indian who had bedeviled pioneer settlers in the Southwest.

Uncle Ted found that he would have to be in New York on St. Patrick's Day for speechmaking. He could certainly take time then to attend Eleanor's wedding, he told her. The middle of the afternoon would be best. The last problem was thus ended.

And so on March 17, 1905, Eleanor and Franklin were married. Their wedding was held at the twin houses of Eleanor's relatives, Mrs. Henry Parish and her mother, Mrs. E. Livingston Ludlow, at Numbers 6 and 8 East Sixty-sixth Street, just off Fifth Avenue. Sliding doors made one room of the drawing rooms of the two houses.

A gala crowd of socialites came, for theirs was one of the year's important weddings, especially since the President of the United States was on hand. There were present the Vanderbilts, Sloanes, Belmonts, Riggses, Van Rensselaers and Mortimers, as well as other old New York

[51]

family representatives. All of them had trouble reaching the wedding scene because of the mammoth St. Patrick's Day parade on Fifth Avenue and the huge crowd that gathered in the area to catch a glimpse of Theodore Roosevelt. Almost a hundred policemen in gray helmets and frock coats formed a cordon at the corners of the block to keep the path clear for Uncle Ted's arrival, but still the crowd pressed forward and invited guests entered the block only with the greatest difficulty. Finally the President came into the block in an open landau and the crowd cheered its head off.

Inside the houses, last-minute feverish activities were going on. When the Reverend Endicott Peabody, headmaster of Groton, who was to perform the wedding ceremony, discovered Franklin's nervous state he took him and his best man, Lathrop Brown, into a small closed room to calm him down. Eleanor had also been engaged in last-minute preparations. She was, as the New York *World* reported next day, "lavishly jewelled. She wore a dog collar of pearls, a diamond bowknot and the veil was fastened with a diamond crescent, which had been worn by the late Mrs. Elliott Roosevelt." She wore a long-sleeved stiff white satin dress covered with rose-point lace that Grandmother Hall had worn at her own wedding several decades earlier. For a wedding present, Franklin had given her a chatelaine watch and pin with her initials in diamonds on the watch.

As the "Wedding March" began, she came down the stairs with Uncle Ted. Guests noticed that the Irish shamrock in his lapel was badly wilted, but he wore a beaming smile on his face, as he held Eleanor's arm. A society reporter noted that she "was considerably taller than the head of the nation, suggesting to many present her beautiful mother."

Eleanor's maid of honor was Uncle Ted's daughter Alice, whose varied activities were minutely reported in the daily papers and who was called by all "Princess Alice." One of Eleanor's bridesmaids was her friend Isabella Selmes, who would later come to Washington as a Congresswoman from Arizona. Isabella had spent most of the week before the wedding mistakenly signing her own name to Eleanor's thank-you letters for wedding presents. Isabella, as well as the other bridesmaids, wore three ostrich feathers in her hair, as further reference to the Roosevelt crest. A young boy named Sumner Welles, distantly related to Franklin and a Groton form mate of Eleanor's brother Hall, was also present.

If the large crowd on the avenue hadn't broken into the block and the band not taken to repetitive blastings of "Wearin' o' the Green," the guests at the wedding might have been able to hear the ceremony. It was

[52]

performed with deep feeling because the Rev. Peabody felt like a father to both Franklin and Eleanor. When he first heard of their engagement he had blessed it with: "I have always particularly liked Miss Roosevelt. She has always been a devoted Sister—you a devoted Son. I can hardly imagine a better training in each case for a happy married life."

When the ceremony finished, Uncle Ted kissed the bride and congratulated Franklin. "I'm glad you're keeping the name in the family," he bellowed. One of Uncle Ted's sons said later, "Father always wanted to be the bride at every wedding and the corpse at every funeral." Franklin's mother with tears in her eyes said she would never forget "how straight and strong and glowing the children looked during the ceremony."

The presence of Uncle Ted was not without its drawback. Immediately after congratulating Franklin, he hurried into the library where groaning boards were piled high with food from Delmonico's. Anxious to be with the President, the guests deserted the newly married couple and followed him. Alone with his bride, Franklin threw up his hands and told Eleanor, "Well, we might as well join the party."

Uncle Ted had to leave early, for he had another speech to make. They watched from a window as the crowd outdoors yelled, "Three cheers for Teddy! Ain't he the real thing?" Uncle Ted in high spirits shook a fist playfully at the ragged urchins who rushed forward to touch their hero. Later Uncle Ted commented on the day in a letter to his son Kermit. "I paid a scuttling visit to New York on Friday to give away Eleanor at her marriage and to make two speeches."

Chapter Seven

A<small>T TWENTY</small>, Eleanor was to find out what it was to be married to a twenty-three-year-old schoolboy who disliked the law he was studying in search of a career. She was also to discover the tenacity of a mother-in-law intent upon dominating her son's household. If there was anything she fortunately did lack, it was financial worries. For Franklin was the recipient of an annual $5,000 interest stipend from the $100,000 trust fund his father left him, while Eleanor had come into a yearly sum of about $7,500. So while she was not free domestically, she was financially.

When they rushed from her cousin's house under a hail of rice, they could take no long honeymoon because of Franklin's studies at Columbia. There was to be only a week and this, at her mother-in-law's insistence, was to be spent at Hyde Park. Young and uncertain, Eleanor made no protest, though she realized that instead of being carefree, she was during that entire week being judged by Sally and the servants. There was, for instance, Elspeth McEachern, an old Scots woman who had been in Sally's employ a long while and considered Franklin as her own. "She was in the house when we went to Hyde Park the day of our wedding," said Eleanor, "and she looked me over critically and appraisingly, wondering if I could come up to her expectations as the wife of 'her boy.'"

After their week, they moved into two small rooms at the Hotel Webster on West Forty-fifth Street. Here until the summer Franklin plowed his way through boring lawbooks and, on occasion, Eleanor brought Hall from Groton to visit with them.

Finally with summer vacation from school, Franklin and Eleanor went to Europe for two months on their belated vacation. One thing she discovered early about her husband was that while his daytime nature was warm and calm, once he closed his eyes he was susceptible to horrible nightmares and sleepwalking. On one occasion during their honeymoon, she was awakened by wild shrieking and found Franklin pulling and jerking on the covers. "Sh-hh!" she admonished him.

"Don't you see the revolving beam?" he bellowed at her in great agitation. Before she could stop him he was out of bed with a wild yell that the entire household must be roused before they were all dead. After a tussle she managed to calm him and push him back into bed. While he was soon asleep, she lay awake worrying.

This characteristic of his caused Eleanor to sleep with her eyes half opened until she chanced on a solution. This came some time later, when, as she wrote his mother, he got up in the middle of one night, "turned over a chair and started to open the shutters! I grabbed his pajama tails and asked what he wanted and received this startling answer: 'I must get it, it is very rare, the only one and a most precious book.' After some persuasion he returned to bed, very angry with me and the next morning he knew nothing about it!"

Another problem the two had was that their name was the same as the American President's. It was little wonder then that when they first came to London, the manager of Brown's Hotel ushered them into the royal suite. The suite was of such glossy dimensions, said Eleanor, that when she put something down in the sitting room, "later I could not find anything." The charge for the suite was far more than they could afford and was based on the supposition that any relative of the President surely had money to burn. Franklin wrote his mother that the rate was $1,000 a day, and while it was nowhere near this, they moved a few days later after they worked up sufficient nerve to face the manager.

Franklin used their honeymoon as a grand pretext to tease his mother about the money he and Eleanor were spending. To the woman who vowed early never to spend a cent of her inheritance but to live solely off the interest, he wrote one day that they had ordered thousands of dollars' worth of clothes, and were going to send her several cases of champagne, "as I know it is needed at Hyde Park." From Paris he wrote, to Eleanor's amusement, "Then we went to Combe and Levy and ordered thousands of dollars of linen, 8 doz. tableclothes, 6 napkins, ½ pillow case and a handkerchief, all very attractive and full of holes or à jour as they say here."

On their sweeping trip, they rushed from London to Paris, Milan, Venice, St. Moritz, Augsburg and then back to England. In a gay mood they did the Continent, Franklin bargaining for rare books at every opportunity and Eleanor taking in the historic sights. Her only general gloom came whenever she visited a place she had once visited with her father when she was a child. They took a gondola out to Murano and she could recall the way her father had stood up in the boat and sung

[55]

with the gondoliers in Venice. At Murano, she and Franklin purchased a set of glasses with the three-ostrich-feather Roosevelt crest invented by their common ancestor Nicholas about 1700. Another sad experience came in the mountains when she refused to climb the jagged, jutting rocks of Faloria, a perpendicular four-hour climb. Franklin was not to be put off and found another girl who would accompany him. "I was jealous beyond description and perfectly delighted when we started off again and drove out of the mountains," Eleanor later admitted.

Franklin made up for this by taking her to Paris and buying her a white cloth evening cloak, a three-quarters coat, an afternoon dress in pastel blue with an extra short skirt, a white net evening dress with a collar and a riding habit. He wrote his mother with more than a hint of honesty: "Today we went to various dressmakers at one of which I distinguished myself by going to sleep, Eleanor got a dozen or so new dresses and two more cloaks."

Franklin enjoyed shocking his prudish new wife. He took her to the *Follies* in Paris just to watch her cold expression. One look about Lido and she wanted to leave. She wrote his mother in horror, "I never saw anything like the bathing suits the ladies wear. Their upper garment could not be called a shirt, it was hardly a frill!"

A sour note greeted them as they left France for England on their last fling before returning home. A report from Columbia Law School notified them that Franklin had failed in two subjects: Contracts and Pleadings. "I thought I had done as well in the two I failed as in those I passed with a B," he grumbled. Hurriedly he picked up textbooks in those fields with the intention of studying them during the rest of his honeymoon and then taking make-up exams upon his return to New York. Aware as she was of his attentiveness toward showing her a good time, Eleanor wrote quietly to his mother, "I am not very confident of his passing." But he fooled her and did when they got back.

Eleanor had a "terrifying visit" at the lovely home of her mother-in-law's friends, Mr. and Mrs. Foljambe, who lived in The Dukeries, at a place quaintly labeled "Osberion in Workshop." Even though it had only one bathroom, the Foljambe home had dozens of rooms, many of which were connected by a small railroad track. The formality of the house was such that guests were never introduced, it being assumed that one's mere presence in the house was sufficient. Added to her withdrawal at such formality was the fact that guests were expected to play bridge after dinner. This proved a sweating ordeal for Eleanor because she played poorly and she got into an argument when she discovered they were playing for money.

/She had much to learn. Franklin called her "Baby," half an endearing nickname and half a description of her immaturity. Later on when she grew with experience, he shortened Baby to Babs, a name he called her until his death. However, the blunt truth was that he was as immature as she/When they visited the Fergusons at Novar, Sydney and Beatrice Webb, the leaders of the Fabian Society and celebrated investigators of England's social problems, came to lunch. Instead of permitting the older couple to hold the floor, with typical youthful brashness "Franklin discussed the methods of learning at Harvard with the husband," said Eleanor, "while I discussed the servant problem with the wife!"/There was little about Eleanor on that occasion that would have prompted George Bernard Shaw, the close friend of the Webbs, to label her as he did years later, "the head of the Women's Movement in North America."/

Their immaturity followed them everywhere. In Scotland, while visiting old friends, Eleanor was asked to open a bazaar. "Talk in public?" Her voice quivered. "Never!" When she adamantly refused despite the plea that as the President's niece she would lend the occasion some needed color and authority, Franklin agreed to save the day with a thoughtful talk. "Cook your vegetables in milk," he chose as his theme and he hammered away at this point before his audience. Unfortunately, milk was a rare commodity in the area and his words brought on only loud guffaws. He managed to sweat out the ordeal, though he ended both hurt and angry.

Not long afterward Franklin got even with Eleanor for not making a fool of herself instead of letting him make a fool of himself. They were at a tea and a woman bent forward and demanded of Eleanor, "Do tell me, my dear, what exactly is the difference between your national and state governments?"

"Well, you see . . ." Eleanor began, only to fall silent. She had nothing to say. The niece of the President knew almost nothing about the American government. Finally after she pleaded with Franklin with her eyes, he reluctantly took over for her. "Not only were women not supposed to know anything about their own government in those days," Eleanor discovered later, "but they even prided themselves on their enforced ignorance." However, in her case she resolved on the spot that when she returned to the United States she would hurry to the public library and find a good book on American government.

It had been Eleanor's hope to parade her handsome husband before the girls at Allenswood and to introduce him to Mlle. Souvestre. Unfortunately, Mlle. Souvestre died shortly before their trip to Europe and

[57]

Franklin never met the woman whose name and thoughts rained down on him relentlessly from his wife.

When their honeymoon came to an end late that summer, both Eleanor and Franklin were slightly wiser in the ways of the world. However, nothing Eleanor learned abroad was of any assistance to her in coping with her mother-in-law's domination of her life. Even from across the ocean the upper hand of Sally Roosevelt was evident. "I am really quite ashamed to send you such stupid epistles," Eleanor apologized for her very existence in one letter to Sally. Once home in New York, Eleanor's first shudder came when Sally commandeeringly announced that she had taken a house for her children at 125 East Thirty-sixth Street, just three short blocks from her own town house. "How thoughtful of Mama," Franklin exclaimed, when he learned she had not only found a place for them but that she had also furnished it and hired their servants. But Eleanor had a queazy feeling that something was amiss.

This feeling brought on no outburst, for Eleanor was physically miserable. She was expecting her first child and was not doing well. "Splendid," Sally congratulated her. "We'll name the baby James after my late husband."

However, the baby who arrived in the world in May 1906 was a girl, and the young mother selected her name. Anna Eleanor Roosevelt, she gave the infant the same name as her own and her mother. The young father proudly dubbed her "Sis."

Until Anna (as Eleanor called her daughter in order to avoid confusion with herself) was born, Eleanor made it a ritual to ride every afternoon with her mother-in-law and to take at least one meal a day with her. There was a formality about the older woman that was in direct contrast to her beloved Mlle. Souvestre. Sally Roosevelt bedecked herself with furs and orchids and used a lorgnette. Eleanor learned that whenever Sally Roosevelt went abroad, she and Franklin were to meet her at the pier on her return no matter what they were doing at the time. She also learned that her mother-in-law was in a constant stew about Franklin's health. She must see him frequently to judge for herself, then return shortly afterward to reassess the physical condition of her boy, who was bursting with good health.

After the birth of Anna, Eleanor leaned even more on her mother-in-law, for she was totally unprepared for the duties of motherhood. She called on her for guidance on almost everything "and never thought of asking for anything which I felt would not meet with her approval." In only one respect were she and Franklin outside her complete domination. "I think she always regretted," Eleanor pointed out, "that my husband had money of his own from his father and that I had a small income of my own." The house at Hyde Park had been left to Sally but she couldn't sell it without approval from Franklin—not that she ever contemplated such a step. This was to be their home as well as hers, Sally informed Eleanor, but everything would be run according to her dictates. When Franklin made some feeble attempts to offer his mother advice about running her establishment, he was quickly slapped down, adding to Eleanor's picture of her mother-in-law as a formidable personality. Even though Hyde Park was to be their base of operations, "Franklin's mother," Eleanor later admitted, "never allowed him to interfere with the running of the place at Hyde Park, or the farm, but the woodland was his and he ran that as his own."

One of the things Sally impressed upon Eleanor was that a well-run home demanded a retinue of servants. People of their class could not sully themselves with the menial aspects of living. "My mother-in-law had a regular staff of cook, kitchen maid, personal maid, housemaid, waitress or butler, laundress, coachman and a chauffeur," Eleanor noted. Servants should be paid small wages and be given gifts, she was told. The small wages would hold them in line and the gifts would make them work hard to please.

Even babies were better off with trained nurses instead of mothers. With this assurance, Eleanor hired a nurse for Anna. Unfortunately, the nurse she hired was morbidly concerned with infant diseases. Ever on the lookout and with great glee for signs of malformities and malignancies in baby Anna, the nurse's avocation held Eleanor in a continual state of jitters. That Anna would ever reach adulthood was beyond belief. The household was soon reduced to tense anxiety while the nurse's further probing was awaited by the terror-stricken mother. Finally, when false alarms piled up and Eleanor wilted, she worked up sufficient courage to fire the nurse.

However, this was only a half measure, for what trooped through Eleanor's home for the next few years was a long list of arrogant nurses for her children. Most of the English nurses she employed immediately recognized her lack of knowledge and self-confidence. Instead of assisting her, they ordered her around as well as the children. Several were Simon Legrees and punished the children, often unjustly, and frowned upon her with blazing eyes on the few occasions when she was courageous enough to object to their cruel strong-arm methods of discipline. If only she had thrown all these nurses out, rolled up her sleeves and taken care of her babies herself, "my children would have had far happier childhoods," she realized when it was too late. Years afterward she

[59]

ruefully admitted, "I don't think many mothers will make the mistakes I made in bringing up my children."

There was one day when she handled baby Anna herself, but the results were so disastrous that she retired quickly from nursery care. She put Anna out for a morning nap in a box outside the back window. No sooner was all this accomplished when Anna took to screaming. "A modern mother," Eleanor remembered from something she had read, "does not pick up a baby when it cries."

Priding herself on being a modern mother, she was severely jolted an hour or two later when the wall phone rang. "How dare you let a child cry like that?" an indignant voice bellowed. "I am going to report you to the Society for the Prevention of Cruelty to Children!"

Anna was quickly retrieved and Eleanor's experiment at direct care ended for the time being.

There was little time now to pay much attention to Anna. As 1907 came in, Eleanor suddenly fell ill. The doctor who was called to the house insisted on an immediate operation. Through an overdose of ether she passed into a coma. Franklin was sure she was dead. The worried doctor stood bent over her and mumbling, "Is she gone? Can you feel her pulse?" as she opened her eyes.

When Anna was less than a year old, Eleanor became pregnant again, and once more she went through several months of nausea. She was to suffer in this fashion carrying each of her six babies. When her waist measurement spread to 34 inches from its tiny normal condition, she was certain that she would present Franklin with twins. Once again the eager look returned to the eyes of Franklin and his mother, and Eleanor prayed that she would have a son in order to please them.

There were no twins. Two days before Christmas in 1907, she gave birth to James. Later when she looked beyond Franklin's and Sally's pride, she regretted not having another daughter to provide companionship for Anna.

They were a family of four now, and in 1908 Sally Roosevelt decided without consulting her daughter-in-law that the fifteen-foot-wide house she had supplied them was too little. They must have something larger, she told the New York architect who built the Freer Gallery in Washington. There must also be closer association between her son's family and herself. The result was ingenious joint houses for the Franklin Roosevelts and for herself at 47 and 49 East Sixty-fifth Street. On the outside, each house was four stories high, of brick and stone construction and with iron balconies off the second floor. Inside, adjoining dining rooms and drawing rooms were turned into single rooms by opening sliding panels.

Here now the servants congregated, nurses controlled the children and the panels moved to admit Sally. Poor little James was quickly diagnosed as a heart case and for some years had to be carried up and down stairs. He was excessively shy and retiring and became a toy for sister Anna, who enjoyed pushing him over whenever she found him upright, Eleanor discovered.

Another Roosevelt appeared. When Anna was still two and James hardly past his first birthday, a third child, named Franklin, Jr., was born in March, 1909. "He was the biggest and most beautiful of all the babies," she said. His disposition was angelic and he thrived no matter what his nursing care. However, in the fall he contracted the flu. Doctors hurried to answer Eleanor's frenzied calls, but they had little to offer and he died in November. Eleanor was severely depressed by his death, unlike Franklin, whose attitude she said was: "This has happened. Now where do we go from here?"

The realization that she had no life of her own came over Eleanor one night shortly after she and Franklin moved into their half of the adjoining houses. She was sitting before her dressing table when suddenly she burst into uncontrollable sobs. The door flew open and Franklin strode into the bedroom.

"What's the matter?" he asked, bewildered. "Is there anything wrong?"

"I don't want to live in this house." She turned toward him and moaned.

"But why not?" he demanded.

"Because it isn't mine in any way. I had nothing to do with getting it and it isn't the kind of house I would have got. I hate it."

"Now, now." Franklin put his arm about her and tried to console her. "I think you are taking Mama a little too seriously," he told her. "You know you're really quite mad"—he patted her shoulder gently—"but I'm sure you'll feel different in a little while."

And so she stayed in the house. It was years yet before she stood up for herself and stopped spending all her time trying to please Mama. But even then she had misgivings. As she wrote in her diary as late as October 3, 1919: "Mama and I have a bad time. I should be ashamed of myself and I am not. She is too good and her judgment is better than mine. But I can live more easily."

For the first five years of her marriage she and Franklin lived a rather aimless existence as they tried to adjust to each other's personality.

Where Franklin was outgoing, Eleanor was shy without his normal outbursts of bubbling joy. His understanding of people and motives expanded during this period, for he was out in the world. Sheltered as she was and fearful of incurring the displeasure of Sally or her children's nurses, hers was blunted. Once she told Franklin that an aunt of his who was intelligent, beautiful and charming seemed discontented and unhappy with her lot. She was amazed that there was more to people than their surface impression. "That is my aunt's form of happiness," Franklin explained to her. "She enjoys feeling that life is not treating her too well, and unless she could complain just a little she would really be unhappy."

Where Franklin was secretive about things dear to his heart, she was naïvely frank. Her code did not permit white lies or hiding one's true feelings. Nor did it permit her to let someone else—even her husband —pay her bills when she had money. When the household budget he prepared showed that $600 was required each month to run their affairs, she insisted that she bear half the burden. While this was not in accordance with the strict Victorian standards under which he had been raised, he quickly agreed.

Neither had yet attained the love of people they later bore as their standard. Letters of this period to Sally are revealing. "We took supper with ——— much against Franklin's will." "Eleanor was overcome by the bad manners and 'revolting appearance' of ———." In 1907 when Sara went to Europe, Franklin wrote her, "In case we don't see ——— all summer, Hymn 684 should be sung—Peace, perfect Peace." Eleanor wrote her about taking someone sailing—"This ought to last ——— for some time; it will us."

There were the little irksome things about Franklin that required a conscious adjustment on Eleanor's part. For instance, he was never on time to meet her for an appointment. Always conscientious, she was on hand fifteen minutes before the scheduled time. The result was that when he finally came whistling down the street, she was furious and they argued. Invariably he promised to come early next time, and invariably he was late. Finally, she studiously became the late arrival.

He was also stingy when it came to spending money on himself. He could not bear to part with money to buy clothes. Once when she delivered a pair of his run-down shoes to the shoemaker, he asked why they were not in the closet. "Oh, I soled them," she told him.

"Sold them!" he wailed. "Why they were still usable—in fact, almost new."

He refused to spend more than two dollars for a shirt. As for ties, he

[62]

let her buy his entire supply for him and accepted them from her as presents. Years later when he was President and was proclaimed as the best-dressed man in the country, Eleanor announced that the news was "disheartening. Now it is more difficult than ever to get him to buy new clothes. Before it required the whole family to wear down his resistance to replenishing his wardrobe. Now it is impossible!" Franklin considered the spending of money an art for experts. He was a sharp bargainer, unlike Eleanor. Even during the bliss of their honeymoon he had relegated her to sight-seeing while he bought old books in the shops of Italy. "You have no gift whatsoever for bargaining," and he had sent her off to look at Roman relics so she would not be hovering about to cramp his sharp style.

While Eleanor had her babies and spent her extra time reading and trying to please Mama, Franklin dabbled at dull law and spent off days rushing off with the boys of his set to play golf, tennis and swim. Sometimes he went away for days with friends on sailing expeditions along the shore in his schooner yacht, *Half Moon*. Without rancor, she was glad that he could get away from domesticity, though she was beginning to harbor her first thoughts that she had to watch out for him and his mother or "develop into a completely colorless echo of both."

Besides having Mama as next-door neighbor in town and spending weekends and holidays with her at Hyde Park, Eleanor also had her continual presence during the summer at Campobello, Sally's island retreat. With the growth of Eleanor's family, Sally had purchased a "cottage" for them at Campobello, close to her own residence. A "cottage" in the Roosevelt lexicon was any country house with fewer than twenty-five rooms.

Here with the retinue of servants looking after their needs, Eleanor and Franklin joined the summer colony in the endless games of bridge and euchre. Alone with Franklin they sometimes spent evenings at a card game called piquet, though cards bored her to tears. She had a gnawing feeling that she must enjoy what her husband did or lose his companionship. When Franklin sweated and strained to lay out a golf course at Campobello, she thought it necessary that she take up the game and walk the course with him. On the sly she practiced driving and putting. Then one morning she informed him that she was a golfer, too, and was ready to play a round with him. He looked at her quizzically and said finally with a shrug, "Well, if you say so."

For three holes she dug up the turf in a torturous effort to propel the little white ball down the fairway and into the cup. Franklin's smile disappeared en route. There was no conversation.

On the fourth hole tee he stared at her beet-red face and said flatly, "Eleanor, why don't you take up some other sport?"

Another person might have dissolved in self-disgust with such browbeating. However, Eleanor was of a stronger nature. There was the summer of 1908 when fragile baby James lay ailing and they went to Seabright, New Jersey instead of Campobello. They took a crowded little house built on stilts on the boardwalk. The beachhouses were so close together that there was a constant din of wailing babies and exasperated parents. Little Anna found it sport one afternoon when brother Jimmy lay sleeping in his carriage to push him off for a long but harmless fall to the sand below. Franklin had to commute daily to New York and bought an early-day Ford for transportation. The car could run only in high gear and presented a real problem since he had to run it onto the ferry if he wanted to cross the Hudson. He could run it onto a ferry only if the boat were empty. He took such pride in his ability to handle this weird vehicle that he insisted that Eleanor learn to drive it and have some fun, too. But he changed his mind when he came home one night and saw the corner of the porch sheared off and the gatepost demolished. Eleanor was so upset by her mishap that she didn't drive again for years.

From her golf and automobile experiences, Eleanor realized that it wasn't vital to have the same interests as Franklin. This conclusion was compounded with still another effort to be adventurous, when she joined him at his greatest joy, sailing. However, she got terribly seasick and retired finally to her babies and books. After that, she let her brother Hall, who was now living with them, take her place. Nine years older than Hall, Franklin treated him like a son, taking him along on a rough cruise to Nova Scotia. On one cruise Franklin incurred Eleanor's wrath by talking Hall into climbing a tree to capture a cormorant's nest. When Hall returned home he smelled so foul that he had to bury his clothes and take a sudsy bath before being permitted to enter her good graces again.

Sometimes Eleanor visited Hall at Groton, where she checked on his progress with the Rev. Peabody and watched him as he played with his two close friends and Groton mates, Sumner Welles and Averell Harriman, the son of the railroad tycoon. On occasion, she and Franklin dispatched her brother to visit with Uncle Ted's family. Generally, he returned from such visits in an exhausted state. Once when Hall returned with some color left in his cheeks, Franklin laughingly observed, "He looks better than he usually does after staying with the strenuous Presidential family."

While Franklin was good-natured in his treatment of Hall, Eleanor took her responsibilities far too seriously. She was in many respects the reincarnation of Grandmother Hall. "Are you sure you washed?" and "Don't you think it's about time you combed your hair?" she nagged at him incessantly. The result was that he came to regard Franklin as his protector.

After an exasperating bout of this sort with Hall, she generally fell into a low moody state. She called this her "Griseldish Mood," a condition that frightened Franklin since it consisted of "shutting up like a clam, not telling anyone what was the matter and being too obviously humble and weak, feeling like a martyr and acting like one." It was not a mood that lasted only for a few hours, and Hall was not the sole source. After a Griseldish Mood had gone on for several days, Franklin would tell her she was acting like an idiot, which, for some unaccountable reason, snapped her out of it.

Sometimes when they wanted a holiday and the feeling of "living" they took the train to Washington. Here they visited Uncle Ted at the White House before he turned over the mansion to his hand-picked successor, fat, jovial William Howard Taft of Cincinnati, in March, 1909. Cousin Alice, who had added to her newsworthiness by dancing the hula, had married Congressman Nicholas Longworth in February, 1906. Uncle Ted foresaw a great future for Franklin in the Republican Party and urged him to get into politics. There was no higher calling than the public service where you worked for the betterment of the lives of your fellow men.

But Franklin did not seem interested and Eleanor saw no reason for pushing him in that direction. Uncle Ted would brush his mustache quickly and then turn fondly toward Eleanor to ply her with questions about herself. For, as Aunt Corinne once observed, "Eleanor was always my Brother Ted's favorite niece. She is more like him than any of his children."

At home Eleanor and Franklin seldom discussed politics. In fact, they had few talks on basic matters. On one occasion, Eleanor fairly startled her young husband when she asked him, "How much should we teach our children about religion, Franklin?"

"What?" He lowered his paper with a quizzical expression in his eyes.

"Don't you think it is our duty to let their minds be free so they can decide for themselves when they are older?"

"They had better go to church and learn what I learned," he sputtered.

"But are you sure you believe in everything you learned?" she asked, concerned.

He rattled his paper and said with finality, "I never really thought about the subject. I think it is just as well not to think about things like that too much."

Franklin failed to pass some of his law courses his last year and did not get his degree. However, he passed the New York Bar in 1907 and went to work for the Wall Street law firm of Carter, Ledyard and Milburn. They took him on as a clerk with no salary his first year. Nor was he given much to do, which was understandable considering that they had a blue-chip clientele and he was without experience. Although he found law somewhat lifeless and dull, nevertheless he chafed under this regime. One Saturday when he came home early in the afternoon, Eleanor expressed surprise that he was home during working hours.

"Mr. Ledyard ordered me to go home," he told her. He had gone to lunch with two other clerks in the office and they had downed stein after stein of beer to drown their sorrow for their lowly status in the office. When they returned, Mr. Ledyard had righteously bellowed at Franklin, "You're drunk, Mr. Roosevelt. Go home immediately!"

Franklin held on to the job despite this incident, but little by little Eleanor noticed that he was beginning to take on the country squire status of his father. Little by little he was pushing himself into the gentlemanly activities his father had immersed himself in at Hyde Park. Though James Roosevelt had left his Hyde Park estate to Sally, Franklin still considered it his home and was developing a strong interest in the affairs of the neighboring village. Eleanor, while she noticed this development, liked her handsome young husband too much to interfere with his desire. It was enough for her that he was finding pleasant ways to occupy his time and that, despite all her own shortcomings, he considered her good-looking and often spoke of her "pretty eyes" and "lovely hair."

What difference did it make that he was proud in 1909 when the Hudson-Fulton Celebration Commission put him in charge of Red Cross relief stations along the route of the parade? He had suddenly seemed older when the bank in Poughkeepsie, next door to Hyde Park, named him a director. He had also become a vestryman at the St. James Episcopal Church of Hyde Park and a member of the Rescue Hook and Ladder Company of the village.

So by 1910 Eleanor assumed, after five years of marriage, that hers would be the life of a fairly well-to-do lady married to a man who would dabble in charities, hobbies and village affairs. That he would

[66]

spend the rest of his life in politics and that she would, too, never entered her mind. He might become an internationally renowned bird watcher, but never, never a politician. In the first place, his eyesight should have barred him from that course. "He always said he was shortsighted when he passed people in the streets and didn't recognize his friends," she once noted. "But he could always point to a bird and tell me what it was."

Politics
last thing
she thought
he'd get into.

Chapter Eight

By the summer of 1910, Eleanor had watched her young husband progress to the point where he was functioning as chief clerk for his law firm in charge of minor municipal cases. In combination with his extracurricular activities at Hyde Park, he should have been happy, she thought. But he was not the least bit happy. As for her, at twenty-five she could measure the enormous progress she had made in the past several years from a poorly educated waif to being a mother and a social matron. However, at twenty-eight, filled as he was with unbridled ambition and vague impatience, Franklin was beginning to act like the man who had missed his boat.

Ironically, he told her, Carter, Ledyard and Milburn specialized in advising corporations on methods for outwitting the antitrust regulations imposed on them by Uncle Ted. Even so, he went on, senior members of the firm considered him too inexperienced to handle such matters. He was good enough solely for the unimportant cases. The result was that she watched the days dribble away with Franklin a trifle sadder each time he came home. Once he handed Eleanor a calling card he had printed to denote his lowly position. "Unpaid bills a specialty," she read. "Briefs on the liquor question furnished free to ladies. Race suicides cheerfully prosecuted."

She watched the storm brewing within Franklin. In the evenings when he was home, he began talking more and more about their many conversations with Uncle Ted, when Uncle Ted had pointedly argued that rich young men owed it to less able citizens to enter public service. "If that is what you want, do it," she urged. That was what he wanted, he said bravely. However, when it came to pin-pointing this decision, how did one go about it?

In the end, after expostulating with Eleanor about the various political posts he believed himself capable of handling, he gingerly wrote from Campobello to friends in Hyde Park. What he should like, he said, was to become town supervisor. While this would not be full-time, he told Eleanor, at least it would place him squarely on the political

[68]

ladder. Eagerly he and Eleanor awaited the reply to his letter, but when it came it was to inform them that there was no election for town supervisor that year.

However, unknown to them, the two Democratic leaders of Dutchess County, John Mack, the district attorney of the county and Mayor John K. Sague of Poughkeepsie, got wind of Franklin's letter and decided he would do well as candidate for another office. The state senatorship of their district, New York's twenty-sixth, was up that year and no established Democrat was willing to run. Overwhelmingly Republican, the district had sent only a single Democrat to the New York State Senate since 1856.

Franklin burst through the doorway with a grin one day. With great excitement he spilled out details of a call paid him at his desk at Carter, Ledyard and Milburn by John Mack. " 'You've got only about one chance in five to win,' " he told Eleanor Mack had said. " 'But even if you lose, it will be a good way to get your name before the voters if you run for office again.' "

"Should I run?" he asked her.

She knew nothing about politics and refused to make up his mind for him. "You'll have to make your own decision," she said. When his mother found out what was brewing, she expressed immediate disgust at his going into politics at all—and as a Democrat! "I was a Republican until I saw the error of my ways," she later apologized. "Many of my friends," she added in retrospect, "said it was a shame for so fine a young man to associate himself with 'dirty' politicians."

Eleanor had never seen him happier. He was suddenly purposeful and she was glad. Despite the admonitions from his mother, he determined to run for senator. However, even with the strong support of Mack and Mayor Sague, the nomination was not his for the asking. Other Democratic leaders in the district would have to approve him, too. The complexities of politics seemed overwhelming to Eleanor.

"Mack and Sague are arranging a picnic for loyal Democrats," Franklin told her, "and if I can pass muster I'll get the nomination for senator."

When she wanted to know if he was supposed to parade before the people at the picnic, he laughingly told her no. Instead, he was expected to make a speech. He had never made a political speech before, yet was not the least bit concerned.

Elliott was almost due to be born, so Eleanor did not go to the picnic with him. All that day she waited anxiously to learn how he had done.

[69]

Was Sally right about politics? Would Franklin be better off if he failed to pass the test?

When he returned home he was in even higher spirits than when he had left. He had given his talk and it had gone over well. "On that joyous occasion of clams and sauerkraut and real beer I made my first speech," he announced happily.

But there was one thing he hadn't liked, he told her. A few of the politicians had expressed the opinion that the only reason they might accept him as a candidate was that he was rich. They evidently believed that the name Roosevelt meant unlimited dollar resources. "They thought I would be a gold mine, but unfortunately, the gold was not there." He had been given to understand that if he ran, he could expect no financial help from the party.

There was another matter that bothered him, he told Eleanor. Ever since he had left the White House to become editor of the *Outlook* Magazine in New York, Uncle Ted had taken over the state's Republicans for his own. Franklin feared that if he ran, Uncle Ted would visit the senatorial district and knock him flying with a single ridiculing speech.

"Why don't you write to him and ask if he plans to speak in the district?" Eleanor advised him.

"But I can't do that."

"Then why not write to Auntie Bye and ask her to find out from Uncle Ted?"

It was a roundabout way of doing things, but Franklin was young and directness was not part of his make-up. He wrote to Eleanor's Auntie Bye and a week later she forwarded Uncle Ted's reply to the inquiry. "Franklin ought to go into politics without the least regard as to where I speak or don't speak," Uncle Ted wrote, annoyed. "He's a fine fellow, but I wish he had ———'s political views."

"What about Mr. Ledyard?" Eleanor asked. "How will he take your running for political office? He probably won't like it."

She was right. Ledyard scowled when he heard about it. If he won, Ledyard pointed out, and that seemed incredible, he would get only $1,500 a year as state senator. "Franklin, my boy," Franklin imitated Mr. Ledyard's voice, "you have too good a start on your legal career with this firm to toss it away now."

Yet despite the lukewarm support from the district's Democratic leaders, Mr. Ledyard's warning and his own slim chances at victory, in the end Franklin decided to run. Whether he won or not Eleanor did not care, so long as he was happier than as a municipal court lawyer.

Elliott was born in September and in October Franklin left Eleanor for his stint at campaigning. Eleanor would always be partial to Elliott because he bore her beloved father's name. That "Bunny," as she called him, was a sickly child who suffered painful accidents, also drew her to him.

Not having paid the slightest attention to political campaigns before, Eleanor was soon appalled at the name-calling involved. She winced at what she read in the papers. Republicans were punching him as a boy trading on the name of his wife's uncle. But what rot to cut him down to their size, Eleanor told herself. They kicked him hard as a Wall Street lawyer and as a wealthy young snob without interest in dirt farmers and country-store clerks. They jibed at what they called his quaint appearance—his nose-pinching pince-nez, extra high collar, flashing gold cuff links, and the bad habit of throwing his head back when he talked.

Worst of all, her idol, Uncle Ted, had been induced to make a speech in the district. One word from him in opposition to Franklin and poor Franklin would be slaughtered. Franklin was uneasy waiting all that day to hear what Uncle Ted would say about him. But Uncle Ted was still her idol when he could not be induced to mention Franklin by name.

The Democratic politicians tried to talk Eleanor into riding with her husband in his rugged campaign. It would do well, they argued, if the candidate's wife were present to sit and sigh and beam while her husband spoke. There might also be rumors if a married man was on the hustings without his wife. However, Eleanor refused. Politics interested her little and, besides, Elliott was only a month old and she wasn't up to the rigors involved. From what she heard, Franklin was bouncing from town to town by car and, as he put it, "at the dangerous pace of about 22 miles an hour in Mr. Hawkey's old red Maxwell, without any front windshield, without any top."

On only one occasion during his campaign did she come out to hear him speak. This was a painful experience for her. Who was more upset by that experience—she or Franklin—she was not sure. It was the first time she had seen him on a political platform and she thought he looked so thin and nervous that the sight of him embarrassed her. The blood seemed to have been drained from his face, he was expressionless and his strong chin jutted out even more than she remembered. The slow manner in which he spoke made her avert her eyes. His frequent long pauses between words gave him a fumbling and groping appearance, and she was both uneasy and sorry for him. Nor was the thin voice the

[71]

forceful tone she knew at home. As for the wooden gestures and flailing arms, Mlle. Souvestre would have dressed him down for ineptitude.

"I know I am no orator, but . . ." he apologized at one point in his address.

"You don't have to be an orator, Roosevelt!" someone in the audience shouted back. The crowd cheered at this exchange and Eleanor felt momentarily better. Franklin also said, "My friends," something she was going to hear thousands upon thousands of times in future years.

That month she saw little of him. On one occasion when he tried to jump on a moving streetcar, he misjudged his leap and fell to the pavement. He was bloody and his clothes were torn when he struggled into the house. Poor, poor Franklin struggling to win. But she stayed up late like a Florence Nightingale to soak his torn arm and leg with disinfectant, and he limped back to the campaign.

In the end it was worth all the agony. During the downpour on election day she walked proudly with Franklin and Sally to the voting center. And when the vote was tallied late that evening, startled Democrats discovered that instead of suffering the usual defeat in the district, young Roosevelt had actually won. His total was 15,708 compared with 14,568 for his Republican opponent, or a victory by 1,140 votes. How much of the victory was his and how much depended on general dissatisfaction with Republicans was not possible to discern. For after a quarter of a century, both the New York State legislature and the governor were Democrats.

Chapter Nine

Albany in January 1911 was an old run-down city. Though it was the center of the state's politics, it was a desert otherwise. Most members kept their families at home while they hung out in Albany hotels all week and subsisted on fried foods until the weekends when they commuted home.

Eleanor was an exception. She would move to Albany to be near Franklin. Although her mother-in-law considered the move unwise, Eleanor insisted to Franklin that it be made. Here was the first opportunity in her entire life to live independently and she was not going to miss the chance. As she put it, "I was beginning to realize that something within me craved to be an individual." Franklin's only doubt about her intention to join him was that perhaps his election was a freak and that his district might revert to its staunch Republicanism by the next election in 1912. But when she persisted he agreed.

They leased a large house on State Street not far from the musty old capitol. It was finely furnished and had a large library where Franklin hung his coat of arms over the fireplace. Besides her three children, Eleanor brought with her two nurses, a wet nurse and three maids.

Her first taste of political life occurred immediately upon her arrival in Albany on New Year's Day, 1911. Franklin had blithely scheduled a reception at home that afternoon, and while she was still moving in, more than a thousand of his constituents came to call. She wore her best dress, which went to the floor in the style of the day. Her high shoes were sharply pointed and her soft brown hair lay piled on top her head. The crowd came to look her over, talk to the new senator and eat all the food on the high-piled tables. Sally was there with her lorgnette and beamed as she stood next to her boy. When the last guest wandered out after three hours, the place looked as though a cyclone had hit it. The babies, kept upstairs throughout the reception, could be heard bawling.

Hardly had Eleanor said good-by to Franklin's mother, who had come to Albany for the day, and begun assessing the damage when the phone rang. It was Governor Dix excitedly requesting her and Franklin to hurry over to the Executive Mansion and join him and his wife and a few friends for evening dancing. All evening Eleanor watched Franklin. He was so gay and relaxed that she realized politics was the right career for him.

She met most of the political leaders either at Governor Dix's dance or during the next few days. They were all excited because of the Democratic swing. "I'm Al Smith," the thirty-seven-year-old majority leader of the Assembly introduced himself to her. She saw a too generous mouth and nose and heard a rather unrefined way of talking, but the eyes were soft and warm. "You're Harvard," he told Franklin with a trace of belligerency. "I'm Fulton's Fish Market."

Eleanor was pleased when the reporters labeled Franklin as the "baby" of the Senate. He was just under twenty-nine and at his handsomest. Not even the brash Albany correspondent for the New York *Herald,* an unkempt gnomelike man named Louis Howe, could dampen her spirits when he scoffingly told her upon first meeting that a state senator was a person who "is of importance somewhere between that of a janitor and a committee clerk." Though Franklin liked this reporter immediately, she was glad to move away from him.

She hardly expected Franklin to run the state government because he had told her that even a veteran of five terms in the Senate was often of little consequence. And when the governor completed his inaugural address and the first roll call was completed, she expected a quiet stay in Albany until the legislature quit in the spring. What she did not know was that her "baby" of the Senate was going to cause the biggest ruckus in the entire state legislature that year.

Even before she had rearranged the furniture in the State Street house, Franklin was the center of an enormous political tussle. U. S. Senator Chauncey Depew's six-year term was to end on March 4 and the state legislature had to select his successor. With the legislature now in Democratic hands, it was assumed by all parties concerned that Tammany Hall boss and owner of four profitable saloons, Charles F. Murphy, would have no trouble winning acceptance for his man, William "Blue-Eyed Billy" Sheehan as next U. S. Senator.

"Blue-Eyed Billy is the last man we should send to the Senate," Franklin ranted at home when Murphy's choice became known.

"What difference does it make who is Senator?" Eleanor asked.

"What difference?" Franklin roared. "Blue-Eyed Billy" had been a bitter opponent of Grover Cleveland, a man Franklin's father had revered. Besides, charged Franklin, he was an unscrupulous party hack, a corporation lawyer who didn't know the national interest on any issue from a hole in the wall; and furthermore, what business did a millionaire utilities operator have serving in the United States Senate?

When he vowed to go down fighting to keep Sheehan from the Senate, Eleanor looked askance. "The rights and wrongs of that fight meant very little to me," she admitted.

She was startled when eighteen other state senators came to the house, all of them filled with emotion as they denounced "Blue-Eyed Billy" and elected Franklin as their leader to fight the confirmation. Without their votes and with a solid Republican opposition, Sheehan could not possibly win.

The fight was on in earnest when Tammany Boss Murphy took away all patronage from the Democratic insurgents. Though the issue escaped her, Eleanor retaliated by opening up her house as the small group's headquarters, where they could plot and talk and give each other courage.

Every morning during the fight the insurgents came to her house to map that day's strategy. Afterward, they marched to the Senate to cast their negative votes against "Blue-Eyed Billy," returned to her house following lunch, sat around talking bravely and smoking heavily and nervously during the afternoon, went out to eat and then came back for more talk. For three months this circus went on, while Eleanor passed out beer and sandwiches and sat with them until long past midnight every night while they talked. Interviewed during this period, Franklin explained, "We just sit around and swap stories like soldiers at the bivouac fire." In time the house got so saturated with thick tobacco smoke that Eleanor had to move Sis, Jimmy and Bunny to third-floor bedrooms to stop their nausea. But as she passed around the beer and listened to the talk, Eleanor absorbed a great deal about political strategy. Now and then she expressed a quiet opinion. Years later Franklin claimed proudly that his wife's "political sagacity" had its beginning at these anti-Sheehan sessions.

When the fight continued unabated throughout January and February, Franklin began getting wide national publicity. Hardly a paper Eleanor opened failed to carry his picture. He was likened to Uncle Ted for his high-principled stand, a description that made Murphy sick but Eleanor proud. Uncle Ted, who was also in the news because of his break with his protégé, President Taft, wrote Eleanor with glee about Franklin's activity. Asked sarcastically on the Senate floor one day if he was an admirer of Theodore Roosevelt, the Republican, Franklin retorted: "Why, who can help but admire him? My uncle-in-law

[75]

will come back all right, no matter what some people believe." Eleanor, sitting in the gallery, was pleased.

As a last resort, Sheehan confronted Franklin one day and asked for a meeting between the two. Franklin told Eleanor that evening, "Blue-Eyed Billy and his wife are coming for lunch tomorrow. We're going to have it out once and for all."

This was something she dreaded. As a hypothetical problem it was exciting, but as an actuality the Sheehan affair made suddenly personal was another matter.

"Blue-Eyed Billy" and Mrs. Sheehan came on schedule. Expecting an ogre or at best some uncouth lout, Eleanor was surprised to find him pleasant as well as cultured, at lunch. Afterward as though on signal, the older man and Franklin rose and disappeared into the study. Left alone with Mrs. Sheehan, Eleanor was suddenly unhappy. Their mouths seemed to be coated with glue as they talked on and on about the weather, furniture and children, while their eyes were trained on the study door. From time to time loud angry shouts came from within. Some were Sheehan's and some were Franklin's. Eleanor and Mrs. Sheehan had to pretend they heard none of it. Finally the door flew open and Sheehan came stalking out, his face clouded and red, with pale-faced Franklin walking silently behind him.

As soon as the outside door closed on the Sheehans, Eleanor asked worriedly, "Did you come to any agreement?"

"Certainly not," Franklin snapped, putting on a too-serious expression that sat incongruously on his young features.

At the end of March Murphy dropped "Blue-Eyed Billy" and on the sixty-fourth ballot Franklin's insurgents accepted Murphy's compromise candidate, James A. O'Gorman, another Tammany candidate. Big Tim Sullivan, Brooklyn's Tammany leader and another saloonkeeper, remarked on Franklin's role, "You know those Roosevelts. This one is still young. Wouldn't it be safer to take him out and drown him before he grows up? If you don't he'll cause trouble sure as shooting before he's much older."

The aftermath of the fight frightened Eleanor. Franklin had formed a new law firm with Harry Hooker and Langdon Marvin who had been clerks with him at Carter, Ledyard and Milburn. Murphy's animosity caused them to lose their first important client. Others among the insurgents with notes outstanding found them mysteriously falling due. One insurgent's ensuing misfortune angered Eleanor. "This man owned a small country newspaper, largely dependent for existence on government printing and the advertising of local merchants," Eleanor learned. "He also had a wife and two children. Persuasion and bribery had been tried and when both failed he was told they would ruin his paper. The government printing was refused him and on one pretext or another the local merchants found it wise to withdraw their advertising. He was a ruined man."

Following the Sheehan fight, the excitement subsided. The house on State Street went back to normal. The insurgents no longer spent their days and nights there and in time the odor of stale cigar smoke disappeared. Still edgy from the emotional pulling and hauling, Eleanor enrolled in a local class on how to relax. She also joined women in Albany in discussing the slums of the city and the wretched living conditions of the poor. Yet, though she was conscious of the world of unhappy lives made so by poverty, she did not join the others in personal inspections. Sally Roosevelt, like Grandmother Hall, warned her insistently that if she went into the slums she was bound to bring home to her children some of the loathsome diseases found there. With the memory of the sad ending of little Franklin, Jr., still preying on her mind, she decided to follow the older woman's advice.

On March 25, 1911, shortly before the "Blue-Eyed Billy" Sheehan affair was compromised, the spectacular Triangle Shirtwaist Factory fire occurred in New York City. When locked doors prevented the working girls from escaping, 148 perished in the blaze. Frances Perkins, who had been secretary to Mayor Mitchell, helped organize socially-conscious and angry women in a crusade for fire prevention. Branching out into other activities, Miss Perkins went to Albany to lobby for the Consumer's League on a bill to provide a 54-hour week for women in industry.

Eleanor and Franklin met her at this time. Of Eleanor, Miss Perkins remembered her then as a quiet housewife. Franklin impressed her otherwise. "Awful arrogant fellow, that Roosevelt," she claimed Big Tim Sullivan said of him because of his lack of interest in taking a lead on the measure. On one occasion, she said, some Democratic senators were trying to make him be "reasonable" on a bill and that "his small mouth pursed up." He snorted when they finished and told them, "No, no, I wouldn't hear of it!" Eleanor was convinced that his action was not prompted by arrogance but because he was still shy despite his surface boldness on the Sheehan fight.

However, it was true that Franklin then was little concerned about social injustices and the means for correcting them. A dutiful wife, Eleanor followed his lead. As she explained her own position, she "took

[77]

it for granted that men were superior creatures." If he couldn't be bothered with labor problems or social legislation, her undeveloped view was that they couldn't be of great importance.

Eleanor had questioned the meaning of love when she was first married. Now she was certain she loved Franklin. In September of 1911, she wrote him from Campobello, "I have loved every minute, until you left, and since then I've felt very gloomy and I wish you were here, dear, all the time."

If anything disturbed her about Franklin's politics, it was that Tammany leaders were calling him a "reactionary"—whatever that meant—and a "publicity hound." For instance when he attacked Tammany for not supporting a forest fire protection bill, State Senator Pro Tempore Robert Wagner grumbled sarcastically in a heavy German accent, "Senator Roosevelt has gained his point. What he wants is a headline in the newspaper. Let us proceed to our business."

But if Tammany despised her husband, other Democrats did not hold the same opinion. In the fall of 1911 she handed him a letter that had come from Governor Woodrow Wilson of New Jersey. "He wants me to go to Trenton to talk to him about national politics," Franklin gasped elatedly.

He returned home all fired from their talk. "I promised to work for his nomination as President," he bubbled excitedly.

She smiled as a dutiful wife should. Yet Franklin's interest in Wilson brought a grave concern to her. Already there were strong reports that Uncle Ted was going to try for the Republican presidential nomination in 1912. What if he and Wilson were to run against each other? How could she remain a Democrat under these circumstances? And how could Franklin, who had voted for him for President in 1904? But this troublesome thought subsided with the ascendency of another thought: A wife must take the opinions of her husband. In a man's world a woman must show no independence. Furthermore, perhaps neither Uncle Ted nor Wilson would be nominated.

Things had a way of working themselves out with time. And in the spring of 1912 when Tammany opposed any support for Wilson at the state convention and refused to name Franklin even as an alternate delegate for the upcoming Democratic National Convention in Baltimore in June, Eleanor breathed easier.

Chagrined, Franklin decided to get away from it all. Eleanor's brother Hall was to graduate from Harvard and marry in June and Franklin proposed that the two go off on a trip to Panama. "You better come with me. This is your last fling," Franklin told him laughingly. They

[78]

were her giant men, Franklin, a healthy six feet two, and yellow-haired Hall, whose face hauntingly reminded her of both her father and mother and who was a 240-pounder at six feet three inches. "And as for you," Franklin told her, "you're going with me to Baltimore when I get back to watch Wilson get the nomination."

While her menfolk traveled down to see the wonders of the Canal Uncle Ted had started, Eleanor left her children and went to New Mexico. Isabella Selmes, her bridesmaid, and Bob Ferguson, who had been so attentive to Eleanor during her "coming out," had married and moved to New Mexico because Bob had tuberculosis. It was Eleanor's first trip alone since her marriage and her first time out west, to the land her father loved, and she caught its contagion. There were many picnics "up by the buzzard's nest," as Isabella put it, and rides into the endless desert. There were also moments to think about Franklin's enthusiasm for Wilson and her own concern about Uncle Ted.

Chapter Ten

I N JUNE, after Hall sported a big Phi Beta Kappa key on his vest and was safely married, Eleanor went to Baltimore with Franklin. The city was alive with flapping bunting and shouting paraders and hotel lobbies were crowded with bargaining politicians. Though Franklin sprang to excitement in this atmosphere, so far as Eleanor was concerned Baltimore was tropically hot and miserable. At the Democratic National Convention Hall where she went with Franklin, sickening smoke billowed from the thousands of cigars and everyone present screamed instead of talking. Unlearned in the ways of a national convention, from her perch in the hard galleries, the floor doings seemed to be in utter confusion. Instead of being a meeting of calm, friendly Democrats it was, from what she saw, a nasty, snarling contest among bitter antagonists.

Bands blared, gavels pounded, favorite sons bowed and one oily speech followed another. Knots of delegates stood in huddles. The hall grew hotter and hotter and the cigar smoke thicker. It was all a puzzle to Eleanor. One of the few humorous notes was what Al Smith did to a ballooned photograph of Champ Clark who was running against Wilson. Under the picture's caption which read *Don't he look like a President?* Al wrote, *No, he do not.*

Franklin's activities at the convention puzzled Eleanor, too. He had opened a headquarters of his own for Wilson and from it had issued a long statement to all delegates. Barred from the convention floor, he was forever in the press stand to get reporters to slant their convention stories in favor of Wilson.

Eleanor did not stay in Baltimore until the forty-sixth ballot that nominated Wilson. She could not recall ever being so bored and confused. When she fled Baltimore the nomination outcome was still in doubt. But at Campobello, where she had gone with the children and the servants for refuge, Franklin's triumphant telegram arrived: ALL MY PLANS VAGUE SPLENDID VICTORY. It was obvious that Wilson had won, but what Franklin's vague plans were, she did not know. The eventuality she had disliked considering was now at hand, however. Wilson would be opposing Uncle Ted.

Franklin's vague plans were cleared up when he got to Campobello. He would do some heavy campaigning for Wilson in the fall, and if Wilson won he would be in line for a top-rate national post. It was as simple as that, said Eleanor, but what if Uncle Ted beat Wilson? And what about the State Senate? Wouldn't it be better to hedge a bit and run for re-election?

Franklin was not sure that he wanted to run again for his Senate seat. But it was fairly obvious to Eleanor that he would because of his alternative, which was a return to stodgy law. Until the last minute he refused to commit himself. However, he finally jumped into the race when an enormous amount of bilge was spread by Tammany in his district against his candidacy.

"But we won't lease the State Street house again," he told her, "because we'll be moving to Washington with Wilson."

Eleanor, who found politics a great mystery, was puzzled by her husband's cockiness that he would win re-election handily. However, shortly before he got his campaign under way, his attitude changed abruptly. For both she and Franklin came down with typhoid fever. A great leveler, sickness brought on pessimism. Eleanor was to recover shortly without too much pain. But Franklin was to lie in bed day after day and week after week and come to resemble, in Eleanor's eyes, Robert Louis Stevenson, her favorite writer, in his last days on earth.

He moaned and groaned and argued with Eleanor that fate was dealing him a dirty trick. He must get out of bed to campaign for himself and he must make those speeches for Wilson. "We'll see what the doctor says," she stalled.

When the doctor ordered him to stay in bed indefinitely and give up any intention of campaigning, Franklin protested feebly. "I'll get out of bed and start my speeches anyway," he told Eleanor in a panic. However, he lacked the strength to do more than shake a weak fist.

"Perhaps you can get someone else to campaign for you?" Eleanor asked naïvely.

"But who?" miserable Franklin replied.

She thought a moment. "Why not that horrid man from the New York *Herald* who asked you for a job?"

Yes. Why not Louis Howe, that astute reporter? Howe knew all there was to know about New York politics, even though he took such a sarcastic approach. Howe had left the *Herald* to work on the Woodrow Wilson campaign in New York, but his job had fizzled out. In a financial emergency he had appealed to Franklin for help. But Franklin had nothing to offer him then. However, now he did.

Louis Howe came running on his short legs and crooked body. Eleanor was sorry she had thought of his name as soon as she let him in the house. He looked sickly with his bulging eyes, pockmarked face and chronic cough. He was never without a vile cigarette between his blistered lips ("I smoke nothing but Sweet Caporals"), and his most common ash tray was his greasy vest. He smelled as though he needed a bath, his fingers were all stained brown with nicotine, his nails were chewed ragged and his collar flopped sweaty and wilted. Eleanor's first thought about him was "that dirty little man" because he smelled up the house so and dirtied a room within a minute after entering.

When Howe walked out of Franklin's bedroom that day and smilingly told Eleanor he was going to run the campaign, she had serious misgivings about having made the suggestion to her husband. "Franklin will be President of the United States someday," the wizened Howe croaked expansively while she frowned in reply.

Nevertheless, Louis Howe and Franklin were soon thick as jungle trees and the "dirty little man" ran an excellent campaign for a candidate who couldn't leave his sickbed. Unable to trot his candidate around in person, Howe concocted a clever campaign based on written material. Democratic papers gave him free space to extol Franklin's virtues, while Republican newspapers grumbled but accepted money eagerly for full-page ads he wrote in Roosevelt's behalf. Howe also sent out to almost all eligible voters "personal" letters on various issues that he wrote for his candidate's facsimile signature.

There was no length to which he wasn't willing to go to improve Franklin's chances. One morning, for instance, Eleanor was astounded to read in the paper that her sick, bedded husband had been the hero the previous evening of the fire that burned the Dutcher House at Pawling. According to the paper he had dashed in and out among the flames to rescue a score of women and children. Only Louis Howe could have put that story across.

There was no question that Howe worked like a demon and he came frequently to tell Franklin of his progress. "I was very disapproving whenever he came down to report on the campaign," said Eleanor. "I was still a Puritan! I felt that his smoking spoiled the fresh air that my husband should have in his bedroom."

It irked her that Franklin did not find Louis loathsome, and that he laughed a great deal when his campaign manager was present. He even laughed when he should have scolded Howe. At the beginning of

[82]

Howe's generalship, Franklin had deposited money in the bank for Howe to draw on for campaign expenses. As the campaign progressed, Franklin asked him each time he came if he needed more money. Howe always insisted there was plenty left in the account. One time shortly before he came to report, the bank called and said that the checking account was overdrawn. Howe slapped his cheek incredulously and insisted that this could not be so.

"Hand me your checkbook," Franklin demanded.

Howe gave it to him and he examined it. The politically wise but financially stupid Howe had throughout added the amounts of the checks he wrote to the balance instead of subtracting them! Franklin laughed until the tears came.

When the results of the election were made known in November, Franklin's margin was even greater than in 1910. How much was due to Louis and how much was due to the split that year of the Republican vote between the Regulars and the Bull Moosers of Uncle Ted was indeterminable. One thing was clear, however. Without Louis Howe, Franklin told Eleanor, he would have had to withdraw from the race. He would be eternally grateful to the man behind the Sweet Caporals.

Louis Howe was proud of two things. The successful campaign had been inexpensive. Of the $2,500 it had taken to re-elect Roosevelt to his $1,500 post, Louis had taken for himself only $300 plus $120.50 for traveling expenses. But a greater pride came with his belief that Franklin's political career was unlimited. When the 1912 campaign was over, he sent Franklin a letter that raised Eleanor's eyebrows. For he called her husband "Beloved and Revered Future President."

In a sense Franklin's illness that fall had eased Eleanor's murmuring dilemma. It had kept him from uttering a single word of praise for Wilson in his race against Uncle Ted. It was on this very point, however, Franklin was convinced, that his chances were small for joining the Wilson administration in Washington the following March. For what reason would Wilson now feel indebted to him? he asked.

She didn't like to see Franklin so sad. November and December found him in a pessimistic mood. Newspapers began reporting rumors of prospective Wilson appointees. Scanning the stories, she failed to find his name mentioned. January came and the state legislature convened. There was still an outside chance, Franklin decided, so instead of taking a house in Albany, he and Eleanor commuted between New York and Albany and lived in two rooms at the Ten Eyck Hotel in the state capital.

In mid-January came a telegram from Joseph P. Tumulty, Wilson's private secretary. Could he come to Trenton to confer with the President-Elect? Eleanor watched his face when he returned and found there no elation. "I had a satisfactory talk with Wilson about New York patronage matters and he asked me to supply him with the names of deserving New Yorkers. But he didn't offer me anything directly," he said, disgruntled.

A few days before Wilson's March fourth inauguration, Eleanor went to Washington with Franklin. If he couldn't get an appointment now, he never would. The city was splitting at the seams with happy Democrats wild with patronage hopes because the party had been out of power since the mid-nineties. One night they went to a party and Eleanor thought how young and serious Franklin looked in the midst of the old solid-looking politicians. He did look young indeed. At the party Franklin told a story and the wife of a naval officer who didn't know him shook a finger in his face and laughed. "Naughty, naughty," she said mockingly. "Little boys just out of college shouldn't say such things." Franklin looked wounded and Eleanor kept quiet.

Rumor had it that the lobby of the Willard Hotel on Pennsylvania Avenue was the center for job hunters. Up and down Peacock Alley, as the hotel corridor that ran between the Avenue and F Street was called, clusters of men buttonholed others. Franklin went there and returned with a sparkle in his eyes. William Gibbs McAdoo, who was to be Secretary of the Treasury, had asked him to pick between being Assistant Secretary of the Treasury or Collector of the Port of New York.

"Which did you take?" she asked.

"Neither," he replied. "I declined both."

She could only stare at Franklin in disbelief.

Inauguration Day told her why. A few short hours before the noontime festivities, he ran into Josephus Daniels at the Willard. "He is the funniest looking hillbilly I have ever seen," he explained to Eleanor. He had met the new Secretary of the Navy at the Baltimore convention the previous June.

"How would you like to come to Washington as Assistant Secretary of the Navy?" Daniels had drawled, despite the jam in the Willard lobby.

So this was it. Franklin wanted the same position Uncle Ted had once held. "So what did you tell him?" she asked.

"How would I like it?" Franklin called out. "I told him I'd like it bully well. It would please me better than anything in the world."

[84]

"Well, I'll talk to President Wilson," Daniels said genially, "and we'll see what he says."

There were anxious days while they waited to hear how Wilson was disposed. When word did not come right after the inauguration, they returned to New York. They heard that Daniels had asked the two Senators from New York if they had any objection to Franklin. Senator O'Gorman, who landed his seat because of Franklin's opposition to "Blue-Eyed Billy" Sheehan, gave a quick assent. Republican Senator Elihu Root, who had been William Howard Taft's convention manager in the last campaign and who was still smarting from Uncle Ted's rump Republican movement, had only words of caution to report: "Whenever a Roosevelt rides, he wishes to ride in front."

President Wilson submitted Franklin's nomination to the United State Senate on March 11 and Secretary Daniels wrote in his diary: "His distant cousin TR went from that place to the Presidency. May history repeat itself."

A national existence had begun for Eleanor.

Chapter Eleven

LEANOR DID NOT MOVE to Washington until months after Franklin
was sworn in. However, during this period they corresponded
with furious speed. "Dearest Babs" or "Dearest Babbie" he wrote her.
Once she forwarded to him warm congratulations from Uncle Ted.
There was no acrimony in her beloved uncle, even though Franklin had
supported his opponent. "It is interesting that you are in another place
which I myself once held," Uncle Ted wrote. "I am sure you will enjoy
yourself to the fullest as Asst Secty of the Navy and that you will do
capital work."

However, from what Eleanor could learn, his mother wouldn't give
him the satisfaction of feeling that he had achieved anything worth-
while. After he had been sworn in, Franklin wrote Eleanor, he had sent
Mama a letter: "I am baptized, confirmed, sworn in, vaccinated—and
somewhat at sea. For over an hour I have been signing papers which had
to be accepted on faith—but I hope luck will keep me out of jail."

The reply came from the fifty-eight-year-old dowager of Hyde Park:
"Try not to write your signature too small," she cautioned him, "as it
gets a cramped look and is not distinct."

As a result, he went to great lengths to impress Sally. In May, for
instance, when Eleanor was at Hyde Park, Franklin came charging up
the Hudson River to the village in Secretary Daniels' official boat, the
1,500-ton *Dolphin*. People came from miles around to stare popeyed at
the first naval vessel in history to anchor there. Sally Roosevelt looked
at it through her forbidding lorgnette and gave the venture mild approval. And in July when the American residents of Campobello were
quietly celebrating Independence Day with a few firecrackers, Franklin
suddenly appeared with one of the Navy's largest battleships, the *North
Dakota,* and anchored the gun-laden monster at Eastport, Maine, across
the bay. Eleanor brought the children down to see the formidable vessel,
but the visit made little impression on her, even though everyone in
the area came running to the docking station to gape at the *North
Dakota*. Sally gave her final approval when Franklin, after a short stay

ashore, sauntered aboard and was welcomed with a jarring 17-gun salute.

Eleanor also needed approval. Shortly after Franklin had taken office, she suddenly became paralyzed with fear that she would not be able to hold up her end as the wife of an important official. There must be awesome responsibilities involved as the wife of the important Assistant Secretary of the Navy. If Auntie Bye had advised Uncle Ted when he held the same post, certainly she could do the same for her.

Auntie Bye was living in Farmington, Connecticut. "You will have to spend a great deal of time making social calls," Auntie Bye smiled, "but remember that your chief duty is to make life pleasant for the young officers' wives who have such a hard time keeping up their position on very small pay."

Eleanor's face must have revealed her dread, for Auntie Bye added, "Here is my philosophy and you can take it for what it's worth. No matter what you do, some people will criticize you. But if you would not be ashamed to explain your action to someone you loved, then you need never worry about criticism, nor need you ever explain what you do."

When she rose to leave, Auntie Bye followed her to the door with her bent back and said, "By the way, why don't you move into my house in Washington? It's so well located in the center of things and not too far from Franklin's office."

It wasn't until the fall of 1913 that she came to Washington with her three children and four maids to move into Auntie Bye's residence at 1733 N Street Northwest. It was a pleasant old house with large windows but rather undistinguished. Yet it had a special aura. Known as the "Little White House," it had housed Uncle Ted while he waited for Mrs. McKinley to vacate the White House in 1901 after the assassination of "Little Napoleon," as her husband was called. Later, through both of Uncle Ted's administrations, the house was a political center because he frequented it to talk to Auntie Bye. William Allen White, the eminent Kansas editor, used to reflect how he and Uncle Ted would come to dinner at Auntie Bye's and when they discussed politics after the meal, Auntie Bye's husband, Admiral Cowles, would sit in their midst in the parlor and snore loudly.

As was expected, Franklin's mother came down to help them move in. She had supplied a chauffeur for the car they bought at Hyde Park and busily rearranged their furniture as she thought it should be placed. She was most concerned about Franklin's nervous stomach that had developed the previous summer. "You saved my life," he had written her facetiously in July when she suggested medicinal remedies. After Auntie Bye's furniture was arranged to suit her own taste, Sally Roosevelt returned to Hyde Park and left Eleanor to her dismal afternoon round of calls on Washington officialdom.

Up one street and down the next the chauffeur drove her, stopping at frequent intervals at house numbers on her long list. On door after door Eleanor would rap and explain grimly to the mistress of the house, "I am Mrs. Franklin Delano Roosevelt. My husband has just come as Assistant Secretary of the Navy." Then after a pause for doorway formalities and the leaving of her card, she would hurry to the next brass door knocker on her list. The different days of the week were rigidly divided for the various classes of officials: Monday was call day on the wives of the Supreme Court; Tuesday, wives of House members; Wednesday, Cabinet; Thursday, Senators' wives; Friday, diplomats.

Louis Howe had come to Washington to be Franklin's chief assistant at the Navy Department and Eleanor frequently took Mrs. Howe along on the calls. Sometimes they also went shopping together. A strange howling sight they made, with Mrs. Howe's baby and Eleanor's children often bundled into the car during these duties. One time Eleanor wrote in her diary, "Took babies in car to market and they nearly blew away."

Besides making her exhausting afternoon calls, Eleanor had a full social life. They dined out almost every evening and entertained at home once a week. Franklin often returned to the house for lunch and brought government officials with him to the dining-room table so they could combine working and eating. Eleanor presided at table with her little silver bell that had belonged to her mother. Her rings would bring the servants to the table with the next course, after which they were to go into the pantry and shut the door so they wouldn't overhear the conversation. This was her contribution to these heady sessions.

In town, the general routine was for the entire family to have breakfast together. Then Franklin walked down Connecticut Avenue six blocks to his office on Pennsylvania Avenue. Anna and James went to school during the day, which left only Elliott at home. With her social life and daily calling schedule so heavy (she made between ten and thirty calls a day), the children's attire was left chiefly to the servants. A visitor to the Roosevelt home early in Woodrow Wilson's first administration noticed that "the young Roosevelts had not been taught to blow their noses or just did not care to blow them."

Three-year-old Elliott Roosevelt's health weighed heavily on his mother's mind those first years in Washington. He was so wan and sickly that there was grave family concern whether he would survive. In addition, his legs were so badly bowed that he had to wear heavy steel braces to keep from rolling. If these were insufficient troubles, the fall Eleanor moved to Washington, little Elliott still suffered severely from the effects of burning his hands and legs badly in a Campobello bonfire the preceding summer. Only belatedly had Eleanor discovered that some hot coals had lodged inside his leg braces.

Generally she spent Sundays without Franklin. Early in the morning she kissed him good-by and he disappeared with his bag of golf clubs over a shoulder. He took the streetcar to the Chevy Chase golf course, where he often played 36 holes of golf without stopping. One day he played 44 holes, an awesome feat considering Washington's muggy weather. There were Sundays when he grumblingly gave up his golf and took Eleanor with him on cruises down the Potomac with J. D. and influential congressmen with whom he had to deal for his Department's appropriation.

Eleanor and Franklin were from the start among the most popular young couples in the capital. A handsome young man who did a fine turkey trot like Franklin and a smiling waltzer like Eleanor were found to be in demand. These were simple days. The Victorian Age was vanishing in the haze of astonishing industrial progress. There was no thought then of any future war; Wilson's domestic "New Freedom" program was the extent of the political ruckus that enveloped the town's conversation; and so social life was gay and carefree.

Many considered Franklin the handsomest man in Washington and referred to him as "the Gibson Man," the counterpart of the then-stylish Gibson Girl. Walter Camp, the Yale coach, went so far as to state categorically, "Mr. Roosevelt is a beautifully built man, with the long muscles of the athlete." A close friend said of Franklin: "He was a perfect example of the English country gentleman." As for Eleanor, a newspaper mentioning their attendance at a wedding in 1914 said that Franklin "came with his sensible little wife, who is a Roosevelt by birth."

They saw a great deal of Cousin Alice and Nicholas Longworth, her husband. Even though her Republican base was now the minor faction in Washington, "Princess Alice" was still the social queen and still set social standards in the capital. Despite her new status as an important member of the "Ins," Eleanor felt self-conscious in Alice's presence, for her cousin's sharp tongue so jolted people that before they could think of a reply they were hit by a steady stream of such remarks. Alice now, for instance, referred to Democrats as "odd beings," though she toler-

[89]

ated a few, such as Cousin Eleanor and her husband. Being invited to her house for "Midnight Eggs" after a show was a convincing sign that the invited had arrived socially. Alice did many daring things that appalled Eleanor, who was still a prude. She refused to take part in the rigid "Call" system of official Washington, calling it nonsense. Instead, she had announced to the world at large that her life was too short to see anyone who was not of interest to her, for having a good time was her reason for existing. She smoked in public, a shocking spectacle in those days, carried a green snake with her that she called Emily Spinach ("Emily in honor of a very thin aunt and Spinach because it is green"), and liked to sit on a piano and swing her legs while talking to the French Ambassador, M. Jusserand.

One place Eleanor was always made to "feel really at home" was with the family of Republican Senator Henry Cabot Lodge of Massachusetts. As a close friend and supporter of Uncle Ted, the Senator felt a protective overseer of his niece. For hadn't Uncle Ted confided that Eleanor was more like him in personality than any of his own children? Nevertheless, the goateed gentleman's relationship with the young Roosevelts was a little strange considering that Lodge was a fierce opponent of Wilson. Talk at that time was that this stemmed from the fact that Lodge had considered himself the scholar in politics and now he had as competition a man who was not only President but a former scholar and college head, too. The relationship with the Lodges was further complicated by the fact that Franklin was especially friendly with Augustus P. Gardner, the Senator's son-in-law, to whom he fed reams of material about the low state of naval power.

Still another friend was the renowned historian, cynical, aging Henry Adams, the direct descendant of the two Adams Presidents, John and John Quincy. Henry Adams sometimes came calling on the Roosevelts, though he sat in his carriage and asked that the children come out and climb all over him and the carriage. Justice Oliver Wendell Holmes of the Supreme Court, who enjoyed having Franklin come to his customary Sunday afternoon get-togethers with young people, referred to Adams as "posing to himself as the old Cardinal and turning everything to dust and ashes." One time when Eleanor and Franklin visited the fine historian of the Jefferson era, Adams shook a thin finger in Franklin's face when the young man waxed enthusiastically on the glories of the new Democratic administration. "Young man," Adams croaked, "I have lived in this house many years and seen the occupants of the White House across the Square come and go, and nothing that you minor officials or the occupants of that house will do will affect the history of the world for long."

Perhaps the closest friends of the young couple were Secretary of the Interior and Mrs. Franklin Lane, the Adolf Millers, and Assistant Secretary of State and Mrs. William Phillips. The Lanes were an older couple, Miller was Lane's assistant, while Bill Phillips and his wife Caroline were of the Roosevelt vintage. Eleanor had known Caroline from her European schooldays.

All these couples got together for informal Sunday suppers at each other's homes on a round-robin basis. Eleanor, who was not a good cook, had as her specialty preparing scrambled eggs on a chafing dish on the dining-room table. That Bill Phillips could unbend even under Eleanor's informality was considered a matter of wonder by the entire group because at the State Department he was accepted as the most rigid and dignified of the Foreign Service lot. It was a source of considerable amusement to Franklin that Phillips had been secretary to Joseph H. Coate, American ambassador to Britain, the post his mother had tried to secure for him to break up his impending marriage to Eleanor.

Others came into this Sunday supper ritual from time to time. Lou Henry Hoover and her husband Herbert, who served Wilson as chairman of the Committee for Relief in Belgium and as United States Food Administrator, were two who joined the group. While Franklin was never enamored of Hoover's personality, he was highly enthusiastic of Hoover's political possibilities as the Democratic successor to President Wilson. One time he wrote to a friend, "I had some nice talks with Herbert Hoover before he went West for Christmas. He is certainly a wonder, and I wish we could make him President of the United States. There could not be a better one." At one Sunday supper while Eleanor made scrambled eggs, Franklin and Lane worked hard on Hoover to go after the Democratic presidential nomination. But despite their pleas, Hoover later announced himself a Republican.

One thing the group had in common was the belief that Congress was a backward organization that impeded the work of the Executive Branch. This, of course, was and is true of government officials who want no outside interference with their work. This feeling spread among the wives of the Sunday night supper group. Lou Henry Hoover once wrote to Eleanor: "Can't keep dinner date because H.H. has Children's Conference in N. Y. on Thursday and Friday. He can't just shrug his shoulders and say, 'Oh, it's a pity—but they'll *have* to die now,' simply because the people on The Hill have gotten tired of *hearing* about their troubles."

The cost of maintaining the household and their gay social life took far more than Franklin earned. While he wore the some clothes year after year and felt like a wastrel whenever he rode in a taxi, Eleanor had no interest in money and little knowledge of its value. When she believed she needed more household help, she simply hired another servant. In time she had ten employees, all of whom required salaries, food, rooms in some instances, and incidentals.

At first Franklin took his salary in cash, but he found this a sorry mistake because in a few days his pockets were empty. Money disappeared as though by magic and long lectures to Eleanor brought only a shrug. When the grocer came calling one day and complained about a long-overdue bill, Eleanor was finally convinced that something had to be done.

Franklin was almost eloquent in his determination to keep them solvent. From that time on he would take his work pay by check. If he did not have the money in his pocket, he would not be able to spend it. When Eleanor agreed, he limited himself to $5.00 a week for personal expenses. But since this meant coming home for lunch, there was no saving. In addition, they held more dinner parties than usual.

The result was that they were always in financial difficulties, despite Eleanor's contribution of the interest from her inheritance. One January when Sally Roosevelt sent Franklin a goodly sum of money as his birthday present, he wrote back breathlessly that the money would be used for "paying the gas man and the butcher lest the infants starve to death."

During Franklin's seven-year tour of duty with the Navy, Eleanor generally spent from September until the following June in Washington. Franklin's attentiveness to his job added indirectly to Eleanor's maturity. Since he was held to Washington except for weekends, she was forced to make all the arrangements for her family's frequent excursions to Hyde Park and summers at Campobello. Not only did she have to shift for herself, but she also had to plan for her children and the retinue of servants she took with her wherever she traveled. It was a wild little army that set forth from Washington that first time to travel north, but such moves became second nature to her after a while.

Sometimes Franklin came along to Hyde Park to work. Sally did not like his working habits. He would put up several tables in one room. When he littered up one table until there was no more elbow room he moved on to another table. The room soon looked like a pig sty.

Apart from this financial worry life was good to Eleanor and Franklin. If Eleanor showed a marked maturity during her stay in Washington, Franklin's personality also seemed to change. He had always been a friendly sort, but now he revealed himself as so completely gregarious that it astounded Eleanor. He had been in town only a short few months when he knew literally hundreds of persons. He was forever in earnest conversations in group after group, she observed. Newton D. Baker, who came later as Secretary of War, said of him, "Young Roosevelt is very promising, but I should think he'd wear himself out in the promiscuous and extended contacts he maintains with people. But as I have observed him, he seems to clarify his ideas and teach himself as he goes along by that very conversational method." Had he observed Eleanor closely he would have reached the same conclusion. Though she was more reserved than her husband, she found that conversations stimulated her thinking and added immeasurably to her knowledge of many subjects. To her it was a matter of "picking other people's minds," and though she thought it unfair to those persons who had spent a good deal of time amassing the data that they spelled out to her and Franklin, it was nevertheless a wonderful way to improve one's mind.

Though the Roosevelts did not see much of President Wilson and his wife because they were not top-drawer, the Wilsons were always pleased to have them in the White House. Wilson liked to have Franklin as part of the group of elated men behind his desk while he scratched his name on a piece of legislation.

Franklin was wildly excited about his job, though he had at first the contempt of the very young for gray-haired superiors. Like all men put into a position of power beyond their years and experience, he was impatient when he could not get his way immediately. This was a repetition of what Uncle Ted had gone through at the same desk almost twenty years earlier. For Uncle Ted used to grind his big teeth and refer to his slow-moving Secretary of the Navy, John D. Long, as "a perfect dear," and he bluntly described him as having as much spine as a "chocolate eclair."

Franklin's superior, Secretary of the Navy Josephus Daniels, was, at fifty, a drawling former North Carolinian small-town newspaper editor in a paunchy attire who smiled easily, moved slowly and wound his heavy gold watch with a ponderous motion as though there were all the time in the world to strengthen the woefully weak Navy he inherited from the Taft administration. In many respects his actions were remindful of the easygoing existence of the antebellum Southern plantation gentleman. Sometimes his manner even invaded Eleanor's home. On one occasion when he came calling he was appalled to find that the servants were white, and he rebuked her sharply. "Negroes are meant to be servants and not white people," he explained to her coldly. Only with difficulty did Eleanor restrain herself from answering.

However, after a while, as her husband's seven-year stay on his job advanced, she came to admire much about Daniels. And although Franklin often walked in the house and sizzled at Daniels in those early years, he, too, came in time to respect the Tarheeler. Before Daniels was finished he was to do much to make the Navy more democratic. This was true when the Secretary opened the Naval Academy to enlisted men and also when he set up an educational program aboard ship for sailors.

On other scores, however, where Daniels tampered with the manly ways of American tars, Franklin thought him far off base. Eleanor tried to suffer with him when the Secretary abolished the serving of wine at mess and forbade sailors to acquire tattoos. But she could see only good in these orders. Franklin took these rulings as upsetting hallowed traditions that had come up since the days of John Paul Jones, and Louis Howe was quick to inform the old-liners that his boss had not minded the old grog routine of the Navy. Secretary of the Interior Franklin K. Lane walked past Eleanor to scold her husband one time: "You should be ashamed of yourself. Mr. Daniels is your superior and you should show him loyalty or you should resign from your office."

Eleanor had a strong distaste for Louis Howe and despite his great help to Franklin in his 1912 state campaign, she could not understand why Franklin had installed him in the next office to his own at the State, War and Navy Building. In a place where naval officers were dressed so meticulously, Howe's disreputable appearance would only serve to cast aspersions on Franklin's judgment. "Ugliest thing you ever saw," one officer labeled him, and the opinion was general. On one occasion when Franklin suggested that Louis Howe be sent to inspect a battleship, an officer bellowed disquietingly that someone else should be sent because if Howe went the first thing that would happen to him aboard ship was that the crew would give him a good bath.

But Louis Howe was invaluable to Franklin and her husband knew it. He would smile when Eleanor questioned their association. Secretary Daniels was in charge of congressional relations, while Franklin handled Navy yards, purchasing, construction and training camps. Louis Howe had a disarmingly blunt manner and a penchant for getting things done that was of enormous aid to Franklin. In addition, Franklin had had no contact with laboring people and the ever-loyal Louis gave him an education in labor matters from the point of view of the workers. In making contracts, for instance, the aristocratic Roosevelt was soon surprising industrialists with his insistence that their workers' rights be protected. Day after day Louis Howe was broadening his associations by bringing delegation after delegation of labor leaders to his desk to discuss their problems with him. Although his efforts resulted in higher wages, better working conditions and new methods of production, actually Franklin Roosevelt found that production increased and costs went down in the Navy yards across the country and he was being called by the strange nickname "The Economizer" by the press.

However, Louis Howe never forgot for a single moment that his goal was the political advancement of Franklin. He was often to be found in Josephus Daniels' anteroom, where he set his big ears to work listening to conversations and keeping up to date with the Secretary's activities and thinking. He also put in long frolicking hours with reporters from the New York papers, especially the bureau group of the New York *Herald* on which he had been employed for twenty years. From this assiduously cultivated friendship resulted a running stream of friendly newspaper stories about the young heir of Hyde Park.

While Eleanor, who always took the side of the underdog unless Franklin came home with reasons why she shouldn't, was pleased with her husband's concern for the lot of workers in the Navy yards, his mother found such hobnobbing with social inferiors abhorrent. One of her strongest notions at that time was that people should be judged by their financial position. Franklin enjoyed teasing her about it, though Eleanor found nothing humorous in this philosophy. Once when Sally Roosevelt sent Franklin a robe as a present, he wrote thanking her and said the kimono was "not bulky to take on visits to the country houses of my rich friends!" She cared not at all for this jibe.

Nor did she believe that he should plunge into employee problems with labor leaders or take steps to improve their lot. The Roosevelts were born to be aloof pace setters of the landed gentry and they had much to uphold by living well and graciously as the lower classes expected of them. He and Eleanor must set an example of upper-class aloofness. "If we love our own, and if we love our neighbor," she told Franklin, "we owe a great example." This was one time when her son found no humor in his mother's *grande dame* remarks and they had bitter words that neither ever forgot. It was Sally's feeling afterward that her children, Franklin and Eleanor, held strange ideas and that only a long and hard effort would bring them back to the fold. As she wrote the two one time: "I am sorry to feel that Franklin is tired and that my views are not his."

Franklin had real zest for administrative work plus an ability of which Eleanor had not been aware. She heard admiringly from varied sources at least several times a week of the fine reputation he had. Even Uncle Ted wrote her that first October she moved to Washington: "Darling Eleanor, give my love to Franklin. I hear from all sides how well he is doing." No other opinion pleased her so much.

Secretary Daniels was so busy arguing with congressional committees about appropriations for the Navy that he sent Franklin out to handle much of the Department's speaking chores as well as the inspection trips. Sometimes Eleanor went along. On one trip when he went alone, Franklin scribbled Eleanor, "Fine parade, lots of bands—ending with an impassioned oration by hubby to 5,000 people in the park!"

She found it painful at first to hear Franklin talking to an audience. On one early occasion she accompanied him to North Carolina to listen to him. It was the first time she had heard him since his 1910 campaign for the New York Senate. An onlooker noted how thin she looked in her long dress and high collar and that Franklin was resplendent in his cuffless trousers, double-breasted suit and stylish derby. The speech was a fiasco, however, for Franklin picked an unfortunate subject, "Stay East, Young Man," and tortured his chief point, which was that neglected farms in the East should be cultivated. Charitably, the local paper wrote up the talk as "a short businesslike message."

Another time she went with him on a hectic inspection trip of the Gulf Coast. Whisked from town to town along the Gulf with blinding speed, they were dined and feted wildly by local lobbyists fighting for her husband's approval of their cities as naval bases. Their itinerary provided at best only a few hours of sleep each night. More than half a dozen times Franklin's smiling face was so pale and drawn that she knew he "really had been half asleep" while extolling the local port. It was a torturous grind with few respites, one of which came the night Eleanor and Franklin's cousin, Laura Delano, who had accompanied them, were escorted to dinner by an elderly gentleman wearing patent-leather, high-button shoes. For comfort he had not tied his shoe buttons and the loose flapping shoe tongues created a sensation wherever they went.

Eleanor learned something important from this trip. It was simply that no matter how tired she and Franklin seemed to be, they could continue on the move without collapsing. Of this and similar trips she concluded, "They were feats of endurance, and in the doing, they built up strength." Both she and Franklin had inordinate recuperative powers, as well as great initial energy. They could do more and keep going when others had long since given up the struggle.

In addition to her worries that she would fail Franklin in her duties as an official's wife, she also feared she would disgrace him in public. On one occasion she accompanied him to naval target practice in Chesapeake Bay. Thoroughly frightened by the roll of a quiet vessel, it was her lot to be aboard the battleship towing the target. Franklin was not even on hand to comfort her because he was far off with J.D. on the vessel doing the firing. With a rough, chopping sea, it was only minutes before she was seasick. Her face turned steadily greener and her eyeballs swayed with the lurching motion of the ship.

A young officer strolling by on deck mistook her agonized expression for one of boredom. "How do you do. I'm Lieutenant Land," he introduced himself. His first name was Emory. "How would you like to climb the skeleton mast?" He pointed enthusiastically to a hundred-foot mast with a ladder climb to its summit. "You could see things much better from up there," he suggested.

"I suppose I could," she groaned shakily while her head bobbed. What difference did it make that it was a vertical 100-foot climb? It was better to die like that than to remain on deck where everyone could watch her disgrace her husband. Miraculously, when she reached the precarious top, her seasickness vanished. "But it took me many more years," she said long afterward, "before I ceased to dread dinner or luncheon on board a battleship."

These were years of learning, questioning and growth for both Franklin and Eleanor. Unfortunately, his ambitions grew faster than his ground-breaking. In 1914, he decided he would make an admirable United States Senator. He was thirty-two now and this would place him among the youngest Senators in history.

Eleanor was pregnant then, carrying Franklin, Jr., and too ill to care what he did. Off to Campobello she went with her brood to await her next child, and left Franklin to fend for himself. Had she been with him, she might have kept him from acting foolishly. But now that the direct election of United States Senators had come into existence with the Seventeenth Amendment, he believed he could overcome the hurdle of Tammany opposition.

It was a wretched mistake from the moment he announced his candidacy. In the first place, the President, who had seemed interested in his move, decided to keep out of the Democratic primary. In the second place, Eleanor was having trouble with her expected baby and nothing else mattered compared with her welfare.

There was concern in his heart when he dropped his Navy work, campaign planning and hurried to her at Campobello. She was in pain and he felt helpless. In the middle of the night of August 16, he had to dash across the bay to find a doctor. He was angry with himself because her own doctor in New York City was not available. When he returned with Dr. E. H. Bennett, the local doctor from Lubec, Eleanor was in hard labor. Sally Roosevelt came bustling over from her house when she saw all the houselights burning. "What's happening? What's happening?" she called excitedly.

It was not until early evening on the seventeenth that the second Franklin Delano Roosevelt, Jr., was born. Dr. Bennett, in remarking on Eleanor's long period of labor and her stoicism during the entire period, scratched his head in wonder and said, "Why, she is just one of us. I never took care of summer people before."

"You mean," Eleanor laughed, "that having a baby is different if you live in Maine all year around?"

As to the reason why two of her sons were named Franklin, Eleanor later explained, "Franklin's family saw nothing wrong in this practice. In fact, Franklin's grandfather, Warren Delano, was the fourth 'Warren'; three of his older brothers by the same name having died successively in babyhood."

FUTURE ADMIRAL ARRIVED LAST NIGHT. Franklin showed her the wire he had sent to Josephus Daniels.

She did not talk to him about his fight for the Senate seat. She knew about his qualms and his hopes. Tammany dealt him a harsh blow when James Gerard, then Wilson's ambassador to Germany, agreed to run in the primary against Franklin. As she played with her new baby, it was painful for her to read Tammany's description of her husband in the New York papers as "a renegade, meddler and bootlicker." Nor was the constant heckling of him as a baby of thirty-two reassuring. For six weeks she did not see him as he ran around the state in a frenzied effort to rally support for himself, but on primary day he was horribly massacred by Gerard in a vote of 210,765 to 76,888.

She said afterward how terribly hurt he was by this devastating defeat. He was in a daze, friends concurred. But the loss taught him two invaluable lessons. One was that he could not hope to win a state-wide New York election without machine support. The other was that he must not act impetuously but should discuss his intent with Eleanor.

In her political thinking, Eleanor was beginning to develop her own views on public matters. Unlike Franklin, she found it more comforting to join the peace ranks of Josephus Daniels and Secretary of State Wil-

[98]

liam Jennings Bryan, who were both ardent pacifists. When the European War broke out in July, 1914, Franklin never for a moment believed that the war was a short little action that would not include the United States. "It will be the greatest war in the world's history," he forecast.

The pacifists would not accept his view. He tried on several occasions to talk to Daniels about the seriousness of the situation. But the jovial Secretary only scoffed. "A complete smashup is inevitable," Franklin wrote to Eleanor. "Mr. D. totally fails to grasp the situation and I am to see the President Monday A.M. to go over our own situation." His sense of frustration was enormous and he had only Eleanor with whom he could discuss his troubles.

He was to find, as he confessed to Eleanor, that Daniels' attitude was not unique in the Administration. Secretary of State William Jennings Bryan held the same opinion. "These dear people like W.J.B. and J.D.," he said exasperatedly to her, "have as much conception of what a general European war means as Elliott has of higher mathematics."

When he went to the White House, President Wilson was ashen and dejected, for he was too concerned about his dying wife to discuss any other emergency. "So I started in alone," he gave Eleanor a summary, "to get things ready and prepare plans for what ought to be done by the Navy end of things." He talked his chief into letting him serve on a board dealing with neutrality problems and he also arranged to send a battleship to Europe to pick up stranded Americans. On August 5, he wrote his wife: "Alive and well and keen about everything. I am running the real work, although Josephus is here. He is bewildered by it all, very sweet but very sad!" Two days later he added, "Gee! But these are strenuous days! I'm going home to bed after three nights at the various Departments up till nearly 3 A.M. . . . Most of the reports of foreign cruisers off the coast have really been of my destroyers."

He seethed at the minute response to his efforts at defense preparations. "I nearly boil over," he confided to Eleanor, "when I see the cheery mañana way of doing business." That he was right and everyone else wrong he believed when he received a letter from Admiral Mahan, the master naval strategist— "I write to you because I know of no one else in the Administration to whom I should care to write."

By the fall of 1914, her husband was leading the demand for strengthening the Navy. Even Uncle Ted, who had advocated strict neutrality, now abandoned his position and joined Franklin. A bitter qualm for Eleanor was that Franklin was obviously opposing the view of his chief and the President. Nor could she have been pleased when she learned that Franklin through the wiles of Louis Howe sent "Gussie"

[99]

Gardner, Senator Lodge's son-in-law, material that formed the basis of a vicious attack on the condition of the Navy and Army which Gardner presented to the House. To Eleanor he explained his bold action with these words: "The country needs the truth about the Army and Navy instead of a lot of soft mush."

By 1915, Eleanor found herself being dragged somewhat reluctantly more and more into her husband's business. He was openly beginning to ask her opinion on things and she in turn served as prodder to an overworked young man. On one occasion a friend heard her ask Franklin at breakfast if he had received a certain letter. He glanced up from his coffee and said quietly, "Yes."

"Have you answered it yet?" she pounced on him.

He lowered the cup, a bit irked. "No, I haven't."

"Don't you think you should?" she persisted.

His eyes showed resentment. "I suppose so," he finally blurted. He set his cup back into the saucer, excused himself and wrote an immediate reply.

In March 1915 President Wilson asked him and Eleanor to go to San Francisco with Vice President Thomas R. Marshall to open the Pan-Pacific Exposition. It would give Franklin a respite from his harried activities to speed defense, and Eleanor was pleased. They traveled across the country by train with Marshall and two members of their Sunday-night supper club, humpty-dumptyish Secretary of the Interior Frank Lane and his wife and the Adolph Millers. In California another member of the supper club, Bill Phillips, was to join them and share Franklin's duties as aide to the Vice President.

Along the way Marshall regaled Eleanor with examples of his running wit. He was, of course, the inventor of the saying, "What this country needs is a really good five-cent cigar." Nor was he ever without a cigar in his mouth. He was proposing to write a book, he told her, that would have the following introduction: "That the tired businessman, the unsuccessful golfer and the lonely husband whose wife is out reforming the world may find therein a half hour's surcease from sorrow." Crossing the Great Salt Lake, Eleanor exclaimed at the beautiful scenery, at which he whipped his cigar from his mouth and dryly snapped, "I never did like scenery."

Franklin and Bill Phillips made a fine pair, thought Eleanor, when she watched them dedicating the pavilions at the Exposition. In their top hats and formal clothes, they looked the epitome of aristocracy; that athletic husband of hers and tall, lean Bill whom a writer had described so aptly as having an "aristocratically petulant mouth . . . and sleek parting of the hair at the top of his high forehead, so cautious and deliberate in his choice of words that he supplied his small world with few bon mots." Despite Bill Phillips' overwhelming formality, he got along so well with Franklin that it was small wonder that years later Franklin made him Under Secretary of State and world-wide trouble-shooter.

The two young men handled all their Exposition duties with ease, but Eleanor felt only embarrassment for poor Marshall who had come from Indiana, where he had been governor, to Washington without the least thought for protocol. For instance, she felt sorry for him when he shook hands with all enlisted men, an action that made officers aboard the ships at San Francisco rear back with utter contempt. And he sat where he wanted to at mealtime, causing gulping and indigestion in the ranks of the rigid admiralty set.

Once back in Washington, Eleanor saw much of Mrs. Josephus Daniels throughout the rest of 1915, though Franklin and J.D. continued their strained relations. Besides demanding a larger Navy, Franklin's attitude was that Germany was an enemy of the United States, the German Embassy was a hotbed of spies. He pounded the dining room table to convince Eleanor. Especially did he distrust German Ambassador Count Johann von Bernstorff, who had been a Washington fixture since 1907 when Uncle Ted lived in the White House. One night in 1915, Franklin dined at the exclusive Metropolitan Club in Washington. Eleanor was out of town and he wrote "Dear Babs" of that experience: "Von Bernstorff was at the next table, trying to hear what we were talking about."

It was not until the British liner *Lusitania* was sunk in May by German submarines with 124 Americans perishing that public sentiment began catching up with Franklin's thinking. Even Eleanor found herself swayed by this dastardly act. When Secretary of State Bryan continued to hold fast to his pacifist precipice, Franklin considered him with contempt. He knew how much Eleanor had admired Bryan's position in the past. "What do you think of W. Jay B.?" he crowed in one letter to her when Bryan finally resigned on June ninth because he opposed Wilson's second sharp note to Germany regarding the *Lusitania* sinking. In his note the President had demanded that the Kaiser end his "ruthless submarine campaign" or in the future the United States would hold him strictly responsible. "I can only say I'm disgusted clear through," Franklin wrote her about Bryan's continuing pacifism. Then he took a deep breath and added disconsolately, "J.D. will not resign!"

Eleanor could not help but wonder why Daniels did not fire Franklin for insubordination. "I just know I shall do some awful unneutral thing before I get through," Franklin told her about J.D.'s efforts to keep the country out of war. But Daniels never considered dropping him. He fondly regarded Franklin as an errant son and also admired the way he took administrative duties off his shoulders. His tolerance served only to whet Franklin into bolder action. Once he wrote Eleanor in exasperation, "I have any amount of work to do and J.D. is too damned slow for words—his failure to decide the few big things holds me up all down the line."

One reason for the end of hostilities between Daniels and her husband resulted from the fact that 1916 was an election year and the two worked hard for Wilson's re-election. Eleanor had her last child, John Aspinwell Roosevelt, in March, 1916, and in the summer Franklin tried to campaign for the President around Maine in order to be near his family at Campobello.

A harsh polio epidemic occurred in the East that summer and Franklin was greatly concerned that all precautions must be taken to safeguard the children. It became an obsession with him. After one visit, he wrote to "Dearest Babs" from Washington upon his arrival to the capital, "The infantile paralysis in N.Y. and vicinity is appalling. Please kill all the flies I left."

It was Eleanor's idea that the family return early to Washington that summer. But Franklin insisted that she not do so, because of the continuing infantile paralysis epidemic. "I am really upset at the thought of bringing you all down by rail. There is much I. P. in Boston, Springfield, Worcester, etc. Also the various villages are keeping motorists with children out."

As a result, Eleanor lingered on at Campobello. When summer passed and autumn came on, she felt "marooned" there when the other summer residents left. But Franklin still insisted that she not come down by train. He had hopes that he could talk Daniels into letting him take the *Dolphin* to Campobello to bring them to Hyde Park, though he wrote her, "The Sec'y was accused in Congress of intention to use *Dolphin* to campaign in Maine—hence he is scared blue" and "won't be allowed within 1,000 miles of Maine until after September 11." This was Maine's election date.

It was only after the election there that he finally talked J.D. into giving him the *Dolphin* and he arrived early in October at Campobello and the family piled aboard. While the commander of the *Dolphin,* William D. Leahy, entertained no opinion one way or the other about this private use of government property, he did find the trip to New

York distasteful. For the over-healthy Roosevelt children raced from stem to stern and up and down stairs all the time they were at sea, besides pulling pranks on the commander and his fellow officers.

Franklin's obsession with polio was still apparent when they pulled in at Hyde Park, for he asked his mother if she had carried out his orders to fumigate all her cars and carriages as a safety precaution. He smiled broadly when she told him she had. Franklin's caution regarding the children permitted Eleanor to take a real vacation from her family, for she left the children with her mother-in-law and returned alone with Franklin to Washington until just before the November election. While she was in Washington, they moved from Auntie Bye's house, which was now too small for her family, to a larger house at 2131 R Street Northwest.

The Wilson victory over Charles Evans Hughes was one that almost gave Franklin heart failure before it became an assured fact after twenty-four hours of uncertainty. "The most extraordinary day of my life," he wrote Eleanor, explaining his pleasure at Wilson's re-election.

But Eleanor was aware that his pleasure was not in the Democratic slogan, "He Kept Us Out Of War." It was in his desire to play an important role in the war he expected to arrive shortly.

Chapter Twelve

O N THE RAINY NIGHT of April 2, 1917, Eleanor Roosevelt went to the Capitol with Franklin to hear Woodrow Wilson ask Congress to declare war against Germany. Almost two months before, on February 8, the United States had severed diplomatic relations with the Kaiser's government following the German announcement of unrestricted submarine warfare. "All sea traffic will be stopped with every available weapon and without further notice," the Germans announced. And when it came, Eleanor no longer clung to her pacifist standards.

The President's address to Congress that evening had a profound effect on her. "I went in and listened breathlessly," she said. Later when she walked back into her R Street house she felt "half dazed by the sense of impending change."

It was as though a way of life was going out and a new way was coming in. Gay, joyful Washington now took on a grim tone. Suddenly it bloomed from a small town to a large city filled with thousands of strangers who, Eleanor noted, "worked from morning until night and late into the night."

With the coming of war, Franklin took to staying so late in the office that Eleanor had to call him each night and remind him that it was time to come home. "I am unreasonable and touchy now," he confessed to her. As soon as the war was on, he frenziedly bought on contract all that he believed the Navy would need for the entire next year. Although he was tremendously proud of his handiwork, he was crestfallen one evening shortly afterward when he came home. President Wilson had called him in that day, he told her, and given him unshirted hell. The President had been abrupt and to the point. "I'm sorry, Mr. Roosevelt, but you've cornered the market for supplies. You'll have to divide up with the Army."

Eleanor was proud to read in the papers that "See young Roosevelt" had become a byword in busy Washington. He had no time for formalities or red tape. Only speedy action without political interference, he told Eleanor, would get the war effort moving.

However, Franklin was not the only Roosevelt who wanted to play a large role in the war. Uncle Ted was another, and he popped up in Washington in the spring shortly after the fighting broke out. A loud and blasphemous opponent of Wilson he had been and there was still no love lost between them, but his country was at war and he wanted to fight. He now referred to himself picturesquely as "an old cannon loose on the deck in a storm." He was blind in one eye and rather ravaged from the jungle fever he had contracted a few years earlier on an expedition into Brazilian jungleland. But his war spirit was high. When Eleanor and Franklin hurried to Cousin Alice's home to greet him, "though he was kind to us as he always was," said Eleanor, "he was completely preoccupied with the war."

Uncle Ted wanted to raise a division of volunteers and lead them overseas against the Germans. This was in direct conflict with Wilson's program for drafting the entire army, Eleanor knew, but Uncle Ted hoped that his prestige from Rough Rider days would oblige Wilson to give way.

She felt dreadfully sorry for her uncle when he announced he was going to the White House to take up his plan with the President. "After he had been to see President Wilson and the President had not immediately accepted his offer," Eleanor noted, "but had said he must think it over, Uncle Ted returned in a very unhappy mood." If the President had agreed with Theodore Roosevelt's demand, the former President would have taken the cream of the officers with him into one division and would have bedeviled the development of the rest of the Army. "I hated to have him disappointed and yet I was loyal to President Wilson," Eleanor told Franklin.

Uncle Ted's pride fell daily during that stay in Washington. One day he came to call on Franklin and, hat in hand, asked the young man to arrange a meeting for him with Secretary of War Baker. Franklin was glad to do so, and even went so far as to argue with Baker to support Uncle Ted's demand with the President. But Baker was obdurate and Uncle Ted came away with nothing.

As a fighting man, Uncle Ted's disappointment led him to turn on Franklin. The sight of him in civilian clothes galled Uncle Ted. Just two years before when he had been involved in a sticky libel suit and Franklin appeared as his star witness he had nothing but praise for him. T.R. had written him then: "I shall never forget the capital way in which you gave your testimony and the impression on the jury."

But that was two years before. He was proud of Eleanor and told her so because her brother Hall had enlisted in the Army Air Service with his son Quentin. However, "Uncle Ted was always urging Franklin to resign," she noticed.

"You're only thirty-five," he jibed. "Why I was forty and had six children when I resigned from the post you now have and organized the Rough Riders."

"I want to, but they won't let me," Franklin answered, for he had asked permission to get into the fight directly. J.D.'s word was that Franklin had to stay on his job because he was too valuable there.

Franklin's disappointment as well as the tension on the job was apparent by the middle of 1917. When Eleanor left with the family for Campobello in July, he apologized for having been grumpy, a condition he felt had made her leave Washington rather than keep the family there this first summer of the war. "I really can't stand the house all alone without you," he wrote sadly, "and you were a goosy girl to think or even pretend to think that I don't want you here all the summer, because you know I do!"

He was very touchy when he heard that the Secret Service, when they opened the safe in the German Consul's office in New York, had found his name high on the list of Americans to be assassinated. The Secret Service had given him a revolver and shoulder holster, he wrote Eleanor. But he wore it only three days before removing it because he "would normally be dead with the assassin half a mile away" before he could get the gun out and fire it. She was concerned about the strain he was undergoing, especially when he wrote her further on July 17, "Last night I thought I heard a burglar and sat at the head of the stairs with the gun for half an hour, but it turned out to be the cat."

The summer of 1917 also found the young Roosevelts the center of local gossip. For four years now Washington social circles had been watching the extremely handsome young man who laughed easily and jested and moved like a fine athlete. It did not seem plausible to many that any young married man in Washington, and especially this one, could be domesticated. And so a triangle was fabricated out of whole cloth to help while away the hours on social occasions.

In 1913, when Eleanor first came to Washington, she had attempted to handle all her duties by herself, "but found that it took me such endless hours to arrange my calling list, and answer and send invitations" that she employed Lucy Mercer as her secretary three mornings a week. Lucy, who came from a fine but impoverished local family, was extremely pretty and vivacious and was soon an accepted member of the Roosevelt family. On the working side, Lucy not only acted as Eleanor's secretary, but on occasion when needed she helped clean up the house.

Trying to break up marriage w/ rumors

[106]

Socially, Lucy joined Eleanor and Franklin on weekend trips down the Potomac on the *Sylph,* President Wilson's boat, met their guests on equal terms and sometimes helped act as secondary hostess in the house when Eleanor was busy.

By the summer of 1917 vicious stories spread through town that Franklin had asked Eleanor for a divorce to marry Lucy and that his mother had come down from Hyde Park to prevent the breakup. As a final twist, the gossip went on that Lucy would not have him even if he were divorced because she was a devout Roman Catholic. Nevertheless, despite these malicious and unfounded tales, both Eleanor and Franklin continued their friendship with Lucy, to the great disappointment of the rumor mongers.

If Franklin's days were now thoroughly involved with the war effort, Eleanor's life, too, changed immeasurably with the war. And she was much calmer throughout than he. By the following fall, returning from Campobello, Eleanor plunged into as many activities as her family schedule permitted. She became a member of the Comfort Committee of the Navy League, a do-good ladies' organization to knit woollies and sweaters for Navy boys. It wasn't long, however, before Secretary Daniels got into a hassle with the Navy League and barred it from further contact with the Navy. "What a mess about the Navy League," Eleanor complained to Franklin, "but I think Mr. Daniels has made a mistake to refuse all garments from them."

"Sit tight, keep on knitting," Franklin replied, "and don't rock the boat."

The knitting was finally taken over by the Red Cross.

She also made regular visits to naval hospitals to take on any needed task, as well as to talk to the sick and wounded lonely young men and provide them with gifts. One woman wrote her about her boy, "He never forgot the ice cold lemon jelly and little cakes you brought him when you found he had no appetite." Many of the boys told her of their problems and provided her with "a liberal education." For she had grown up in an atmosphere where certain things were right and others wrong. "Out of these contacts with human beings I became a more tolerant person," she acknowledged, "far less sure of my own beliefs and methods of action, but I think more determined to try for certain ultimate objectives."

She found in her new outlook an ability to get things done. One time she went out to St. Elizabeth's Hospital in Washington, which was a federal hospital for the insane. When she was shocked by the conditions she found there, she rushed to Secretary of the Interior Lane, whose

Department was responsible for the hospital, and demanded an immediate investigtaion. Although Lane was too squeamish to return to the hospital with her and see things for himself, he did appoint an investigation committee. The result was that the appropriation for the hospital was increased so that it could become a model for all such institutions in the nation.

Deep down, Eleanor's desire was to go overseas, but she had too many obligations to undertake such a venture. Instead, she added to her work by slaving sixteen hours a day, two or three days a week, in an iron cook-shack Red Cross canteen in the Washington railroad yards. Here she mopped floors in temperatures nearing 100°, made sandwiches and coffee and distributed food to soldiers coming through Washington. She was known as the human dynamo because of her tireless work. This was not a place for humor, though it did crop up occasionally. One time some boys came running into the canteen to say they were AWOL and were being chased by the Military Police. They were properly hidden from view by the wives of an admiral and a Marine general. Later, after the suspicious Military Police finally exited, the women were almost hysterical with laughter thinking of how they could explain their kind deed to their husbands.

In addition to her work, Eleanor still maintained a heavy social schedule. Many were the dinners she held for French and British emissaries who had come to Washington for war aid. Often she returned home with only minutes to change her attire. But she "learned to dress with rapidity," a habit that stayed with her thereafter.

There were occasions when the prominence of her husband troubled her greatly. One time after she was interviewed by a reporter from *The New York Times* on the way she managed her household in Washington, the paper reported that "the food-serving plan adopted at the home of Franklin D. Roosevelt, Assistant Secretary of the Navy, has been selected by the conservation section of the Food Administration as a model for other large households."

"All I can say is that your latest newspaper campaign is a corker," Franklin told her, with harsh sarcasm, "and I am proud to be the husband of the Originator, Discoverer and Inventor of the New Household Economy for Millionaires! Please have a photo taken showing the family, the ten cooperating servants, the scraps saved from the table and the handbook."

"I do think it was horrid of that woman to use my name in that way," Eleanor replied tearfully. "I'd like to crawl away for shame."

But the storm soon blew over and she forgot it. There were so many worth-while things to do in wartime Washington, though Franklin was beginning to loathe the city and was calling it "the Saloon, the Salon and the Salome." From his earnest talks with her at home and from his frequent conversations with foreign visitors, he was more anxious than ever to leave the capital and get into the fighting.

Even so, these years were the best family years. When John was born in March 1916 the family unit had become complete, and there were to be no more protracted periods of nausea for Eleanor, nor concern about frail infants catching fatal diseases, as did her little brother Ellie and the first Franklin, Jr. These were hardy children she had, except for wan, suffering Elliott. They were seldom at rest, especially Franklin, Jr., who enjoyed talking so much that Eleanor laughingly said he made up for shy Jimmy and then some. Franklin, Jr., bore a startling resemblance to his father in more than appearance, she thought. "He had a very warm heart and emotions you could appeal to very quickly," she noted. Others agreed that John looked like her. With her long blond hair, Anna, who found little companionship with her rough-playing brothers, was the link in appearance with the handsome and beautiful Hall branch of the family.

There were meals, baths, games, prayers and high jinks in endless array, all accomplished without any semblance of family formality. Eleanor and Franklin were "Mom" and "Pop," and were treated to no greater show of respect than a brother or a sister. Eleanor made it a point to spend at least an hour with them before bedtime and seldom broke her rule. Franklin, so busy at the office, nevertheless found time to take his "chicks" sailing, tobogganing and on sight-seeing expeditions. He was another Uncle Ted in enthusiasm and getting down to the level of children.

The result was that family life was always noisy. Graduated from thumb-sucking (each had the habit to Eleanor's despair), the children were great yellers, wrestlers and pranksters. Eleanor said she learned to concentrate by reading in the midst of their playing. On rare occasions, when they lay flat on their backs and panted and sweated, she read Kipling and Stevenson poems to them. Unlike the boys, Anna was raised strictly and had to take a maid, Connie, with her to parties and to stay with her through the night. When Anna wanted to keep Chief, a police dog she had won at a county fair, Eleanor and Franklin held a serious conference before they agreed. "I own him. May I keep him? He is so sweet in my lap," Anna sent Eleanor a telegram as a clincher.

When the children were stumped by homework problems, once they started school, both Eleanor and Franklin helped, though Eleanor admitted she was of little assistance in arithmetic. Franklin was a shining star here. Home alone of an evening, which seldom happened, Eleanor and Franklin often played Hearts with the children. Here again Franklin was a star. However, as the boys grew older, he was a flat failure in another field. Too shy to explain sex to them, he turned over the job to Eleanor.

Nor did Franklin have it in him to discipline the children, no matter what wrongs they committed. "I can remember once punishing my youngest son, who had a very violent temper, by sending him to his room," said Eleanor. "Not finding him there, I went straight to the study where I found him crying his heart out in his father's arms, with his head buried in his father's shirt front. My husband sat tipped back in his desk chair looking entirely miserable and quite guilty because he knew he was not upholding discipline."

Because of her own upbringing, Eleanor was inclined to be a weak disciplinarian. Nevertheless, with a husband who would not spank no matter what the provocation, she had to do it all. Once when she was away with the family, she wrote to her husband that Elliott had bitten James hard. She explained that no matter whose fault it was boys didn't bite. "His feelings were much hurt and he made such a long upper lip, he looked like a rabbit, but at the end of the spanking (with my slipper) he said, 'It didn't hurt very much, Mother!' " Franklin's reaction was to treat it as an amusing story without a moral and one that would not have had as bitter an ending had he been present.

The result was that the Roosevelt children gained a rather unsavory reputation for their uncontrolled ways. The boys considered it great sport to drop bags of water from their second-story windows onto the heads of the stylishly dressed ladies who came to Eleanor's teas. Once when Eleanor and Franklin gave a formal dinner, the children dispersed the entire group in wild confusion by setting off stink bombs. On another occasion when son Jimmy could not be found, his parents were convinced he had met with foul play. Hourly their agitation grew as they searched without success. Finally they notified the police who started a city-wide search. Almost half a day later when Eleanor and Franklin were almost prostrate with concern, Jimmy was found riding on the back of a speeding motorcycle driven by Crown Prince Leopold of Belgium.

Nor did Franklin's mother help the discipline problem. She doted on the children and undid with great glee whatever punishment Eleanor decreed. She often took the children to Hyde Park when Eleanor accompanied Franklin on a trip and turned them loose to do whatever they desired. On one occasion Eleanor punished her boys when they misbehaved by taking away their pet pony and giving it to some children who lived at the other end of Hyde Park village. Undaunted, Grandmother Roosevelt immediately bought them two fine horses to replace the loss of their little pony.

Eleanor never found this or any of the actions of Sally to undermine her parental authority the least bit amusing. Yet there was never anything she did about them. It was an inward burn that was not outwardly expressed, a sunken feeling that the foundations of her family and their security were in jeopardy from the doting largesse of Grandma.

To cope with her mother-in-law's "kindnesses" toward the children, she needed Franklin's aid. But Franklin would not argue with his mother. Besides, he claimed, he was too busy to do more than be disgusted. The result was that they let this situation ride throughout the rest of Sally Roosevelt's long life.

There was little doubt that her husband was busy during the war. In addition to his work on naval production and strategy, he was a busy salesman of Liberty Bonds. Sometimes she went with him to listen to his appeals. She also went to the station to see him off to make his inspections and to plead with audiences to donate needed objects, such as binoculars, to the Navy. She ransacked her own possessions in a burst of patriotism. But Franklin was sick at heart when J.D. issued a national call to owners to turn over their private yachts to the Navy for coastal work. It meant giving up his *Half Moon* on which he had had such splendid trips. His mother, however, was pleased to see the boat go because it had been purchased by her husband shortly before his death and it brought back too many memories.

By June 1918, Murphy of Tammany wanted Franklin to run for governor of New York. Franklin turned him down because if he couldn't get into the war, it was his duty to stick with war work and not take on a civilian task. He did suggest Al Smith, however, as a worthy candidate.

The war looked without end at that time. The Germans had come close to taking Paris in June and were far from a defensive fight on their own soil. Franklin met with J.D. and suggested that one of them go to the battle lines and see the war firsthand. "A good idea," Daniels drawled. "You go."

"But I want to become a naval officer when I get back," Franklin told him. J.D. agreed to his demand.

When he left, Eleanor told him not to eat rationed sugar in English homes. He was careful not to do so when he ate with the king and other high officials. In France, he wrote Eleanor, he found a naval battery in Army uniforms under Admiral Plunkett. On the spot he asked Plunkett if he could join his outfit after making his report on the fighting to Daniels. The Admiral offered to accept him as a lieutenant commander.

While Franklin was overseas, Eleanor went to a funeral of Aunt Corinne's husband, Douglas Robinson, in New York and encountered Uncle Ted there. Her uncle was still bitter about Franklin's civilian status. Only shortly before he had learned that his son Quentin had been killed in the fighting. "Use your influence to get Franklin to enlist," he demanded.

Eleanor flushed. "It's Franklin's own business what he does," she replied, angry for the first time in her life at the uncle she adored.

Franklin raced from front to front and held meetings with prime ministers, generals and front-line soldiers. Meanwhile, at home, Eleanor labored in the hotbox of a corrugated tin shack over the old army stove in the Washington railroad yards. By the time Franklin got on the *Leviathan* for his return trip home he had double pneumonia and a bad variety of influenza. The ship became a floating hospital when not too far into the Atlantic and several died aboard. Franklin left the ship in New York on a stretcher. Before he recovered, Eleanor was nursing him, their five children and three servants who also came down with flu at one time. Poor little Elliott had double pneumonia in addition to the flu.

Uncle Ted wrote Franklin on September 23, "We are deeply concerned about your sickness and trust you will soon be well. We are very proud of you. Later, Eleanor will tell you of our talk about your plans."

However, Franklin's plans were simple, Eleanor knew. He was to join up with Admiral Plunkett's naval railway battery of fourteen-inch guns at the French front. When he was able to get on his feet in October, he asked J.D. for his release. Daniels sent him to talk it over with Wilson.

Excitedly he walked into the President's oval office in the White House and pleaded to be released for active duty. However, Wilson cut through his arguments to announce that the Germans had already asked for an armistice. Franklin was too late. When he came home Eleanor knew that something was up because his face was so long. "I've missed my opportunity," he told her glumly.

Chapter Thirteen

THE KAISER HAD FLED to Holland and the Armistice was signed on November 11. Woodrow Wilson set off for Europe with a vision to make the hard war just finished, the last war. There would be everlasting peace from then on.

When Franklin was asked to go to Europe to close out American naval operations on the continent, Eleanor went with him. Everyone remarked how tired she looked after nursing him, the children and the servants through the influenza epidemic of 1918. But there was still another reason for her weariness. Franklin had discovered that while she nursed her own brood, in the evenings when they were all properly dosed and covered with extra blankets, she had slipped from the house to nurse government girls who were alone and sick in Washington. How many she nursed he never did find out, though a dozen or more later claimed that she had sat beside them and fed them medicine.

It was to be a gay, carefree trip across the Atlantic in the crisp wintry air. She deserved it, he said, away from family concerns and her hectic wartime activities. However, it was otherwise. Amidst their shuffleboard playing on January 6, 1919, came a radio report of Uncle Ted's death. The announcement was a great shock. Outside of Franklin there was no man to whom she had been closer in the past two decades. She could not find the right words for her diary as she wept. Indestructible Uncle Ted. "Another great figure off the stage," she wrote finally in her diary in a shaky hand.

It was a gigantic undertaking Franklin hoped to clear up in a month or so. His task was to dispose, at the highest prices, of 54 shore bases, several radio stations, 359 ships, as well as determine an orderly schedule for returning 80,000 men to their homes in the United States.

In Europe, in the midst of such hectic activities to liquidate naval assets and to sit in unofficially at the Paris Peace Conference then in progress, Franklin somehow found time to take Eleanor along on several trips. In Paris they were ensconced at the Ritz, a good spot for hearing the latest gossip about the arguments Wilson was having with the British, French and Italian premiers. From the Ritz, she went on occasion with Aunt Dora, Franklin's aunt, to visit the American wounded in nearby hospitals. Once they went to a hospital specializing in plastic surgery. Eleanor, who prided herself on her ability to look at any medical case without becoming queasy, found that when it came to visiting men who had lost parts of their faces she "couldn't bear to look."

On a visit to battle fields with Franklin she developed a bad case of pleurisy with stabbing pains and a high fever. But she didn't see why this should interfere with her examination of the pockmarked countryside and the front-line trenches. She gasped, held her side, but all the time managed to hide her pain from Franklin until it was over. Only afterward did she confide in him that she was not exactly up to par. He was horrified that she would abuse her body in this fashion. "To my rage," she wrote in her diary, "Franklin wouldn't let me go calling with him. He dines with ———. He made me back out." When they returned from their tour of the battle zones, Franklin was severely criticized for taking Eleanor to the restricted area which still contained dangerous explosives.

Franklin's task was done in February. Eleanor and he traveled home on the *George Washington* with President and Mrs. Wilson and their party. Though Franklin observed all protocol, naval officials were appalled when Wilson would not walk onto the ship before his wife. One day at sea Eleanor lunched with the Wilsons. The President expressed pleasure at Franklin's fine work in Europe, but he was in full glow regarding what he considered his own crowning handiwork, the contemplated League of Nations. "The United States must go in," Eleanor scribbled in her notebook the words Wilson spoke so seriously at lunch, "or it will break the heart of the world, for she is the only nation that all feel is disinterested and all trust."

Before the *George Washington* reached Boston, Franklin had emerged as a minor hero. In the heavy fog the vessel wandered far from its course. Franklin not only identified their position but also helped navigate the ship safely back on its proper route, as Eleanor assumed he could. When they docked in Boston, the thin small-faced Governor Calvin Coolidge joined the mass greeting for the returning President. It was a sight—with the Wilsons, Coolidges and Eleanor and Franklin driving in the caravan mid the wildly cheering crowd to the Copley Plaza Hotel. Eleanor sat next to Governor Coolidge at lunch and squirmed uneasily as the governor ate in complete silence without any chitchat for his lunching companion. Later, carried away by his own enthusiasm, Coolidge told the immense crowd that had assembled to listen to the President that he "was sure the people would back the President."

The wartime excitement had disappeared from Washington by the time she returned there. Though she still busied herself with Red Cross and hospital work, a general exodus from the city had already begun. However, Franklin remained busy, too busy still, thought Eleanor, even though he sometimes found time to play golf with easygoing Senator Warren Harding from Ohio and to go hunting on occasion with handsome young Lt. Dicky Byrd, who served on the *Dolphin*, J.D.'s boat, and who had become a warm friend of both Eleanor and Franklin.

As vociferously as he had earlier argued for a mighty armada, Franklin now labored for a deep cut in naval strength. Also in the early months of 1919 he undertook a heavy speaking engagement in favor of the League of Nations. He did not agree privately with the President's stubborn stand against any changes in the League Covenant. Wilson wanted the whole cake or not a crumb, he told Eleanor. It was more logical, he added, to compromise with Senator Lodge's reservations and get the show on the road.

As 1919 moved along, and Eleanor was caught in the emotional national battle over the League of Nations, it was more than a bit disconcerting to her to watch her Cousin Alice cavort. While Eleanor was a quiet supporter of the League, Alice was a loud, outspoken opponent. During the war, Alice's name had been in the papers chiefly because she stopped wearing corsets and liberated American women followed suit. Now not only did she occupy a front-row seat in the Senate galleries daily and nod approval as Lodge, Borah and the other opponents of the League denounced Wilson and his proposal, but she was also commonly referred to as the inspiration of the "Battalion of Death," as the Senate opponents were called. She held open house for the Battalion and joined in the master strategy to return the nation to isolationism. Alice said that when President Wilson passed her one time, she stood "with fingers crossed, making the sign of the evil eye and saying a murrain on him."

The year 1919 saw many signs of postwar national hysteria. Anti-Negro riots broke out in many cities across the nation as a forerunner of the bigoted Ku Klux Klan. Even Washington got a taste of such disorder in July. "The riots seem to be about over today," Franklin wrote Eleanor about the capital's distemper. "Only one man killed last night. Though I have troubled to keep out of harm's way I have heard occasional shots during the evening and night. It has been a nasty episode and I only wish quicker action had been taken to stop it."

The readjustment brought on strikes, unemployment and a red scare. The newly appointed Attorney General, A. Mitchell Palmer, who lived across the street from Eleanor's house, had immediately plunged into a campaign against radicals that, his friends hoped, would catapult him into the White House in 1920. One night in June 1919, Eleanor and Franklin were returning home. Just as they turned into their block an enormous explosion occurred. Frenziedly they raced ahead, fearful that the explosion occurred in their own home. What had happened, they discovered, was that bombers had blasted Palmer's house and most of it was in ruins. Fortunately Palmer had gone to bed at the rear of the house and was uninjured. Cousin Alice, who hurried over, found arms and legs of the two bombers strewn all over the Roosevelt lawn. Eleanor rushed inside to see if her children were all right. "I remember it so well," her oldest son Jimmy recalls, "because Mother gave me hell for being out of bed."

When 1920 came, the great expected fight arose among the Democrats to win places on the national ticket. Eleanor knew that her husband wanted to be governor of New York, but since Al Smith planned to run for re-election, this was out of the question. Col. Robert R. McCormick, editor of the Chicago *Tribune* and an old friend of Franklin's from Groton days through the more recent years when Franklin fed him material for the campaign against Daniels for a large Navy, now went so far as to promote her husband editorially for President. However, few considered him old enough for the job. Nevertheless, there was a great deal of national interest in Franklin, she could tell from the papers, especially for a Democratic ticket of Herbert Hoover and her husband.

In June the Republicans in convention put up Senator Warren Harding of Ohio and Governor Calvin Coolidge for President and Vice President. Cousin Alice described Harding as "just a slob" and Coolidge as "looking as if he had been weaned on a pickle." It was not until the end of the month that the Democrats held their national convention at San Francisco. Franklin wanted Eleanor to go with him but she preferred staying in Campobello. Treasury Secretary McAdoo and Attorney General Palmer were the leading candidates, with a strength so equal that neither could command the necessary two-thirds vote. The result was a wild convention which required 44 ballots until delegates compromised on Governor James M. Cox of Ohio as presidential nominee.

Because Cox had not been associated with Woodrow Wilson's fight for the League of Nations, political managers at the convention searched for a running mate for Cox who was a strong League man. They stopped their hunt when they came to Franklin Roosevelt. There was, however, one unanswered question that might have disqualified him.

One day at the convention, Franklin later told Eleanor, he had been accosted by Judge Timothy Ansberry of Ohio. "How old are you?" Ansberry demanded.

"Thirty-eight. Why?"

Ansberry smiled and wiped his brow. "That's good because you know the Constitution says a Vice President has to be at least thirty-five. I'm going to nominate you."

Nonplussed, Franklin asked, "Do you think I ought to be around when you do?"

"No, I'd leave the hall."

A short while later the judge was telling the convention, ". . . He has crowded into that short period of time a very large experience as a public official. . . . His is a name to conjure with in American politics—Franklin Delano Roosevelt."

After a seconding speech by Al Smith, who believed that Franklin's name on a national ticket would help his own re-election fight in New York, Franklin was nominated by acclamation.

Eleanor was not excited when she heard the news, for Franklin was not optimistic regarding the chances of the Democrats that year. Besides, as she put it: "Personally, I had wanted Franklin out of government service for a few years at least."

Nevertheless, it was fun going through the mountain of congratulatory letters and wires that arrived. One from Lt. Dicky Byrd had only a single word—GOOD. Herbert Hoover wrote that he considered "it a contribution to the good of the country that you have been nominated and it will bring the merit of a great public servant to the front." Eleanor Lansing, the wife of Wilson's Secretary of State, wrote Eleanor, "Although an anti-suffrage, I am glad to have a vote to cast for your husband."

But many old Republican friends turned on them. Two Republicans who still felt warm toward the young Roosevelts wrote, "Congrats! I wish we could elect Harding and Roosevelt"; and "Please refuse to allow Franklin to don overalls and be 'taken' with a plough grasped to his breast."

However, Senator Lodge was now bitter. Having called Eleanor and Franklin to his home and treated them graciously, he now blasted her husband as that "well-meaning, nice young fellow, but light." Colonel McCormick now called him, "the one-half of one per cent Roosevelt. If

Franklin was Theodore, then Elihu Root was Gene Debs and William Jennings Bryan a brewer!"

Insults from the other Roosevelts came fast and furious. Cousin Alice, according to some people in Washington, described Franklin as "two thirds mush and one third Eleanor." Her brother, Theodore Roosevelt, Jr., who with his wife had been close to Eleanor and Franklin, now denounced him with, "He's a maverick. He doesn't have the brand of our family." Eleanor wrote Franklin that "Mama is wild over Nick Longworth having called you in a speech a 'denatured Roosevelt.' "

Eleanor wouldn't answer such mouthings but her mother-in-law did. Asked why the other Roosevelt branch was so antagonistic toward Franklin, she said haughtily, "It must be because our side of the family has all the looks!"

As soon as Franklin was nominated, reporters descended on Hyde Park for interviews and stories. Eleanor was uncomfortable under the glare of a news spotlight. Part of her discomfort was due to her displeasure with her own appearance. This was strange considering that her friends thought her an attractive young lady and modishly attired. Asked by Louis Howe to send him a photograph of herself for publicity purposes, she wired back, "Are no pictures of me." For two months afterward, newspapers ran another woman's picture as hers. She had had her picture taken at a Washington baseball game with Franklin. Resurrected by a photographer, the picture was trimmed to cut off the woman on Franklin's right while retaining the woman on his left. Unfortunately, Eleanor was the lady on his right. Finally, when the campaign was well under way, she did hand out a photograph of herself, but an old one, with the following deprecatory remark, "I take such bad photographs that I've not taken any for years and years."

Franklin did not return immediately to Hyde Park after the San Francisco convention. First he went to Dayton, Ohio, to meet Governor Cox. Then the two later met in Washington so that Franklin could introduce the governor to President Wilson. The President lay sprawled in his wheel chair on the portico of the White House, Franklin related the sad scene to Eleanor. He was still ravaged by the stroke he had suffered the preceding September in Colorado while on a cross-country speaking tour to whip up public support for the League of Nations. Wilson's appearance was ghastly and he kept his paralyzed left arm covered with a shawl. With tears in his eyes, Cox told Wilson he would make the League his key campaign issue. Wilson in a hoarse little voice mumbled, "I am very grateful. I am very grateful."

Eleanor went to Washington to close up their residence while Frank-

[118]

lin finished last-minute work at the Navy Department and resigned. Two thousand employees came out to cheer him when he left and gave him a loving cup. And it was on August 9 that she stepped on the front porch of her mother-in-law's Hyde Park home for Franklin's formal notification ceremony.

The Poughkeepsie *Enterprise* wrote: "Hyde Park was dressed within an inch of its life for the debut in the great affairs of the nation." The crowd, it reported, came pouring onto the Roosevelt grounds in everything from "limousines, to ox-carts, taxicabs, omnibuses and 'shank horses.'" This was the first of many political celebrations to take place here. It was a neighbor, Henry Morgenthau, Jr., who arranged the home-coming and notification and he did his job well. With graciousness, Eleanor and proud Sally Roosevelt handled the immense crowd that crushed the carefully tended grass and flowers, while Franklin denounced Harding's campaign to restore normalcy with— "We can never go back."

Eleanor went on one campaign swing with her husband. In October she climbed aboard his private car, *Westboro,* for a free-swinging trip across the nation. She had sent her children to Cousin Susie Parish with a detailed account of what pranks to expect from the young ones. Although Louis Howe considered her a great asset to have along on the campaign train, Eleanor thought of it primarily as a means of seeing to it that Franklin did not get too exhausted. He had been running top speed ever since his Hyde Park notification. In fact, even the servants had called this to her attention. Her cook Nora once complained that she had made a special gingerbread in his honor, "but the people didn't give him time to eat it."

She was the only woman aboard the *Westboro* and it was her first real contact with reporters. Grandmother Hall's admonition when she had first gone to Washington in 1913 "that a woman's place was not in the public eye" had set Eleanor's tone in meeting with the press. She had never offered information in an interview—even in that ill-fated wartime one where she was acclaimed as a "model" housekeeper. Her whole approach had been to make it difficult for reporters by saying as little as possible. Now she found that reporters could serve as a positive good and that they were hard-working and honorable. It was Louis Howe who pointed this out to her by using one reporter, a drawling Irishman named Stephen Early, as his example.

She also learned a great deal by watching Louis Howe and Franklin in action. Franklin averaged more than ten speeches a day and "the dirty little man" with the asthmatic cough worked like a beaver on these speeches to give them life and sparkle. Nevertheless, there were just so many different speeches a candidate could make and Eleanor, who had to listen to all of them, said after a while that Franklin's voice sounded like "that of a crow." As for Louis Howe, Eleanor still found it difficult to accept him as Franklin did. "I was as determined that I would not like him, as he was that I should . . . I could not see what Franklin saw in him, nor why everyone thought him such a genius."

At one point she almost deserted the campaign train. Word came that Jimmy was ill with a stomach ailment at the Groton infirmary. "I must go to him," she cried.

"I need you," Franklin told her. "Besides, Mama is already on her way there."

She stayed, with misgivings. Later she was to call this trip "the start of her political education." Long past midnight, the men aboard discussed politics and in their discussions they often asked for her opinion. They also played a lot of poker, smoked heavily and used unsaintly language at times. Amidst all this, Romeo the porter was kept running back and forth bringing his Bible so they could check quotations. She was appalled by such carryings-on, especially since they served no good purpose and only added to Franklin's growing weariness. Sometimes their high jinks got as rough as with her boys at home. On one occasion when all agreed that Louis Howe needed a bath, he wouldn't take one. Franklin and two others finally seized Howe, pulled off his trousers and threw him in the tub.

It was Eleanor's duty to sit close to Franklin when he spoke and cast a fond continual stare at him as though every word he uttered was of the greatest interest and surprise to her, though she had already heard the same speech a dozen times. Hard as this task was, it was made more difficult when the newsmen stood in the rear of the crowd and made grotesque faces at her in an effort to make her burst out laughing. Once when Franklin walked down a center aisle after a speech and woman after woman gushed, "My, isn't he handsome?" reporters surrounded her and chorused, "Aren't you jealous?" Louis Howe sometimes ribbed her by chuckling, "Women go mad about Franklin." But when he thought such horseplay had gone far enough, Howe would try to make up for it by taking one of Franklin's speeches to Eleanor's compartment and asking for her advice and comments.

Even though Franklin worked hard during that campaign, Eleanor said afterward from her experience, "Campaign trips by anyone except the presidential candidates themselves are of little value." The final outcome proved her point when the Democrats were swamped by a 404 to 127 electoral vote.

It was the first time in ten years that thirty-eight-year-old Franklin was out of public service. While he considered politics his life by now, Eleanor was pleased that he would have the time to become a family man and make up for his inattention to the children. As Franklin moved out of the political scene in 1920, he called himself in a letter: "Franklin D. Roosevelt, Ex. V. P. Canned. (Erroneously reported dead)." But both he and Eleanor knew that sooner or later he would be back in politics, though she hoped it would be later.

"It was a damn fine sail," Franklin referred to the campaign. For he believed that the race had done him good personally by getting his name before the people from coast to coast. From Louis Howe, who had returned to Washington to help break in Harding's new Assistant Secretary of the Navy, who was Eleanor's cousin, Teddy Roosevelt, Jr., Eleanor heard no pessimism. In fact, she heard that one day Louis had passed the White House with friends and had confided, "That's where Franklin is going some day . . . Franklin and I!"

Chapter Fourteen

AFTER HIS DEFEAT, Franklin took Eleanor's brother Hall along on a hunting trip to Louisiana. Following this, Eleanor watched him make his change to civilian life. He spent his mornings as the $25,000-a-year vice-president of the Fidelity and Deposit Company of Maryland in charge of its New York office on Wall Street. His afternoons he gave to his old law firm, now called Emmet, Marvin and Roosevelt with the withdrawal of Harry Hooker and the addition of Grenville Emmet. Unrested as he was, he nevertheless took on extra duties as the chairman of several drives for funds, as an overseer of Harvard, chairman of the New York Boy Scouts, the big wheel behind the Wilson Foundation and board member of a half-dozen organizations. By midyear, a concerned Eleanor was saying, "My husband is working hard."

Family arrangements were complex. Little Franklin, Jr., and John stayed full-time with Sally at Hyde Park. James was away at Groton except for vacations. Eleanor spent most of the week in New York and brought Anna and Elliott with her to Hyde Park on Thursday for the weekends. Franklin came up on Fridays to join them at his mother's place. In 1915, her mother-in-law had expanded her Hyde Park residence greatly with the hope that her son's family would make it their home as well, and they had. Along one narrow corridor in the remodeled house's second floor she had lined three bedrooms in a row; for herself, Eleanor and Franklin, in that order.

Bored by her years of afternoon calls and teas in Washington and exhilarated by her campaign trip with Franklin, Eleanor was determined to make better use of her time now that her children were getting older. One thing she determined to master was the art of preparing a decent meal. She found an ex-cook who had married and twice a week she went to her apartment and cooked an entire meal "which I left with her for her family to criticize." She also spent four days a week taking courses in typing and shorthand at a New York business school. In addition, when Mrs. Frank Vanderlip, chairman of the League of Women Voters for New York State, asked her to join the board, Eleanor did, and took on the job of making reports on national legislation. When her mother-in-law scowled at such carryings-on for a woman of her background, Eleanor joined the elite Monday Sewing Class of which her husband's mother was a longtime member. Nevertheless, Eleanor realized that she was really independent now and her own master and "was thinking things out for myself and becoming an individual."

When she took her family to Campobello for the summer of 1921, Franklin could not join them immediately. At the close of the first week in August, he came to Campobello with Mr. Van Lear Black, the head of Fidelity and Deposit. Black insisted he looked too tired to work. They sailed for a few days and Franklin seemed to be relaxing. However, on August 9, he fell overboard and when fished back on Black's boat, the *Sabalo,* he developed a bad chill.

On the tenth, after Black left, Eleanor and the children went sailing with Franklin aboard the *Vireo,* the small sailing boat he had purchased to replace the *Half Moon.* He claimed to have suffered no ill effects from his dousing the day before, even though he had told Eleanor the water "was so cold it seemed paralyzing." On their way back home, Jimmy spotted a forest fire on an island off Campobello. "Of course," said Eleanor, "we must make for shore at once and fight the fire."

It took several hours before the fire was out, but by that time they were all sweaty and grimy. "How about a race across the island and a swim in Lake Glen Severn?" Franklin called out eagerly.

They took him up and started off. After the swim, Elliott demanded that they all dive once into the freezing Bay of Fundy. Franklin was reluctant, but he finally agreed. Back home he told Eleanor that he was tired. He sat in his wet bathing suit while he read the batch of mail that had come that day. Eleanor glanced at him after a while and saw that his lips were purple and he was shivering. "You must go to bed and get warm," she told him.

"But I've promised the chicks that we're going camping tomorrow."

"You should be better by then," she said.

However, the next day he felt much worse. He had a fever and his joints ached. Now concerned, Eleanor called the local doctor, E. H. Bennett of Lubec, who had delivered Franklin, Jr. Dr. Bennett looked him over and diagnosed his difficulty as a bad cold. Mrs. Louis Howe who was visiting the Roosevelts wired her husband in Washington to come because his friend was ill. Louis, who was quitting the Navy to take a job with an oil company in New England, came as fast as he could.

The next day Franklin felt worse. When he got up to go to the bathroom, his legs failed him on the way back to bed. He let out a yell and Eleanor came running and helped him back into bed. It was no longer a minor business.

On the fourteenth, she wrote anxiously to Franklin's half brother: "Dear Rosy, We have had a very anxious few days as on Wed. evening Franklin was taken ill. It seemed a chill but Thursday he had so much pain in his back and legs that I sent for the doctor, by Friday evening he lost the ability to walk or move his legs but though they felt numb he can still feel in them. Yesterday A.M. Dr. Bennett and I decided we wanted the best opinion we could get quickly so Louis Howe (who, thank heavens, is here, for he has been the greatest help) went with Dr. Bennett to Lubec and they canvassed the nearby resorts and decided that the best available diagnostician was the famous old Dr. W. W. Keen of Philadelphia and he agreed to motor up and spend the night. He arrived about 7:30 and made a most careful, thorough examination and the same this morning and he thinks a clot of blood from a sudden congestion has settled in the lower spinal cord temporarily removing the power to move though not to feel. I have wired to New York for a masseuse as he said that was vital and the nursing I could do, and in the meantime Louis and I are rubbing him as well as we can."

Dr. Keen's diagnosis was wrong. The rubbing that Eleanor and Louis Howe did was the worst possible treatment for what really ailed Franklin. For he did not have a blood clot but infantile paralysis instead. Nevertheless, when Dr. Keen sent her a bill for $1,000 a few days later, Eleanor paid it though she knew he had done wrong. He had changed his first guess to a new diagnosis of a "lesion on the spinal cord." But when Franklin's bladder and rectal sphincters became paralyzed, the thought came to Eleanor that her husband might have polio.

Even with improper treatment and incorrect diagnosis, Eleanor could not help but marvel at her husband. She wrote Rosy eight days after the onslaught that "he's getting back his grip and a better mental attitude." Years afterward Franklin admitted to a friend that at the time Eleanor believed him cheerful he had actually been in complete despair.

It was on the twenty-third "that I have asked Dr. Keen to try to get Dr. Lovett here for a consultation to determine if it is I. P. or not. Dr. Keen thinks not." Nevertheless, when Eleanor kept insisting that Dr. Robert W. Lovett, the Boston expert on infantile paralysis, be brought into the case, Dr. Keen finally agreed to bring in Lovett even though Lovett had a large and important dinner party at Newport—"and you know that Newport is exacting in its social forms." Dr. Lovett's quick diagnosis was I. P.

Two immediate problems presented themselves with Franklin's paralysis. One was Louis Howe's concern that nothing appear in the papers about Franklin's affliction because of the effect such news might have on any future political career. When he told this to Eleanor, she asked him in amazement, "Do you really think that Franklin has a future in politics?" She had been sleeping on a couch in Franklin's room and acting as a nurse on 24-hour duty and the thought that a man wracked with such pain and with two paralyzed legs would ever be able to meet the demands of a rigorous political campaign sounded preposterous.

"Let me tell you what I believe." The little man let cigarette ashes fall on his vest. "I believe that your husband will one day be President of the United States."

The other concern was about Franklin's mother. She had gone to Europe on a vacation jaunt and was expected back at the end of August. The custom was for Franklin to meet her at the dock when she arrived. How would she take his absence when she landed and what would be her reaction when she learned about his condition? Eleanor wrote her a letter to be delivered to her by her brother, Frederic Delano, when he met her in Franklin's stead: "Dearest Mama, Franklin has been quite ill and so can't go down to meet you on Tuesday to his great regret. . . . You don't know what it means to feel you near again."

Sally was shocked to hear about Franklin, but she was dowager enough to make the best of it. She wrote to her brother about her arrival at Campobello: "I got here yesterday at 1:30 and at once . . . came up to a brave, smiling and beautiful son, who said: 'Well, I'm glad you are back Mummy and I got up this party for you!' He had shaved himself and seemed very bright and keen. Below his waist he cannot move at all. His legs (that I have always been so proud of) have to be moved often as they ache when long in one position. He and Eleanor decided at once to be cheerful and the atmosphere of the house is all happiness, so I have fallen in and followed their glorious example. . . . Dr. Bennett just came and said, 'This boy is going to get all right.' They went into his room and I hear them all laughing. Eleanor is in the lead."

By this time Louis Howe confided in Eleanor that he was not going to take the job offered him by the New England oil company. In fact, he was not going to take any job, for he was going to devote all his energy to Franklin. This seemed to her rather foolish considering that

[125]

Howe had a family and they would need some income to get along. But he was adamant and she did not argue.

He confided in her his plan for preventing Franklin's political career from ending at this point. As long as they could, they were to keep the nature of his catastrophe out of the papers. "If the papers say that he has infantile paralysis before we can break the news gently," Howe rasped, "Franklin's finished. Why, people will think paralysis means spinal meningitis or else some disease affecting the mind."

Both he and Eleanor carried out the fiction of telling the press correspondent who came over from Eastport almost daily to inquire about Franklin that he had nothing worse than a cold. "It's a bad one all right," Louis would add. It was not until almost three weeks after Franklin's legs were paralyzed that Louis finally told reporters that "Mr. Roosevelt has really been sick. However, he is now improving." This latter remark was, of course, to offset the first sentence.

The problem hit Howe and Eleanor full-face in mid-September when it became necessary to move Franklin to a New York hospital for better care. Eleanor made arrangements with Franklin's uncle, Frederic Delano, to bring a private railroad car to Eastport. Franklin would be brought across the bay by boat and lifted into the railroad car. But how to keep the reporters from viewing his helplessness? Louis Howe had the answer. He passed word along that Franklin's boat would come into Eastport at a certain dock. By bringing Franklin in at another dock on the opposite side of Eastport, he would not only keep the reporters and the expected crowd from guessing the truth but he would also save Franklin from the shame of being carried along on a stretcher, in full view of curiosity seekers.

The plan worked to perfection. Franklin was laid on the floor boards of a motorboat. Eleanor sat with the five children in the bow and kept them quiet. Franklin was in excruciating pain, but he managed to smile at them, amid gasps and groans. When the boat reached the deserted end of Eastport, he was put onto a baggage cart and Eleanor walked alongside him to whisper words of encouragement. Up a bumpy incline they went until they reached the private railroad car in the siding. And even though a window had been removed so that his stretcher could be passed into the car from the baggage cart, it required an enormous amount of maneuvering before he was safely passed through. Finally when he was in bed and Eleanor had wiped his heavily perspiring face, Howe informed the reporters and the local citizens that Franklin could be seen in the railroad car. The crowd came over and he managed to smile at those he knew. A reporter from the New York *World* wrote: "Mr. Roosevelt was enjoying his cigarette and said he had a good appetite. Although unable to sit up, he says he is feeling more comfortable."

Once in New York, Franklin was again passed through the train window and Eleanor and Howe rode in the ambulance with him to the Presbyterian Hospital. Here he was put under the care of Dr. George Draper, a Harvard classmate of his and an associate of Dr. Lovett. When Eleanor and Howe met reporters outside the hospital later, Howe told them: "Mr. Roosevelt is suffering from poliomyelitis. His doctor, George Draper, has the following announcement to make, 'I cannot say how long Mr. Roosevelt will be kept in the hospital but you can say definitely that he will not be crippled. No one need have any fear of permanent injury from this attack.'"

When a month passed and Franklin showed no signs of improvement, it came over both him and Eleanor that he would probably never regain the use of his legs. Dr. Draper was even more pessimistic. Watching Franklin's agony daily, he reached the conclusion that Franklin's back muscles were so badly damaged that he would never be able to sit up unaided. He was wrong in this conclusion but he was right in another when he told Eleanor, "Franklin has such courage, such ambition, and yet at the same time such an extraordinarily sensitive emotional mechanism, that it will take all the skill we can muster to lead him successfully to a recognition of what he really faces without crushing him." Dr. Lovett put it more succinctly: "There is likely to be mental depression."

But Eleanor knew that her husband's will was indomitable. At a time when it pained him to have anyone touch his bed sheets and when plaster casts were on both legs and wedges were driven in deeper each day to stretch the leg tendons, he took pride in pulling himself up by a strap hanging over his bed and turning himself over.

The worst crisis came at the end of October when she brought Franklin home to their Sixty-fifth Street house adjoining Sally Roosevelt's. "My son must come home to live in Hyde Park," Franklin's mother told Eleanor. "He's going to be an invalid the rest of his life and he needs rest and complete quiet."

"That's the last thing he should do," Eleanor told her. "And I won't let him."

Sally turned to Louis Howe for support. "You have good common sense, Louis. Can't you see that a political future is now out of the

[127]

question for my son? He always wanted to write and when he comes home to Hyde Park, he can keep busy doing that or reading books and collecting stamps."

Louis Howe snapped at her, "I expect him to be President." Then, staring at Franklin, Howe said angrily, "Sure you can retire and become a country squire like your father, or you can take up where you left off and go right on. So far as I'm concerned you're a man of destiny." Eleanor watched a friendly light come into her husband's eyes.

"I ought to know what is best for my son," the older woman went on. "Those wild political friends will sap his strength."

Eleanor turned wearily to Dr. Draper. "What about it, George? Should Franklin be relegated to the wheel chair for life?"

Dr. Draper stared at her and at Franklin's mother. Finally he said, "His recovery will be speeded if he becomes active again. He isn't an invalid, and there is no reason why he should be treated as one."

Sally Roosevelt would not give up, however. She was determined to have Franklin to herself again. All that winter she came through the sliding doors separating her place from Eleanor's to charge that there was too much noise going on for poor Franklin. She also worked on her son to undo the encouragement he was getting from Eleanor and Louis Howe by telling him constantly that he would always remain a helpless invalid.

In addition, she pitted the children against Eleanor in order to bring about her hoped-for victory. Eleanor had given Louis the big room on the third floor because he lived with them during the week and went home to his family in Poughkeepsie for the weekends. The children were all put into small rooms on the fourth floor. Eleanor slept on a cot in one of the boys' rooms and dressed in Franklin's bathroom. The old lady talked to the children about this peculiar arrangement where Howe got the best of things. "We used to look forward to Sunday breakfast," said Elliott, "not because of the extra large meal but because that was the only day of the week Louis wasn't on hand."

"It's not fair to you," Grandmother told fifteen-year-old Anna, "that you should have such a small room while that man has such a big room on the third floor. And besides, he has a bathroom."

Eleanor noticed the change in Anna. "The situation grew in her mind," she said of her daughter, "to a point where she felt that I did not care for her and was not giving her any consideration. It never occurred to her that I had far less than she had." At dinner sometimes, when Franklin had been carried to his place at table, Anna would act poorly, Franklin would reprimand her and she would run sobbing from the meal.

The tense tug of war in the house exploded at last in the spring of 1922. Eleanor was reading to Franklin, Jr., and John when suddenly she burst into tears. Her sobbing was soon uncontrollable. Elliott walked in from school, took one look at her and ran out of the house. Louis Howe, who had been with Franklin in his bedroom at the third floor rear, came down when he heard her sobbing. "What's the matter, Eleanor?" he asked, bewildered. But she only continued crying and he hurried away. When the two boys went off to bed, she sat on the sofa in the living room still wailing. Finally she went to the empty house next door, for her mother-in-law was away in the country, scrubbed her face with cold water, and finally stopped crying.

It was only after that letting off of steam that Anna realized that she had been wrong and that her mother loved her. The result was a firm foundation of friendship that never abated. As for her crying jag, Eleanor Roosevelt said, "From that time on I seemed to have got rid of nerves and uncontrollable tears, for never again have either of them bothered me."

By the spring, Franklin could wear a seven-pound steel brace on each leg. It was pitiful to watch him as he swung each braced leg clumsily from hip muscles in order to hold himself erect. But he was determined to re-enter the society of men. Eleanor smiled encouragement as he practiced moving about with crutches and stopping from time to time to rest upon the rigid braces. Louis Howe would read to him by the hour, from history books to daily papers, as he lay in bed and tried to move his toes. Asked years later how he could take the strain of the Presidency, Franklin laughed. "Once I spent two years lying in bed trying to move my big toe. That was the hardest job I ever had to do. After that, anything else looked easy."

Eleanor realized while it was going on that "the experience, above all others, which shaped my husband's character along more definite lines and gave him a strength and depth that he did not have as a young man, was the long struggle with infantile paralysis. As he came gradually to realize that he was not going to get any better, he faced great bitterness, I am sure, though he never mentioned it. The only thing that stands out in my mind as evidence of how he suffered when he finally knew that he would never walk again, was the fact that I never heard him mention golf from the day he was taken ill. . . . That game epitomized to him the ability to be out of doors and to enjoy the use of his body. Though he learned to bear it, I am afraid it was always a tragedy."

Franklin's thought on the subject was one he tried to put humorously. "It was rather humiliating to contract a disease of which seventy-five per cent of the victims are children."

In the summer of 1922, Eleanor took her family to Hyde Park. Franklin's doctor had recommended that he get plenty of sunshine and swim in water heated to seventy degrees. Their friend Vincent Astor had promised the use of a nearby pool. Even though such advantages were available at Hyde Park, Eleanor feared a further outbreak of battle between herself and his mother.

Nor was she wrong. Several times a day Sally Roosevelt cautioned Franklin to quit exercising so strenuously. Sometimes she told him that he should give up exertion entirely. Above all he should not do any thinking about politics or pay any attention to that despicable Louis Howe whom he had brought to her house and who talked to him as though he were running for office.

Sometimes she discouraged him. Once after such a browbeating, he sat in his wheel chair and supervised Anna as she put books into the library wall. When she dropped several, he scolded her and she ran off sobbing to her mother.

Eleanor Roosevelt put her arms around her daughter and tried to explain his outburst. "Mother talked of the battle Father was fighting against great odds," said Anna, "of the naturalness of his nervous reaction; how lucky we were to have him alive and to be able to help him get well; how much more patience and grit he had to have than we; until I felt very sheepish and even more ashamed—but in a different way, a more adult, understanding way. Back I went to the library where, of course, I not only found forgiveness but also a sincere and smilingly given invitation to resume my place on the ladder."

Eleanor watched Franklin exercise at Hyde Park that summer by the hour. Sometimes he relaxed on the living-room rug with the boys and played marbles with them. But most times he was on the parallel bars in the garden going back and forth and supporting his weight with his shoulders and arms. Every morning he would set off down the driveway to the gate on crutches. It was terribly painful but he would not give up this effort until his doctor warned that it would wreck his heart. He must have known that it was a losing battle so far as the re-use of his legs was concerned, for they grew thinner each day. It made Eleanor sad and yet proud the way he would swing himself from his chair to the floor and crawl across the wood boards until he reached the object he wanted.

There must be something more constructive to do for someone with such unbeatable spunk, she told Louis Howe.

He agreed. There was.

Chapter Fifteen

Louis howe devised the master plan. First, he informed Eleanor, they would develop all sorts of hobbies and get Franklin interested in them.

Louis was an excellent carpenter. Since Franklin had always loved the sea, Louis began making model sailboats. When Franklin saw some of them, he immediately set to work designing models of his own. Louis winked at Eleanor when this phase of his plan caught on.

Before long Franklin and Louis and the boys were racing the model boats on water as though, thought Eleanor, they were all the same age schoolboys. They tried them across the Hudson and Louis proposed an annual toy boat race across the river. "The winner will get a loving cup," Franklin joined in, "the Krum Elbow Cup!"

It was good to see Franklin so excited. They yelled and screamed and applauded as their boats moved on the water. Once when Louis won the silver cup, Franklin derided his effort to friends. "The race was held in a gale," he explained, "and his boat was the only one that wasn't dismantled."

Eleanor laughed when Louis tapped Franklin's shoulder. "That's the Roosevelt story," Louis growled, "and anyway who has the cup?"

Louis had time to work on Franklin because all the children were not at home. One by one they were going off to Groton. Elliott joined James at Groton in 1922. This was Franklin's wish as well as Sally's. Anna was at Miss Chapin's School in New York; while Franklin, Jr., was enrolled at the Buckley School until he was old enough for Groton. Little Johnny was still at home and, of all the boys, Johnny was his father's favorite. Sally also doted on him. As a child he had not grown properly and was called "Runt" by his brothers, a nickname his mother despised. Small as he was, with no indication that one day he would be the tallest of Eleanor's giants, he was nevertheless an optimistic child whose vocabulary was almost entirely slang. Asked by Eleanor one time to help his grandmother across a rough beach, John took her arm and shouted, "Come on, Toots." The old lady howled with glee. Franklin also acquired slang from Johnny. Throughout his life whenever Franklin used slang and saw that his visitors looked shocked, he would pin the blame on John. "Oh yeah, or so what," Franklin would say and then add, "as my boy Johnny says."

Another step Louis took in his campaign was to rummage through bookshops to find rare old books that might interest Franklin. He learned from Eleanor the types of books Franklin relished. He also scoured art stores for prints of early American sailing vessels. One time he deposited on Franklin's bed an original painting of John Paul Jones that had cost him only $25, he announced cagily. And of course there were stamps. Louis pored through catalogues and became a minor expert in philately, in order to be able to talk sense on the subject with Franklin.

All these were to the good, said Eleanor. But a life of hobbying was not much more than Franklin's mother had in mind. When she encouraged Franklin to return to work he jumped at the suggestion. He gave up his law partnership because he could not maneuver his wheel chair up the stairs to the building and he refused to embarrass himself each day before others. However, he stayed with Fidelity and Deposit because there was only a single step at the front entrance. He found that outside of the fact that his legs were paralyzed, his general health was good. Friends found that he was a different person once he emerged back into life. At the end of a work day when others developed short tempers from hurrying to and fro, he was calm, untired, and he maintained a judicial mind to the end. One reason was that he did no running around. Everyone had to come to him.

Eleanor watched over him to see that he did not grow tired. But he never did. His routine in New York was to receive callers while he was at home and still in bed from eight-thirty until ten-thirty; go to work until five, with lunch at his desk instead of rushing on the street to find a place to eat; and afterward, return home for his exercises, dinner and conferences.

But hobbies and work were not enough for Louis Howe. Franklin's life was politics, he argued with Eleanor, and he must get back his interest in it.

"But how are you going to do that?" she asked.

Howe laughed. "I know the best way to get him back into what he must be doing. You're going into politics," he announced calmly.

"Me?" she asked incredulously, for she had never been involved in politics even when Franklin had held office.

"That's right," Howe repeated. "You're going into politics."

[133]

The mother of five and the wife of a handicapped man soon realized that Louis Howe meant business. Her work in analyzing legislation for the League of Women Voters was not enough for him, though he was impressed with how much she had learned there about good working habits from Elizabeth Read. Miss Read had "instilled in me," said Eleanor, "the necessity for setting up a standard to be met in whatever work one undertook." Louis found out that Eleanor was considered the most efficient worker the LWV had.

"But that isn't the only place where you should be active," he chided her. "There are lots of other deserving places you could fit in."

Although she was "upper class" socially, she plunged into the activities of the Women's Trade Union League. She found several women in this organization who fought as hard as male labor leaders to organize the women in industry. Some were extremely well grounded in labor history and theory.

Two of them, Maude Schwartz and tiny, redheaded Rose Schneiderman, immediately took up with Eleanor and they became good friends. "Bring them home to Franklin," Howe growled, and she did. They came in cautiously that first time, but once at ease they returned frequently to argue with Franklin and Eleanor about trade unionism and its place in an industrial society. Maude had been a member of a printer's union in England where she was born and she had endless funny stories about organizing British workers. Little Rose, with her grammar-school education and her background as a capmaker and organizer for garment workers, was excitable and determined and talked of the many dire things that happened to unorganized workers and to the unemployed. Franklin came alive and his eyes sparkled as he laughed at Maude's stories and commiserated with Rose. To Eleanor they were a tonic, too.

At Howe's further suggestion she also joined the Women's Division of the Democratic State Committee. This was done when Marion Dickerman, a schoolteacher, lady politician and an active member of the Women's Trade Union League, introduced her to Nancy Cook of the Democratic State Committee. Miss Cook was so pleased to have a Roosevelt in the organization that she asked her to speak at a fundraising lunch for Democratic women. Many members were surprised to find that Franklin Roosevelt was married.

The thought of rising before a large group of people and speaking appalled her. But Louis Howe said she needed such experience. Somehow she got through this ordeal, though she felt clammy and tongue-tied. The occasion itself was a great success, for she raised $12,000. She was asked to speak at other meetings. Louis Howe came and sat at the rear of the halls while she spoke. Afterward, he would rip into her effort and tell her where she had gone wrong. He was especially irked by the nervous laugh and the high-pitched giggle which she interlarded between sentences. "Why do you laugh when you're making a serious speech?" he bellowed at her one time.

She hadn't even known she had laughed.

"There wasn't anything funny," he scowled. "So don't do it again."

It took her years before she overcame the nervous laugh and the giggles when she faced a sea of listeners.

When Al Smith ran for governor against Nathan L. Miller, then serving as governor, Louis Howe got her to make a speech in Smith's behalf. It was a speech he had written and he made her memorize it and repeat it to him dozens of times. Throughout his criticism was derisive. And when she finally made the speech, fumbling her way through it and laughing nervously while she tried to recall the next line, he came to her afterward and scolded her as though she were an errant child.

Howe also showed her how to read a newspaper. "Read the first paragraph of a story and it will give you a good summary. Don't waste time on anything further unless it's of importance." He practiced going through entire papers with her page by page and scolded her gruffly until she could handle *The New York Times* in thirty minutes.

But Eleanor did not mind the berating, for she was becoming much interested in politics and wanted to improve herself. Besides, she was growing fond of the strange little gnome who was so intent upon renewing her husband's political career. He began to treat her as a friend and not as part of the political appurtenances necessary to a candidate for office. While in private he was often cruel in pointing out her shortcomings, in public he showed her the greatest deference. "I remember," she said later, "Louis Howe taking me out to dinner at a restaurant, sitting at a table he did not like, and eating food he did not like, simply because he said he knew I would be uncomfortable if he made me conspicuous by getting up and changing to another table or complaining about the food."

Only a year after she joined the Women's Division of the State Democratic Party, Eleanor was chairman of the Division's finance committee. Prominent Democrats were beginning to seek her counsel. They had discovered that she had an intuitive ability to find the right answer to a complex problem. She was always on the move now, just as Howe had hoped, and the effect on Franklin was enormous. The sight of his wife moving in political circles made him positively jealous! Politics was a man's game and was he not a man? He would show her how good a politician he was. Sitting slouched on the chair next to Franklin's carved double bed and letting the ashes from a Sweet Caporal fall where they would, Louis Howe smiled and said nothing.

Franklin started out cautiously by insisting he be permitted to help out at the Women's Trade Union League. What the women concocted for him was to appear at the League headquarters at Christmas time and read Dickens' *Christmas Carol* aloud to union children.

"At home we discussed politics violently," Eleanor recalls the change that took place. In September 1922, Franklin held a reception for Al Smith at his mother's Hyde Park home. It was his formal return to the political arena. He could sit and shake hands with party bigwigs and laugh heartily at the tales of the State Democratic Convention, where Eleanor and their neighbor, Elinor Morgenthau, marched three times around the hall with the Smith banner held high when Al was nominated.

But now that he was started on the road back into politics, there was no reason for Eleanor Roosevelt to drop out. She edited the Women's Division paper, a trial at first because she lacked journalistic experience. But Louis Howe taught her how to make up the sheets and proofread. When Franklin saw the first edition, he was full of praise. "Louis wrote every headline," she had to admit, "because he said mine were terrible." But it wasn't many months later before she was an old hand at that sort of thing.

Though her speaking mannerisms were hard to alter, Louis Howe did effect a great change in her speeches. "Keep this in mind and you won't go wrong," he told her. "Have something to say, say it and then sit down!" She found this was a blessing.

Eleanor Roosevelt also took on the task of political organizer. She finally learned to drive though she had two accidents at the outset. Once she drove into a stone gatepost. Another time with her entire family along, she backed the car down a steep bank and was fortunately stopped by a stout tree. But after these mishaps she drove all over the state to organize women voters into the Democratic Party. Everywhere she stopped to address women she told them that the Democratic Party "seems to have been more concerned with the welfare and interests at large and less with the growth of big business interests."

When the men Democratic leaders refused to take their female counterparts seriously, she set out to change their minds. A chief problem was getting them to sit still long enough to hear her out. Franklin had argued: "Democratic women have too often in the past been rather apologetic for calling themselves Democrats. This should end, and they should let the world and their neighbors know that they take great pride in their Party."

On one occasion she and Caroline O'Day called on a party leader. They were told by the man's wife that he wasn't home. "That's all right," said Eleanor, who thought the woman's eyes were too furtive, "we'll just wait on your porch until he comes."

She and Caroline made themselves comfortable and waited relentlessly. An hour later the woman came out again. "I don't know when my husband will be home," she said, annoyed.

"It doesn't matter," Eleanor laughed. "We haven't anything else to do. So we'll wait."

The woman went back into her house and closed the door with a slam. An hour later the door creaked open and a man's face appeared. "You win," he said morosely. He had been hiding indoors all the time. Eleanor laughed and proceeded to win his support for adding local women to his group.

Besides her new interest in politics, Franklin's infirmity resulted in another great change. Since he could not take part in outdoor activities with the children, she had to do so. She went to the Y.W.C.A. for swimming lessons and learned to overcome the fear of water she had picked up at Sagamore Hill in Oyster Bay, where Uncle Ted had delighted in throwing non-swimmers off the dock into deep water. She also took up horseback riding again so she could join the children, who were proficient in this sport. She even went so far as to brave the wilds of the woods on a long camping trip with her two youngest sons and some of their friends in 1923. When Franklin, Jr., cut himself with an ax, she calmly administered first aid. She also found time to become a lay person admissible for aid in the delivery room of a New York hospital—in case the necessity ever arose.

Sometimes Eleanor's political activities were on an everyday level and sometimes they were on a more complex plane. For instance, on election days she drove people to the polls to vote. She saw with shock the extent of open bribery to enlarge a candidate's support. Once she drove a wizened old man to the polls and he told her proudly that he had sold his vote several times during that day. "When I suggested that it was really selling your right to be an equal with any other citizen," said Eleanor, "he remarked, 'I vote as I please in the end anyway.'"

She was also going to political conventions where she made strong attempts to prod male politicians to give some attention to the ladies.

When she demanded to know why more women weren't permitted to serve on local committees, one man barked at her, "No, we don't want women to serve on local committees. We'd never be sure what they'd do." "For forty-eight weeks a year," Eleanor told him in reply, "women are entirely forgotten as potent political factors. Then four weeks before the election men wake up to their importance." Louis Howe was especially gratified when Eleanor could report she had seen Al Smith at some of these Democratic get-togethers. To Louis any personal link with Al was important for Franklin because Al was going places in the party. Once Smith wrote Franklin that he had seen Eleanor at a convention. She also corresponded with him on political matters. Once he wrote Franklin, "I was awfully pleased to hear from Mrs. Roosevelt of the progress you are making. I just got all worked up over it."

When Al became governor of New York, Eleanor on occasion went to see him to lobby for legislation she wanted. For a shy person this was quite a step forward for her, though many of the women who lobbied with her were excellent teachers and gave her courage. Once she accompanied Mrs. Florence Kelly of the Consumers League to pressure Governor Smith into supporting the Child Labor Amendment. Florence was the daughter of W. D. "Pig Iron" Kelly, a high tariff congressman, and a strong personality in her own right. They knew that Al Smith, though generally strong on labor legislation when pushed by his adviser, Mrs. Belle Moskowitz, was adamant against the Child Labor Amendment, with the quaint notion that it interfered with the rights of the family.

On that occasion, Al Smith was not in a mood to let them argue with him. Nor did he wish to divulge the reason for his opposition. "He did not quite like to tell Mrs. Kelly," said Eleanor, "since she could be caustic on occasion! The way he walked up and down his office and stormed at Mrs. Kelly about the evils of social workers, and putting into legislation things which did not belong there, was clever but unconvincing. I came away feeling that there were weaknesses as well as strength in Alfred E. Smith."

She was learning fast about politics and politicians. On a higher plane she served in 1923 as a member of the jury of award for the Edward Bok competition for the best plan for world peace. Esther Lape, who was Eleanor's good friend, was the manager of the Bok Foundation. Louis Howe and Eleanor got Franklin interested in this award and he seriously spent a great deal of time writing a long essay on the subject under consideration. However, when Eleanor became a member of the award jury, he did not submit his plan. Nevertheless, he did show his essay to Esther Lape and in 1945 pointed out that his plan was basically that of the United Nations.

Throughout all this long period of illness and mental recuperation, Eleanor never once mentioned his troubles to her husband. He would not go to Campobello, but she accepted this determination as based on the difficulty he would have maneuvering about there rather than on the fact that it was where he had contracted infantile paralysis. She would tell him of incidents that happened there when she took the children at vacation time and he would laugh heartily at her humorous tales. She had bought a small donkey on Campobello that everyone could ride except herself. Whenever she got on the beast, he would lie down and roll over, to the great merriment of all spectators. Franklin expressed an interest in seeing sometime whether the same experience would befall him, though he did not say when he would go to Campobello.

The entire family, with the exception of his mother, talked to him as though nothing ailed him. "We didn't do anything," Eleanor recalled, "except treat him as a perfectly normal, able-bodied man which was what he made us all feel he was, and never let anyone intimate to him that he was trying to do too much. Once when he was planning to go South, I think it was the winter after he had infantile paralysis, he said he thought it would be easier for him to go by boat than by train. That was the only time I ever heard him acknowledge that he was not just as he had been before."

As the years passed after Franklin's attack, his mother still refused to give up the notion that he would become her little boy again at Hyde Park. Though she never quite understood that Eleanor's entrance into politics was part of a plan to restir Franklin's political interest, she concluded that Eleanor and Louis Howe were pitting themselves against her. Howe she detested for breaking up her fond dream. Eleanor she thought a modern woman without true respect for the old gracious ways. And poor, poor Franklin. To the end of her days, said Eleanor, Sara Roosevelt could never "let him leave the house without inquiring whether he was dressed warmly enough or urging him to wear his rubbers or put on a sweater under his coat. The older he got the more it annoyed him."

Chapter Sixteen

THE YEAR 1924 heralded the return of Franklin to active politics and the emergence of Eleanor into political prominence. The catalytic agent for both was a whisky-drinking, cigar-smoking, derby hat wearer named Al Smith.

In late spring of that year Governor Smith came to the conclusion that he would make an admirable presidential nominee for the Democratic Party and he asked Franklin to take charge of his preconvention campaign. Louis Howe let out a loud hurrah, though Franklin's mother told him furiously that Franklin must not undertake anything so strenuous. Besides, she went on, the governor was an uncultured man and without any ability. It was true, Eleanor knew, that whenever Al Smith came to Hyde Park, he recognized the old lady's contempt for him and in his embarrassment he reverted to ungrammatical and loud talk.

Al Smith's request was not based on altruistic motives but Louis Howe didn't care. As he discussed it with Franklin and Eleanor, Smith wanted to get out from under the general impression that his support was entirely Irish-Catholic. What better way than to land a Roosevelt?

When Franklin accepted, Eleanor also found a role for herself. She was asked to present platform planks of importance to women to the convention's resolutions committee. Unfortunately, the all-male committee would not let her into the room. She sat outside the door and knitted most of the night until she was able to prevail upon James Farley to deliver her resolutions to the committee.

But most important to her was the opportunity to hear Franklin nominate Al Smith. Howe had admonished everyone around Franklin, "Don't carry him up on the platform. If people see him being carried, they'll have only pity for him and he'll be dead politically."

On that hot June day in Madison Square Garden in New York, unknown to the crowd and out of its view, Franklin was carried in his wheel chair to the speaker's platform. He had asked a friend to shake the speaker's stand to see if it would support his weight. Then his time came.

Eleanor watched, her hands clammy and her breathing uneven. With crutches under his arms and holding onto their seventeen-year-old son Jimmy, he swung himself along slowly toward the stand. A hush fell over the boisterous crowd as it waited to see if he could make it. And when he finally did, Eleanor smiled with pride as he gripped the stand and jutted his chin out toward his audience. For almost five minutes the crowd stood and cheered him.

And after he spoke for Smith and extolled him as the "Happy Warrior," the suggestion of Judge Joseph M. Proskauer, Smith's speech writer, the delegates went completely wild. Louis Howe told Eleanor that he was afraid the delegates would go ahead and nominate Franklin for the Presidency, which would be too much of a good thing. Will Rogers, who was reporting the convention for *The New York Times,* said that when Franklin finally "did get to the end and named Al you would have thought somebody had thrown a wildcat in your face." It was only after Franklin put up his hand and asked the crowd to stop cheering and applauding that it did.

With Smith's strength about equal to William McAdoo's, neither got the nomination. In the fall when the Democratic nominee, John W. Davis, the Wall Street lawyer, faced Calvin Coolidge, he lost as Franklin anticipated.

Despite Smith's failure to land the presidential nomination he did run for re-election that fall for governor. His opponent was Eleanor's first cousin, Teddy Roosevelt, Jr. And it was Eleanor's turn now to act toward him as unmercifully as he had acted against Franklin in the 1920 election. Cousin Ted had served as Assistant Secretary of the Navy during the Teapot Dome scandals and though he had not been involved he had taken no part in exposing the skulduggery.

To weaken Cousin Ted's fight, at Louis Howe's suggestion Eleanor devised an enormous teakettle which spouted steam and had it set on top an automobile. Wherever Cousin Ted campaigned in the state the spouting teakettle followed him. Though this stunt played an important role in defeating Cousin Ted, Eleanor later regretted such roughness and said, "I never blamed my cousin when he retaliated in later campaigns against my husband."

After Franklin's "Happy Warrior" speech to the Democratic National Convention in the summer of 1924, Eleanor became aware of a gigantic effort on his part to learn to walk again. It was not that he was any longer embarrassed to be seen on crutches. Actually, one day when he went to work he fell on a slippery lobby floor. Not the least bit mortified, he called to passers-by, "How about a hand so I can get back on my feet?" He wanted to walk because walking meant the independence he had always known.

He tried that summer to ride an experimental tricycle his mother bought him. Eleanor was worried when he turned to horseback riding, which she considered a danger since he could not use his legs to help himself stay on. Franklin himself exclaimed that the type of horse he required was one that "is constitutionally unable to trot, and which is also guaranteed against any sidewise motions."

It was in the fall of 1924 that George Foster Peabody, a New York banker and philanthropist, wrote Franklin and extolled the curative powers of a swimming pool he owned in Warm Springs, Georgia. When Peabody sent along a testimonial from a victim of infantile paralysis who claimed that in three years he had progressed from leg paralysis to locomotion with a cane, Franklin insisted that Eleanor go to Warm Springs with him to see for themselves.

When they arrived early in October for a three-week exploratory visit, Eleanor's first reaction was that they had made a mistake. "It was then a very run-down southern summer resort which had seen much better days. The old hotel with its piazzas called to mind the southern belles of Civil War days." Its only redeeming feature was its swimming pool where the water coming out of the ground had a high content of mineral salts and was a natural 88 degrees.

When Franklin got into the water, he found he could not only stand without braces but he could walk about in the water. The effect was exhilarating, though he believed then that the water had healing power and not, as he found later, that it was the high mineral content and the warmness that made his body buoyant and comfortable. Eleanor, always a skeptic about unproved conclusions, left him after a few days to continue his experiment. "It is too bad Eleanor has to leave so soon, but she and I both feel it is important," he wrote disappointedly to his mother, "for her not to be away the end of the campaign."

In New York, she learned by letter that a delightful thing had happened to him. He managed to feel life in his toes as he walked in the water. "It is just a week since you left," he wrote Eleanor excitedly. "The legs are really improving a great deal. This is really a discovery of a place and there is no doubt that I've got to do it some more." He didn't seem to realize then that water in general reduced the weight of gravity and permitted one to exercise unused muscles for a great length of time. It was Warm Springs alone, he felt, that had that power.

He remained there for six weeks that trip. While he was there a newsman wrote a syndicated feature, "Swimming Back to Health," which spread the story of Franklin's efforts at Warm Springs around the nation. Franklin was embarrassed and angry, though Louis Howe told Eleanor gleefully that it was wonderful publicity. The following spring when Franklin returned to Warm Springs, he found that several other polio victims, attracted by the newspaper article, had come to be cured.

Eleanor was not very enthusiastic when he broached the idea to her of sinking most of his money into the establishment of a Warm Springs Foundation to treat polio victims. When he addressed the national convention of the American Orthopedic Association in Atlanta early in 1926 and won from them a reluctant agreement to send an investigating committee to Warm Springs, she realized he meant business. "I know you love creative work," she told him. "My only feeling is that Georgia is somewhat distant for you to keep in touch with what is really a big undertaking. One cannot, it seems to me, have vital interests in widely divided places, but that may be because I'm old and rather overwhelmed by what there is to do in one place and it wearies me to think of even undertaking to make new ties."

Despite her further objection that he might put so much money into it that there would not be enough left to see the children through college, when the orthopedists declared that every patient at Warm Springs had shown some improvement, he went ahead and put up the initial money to start a nonstock, nonprofit foundation. He never divulged to Eleanor what money he put in, though it became known to her that it was about two thirds of his wealth, or about $200,000. He also had to raise another $500,000 to improve the property he purchased from Peabody, and in addition he later took out a $500,000 life insurance policy making the Foundation the beneficiary.

The Warm Springs Foundation was important to Franklin, Eleanor knew, even though it put him on a precarious financial basis. It gave him a chance to help others, especially children, and she marveled at the peace that came over his face when he spent a few weeks with his fellow polio victims. It was ironical, though, that while he praised Warm Springs to the sky, his own signs of improvement came at a snail's pace. One friend recalls how in 1926, two years after he started treatment at Warm Springs, "Franklin and Eleanor came to visit with me in Mattapoisett. Two men carried him in to a seat at the dining room table. He told the men not to return until 9:30. When dinner was over, Franklin pushed back his chair and said, 'See me get into the next room.' He got down on the floor and went in on his hands and knees and got up into another chair himself."

While Franklin was busying himself with Warm Springs, Eleanor continued her political activities. Both she and Louis Howe kept him informed of the details of New York happenings. Franklin had begun a new law partnership with Basil O'Connor in 1925 and Howe worked in the same building where their office was located as secretary of the National Crime Commission.

It was through Eleanor that Franklin maintained contact with many influential politicians. The people she brought home helped educate him on a variety of subjects, and her reports on her various activities brought on a sharpened interest in new matters. She began carrying little black notebooks with her, a practice she maintained thereafter. The notebooks were reminders of her engagements day by day and often covered events five or six months ahead. About a dozen items were entered for each day and crossed through when completed.

There were talks to give to county conventions; typing to be done on national and state legislative summaries for the League of Women Voters; lobbying letters to be sent to U. S. Senators to win their support for the entrance of the United States as a member of the World Court and an analysis of their replies. There was one reply from Senator Walter F. George of Georgia who complained, "My support of it brought on vigorous opposition to me in my re-election fight."

She was now deeply involved with state and local civic work and with welfare problems. Women's clubs began asking for her to buoy up their membership and give them courage. The head of one organization said she liked Mrs. Roosevelt's "high-mindedness, or disinterestedness or something." She was never hard-boiled, as were so many of the women active in public matters, but was always feminine and a lady.

She wrote Franklin from the "road" as if she were a traveling salesman: "March 3rd. Wednesday A.M. Mrs. O'Day and I saw the Governor, our assemblymen and others and then Mrs. Greene and I went over to Saratoga, where we had a fine democratic tea. We dined at Skidmore College and I spoke afterwards to the girls on the World Court and League. . . . Caught the midnight in Albany and had a busy day Thursday with a lunch for Miss Smith, dean of the Bryn Mawr Summer School, International co-operation meeting and a visit to Tissie and her baby. . . . I read at the Women's Trade Union League in the evening. . . . This morning went to see Elizabeth Read as I'm to be treasurer for City, State and Nation, don't laugh! . . . I've written or am writing to every Democrat in the state."

Her enthusiasms were so infectious that her husband, who had a retentive memory, could repeat to others what she told him as though he himself had been directly involved. Yet she disliked being told that she was putting her emotions into her "causes." One time when a visitor praised her "passionate interest" in welfare legislation, she quickly replied, "I hardly think those words apply to me."

In 1926 she became directly involved in a political campaign as a speaker. Throughout the state of New York she made speech after speech for Robert Wagner, Franklin's old opponent from his State Senate days in the "Blue-Eyed Billy" Sheehan fight. Wagner was running for the U. S. Senate against James Wadsworth. Wadsworth she tellingly ridiculed as "a country squire of the Seventeenth Century." Wagner she painted as a great champion of social legislation. When Wagner won, he said publicly that her aid was the most important factor in his success.

The more activities she took on, the greater seemed her energy. When Franklin bought a small farm about a mile and a half from his mother's place in Hyde Park, Eleanor erected a cottage on the property. Here she could bring her friends for talks and relaxation without the eye of Sally Roosevelt over all that went on. Franklin served as architect and later erected a swimming pool on the front lawn. He enjoyed this diversion. "My Missus and some of her female friends," he joked, "want to build a shack on a stream in the back woods and want, instead of a beautiful marble bath, to have the stream dug out so as to form an old-fashioned swimmin' hole. Apparently the girls think that this will get them more closely back to nature and I foresee that I shall have to put a substantial board fence around the swimming hole to keep interested neighbors from seeing how close they get back to nature when they take their morning plunge."

In 1926, the year the cottage went up, Mrs. Roosevelt and her closest political associates, Nancy Cook and Marion Dickerman, got a bright idea for alleviating the growing unemployment problem around Hyde Park and constructed a furniture shop in partnership on the property. They called their factory Val-Kill, after the creek that ran along the farm. Val-Kill, from the Dutch, meant "Brook in the Field." Although Franklin found the idea of manufacturing reproductions of early American furniture quite boring, he thought it grand that the girls were trying to solve a fundamental problem instead of sticking to generalized discussions. On a basis nonprofit for themselves, the women were soon providing employment for out-of-work farm men.

Despite her own lack of higher education, Eleanor had had a yearning for years to try her hand at teaching. In 1927, when her youngest child John went off to boarding school, her opportunity arrived. Marion

Dickerman was the assistant principal of a school in New York City, Todhunter School, and that year when Miss Todhunter wanted to return to her native England, Eleanor, Marion and Nancy Cook bought her out. The school was a fashionable private institution for girls. Nevertheless, Franklin's mother called it beneath dignity when Eleanor announced that she was to be a vice-principal. But Eleanor disregarded her.

Because of her own absence of teaching experience, she taught only the senior girls who were more mature. Three days a week she commuted to the city to give courses in American history and English and American literature. She also gave a course she called "Happenings" that dealt with current affairs. Not content to have the girls discuss what they read in their papers, she took them on expeditions in the city to see things firsthand. She led them into courtrooms, to police line-ups, and she took them to walk inside the various slums of New York so they could see how other people live and get a better understanding of the problems faced by others. These were girls from Central Park and Park Avenue homes and she knew that their experiences in "Happenings" might well constitute their only experiences with less fortunates.

By 1928, Eleanor Roosevelt was one of the best-known personalities in the state of New York. Quietly, and then with a burst after her husband was stricken with polio, she had impressed herself as a being independent of her husband and yet as a partner in a high-powered team of politicians. All this portended big things that were to erupt in 1928.

Chapter Seventeen

HE GROWING EASE with which Eleanor Roosevelt raised money for the women's division of the New York State Democratic Committee and the admiration both men and women in the party had for her did not escape the attention of Al Smith, the governor. Though he felt ill at ease at the Hyde Park home of Sally Roosevelt and Eleanor would not stock liquor there during Prohibition, Smith came to believe that both Eleanor and Franklin were important to his presidential aspirations. And they in turn believed him to be a good, liberal person, an excellent administrator and a man whom they must support, especially because he was under attack for being a Roman Catholic.

In 1928 he asked Franklin to travel to the Democratic National Convention at Houston to place his name in nomination and to serve as his floor manager. Franklin did so in June and his own triumph was evident. He came, not swinging himself along on crutches but walking gingerly along with leg braces and a cane, and he held onto his young son Elliott's arm as though he wanted the boy to see what was going on, instead of gripping him for support. Nor did he look pale and sickly as he had four years earlier. His upper torso was powerful and his voice was rich throughout the speech, which was the hit of the convention.

After Franklin had done his part so nobly in helping Smith win the presidential nomination in a single ballot, the governor now concentrated on Eleanor. As Louis Howe was working ceaselessly to advance Franklin's cause, so was a plump little brainy woman named Belle Moskowitz performing a similar stint for Al Smith. At Al's request, she came to see Eleanor one day and asked her to head up women's activities for the campaign against Herbert Hoover, who had won the Republican nomination. Eleanor agreed and became director of the Bureau of Women's Activities for Smith's campaign.

It was Louis Howe's opinion that until Eleanor Roosevelt moved into her office at Democratic Campaign Headquarters in New York's General Motors Building near Columbus Circle, American women were not politically minded. How much was due to her work is problematic, especially since the two burning issues in the campaign were religion and whether or not to repeal the Eighteenth Amendment and bring back whisky.

Whatever the case, Eleanor put on an energetic show. Mrs. Nellie Tayloe Ross was given the job of handling the field work, Congresswoman Mary Norton of New Jersey ran the Women's Speaker's Bureau and Mary W. "Molly" Dewson, a tall aristocratic woman who had been civic secretary of the New York Women's City Club, was dispatched to take charge of the important St. Louis office.

Eleanor never felt the absence of Belle Moskowitz's hot breath on her back, for Mrs. Moskowitz wanted every ounce of energy expended to put Al Smith into the White House. From the time when she accepted the payless job until the election ended in November she was to work such long hours and with such gusto that even Belle Moskowitz tired in the tide of her energy.

Eleanor packed as many visiting women into Democratic headquarters for tea, brief talks and handshakes as space allowed. She made the entire staff take part in a constant whirl of such activities. On one occasion when Mrs. Ross, who had served as governor of Wyoming after her husband's death and as such was a stellar attraction, could not be found to go through the handshaking routine, Eleanor sent out a search party for her. The Lady Governor was finally located lying on the bare floor of the ladies' rest room in a state of exhaustion from previous sessions with handshakers.

Eleanor also went on speaking trips. Once her partner was Mrs. Charles Dana Gibson of Virginia, whose husband had used her beautiful face as his model for the "Gibson Girl." Wherever they traveled Eleanor got up and recited facts and figures to demonstrate that Smith should be elected President, while Mrs. Gibson concentrated on drawing "oh's" and "ah's" from each audience. Women questioned how a Dry like Eleanor could support a Wet like Smith. When Franklin received a picture of Eleanor through the mail, and one that did not do her justice, he replied, "Thanks for sending me that awful picture of my Missus. She is apparently looking at a fly on the ceiling with the hope of finding out how to be wet and dry at the same time."

One time Al Smith insisted that she come with him to St. Louis to help him evaluate the way the campaign was going in the Midwest. She was besieged by letters from women Democrats across the nation asking her for advice. Louis Howe carefully wrote all the names and addresses down for future use. One lady in Kentucky wanted to know

[148]

how to answer a speech. "Write letters to the papers taking up point by point whatever he said and disproving it," Eleanor advised her.

She made a national report on the organization of Democratic women in mid-September and it was from this that she concluded that Smith's chances were poor. She analyzed "My office, Publicity, Gov. Ross's Office, Smith For President Clubs, Women in Industry, College Leagues, Business and Professional Women, Social Welfare Workers and Educators." Of the South, she said sadly, Florida, Mississippi, Alabama and Virginia looked unsatisfactory. As for the West and Middle West, she considered them hopeless. "I feel no real organization exists. What is being done is more or less haphazard."

In the fall of 1928, Eleanor took the time to go to Rochester to attend the State Democratic Convention. Despite her hectic existence, she felt lonely. Franklin was in Warm Springs working up an animosity for Al Smith for talking in more generalities than Herbert Hoover, whom Franklin admired. Sally Roosevelt had been in Europe, the boys were in school, and her daughter Anna, now twenty-two, had married Curtis Dall.

She had no intention of staying long at the convention because she had to get to her classes at Todhunter, which she still continued despite the political campaign. She was aware that Al Smith had confided in others that he wanted her husband to run for governor in order to pick up extra New York votes for himself in the presidential race. But she had agreed with Franklin and Louis Howe that it was a bad time to be running for governor. Howe's reasoning, always political, was that the continued prosperity might bring a Republican landslide and bury Roosevelt as well as Smith. It was best, he believed, to run for governor in 1932 and then for President in 1936.

Whatever Howe thought, Franklin and Eleanor agreed that for the next few years at least he should continue his treatment at Warm Springs. And when Democratic leaders began beseeching him to run for governor, he turned down the offers flatly on the ground that he wanted to better his health.

But the pleading continued when Smith grew even more convinced that he needed Roosevelt to carry New York. The only other possible candidate was Townsend Scudder, a justice of the New York Supreme Court. But Smith would have none of him because he found him cold and unfriendly. "You just can't talk to him," Al scowled. It was Roosevelt or nothing.

And this was the situation when Eleanor arrived in Rochester for the state nominating convention. Smith and John J. Raskob, chairman of the Democratic National Committee, asked her to come visit them at the Hotel Seneca. It was obvious to her that they planned to use her to make Franklin run.

"That's impossible," she told them after they asked for her help. However, she did put in a call to Franklin at Warm Springs so he could tell them himself. "Yes, I know, Franklin. I did tell the Governor you wouldn't," she said.

"I'm not well enough to run and that's all there is to it," Franklin told her.

She put Al Smith on the phone but he made no progress. After he hung up dejectedly, Smith and Raskob went to work on her again. "We have to have him," Smith said. "Tell us for sure, do you really think campaigning would ruin his health?"

"I don't know," she admitted. "The doctors feel that if he continues with his exercises and swimming at Warm Springs he might improve."

"Is it that he wants to walk before he will run, or what?"

She smiled. "My husband told me laughingly not long ago that if he lived long enough he might be able to walk again. But I sometimes wonder if he will ever get further than he is right now."

One of Smith's ideas was that Herbert Lehman, whom he wanted to run for lieutenant governor with Franklin, could take over the governor's job whenever Franklin didn't feel up to it. Eleanor knew that Franklin would be angered if he heard about this, even though he didn't plan to run.

By now excitement hit the convention on whether Al Smith would be able to convince her husband. Even when Franklin wired Smith, "I must therefore with great regret confirm my decision not to accept the nomination and I know you will understand," Smith did not give up. Eleanor's daughter got into the act by sending her father a telegram: "Go ahead and take it." Back came a wire to Anna: "You ought to be spanked."

The next day Smith and Raskob talked to Eleanor again. "Are there any other reasons besides his health why your husband won't run?" asked Raskob.

She mentioned the heavy financial obligation he had undertaken at Warm Springs. Even though when his half brother Rosy died the previous year and left Franklin $100.000 (plus his fishing equipment), Franklin stood on shaky financial ground because of his investment in Warm Springs.

"Would it make any difference to Frank if he were relieved of all financial anxieties?" Raskob went on. She shook her head, but Smith said, "Would you be willing to put in another call to your husband so we can try one more time?"

She told Smith that she would do nothing further than say hello and turn the phone over to him. But it wasn't so easy to make connections. Franklin had gone to Manchester, Georgia, to make a speech in the school auditorium. Eleanor had a messenger climb the three flights of stairs to the hall and tell him to come to the town drugstore's phone. She would be waiting for him on the other end of the line. He took his sweet time in coming, he told her later, because he guessed why she had called.

"Hello, Franklin," she told him.

He laughed. "I've been keeping out of reach all day and I wouldn't have talked to anyone else but you . . ."

"I'm calling because Mr. Raskob and Governor Smith begged me to. And I'm leaving you to Governor Smith because I have to catch the train."

With that she handed the phone to Al Smith and rushed out of the room. The last thing she heard was Smith yelling, "Hello, Frank!"

The morning paper brought her the news. Franklin had been persuaded to run for governor. She had hoped that he would be able to withstand the pressure. "I don't want Franklin to be governor," she told a reporter who came to interview her that morning. There were tears in her eyes. "It will spoil our lives. He doesn't want to be governor. What shall we do?"

But she calmed down and sent him a wire: "Regret that you had to accept but know that you felt it obligatory." Later she told other newsmen, "In the end you have to do what your friends want you to do."

Louis Howe was furious when he heard. Eleanor laughed at him when he slapped his forehead and let out with his outraged "Mein Gawd!" The acceptance was pure political folly to him.

"You can't plan every move in this world," she told him. "You have to accept circumstances as they develop and make the best of them."

"You don't have to accept circumstances," he retorted. "You dominate circumstances, that's what!"

Franklin hurried back from Warm Springs for his four-week campaign against Albert Ottinger, the Republican opponent who had amassed a fine record as the state's attorney general. Eleanor went to Hyde Park to meet him. When he arrived his mother greeted him unhappily. "You haven't the strength to run for office," she told him. But he nodded and smiled.

In his month-long campaign throughout the state by car and train,

Franklin and Louis Howe were on their own. Eleanor played no part in their barnstorming effort, but continued instead her concentration on the Smith campaign for the Presidency. She went on more speaking trips for Smith that last month. But everywhere she ran into ugly religious prejudice. She grew convinced that he could not win when she heard reports from other Smith workers throughout the South.

Great tension worked up at Smith headquarters as the campaign headed into its final weeks. There were some workers who brought out Eleanor's wrath because they were using their jobs to enrich themselves. One speaker whom Eleanor employed bought four new tires and put the bill on her expense account. Another lady speaker found the air chilly and charged her $150 coat to the Democratic Party. Some of Eleanor's co-workers suddenly found themselves irritated by their associates in those last days and Eleanor spent much of her time applying balm to wounded feelings. Nancy Cook and Elinor Morgenthau, both sweet personalities and dear friends of Eleanor who worked at state headquarters, somehow managed to work up a bitter row and Elinor Morgenthau resigned. Nor was this all. Governor Smith, anxiously concerned about his dwindling chances, was not now all sweetness and light. Coming down the stretch he was angry for no apparent reason with all the women, including his chief adviser, Mrs. Moskowitz. More than once he blistered the group with unreasonable excitement.

Under these circumstances, it occurred to Eleanor that if Al Smith lost, all of Franklin's efforts would also be in vain. She heard from him and Louis Howe occasionally of the large crowds that came to hear him. Campaign crowds, it was true, did not always mean voting crowds. Franklin's friends, however, swore to her that his crowds were different and that he shouldn't be counted out with Smith.

Eleanor went to hear him a few times, and what impressed her most was his vigor and his sincerity. As he held aloft and waved the old brown campaign fedora he first campaigned with in 1910, he was radiant and the crowds cheered.

When she went with him to vote at the Hyde Park Town Hall on November 6, he was terribly concerned about having his picture taken as he struggled from the car. "No pictures of me getting out of the machine please, boys," he pleaded with the photographers. To a man they turned away until he was on the sidewalk and his braces were set in place. Then they snapped him. Thus began a tradition never to photograph him in an embarrassing position. Eleanor was pleased with the display of courtesy on the part of the reporters, and it bore out Louis Howe's frequent assertions on the honorable state of newsmen.

[152]

That night, Eleanor went with Franklin and his mother to the campaign headquarters in the Biltmore Hotel in New York City. Almost from the outset there was sadness as early returns trickled in. Louis Howe's face had a blackish tinge as Hoover and Ottinger piled up a quick lead over Smith and Franklin. Eleanor saw all their work going for naught and watched the tired lines form on her husband's disappointed face. But Sara Roosevelt who had wanted to push her son into an invalid's bed for life now sat with her jaw jutting out and announced to all her conviction that not only would Franklin win but that he would make an excellent governor.

By midnight it was obvious that Al Smith was hopelessly swamped and that Al Ottinger's lead would probably be enough to send him to the Governor's Mansion in Albany. Eleanor left with Franklin, who was dejected by the returns, for their city residence. "Come along, Mama," she said to her mother-in-law.

But Sally Roosevelt refused to go with them. "I'm going to stay right here until it's all over and you are Governor," she insisted to Franklin. He shook his head and pointed out that the morning papers were calling Ottinger "Governor." "They won't tomorrow," she snapped.

"No they won't," agreed one of Eleanor's friends, Frances Perkins, who was seated nearby.

Sally Roosevelt and Frances Perkins stayed until four A.M. when late returns showed that Smith had lost the state by more than 100,000 votes and Franklin had won by 25,000. The two women came boisterously into the house at sunrise.

"I told you we had a governor in the family," Sally Roosevelt told Eleanor proudly when she walked in the door.

Chapter Eighteen

INAUGURATION DAY, January 1, 1929, turned out to be raw and cold in Albany. First a snow flurry, then a howling wind, and the streets were slick and treacherous. Eleanor Roosevelt in her new gown and Franklin in his formal clothes and top hat made their way carefully by chauffeured car to the capital.

The weather was so horrid that the inaugural ceremony had to be transferred to the Assembly Chamber, now jammed with 600 guests. Al Smith was everywhere in evidence with his cigar slotted into the corner of his mouth, while he took handshakes and slaps on the back as though the day were his and not her husband's. In fact, Franklin, in his inaugural address, helped carry on this mirage by heaping encomium after encomium upon Al, the "Happy Warrior" who had been snowed under for the Presidency by Herbert Hoover, and who was now relinquishing his post as governor of New York to his protégé.

Eleanor was forty-four years old as she watched the scene. Franklin, with his hair cut short for the occasion, maintained a heavy, serious air, so unlike himself. But as she watched him in his moment of half-hidden triumph, it must have come over her that they had already lived more than a lifetime together. When she recounted the trials of their early years of married life, their years in the State Senate, the packed eight years in Washington, the race for the Vice Presidency, the long heartbreaking bout with polio and Franklin's triumphant return to politics, it seemed impossible to crowd all those into her forty-four years.

There was little concern within her that he would be unable to attend to his duties as governor, though he had told her and others before the campaign began that he did not believe himself up to it. Even after he won, following headlong electioneering, he had expressed personal doubts whether his stamina was sufficient. "But here I am," he said with a shrug, as though he would have to make the best of things. However, there were important gains that she had discerned. In the first place, politics exhilarated him. Public matters made his gray-blue eyes shine and added zest to his living. Second, he was actually stronger

[154]

physically than he had been a year ago. Earlier, he had needed to lock his braces to stand; now he could remain upright in one position without the braces.

They presented a striking picture as they left the capitol for the Executive Mansion where they were to live during the next four years. For she stood five feet eleven inches and he almost six feet two. But little was expected of them, even though his victory was one of the few bright spots in the Democratic debacle of 1928. How could anyone rival the spectacular Al Smith? As for a politician's wife, who could picture one who didn't sit in back rooms and pat dogs and oversee the kitchen?

As things turned out, their four years in Albany were far from tranquil. Al Smith trouble hit them at the outset. After his abysmal defeat by Herbert Hoover for the Presidency, Al went into a state of shock, angry and hurt at his disgrace. Insult to his injured pride came with the reminder that Franklin had carried the state of New York, while he had failed to carry even his home ground. Louis Howe wandered into the room with a Sweet Caporal dangling from his cracked, dried lips, shook his head at Eleanor and Franklin and croaked, "Al isn't going to like this a damned bit."

And Al didn't. During those last few weeks before he turned over the Executive Mansion to Franklin, he sat at his desk in the Albany capitol and angrily compared his fate to that of his successor. A puff on his long black cigar, a swipe at the spittoon and a slap on his derby and he knew what was right, by God. Where would Franklin have gone without him? a little voice inside him asked. Nowhere, that's all. That Hyde Park rich man's boy owed everything to Al from Fulton's Fish Market. So why not, even though you were no longer governor, run the state by manipulating and controlling this blueblood?

In theory, all this looked practical and reasonable. And why shouldn't it? Hadn't Frank always talked and written to Al as though he were the older man's inferior? There was no reason why this relationship should change.

First off, Al asked Frank in a friendly way to take on Mrs. Belle Moskowitz as his chief adviser. "Absolutely the best move you'll ever make," he assured him. Since this short, stout and forceful woman had served as Al's closest adviser, putting her in Franklin's office would provide Smith with a ready access to all of the governor's thinking and plans and would give him a prime agent for controlling his activities.

Eleanor Roosevelt recognized this Smith design as the crisis in her husband's political career. Having worked with Belle Moskowitz in the 1928 Smith campaign, she was well aware of Mrs. Moskowitz's devotion to Smith. She knew that Mrs. Moskowitz was a decent liberal person, for it was she who had forced the liberal social legislation program on a reluctant Smith. She also knew that Mrs. Moskowitz provided Al Smith with his stand on other political matters. Newsmen used to joke, "Let's go up and talk to Belle and find out what's on Al's mind."

It was Eleanor who persuaded Franklin to turn down Smith's "suggestion" that he employ Mrs. Moskowitz. The situation was not helped afterward when stories passed around that Eleanor had said that the Smiths had lived it up at the Executive Mansion by keeping their cook busy making "monumental desserts." The Smiths angrily retorted that their Japanese cook had made a huge three-tiered cake for them before they quit the mansion and they had left it behind because it was uneatable.

Nevertheless, there was no open break between the Smiths and the Roosevelts for a long time. This did not happen until 1931 when Smith to Franklin's amazement opposed a reforestation amendment to the state constitution. The amendment would have given the state the power to buy up abandoned farms and reforest them. That Smith would have chosen a conservation measure to come out strongly against his successor caused Eleanor and Franklin to stare at each other in disbelief. But he had. And early in December of 1931, Smith, sitting in his office as president of the Empire State Building, turned on an interviewer, rose, stamped his foot and screamed, "Do you know, by God, that he has never consulted me about a damn thing since he has been governor?" The interviewer later revealed to Eleanor that Al then slammed his fist on the desk and called Franklin a dodger on the prohibition issue. "Why in hell don't he speak out?" he demanded.

Louis Howe had done his work well. He had taken the political raw material he found in Franklin and had fashioned it into the governor of the most populous state. He had also taken the frightened and lonely Eleanor and had pushed her out into a busy and cynical world, watched her bumble and stammer and taught her so thoroughly that she emerged as a strong independent force.

She had come upon a new word: DUTY. Self-indulgence was a pitiful waste of time. You didn't do things for self-enjoyment or for praise. You did things because they had to be done. If you didn't do them, they might not get done. What difference did it make if it kept you in the middle of crowds, when you really liked privacy? Or that you had to be a leader when you were constitutionally built to be a follower? Or that your name would be associated with underdogs of all sorts, many of whom considered you a fool for helping them? The happiness of others was all that mattered.

This concept of DUTY was Victorian, soft-headed and entirely un-American in the brassy 1920's. But Eleanor Roosevelt had it and it guided her entire existence. What before had been only a part-time philosophy now became her full-time credo. With her daughter Anna now married and a mother, James at Harvard and Elliott, Franklin, Jr., and John at Groton, her time was now her own. The thought of spending hours each day directing housekeeping was repulsive to her. "I rarely devote fifteen minutes a day to it," she told a reporter. A friend laughingly remarked, "She would have starved in a kitchen."

Though the governor's regime forced a framework of living upon her, Eleanor managed through sheer will power and enormous vitality to carry on several lives of her own. From January through March or April, Franklin's responsibilities kept him in Albany. In the spring there was the inevitable sojourn at Warm Springs in Georgia. The summer found him back at his desk in Albany with weekends at Hyde Park and excursions throughout the state. The fall brought them to Hyde Park and to Franklin's mother; Thanksgiving at Warm Springs; Christmas at Hyde Park; and then the return to Albany for the new legislative year.

Within this framework Eleanor rounded out her existence. And what emerged was a helter-skelter of duty activities that amazed her friends and baffled those who expected the state's first lady to remain within the inner recesses of the Executive Mansion. She never seemed rushed. Ida Tarbell said, "She has a capacity for carrying an enormous amount of detail in her mind and of seeing that this detail is executed without fluster." Three days a week she continued teaching at the Todhunter School in New York City. On a typical Sunday night, she rushed down the stairs of the Executive Mansion in Albany and clutched her heavy briefcase filled with teaching matter. When she reached the landing, the pantry door opened as though on signal and a servant handed her crackers and a glass of milk. She gulped the milk and munched the crackers as she dashed out the back door to the car that would carry her to the station. "I prepared my lessons on the train going up and down," she admitted.

Once in the city at midnight, she made her headquarters in the house on East Sixty-fifth Street that had been a bone of contention between her and Franklin because it was forced on her by his mother. Her teaching hours at Todhunter now lasted from nine to one on Monday, nine to five on Tuesday and nine to eleven on Wednesday. Whenever she could not make a class, which was seldom, she detailed copious teaching notes for substitutes. There were always added reminders: "Do not allow them to pass notes or talk; get them to state their opinions."

Wednesday afternoons the schoolmistress was back again at the Executive Mansion, a gracious and charming hostess at the weekly public reception that lasted from four until six P.M. During the rest of the week there were several teas and at least one formal dinner, all of which she attended as though they were the only thing on her mind.

Eleanor knew Al Smith's fear was that Franklin might win the Democratic presidential nomination in 1932, which Al considered his own stakeout. But Franklin was too busy in those first few years in Albany to concentrate on this subject. For one thing, he took power in January 1929 with a Republican majority in control of the state legislature. And the Republicans were determined to make him look bad so he would not make an effective candidate against Hoover in 1932. Even before he took office, Eleanor and Franklin could smell the Republican opposition out for blood. Franklin wrote to the widow of the Old Commoner, William Jennings Bryan, on December 19, 1928, "Eleanor and I are getting ready for a strenuous two years. I expect to be the target of practically all of the Republican artillery, but, as you know, I am a little like my dear friend, Mr. Bryan, in liking a good fight."

In the spring, Franklin ran head on into the stubborn opposition when he sent his budget to the legislature. In his anguish he wrote to a friend: "This family is going through the usual tribulations. James is getting over pneumonia; Elliott is about to have an operation; Franklin, Jr., has a doubly broken nose and John has just had a cartilege taken out of his knee! Anna and her husband, Curtis Dall, are taking a short holiday in Europe and their baby is parked with us at the Executive Mansion. Eleanor is teaching school two and a half days a week in New York, and I am in one continuous glorious fight with the Republican legislative leaders."

Nor was the political turbulence confined by any means to his Republican opposition. Besides the Al Smith rancor and the carping by Al's loyal friends, there were graft troubles boiling away inside the Democratic regime of Mayor Jimmy Walker in New York City. Although Franklin was openly anti-Tammany, Walker's shenanigans reflected upon him. Yet upon the advice of Louis Howe, Franklin shied away from taking direct action until it was forced upon him in 1932. As an interim stopgap, he listened to Louie and sent Eleanor to the mayor's office to admonish him. However, despite her visits to Walker, he did not change his ways and the trouble continued.

The Executive Mansion was a Victorian monstrosity of gloom. Eleanor's sitting room was considered the only pleasant room in the place. The informal meals were generally taken in the sun porch off the depressing state dining room. A Groton master who came to visit reported afterward, "When we reach the Mansion tea is served in Mrs. Roosevelt's living room upstairs and there about her are gathered the two Groton boys, Franklin, Jr., and John, and with their colored mammy, the two grandchildren—Anna's little girl and boy, Sistie and Buz. Political or government talk is banned, except now and then a humorous incident or echo. After this . . . we disperse to dress for eight o'clock dinner."

Life in the Executive Mansion was a madhouse. The evening noises from inside were only exceeded by the din after midnight from the poor Italian neighborhood close by. When the children were home for holidays or weekends, they played ball in the yard, rode horses, wrestled or vented their enthusiasm with shouts. Often their father joined in by teasing them. There was never a clear idea of who was coming to dinner. "I've laid places for six . . . and eighteen sat down twenty minutes later," Eleanor said. And almost all who came to dinner expected to be put up overnight. This was always jarring to Eleanor because several others besides the family lived on a fairly permanent basis with the Roosevelts. Of course, a room was always available for Louis Howe. But besides him, there was Franklin's counsel, Sam Rosenman, who had helped write speeches for him in the 1928 campaign. The Rosenmans lived with them for long periods at a time. Then there was pretty Marguerite LeHand, Franklin's secretary, and her assistant, Grace Tully. Miss LeHand, nicknamed "Missy" by Eleanor's daughter Anna, had originally come to Hyde Park after the 1920 campaign for the Vice Presidency to help Eleanor temporarily in the task of cleaning up her correspondence. When this was completed she had transferred to Franklin as his secretary, and as second-string hostess for him whenever Eleanor was absent. Grace Tully had also begun as Mrs. Roosevelt's aide in her work in the 1928 campaign, after a service as secretary to Cardinal Hayes. In addition to these there was Malvina Thompson, a short, energetic former Red Cross employee who had served as secretary to Eleanor and to Louis Howe in the 1928 campaign. "Tommy," as she was quickly and permanently dubbed, stayed on with Mrs. Roosevelt as her permanent secretary. Proficient and mature and untiring, Tommy brought forth the following encomium from Eleanor: "The woman who makes life possible for me."

The chief memories of those who ate with the Roosevelts were the poor quality of the cooking and the variety of subjects discussed. Meals were punctuated by frequent phone calls for Franklin and Eleanor and by the loud talking of the children, who were permitted to express themselves freely. Once asked by a magazine editor to let the rest of the country learn of their eating habits, Eleanor replied: "I am sorry to tell you that my husband and I are very bad about food. I do not know of any particular dish which he likes unless it is wild duck and the only recipe for this from his point of view is that it should fly through the kitchen."

At dinner Franklin often gave vent to a streak of Dutch thrift on personal spending, to which Eleanor was in full agreement, for she was still wearing the tweed coat Franklin purchased for her on her honeymoon in 1905. One time he grumbled about his light bill in Warm Springs, which was 18¢ per KWH, or about four times the prevailing rate at his mother's place at Hyde Park. Another time he and Eleanor engaged in a long dinner conversation on the subject of buying the cheapest and yet passable first dinner coat for Franklin, Jr. They finally agreed to spend not more than $15. The other guests sat engrossed throughout the debate.

As her stay in Albany lengthened, she became a familiar sight to the townspeople as she rushed about looking for underdogs whom she could help. Any halfway honest story drew her immediate concern and aid. In warm weather as she poked about, she was easily recognizable in her white dress, tennis shoes and the velvet band tied around her light brown hair. In the day of flappers, she wore no make-up; her eyebrows were straight and her eyes drooped at the edges like Uncle Ted's, and she had his famous smile.

Unlike other Good Samaritans, her charities were not simply a matter of handing out money. Normally, they required this plus an expenditure of time and physical effort. Sometimes she devoted months to single cases. On one occasion, when she was getting ready to take the late Sunday evening train to the city, she called in Grace Tully and said, "Tully, please ask Whitehead to get some eggs and milk and a few other things and will you please take them to this address? Here is a small check for her besides." Further evidence revealed that she had come upon a poverty-stricken young mother and she was taking over the duty of straightening out the girl's existence. Later she not only saw to it that the young mother got a thorough grounding as a seamstress, but she also landed a job for her.

However, local charities and her teaching at Todhunter were not her only extracurricular activities. She kept up the Val-Kill furniture fac-

Five-year-old Eleanor Roosevelt in a pose characteristic of her chats with Papa Elliott, who delightedly captioned this shot "Scolding Father."

Childhood and School Days

As a child Eleanor adored her doting father, Elliott Roosevelt (brother of Teddy), but was awkward and shy with her beautiful mother, Anna Hall Roosevelt, who took her daughter's plainness as a personal affront. Within two years, Eleanor lost her mother, her four-year-old brother and her father. Grandmother Hall, a strict disciplinarian and staunch believer in cold baths and long flannels, took in Eleanor and brother Hall. Eleanor loved to escape to her warmhearted Uncle Teddy's house. At fifteen she was sent to England for her only formal education, three years at the Allenswood School.

Absorbed in the glittering whirl of High Society, Anna Hall Roosevelt deplored little Eleanor's solemnity and nicknamed the child "Granny."

Elliott Roosevelt with Eleanor and the boys, Hall and Ellie; soon after, he began his self-imposed "exile" to Abingdon, Virginia, because of his excessive drinking.

At fifteen Eleanor (third from right, back row) began her schooling at Allenswood, where the kindly headmistress, an early-day feminist, influenced her thoughts on every subject from politics to fashion.

Debut, Courtship, Marriage

Fetched home at eighteen by Grandmother Hall (". . . because you must come out!"), Eleanor dutifully followed the prescribed round of parties, where the attentions of her handsome distant cousin, Franklin Delano Roosevelt, helped to melt her initial shyness. In the fall of 1903, Eleanor accepted Franklin's proposal of marriage, but his possessive mother succeeded in delaying the wedding until St. Patrick's Day, 1905.

In the summer of 1904, Eleanor visited Franklin at his mother's "cottage" on Campobello.

Eleanor with her awe-inspiring hostess, Mrs. James Roosevelt, who had in the previous spring temporarily diverted Franklin from the road to romance with a cruise to the Caribbean.

Eleanor was married in Grandmother Hall's white satin wedding gown. Walking down the aisle on the arm of her beloved Uncle Teddy, now President of the United States, the bride was "considerably taller than the head of the nation."

Their two-month honeymoon tour of Europe covered the continent. In a Venetian gondola, Eleanor was model and hatholder for camera-wielding Franklin.

Wife and Mother

Eleanor remained the retiring wife and mother, as Franklin turned from law practice to politics, attracting national attention as an insurgent New York State Senator. With his appointment as Assistant Secretary of the Navy, the post from which her Uncle Teddy had climbed to the presidency, family tradition fitted Eleanor for her position as the wife of a public official during the strenuous years of World War I.

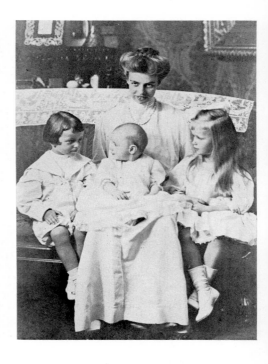

1911: Eleanor was busy with Anna, James and Elliott; the first Franklin Delano Roosevelt, Jr., had died in infancy.

Four generations: Eleanor with her grandmother, Mrs. Valentine Hall, her mother's sister, Mrs. Stanley Mortimer, and daughter Anna. 1913.

By 1916 the family had outgrown their first Washington home, the "Little White House" of Eleanor's Auntie Bye, where Teddy had lived before his inauguration.

In 1919 Eleanor stood by as President Wilson and Franklin reviewed returning Marines.

In 1920, Eleanor shared the defeat of Franklin, nominated for Vice President to run with Cox against Harding. Her worst days came when Franklin was stricken with polio at the summer home on Campobello. During his long illness, Eleanor was goaded into minor political activity by his gnomelike adviser, Louis Howe. Together, they reawakened Franklin's interest and kept the Roosevelt name alive.

Franklin joined the family at Campobello before launching his vice-presidential campaign. Here, the following summer, polio struck him down.

On the 1920 campaign trip, Eleanor accompanied the nominee and Louis Howe (left), the man who was to change her way of life.

While Franklin fought to regain his health, Louis urged Eleanor into the 1924 campaign to elect Al Smith governor of New York over her cousin, Teddy Roosevelt, Jr.

and Recovery

In reporting on the affairs of the world to her chair-bound husband, Eleanor sharpened her own awareness and observations. The long mutual struggle ended triumphantly in Franklin's election as governor of New York in 1928. But the onslaught of the depression drew them toward a still higher goal.

Her behind-the-scenes efforts contributed to Franklin's election as governor in 1928 and (above) 1930.

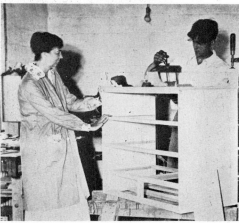

After the crash, Eleanor and two friends established the Val-Kill furniture factory to provide employment for skilled workers at Hyde Park.

The governor's mansion at Albany, another temporary residence for Eleanor, was only one step from the White House.

Depression

On March 4, 1933, Eleanor became the First Lady of a nation frightened and dazed by the depression. Her determination to remain in the background soon gave way before the rush of events into which she was plunged.

At Louis Howe's urging, Eleanor began a series of press conferences to attract the interest of women. Ridiculed at first, the meetings eventually paid off in national publicity.

Another Howe stratagem led Eleanor without warning to the rebellious Bonus Army camp, where her common-sense approach ended a national crisis.

"The eyes, ears and legs" of the President, Eleanor left news-women panting behind as she investigated housing conditions in the Virgin Islands.

Her influence boosted the career of Jim Farley, who said later, "If it hadn't been for her, I would never have gotten where I am, for she gave me my first big chance."

Franklin had vetoed her idea of becoming a pilot, but on his missions Eleanor became a veteran passenger of commercial planes.

Where others had failed, her persistent efforts brought about the long-delayed clearance of the notorious Alley-Dwelling slums in Washington.

Over the Years

To her social and political chores as First Lady, Eleanor added a daily newspaper column and weekly broadcast, through which she could report her world-covering activities and plead her favorite causes.

As mistress of the White House, Eleanor banished the cuspidors, put a swing on the lawn, remodeled the kitchen, neglected the cuisine.

In every campaign she never failed to champion women's political representation.

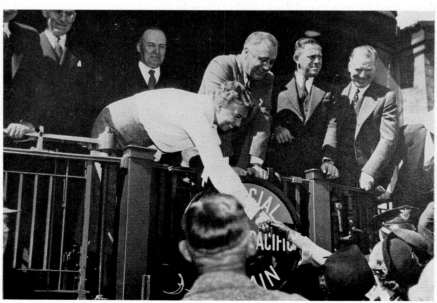

Her enthusiasm for Warm Springs was more cautious than Franklin's, for it had at first almost captured his whole attention; but she was a frequent and sympathetic visitor there.

Aboard the *Amberjack II,* the family stole out of the spotlight for a cruise to Campobello.

For photographers, a smiling truce with Westbrook Pegler, whose slashing attacks on her column appeared regularly.

When the King and Queen visited Hyde Park in 1939 to demonstrate British-American solidarity, Eleanor made headlines by serving them hot dogs.

Although opposed to a third term, she singlehandedly restored the bickering 1940 Democratic convention to unity and order.

Asked by reporters how she would conduct herself during an unprecedented third term, she posed as "Whistler's Mother" at the Gridiron Widows' annual party.

Wartime

The shadow of Nazi aggression darkened the American scene. After Pearl Harbor Eleanor's energies were channeled almost exclusively into wartime activities. Her fabulous travels now included a trip to war-ravaged England and a grueling five-week tour of the South Pacific, during which she lost thirty pounds.

From wounded boys in the Pacific she personally delivered messages to startled wives and sweethearts.

Fala, a famous member of the Roosevelt household, brought rare moments of relaxation to tiring F.D.R.

With perhaps a premonition of the end, Franklin asked Eleanor to assemble all thirteen grandchildren for his fourth inauguration in 1945.

On Her Own

Despite her grief at Franklin's death, Eleanor was soon recalled to the public scene. As a United Nations delegate, she became the outstanding opponent of Russian tactics of confusion and delay. Busy as ever today, Eleanor explains, "You see, I have nothing to do but work."

Winston Churchill and his wife were among the many visitors Eleanor accompanied almost daily to Franklin's grave at Hyde Park.

Truman praised her "poise and patience" during her years of work to bring about the UN Declaration of Human Rights.

Of her consuming interest in children, Eleanor once wrote, "Sometimes I despair of grown people, but if there is any point in saving civilization, certainly it is the children we want to keep alive."

tory 2 miles east of Sara Roosevelt's Hyde Park estate. Officials of the Metropolitan Museum in New York who scoffed openly when she first approached them for help in designing salable Early American furniture now accepted her seriousness and co-operated fully. In order to keep the local Hyde Park citizens who were working at the factory at full-time employment, she often popped into the offices of furniture buyers in New York. Here, with a strong sales line and with her kit of photographs of Val-Kill productions, she tried in her fervent but ladylike way to get them to carry her wares. Often, when it was necessary to meet a financial crisis, she turned into a large self-purchaser of the large and somber furniture pieces.

There were also many organizations to which she devoted time. Several tried to get the use of her name, but she insisted that unless she did some actual work, she would not allow her name to be used. She was a board member of the Foreign Policy Association, the Women's Trade Union League—she once help picket a place for anti-union activities—and the Women's City Club. Asked to serve with a committee of women to advise Cornell University on its College of Home Economics, she worked like a beaver to raise funds for a new building and an increase in the staff. She also wrote many magazine articles replete with simple wisdom but without any regard for punctuation, and served on the board of a junior book club where she proved a harsh judge of its selections, labeling one "pleasant trash."

On top of all these activities, there were many things Franklin asked her to do for him. Because of his crippled condition, she often substituted for him at fairs or on speaking engagements. "The best I can do is send Eleanor," he wrote one beseecher for a Roosevelt speech. One time she gave nine speeches in three days. After another heavy speaking load, she wrote in reply to a request, "I'm floored at the request for another speech."

Franklin discovered that one of the perquisites of his job was a glass-bottomed boat called the *Inspector*. Al Smith had never paid attention to upstate voters. So far as he was concerned they were blockhead Republicans whose voting power could be overcome by concentrating on the big cities. Franklin decided that Al was wrong.

The *Inspector,* dingy as she was, held all the attributes of political perfection for Franklin. She could first of all provide him with a vacation on water, for she traveled the inland water routes of the state, which were fairly extensive. In addition, she provided him with an easy route upstate. Finally, and equally important, the *Inspector* gave him the opportunity to inspect the large collection of state institutions.

So in the summer, he, Eleanor and the children traveled on the *Inspector* to meet the people and also to learn the truth about the institutions for the blind, deaf, insane and aged and the state's prisons and reform schools. Because of his physical handicap, Franklin could not do the inspections himself. It was necessary that Eleanor do it for him, mosey about, take in actualities and report back to him. "It was the best education I had," she later said.

But unfortunately, it was a skill she had to learn by long experience from a tough taskmaster like Franklin. The first stop of the *Inspector* was at an insane asylum. "All right," he told her, "go in and look around and let me know what's going on there. Tell me how the inmates are being treated."

She went inside and returned in a little while with the day's menu. "Did you look to see whether they were actually getting this food?" he scolded her. "Did you bother to lift a pot cover on the stove to check whether the contents corresponded with this menu?"

She shook her head.

"Next time, if you are going to inspect, then really inspect."

She agreed she would.

However, it took some time before she trained herself to be observant. Her mind took in the whole picture without the little details. "But these are what I need," he bluntly told her.

"I'm not really well educated," she told a reporter, "and I never remembered things until Franklin taught me. His memory is really prodigious. Once he has checked something he never needs to look at it again. One time he asked me," she said with self-reproach, "to go and look at the state's tree shelter-belt plantings. I noticed there were five rows of graduated size, increasing in height up to the cottonwoods which formed the top tier.

"When I came back and described it, Franklin said, 'Tell me exactly what was in the first five rows. What did they plant first?' And he was so desperately disappointed when I couldn't tell him, that I put my best efforts after that into missing nothing and remembering everything."

In time she came to serve as his eyes and legs and to be his best reporter. He was proud of her. Where evidence was not available, she learned how to judge facial expressions, flickering eyelashes and hand motions to determine the truth. "At the institutions I inspected I learned to notice whether the beds were too close together, and whether they were folded up and put in closets or behind doors during the day, which would indicate that they filled the corridors at night; I learned to watch the patients' attitude toward the staff; and before the end of our years in Albany, I had become a fairly expert reporter on state institutions."

There were some occasions, however, when she was fooled. One time when their car approached a mental hospital, a man cutting the grass halted in his work, removed his cap and bowed low to them. Franklin was pleased with their reception. But as they passed him, they glanced back and watched him thumbing his nose at them.

Eleanor also performed other duties for him. He often asked her to read reports and report their gist to him. There were also the innumerable ceremonial functions which she attended as his substitute. She could lay a cornerstone as though it were an everyday exercise. She went to charity balls, horse shows, flower shows, political gatherings, and was on hand for the ceremonies involved in opening new bridges. Even when he went to a state or local fair, he wanted her along to take over part of his work. While he drove around the fair grounds and made himself available for handshakes, she went through the buildings systematically. She had comments to make about each exhibit and talked to the people there about their schools, local health problems and whatever else was on their minds. This was especially effective in upstate New York where the sight of a Democratic governor and his interest in local matters was a distinct novelty. Everywhere she went she added to his popularity.

Chapter Nineteen

F ELEANOR WAS INVOLVED in the peripheries of politics, it was only natural that she would also plunge into the vital political issues involved. Although she disclaimed any credit, she was chiefly responsible for the selection of Frances Perkins as head of the State Labor Department. She was everywhere throughout the administration when it came to promoting the interests of women. It was a fetish with her to overcome the old prejudices against women in politics. "In order to keep the women quiet," she observed, "the men occasionally give them small positions or listen to their counsel in small matters."

Oddly, though the blatant feminists of her day agreed with her that women were capable of holding important political posts, they disagreed with her violently when it came to legislation affecting women. On one occasion, she testified before the Assembly Commission in favor of the 48-hour week for women workers. "Women are only women," she argued, "and need the protection of government." The feminists screamed that she was a traitor, and that women should be treated on the same plane with men on all scores. But Eleanor was soft-spoken, warm and always feminine and would not accept their basic premise.

She also spoke and testified on housing and other legislation and took a stand often at variance with what her husband was promoting. But Franklin was not offended because he realized that they complemented each other well. Where she was compassionate about all human ills and the need for redoing the world, he preferred judging programs in terms of political feasibility. One time when she argued bitterly with with him about the need for a state unemployment compensation act, he turned on her sharply and exclaimed: "I agree with Uncle Teddie that you can't get too far ahead of the people. Although a man can be ahead of his constituents on a couple of objectives and still be their leader, if he gets in advance of them on too many points, he ceases to be their leader and becomes separated from them."

He never deviated from this principle of Uncle Ted's. Another time in Albany, for instance, when a friend of hers asked her to remonstrate

[164]

with Franklin about his slowness in pushing for old age pensions, she threw up her hands and remarked grimly, "We have argued so long that we are no longer on speaking terms on the subject."

Actually, Franklin was far from the liberal he was to become later, and needed her constant prodding and conscience to move him in that direction. When he became governor, he believed firmly that the government is best which governs least, or, as he put it, "After all, the best government is the least government." On the question of the power of the Federal Government, he was outspokenly a states' rights man. As governor he opposed government insurance of bank deposits. With him government was not the tool that it was to her, to help the underdogs of society.

So there was conflict in their relationship as well as admiration. But this was to be expected from two with such strong personalities. Outsiders considered them alike, but they differed in more than social outlook and political methods. Eleanor would tell exactly what she believed on any subject. With his political career at stake, he would not. A close associate of his during the Albany days noted, "No one could tell what he was thinking, to say nothing of what he was feeling."

He called everyone by his first name. It was his way to break the class barrier with politicians not of his social stripe. Often he employed nicknames. Colonel House, who had been President Wilson's adviser and was now trying to influence Franklin, became "Colonel Mouse." On the other hand, Eleanor was never able to transcend the "Ladyship" level. First names stuck in her throat. She had none of her husband's surface affability. "It is not easy for me to make friends," she confessed. "I was brought up in an era when you did not casually call people by their first names and always remained on a more or less formal basis."

She was always the same, always natural and with a high dignity wherever she went. He could change as the situation might require. She had no time for superstitions; he was full of them. He would never travel on the thirteenth of the month, and lighting three cigarettes with one match was a most dangerous undertaking. She needed no diversions from her duty outlook on life. Her sole interest was people. She needed no hobbies; he couldn't get enough of them. Even when she knitted she always did so while doing something else, such as dictating a speech or being interviewed. After a trying day he liked to play cards. On the night a murderer was electrocuted, he was invariably grim and grumpy and worked himself out of this state by smoking heavily and playing cards all evening. He was an avid collector; she collected nothing. In 1929, he wrote a dealer, "My Missus says that if I get any more models

[165]

or pictures something drastic will have to be done about household arrangements!"

During their stay in Albany Eleanor and Franklin derived a great deal of satisfaction from their children, despite the fact that at times personal problems plagued their youngsters. Daughter Anna's marriage to Curtis Dall in 1926 was not turning out well. Dall had gone to work for Lieutenant Governor Herbert Lehman's investment firm, Lehman Brothers, yet both Franklin and his mother continued to give Anna an allowance. Although Eleanor was thrilled when she became a grandmother in 1927 with the birth of Anna Eleanor (Sistie) and again in 1930 when Curtis, Jr. (Buzzie) was born, the marriage could not be saved.

When the entire family was together the composite picture was one of deep devotion and pleasure. But Eleanor suffered anguish for her four boys, despite all their energetic family fun. Franklin later blamed himself for not helping them over troubled times. All were lively and compassionate, but they needed a strong guiding hand from their father. However, he was seldom available to answer their growing number of questions. "I often think of my own sons," he said regretfully. "From the time I became governor onward, I did not have enough time for them. Both Eleanor and I were so desperately busy. . . . If I had been less occupied a lot of things might have been different."

One of the difficulties stemmed from Franklin's unwillingness to discipline them when they were small. "When they were very small," Eleanor confessed, "I took them on a number of occasions to their father at the end of the day and asked him to spank them. I knew they would receive a mild spanking." Born into a well-known family, they felt little need to take their studies seriously. When Eleanor enrolled Franklin, Jr., in the Buckley School before sending him to Groton, he failed badly at his entrance examination. On questioning him, she found he had failed on purpose. "I thought if I didn't answer the questions I wouldn't have to go!" he wailed. They generally "just got by, which always used to make me very angry," said Eleanor, who had had her heart set on going to college but was deprived of that opportunity by her grandmother. Franklin, too, in examining the Groton reports on his son James, noted his poor grades and said cynically, "He did very well . . . in athletics and leadership."

Her second son, Elliott, hated Groton. As Eleanor viewed his problem, "My mother-in-law sided with my husband in making him stay there and I was too young to take any stand. Every time Elliott went back to Groton he remonstrated with us and my husband said he was just a rebel and did not like discipline and that whether he realized it or not, he was getting a great deal out of it. My mother-in-law almost died at the thought of taking him out."

The family squabbles concerning Elliott were disconcerting indeed, considering that Franklin was saddled at the same time with the job of running the state of New York. In 1929, when Elliott graduated from Groton, he failed two college entrance subjects on purpose, Eleanor discovered.

"That summer I took the two younger boys to Europe and left Franklin to persuade Elliott, as I did not want him to start out by having failed." She hoped that during her absence, Franklin would have some man-to-man talks with Elliott and convince him of the essentiality of going to college.

Her trip abroad with Franklin, Jr., and John, then fifteen and thirteen, was filled with foreboding about what was going on between her husband and Elliott. Nevertheless, she tried to show her younger sons a good time. Even this was marred by their boredom at seeing the sights of Europe and their keener desire to wrestle each other. "In every city where we stayed, we climbed bell towers, and I tried to walk my sons in the evenings. I wanted them to be so weary that they would not start roughhousing before they went to bed, since roughhousing usually turned into a battle royal and I got my exercise separating two very angry brothers." She wrote to Franklin how nervous they were making her. And at one point, he wired her, "Hope you have a good trip. What shall I do with your casket?"

Upon her return she found that what she had dreaded had taken place. Franklin was of the opinion that Elliott should not go to college. "Franklin was overwhelmed by Elliott. I said he had to pass his exams and took him down to Hun School [a preparatory school in New Jersey]. He never spoke to me for three months. At the end of that time he was ill and had to come home and then he deigned to make up with me."

Elliott did pass his college entrance exams but he refused to go to college, despite Eleanor's many pleas. He wanted to work and earn his own way, but he wanted help in getting a good job. Both Eleanor and Franklin considered this notion abhorrent, and neither would help him in his design. However, Elliott went to his grandmother and asked for her aid. He was only twenty at the time. "My mother-in-law went to Mr. Bernard Baruch and said that Franklin wouldn't do anything about helping Elliott get a job. Elliott was put into a job as a sort of semi-partner [the Albert Frank & Co. advertising firm in New York]. He

[167]

knew absolutely nothing about the business and was only there because of Mr. Baruch. Little by little it dawned on him that he did not know anything about the business and was able to do very little of real value."

Her oldest son James also had a similarly disheartening experience. After he graduated from Harvard in 1930, after a six-months delay when he failed German, he enrolled in Boston College Law School, but he did not remain there long. This bitterly disappointed Franklin who wrote him, urging him to get his law degree. "Take the advice of an old and experienced bird," he made a last-ditch appeal.

Eleanor, in the midst of her frenetic activities, watched James's progress gloomily. "James went into several businesses with people and really had no background. They wanted him for his name and he was too young to realize it." The head of an insurance firm with whom he went in September, 1930 remarked incredulously, "Big men and big interests began to swarm down on us, begging us to insure them."

Old Henry Morgenthau, Sr., a close friend of the Roosevelts', remonstrated with Franklin for letting James and Elliott use the family name as an easy steppingstone to wealth. But Franklin just held out his hands in utter resignation and replied, "They will have to learn since they are high-spirited and obstinate. If I interfere it will only make matters worse."

Also a sore point with Eleanor was that her boys married very young, though Franklin pointed out that he had been just as young when he married her. She explained their early marriages on the basis that her boys "were not really rooted in any particular home and were seeking to establish homes of their own." The Hyde Park home was their grandmother's; the New York City house was a joint enterprise with Grandmother; and the Executive Mansion in Albany was hardly a place one would call "home." How could they possibly feel relaxed in any of these places?

Franklin was taken with James' bride, Betsy Cushing, whom James married in September, 1930. Dark, pretty and friendly, Betsy was the second daughter of Dr. Harvey Cushing, the renowned Boston brain surgeon. When the wedding was coming up, Franklin wrote Dr. Cushing, "My better half has made a demand that within three days I give her a complete list of all political and business associates whom I have shaken hands with during the past twenty-five years, in order that they may be invited to your wedding! I want to go on record as expressing my gratitude to you for paying for the event!"

Elliott married Elizabeth Donner of Philadelphia in January, 1932. A year and a half later they were divorced after the birth of a son,

William. Eleanor Roosevelt, who worried so much about Elliott, said of that marriage, "His first marriage had been a quick disillusionment. He had found no community of interests with his wife and realized rather soon that he had mistaken a feeling of sympathy for love."

But if the older two boys concerned her, what of the younger two? The difficulties of Franklin, Jr., and John were easily stated in one word: Grandma. She spoiled them at every turn. And they, said Eleanor, "always treated her with an affectionate camaraderie which won from her almost anything they desired." Behind her back, they called the screen porch where she spent much time "Grannie's bughouse." They ran to Grandma more and more to get the things Eleanor and Franklin said they should not have, knowing, said Eleanor, "that whatever they wanted would be forthcoming." On one occasion Franklin, Jr., smashed a small car his parents had given him. Both Eleanor and Franklin decided that he would not get another one. But "Grandmother, at his request, had replaced the car with a much more expensive one. When we objected, she looked at us quite blandly and said she had not realized that we disapproved."

With his penchant for speeding and daredevil driving, Franklin, Jr., brought many a queasy moment to his parents. One time he bet that he could ram a tree at thirty miles an hour without damaging his car. He came through this experience personally unscathed, although he destroyed the tree and ruined a fender. John in turn once accidentally sideswiped a train.

On one occasion when Franklin, Jr., drove a great distance in a short time, Eleanor called it reckless driving and insisted that Franklin take his license away. Franklin agreed, with the assurance that he would give the boy a dressing down. To make certain, Eleanor sat just outside the study, "angry and determined," she said, "while Franklin talked to Junior." Franklin spoke in a loud voice, but he shifted responsibility to her by beginning every sentence with— "Your mother says." After a dozen such scolding remarks, he suddenly banged on the desk top and shouted, "Your mother wants me to take your license away for a while, so give it to me!"

Pleased with the outcome, Eleanor was startled two days later to discover that Franklin had slipped the license back to Junior with the soft admonition to "drive more slowly."

It was Eleanor's contention that if they were treated as ordinary traffic violators, they would learn a lesson and calm down. Unfortunately, traffic officials let them off free when they got a ticket because their father was an important public official. This happened in Providence, Rhode Island, when Franklin, Jr., was found to be driving with an expired license. Another time when he was speeding between Albany and Boston, the arresting officer upon learning who his father was took him to dinner. Eleanor and Franklin were utterly dismayed when they heard about his favored treatment, though they realized his driving speed would lessen with age.

Sara Roosevelt, finding that she had lost control over the lives of her son and Eleanor, had transferred her attention to the boys. Franklin's election to the governor's seat, while a matter of deep pride to her, had upset her household beyond repair. Gone was her normally quiet existence where she sat listening to music while the butler stood at attention next to the phonograph, ready to wind it when the spring ran down. Now, when Franklin came to Hyde Park, he brought along a houseful of politicians and reporters.

Despite the influx of these strange people, whom she considered a trashy sort, she maintained dominance of her home and said whatever she wanted to. A friend of her son's said that "Eleanor and Franklin lived in fond fear of her remarks." When Governor Huey Long of Louisiana ate one time at her table, she exclaimed in a loud whisper, "Who is that dreadful person sitting next to my son?" "Anna and I immediately began to talk at the top of our lungs," said Eleanor.

Eleanor always felt like a guest at Sara's Hyde Park house. Franklin, however, considered it his home, and though he and his mother had little in common now that he was governor, he maintained a strong sense of loyalty to her. In May of 1931, when Sara took sick while on a visit to Paris, he dropped his duties and rushed across the ocean to be at her side. It was an act of love.

Still another concern was Hall Roosevelt, Eleanor's younger brother, whom she and Franklin considered as one of their children. When Hall and his first wife, whom he had married in 1912, were divorced in 1922 after having four children, it came as a great shock to Eleanor. Franklin handled many of the legal details involved in the divorce as a sort of fatherly adviser to Hall. A bright student at Harvard, Hall had no definite focus in his existence, nor could he maintain interest in anything for long. During the twenties, after Franklin was on the road back from paralytic polio, he and Hall entered into many speculative ventures. Hall wrote him frequently about deals that might bring them in quick and high profits. Among his proposals were those involving stock market so-called killings, rice fields in Louisiana, power companies and aviation companies. Nothing ever panned out, though they helped keep Franklin's mind off his ailment. One of Franklin's ventures in Hall's behalf was a long-drawn-out effort to get him $75 from a motor car company. From the legal correspondence available in this instance, Hall had been promised a new car with a trade-in discount for his old car. But when Hall tried to consummate the deal, the car dealer changed his mind. It was a foolish and embarrassing business for Franklin, but at Hall's behest he wrote and demanded that the firm give Hall $75 for wasting his time. After several fruitless letters, Franklin told Hall to forget about it.

After going from job to job, during the time when Franklin was governor, Hall had found a position in Detroit as city controller under Mayor Frank Murphy. He had already begun to overindulge in gin, a matter of harrowing concern to Eleanor, who took the blame on herself for not having brought him up better. "By the time he realized that he could not stop drinking whenever he wanted to," Eleanor said ruefully, "he had been through so much that he no longer wanted to stop." Nevertheless, he worked hard at this job under Murphy and staked out Michigan as his territory for swinging the Democrats behind Franklin for President. He found a new hero in Detroit, Father Charles Coughlin, and wrote Eleanor a letter beseeching her to get Franklin to invite Father Coughlin to a Saturday conference at Hyde Park. "He has the largest following of any man in the United States," he assured her. The meeting did take place and for a short while Franklin felt indebted to Hall.

The local saying was pertinent to Eleanor Roosevelt, "When they are young, they break your arms. When they grow older, they break your heart."

Chapter Twenty

However, there were too many activities of interest going on to permit her time to sit and mope. In 1930, for instance, little Louis Howe reached his grand decision. His timetable for Franklin's try for the Presidency had called for Franklin to run in 1936. Suddenly 1932 became the year of decision.

But there was first the hurdle of a re-election race in 1930. Considering the tenacious opposition of the Republican legislature, Franklin had done more than passably well in his first term. Besides, Eleanor, in her many appearances and speeches in upstate New York, had dented the solid Republican stronghold there. With her clothes worn loose around the middle, her old-fashioned watch pinned on her bosom and her genuinely interested manner, she had captivated group after group. A reporter noted that "the camera misses her freshness, charm and intelligence."

She and Franklin were a close-working team during that campaign. He covered 12,000 miles and spoke in every county. To offset the whispering effort of the Republicans that he was really in poor health, Louis Howe concocted a brilliant move. Franklin applied for $500,000 worth of life insurance with the Warm Springs Foundation as beneficiary and sailed through his physical examination with widespread publicity given to the results. Eleanor believed it undignified to campaign openly for her husband. Nevertheless, as she put it, she could not "sit in one's chair and calmly survey the wall paper opposite." Behind the scenes she worked with Mary (Molly) Dewson who ran the women's work at Democratic headquarters. Superefficient and always charming, Eleanor helped plan strategy, arranged for speakers and meetings, answered mail and battled with the men working with Franklin to give the women a strong role to play in the campaign.

The final vote in November was an enormous landslide for her husband, a whopping majority of 725,001. Both she and Franklin claimed joyfully that "that last one was my vote." Louis Howe announced frankly that Franklin would be President for certain in 1932.

And there were good reasons for his optimism. Franklin's magnificent victory made all other Democratic aspirants look pale in comparison. But there was an even more important reason. It was the devastating depression that had fallen out of the skies to end the wild, speculative twenties.

The depression brought a great change in Franklin and Eleanor, though in Franklin's case the change came late. Even in December, 1929, he called the stock market crash and the ensuing unemployment a "little flurry." Not even the fact that his mother lost heavily in the crash changed his mind. When a magazine editor asked him to write an article attacking the inactivity of Herbert Hoover, Franklin turned down the request and gave as his reason, "He happens to be on old personal friend of mine."

It was only later, at the continual imploring of Eleanor and Louis Howe, that he took his first cautious steps in breaking with tradition and formulating a state-wide program to cope with the economic tragedy. Part of his change was attributable to the do-nothing approach of President Hoover who was convinced, first, that the depression would be short-lived, and second, that government aid to economic unfortunates was a violation of the Constitution. Another reason was his growing belief that if he held to the same approach in New York State, he would dissipate his 1930 victory.

In Washington, a vital national issue revolved around Eleanor's first cousin, Alice Roosevelt Longworth. Since the wife of President Hoover's Vice President, Charles Curtis, was an invalid and could not attend social functions, Alice claimed that as the wife of the Speaker of the House *she* was entitled to her social status. As such, she demanded that she take precedence at social affairs over Dolly Gann, the half sister of Curtis, who acted as his hostess.

While this battle of who sat higher above the salt raged in Washington, Franklin was quietly asking professors to teach him the economic facts of life and to advise him on legislative means to cope with the depression in New York State. Chief among these advisers were Raymond Moley, Rexford Tugwell and Adolf Berle. Of an evening, Eleanor would find him arguing with the professors while he sat in shirt sleeves and ate peanuts.

Louis Howe gave them the name "Brain Trust," as they worked with Franklin to set up a state program for farm relief, unemployment relief, conservation and social welfare. It was through their guidance that he used the term "Forgotten Man" in a speech in April, 1932, in which he expounded the revolutionary view that government aid should

[173]

go to men at the bottom of the economic heap and not to those at the top, as Hoover was proposing. When he established a state relief program in 1931, it was Eleanor who induced Franklin to take on Harry Hopkins, who had worked with her as the social worker advisor to the Women's Division in the 1928 campaign. Henry Morgenthau, Jr., publisher of the widely read *American Agriculturist,* Franklin's partner in a squash-raising venture, and the husband of Elinor who worked with Eleanor Roosevelt in 1928, became Conservation Commissioner.

Besides promoting far-reaching programs with Franklin, and moving him to action, Eleanor attempted to fight the depression singlehandedly. By 1931, there were 8,000,000 Americans unemployed. Walking through Times Square when she was in the city, she felt the shame and the degradation of the crowds of beggars and the shocked sullenness of the hordes in the emergency breadlines. She handed beggars cards informing them that free meals awaited them at her house. She also bombarded state and local officials with personal requests to aid individuals who were writing her by the thousands. In one instance, she pleaded with the State Commissioner of Mental Hygiene to help one woman—"Poor thing, she does not sound very happy." She wrote to the head of the New York City Board of Child Welfare, "I am enclosing this pathetic letter as the woman says she is a widow, and I wondered if she would not be entitled to a pension." When state agencies could not help, she went after private organizations. Her name brought quick results. "The man is a carpenter but has been unable to get any work. I wonder if you could have your organization look into this and give him any help possible." He was given a job. She got worthy people out of insane asylums and worked on Sam Rosenman, Franklin's counsel, to go over parole possibilities for others. When several persons wrote her about the hardships they were undergoing living on firemen's pensions, she wrote back, "I will find out about the firemen's pension and see if there is any chance of it being raised." Legislative committees found her a difficult person to turn aside.

At times when all avenues of aid proved fruitless, she became a one-woman employment agency. She considered herself a last resort and her heart was big enough to encompass even those who tried to trick her or were unworthy of aid. There were many of these, but she shrugged them off when she learned that she had been used, because she knew that most people who came to her were worthy of her aid. On many occasions, members of her family were appalled with her generosity that knew no bounds. One time she brought a young hobo to the Sixty-fifth Street home and put him up overnight on the fifth floor. When others in the house expressed fear that he might rob the house and kill them during the dark night, she reluctantly locked the attic door on him and lowered the elevator between floors. In the morning they breathed a sigh of relief when she fed him breakfast and sent him to Bear Mountain where she had arranged a job for him.

Sometimes people tried to take advantage of her generosity. "One of my most touching and regular correspondents," she said, "was a mother whose son was in an institution. When she found I could not help her free him she begged that I go to see him, which I did. Then she demanded that I go weekly and read the Bible to him!"

Only Eleanor and Louis Howe would talk to Franklin on a person-to-person basis during this period of frenzied efforts to ease the great social and economic calamity. When Louis Howe would come up from his New York City headquarters and find the Brain Trust in Franklin's office, he would eye them with half contempt. Though the professors were important, they were obsequious in their manner when talking with the governor. To Louis, the governor was always "Franklin," and he told him exactly what was on his mind. When he was angry he called Franklin "Pighead." Once he yelled at him, "Franklin, you idiotic fool!" Another time, while trying unsuccessfully to get his point across, he pounded on Franklin's desk in disgust and snarled, "Can't you get anything into that thick Dutch skull of yours?"

There was never any trouble between them, Eleanor knew, because Franklin did not take offense at any of his remarks. He knew that the little gnome was dedicated completely to his welfare. It was Louis, irascible or not, who relieved him of the load of preparing the way for the 1932 presidential race. "Louis really loved power," Eleanor said of him, "not for any advantage to himself but simply to show those of us around him that he could accomplish what he set his mind to do." Nor was Louis any easier with Eleanor. "Mrs. Roosevelt and I," he told friends, "are running a race to see which one can find the ugliest pictures of ourselves."

Franklin was not above using Louis as a foil. Once when a banking crisis hit the state, Lieutenant Governor Lehman arrived ashen-faced to discuss the situation with Franklin. Louis lay back on the sofa and smoked calmly while Lehman nervously paced the floor in great agitation. "What are we going to do?" Lehman's voice shrilled. In the midst of his wailing the phone rang and the wizened little man rose slowly to answer it. "Louis, will you please sit still?" Franklin bellowed at him. "Stop moving about so much!" Later, when Lehman was gone,

[175]

Franklin smiled at Louie and said, "Herbert isn't going to be able to work tomorrow."

She watched Louis prepare for 1932 and was amazed at his industry. His body was puny but his agile mind was alive with ideas. As Franklin's chief of staff he kept up a running correspondence with 2,000 political leaders throughout the country. Each person had to be treated individually, as though he were a major cohort of Franklin's. Louis carefully plotted each state politically and kept cards with pertinent details of those who might be going to the national convention as delegates or alternates. By early 1931, he had already moved ahead to the point where he was operating out of a six-room headquarters on the sixth floor at 331 Madison Avenue, across the street from the Biltmore, which he viewed as Franklin's presidential headquarters. Here he stepped up the frenzied pace of his letter writing, undertook a large-scale effort to raise the necessary funds for Franklin's nomination fight and began to sift through his intelligence files to determine Franklin's campaign managers in the various states. Once when he took a short vacation to get away from these activities, Franklin wired him, "Keep away from the deep water."

Louis had worked for Eleanor, too. As early as July, 1931, she wrote at his request to Molly Dewson of the Democratic Women's Division, "Franklin has asked me to get busy on this organization work and I have written the enclosed letter which is to go to all women whose names are sent in to us from different states."

Now that Louis was coming into the limelight, Eleanor grew concerned with his slovenly appearance. For months she nagged him about getting a new hat to replace the misshapen headgear he wore. "Oh, yes, and now about my hat," he said to her puckishly whenever he saw her staring at his head. However, he would not buy a new one. On one occasion she insisted that he wear a tuxedo to an important affair. "Mein Gawd! What will my friends say?" he protested unsuccessfully. When he came to get her, he was hardly recognizable without his potato-sacklike trousers. And all evening his pockmarked face grew smaller and smaller as he squirmed in agony. Despite this and the fact that cigarette ashes fell relentlessly on his jacket front, Eleanor sat and beamed at the transfiguration. All her satisfaction disappeared, however, when she happened to glance down and discovered that he was wearing one black and one white sock.

Louis was never cruel to her, though he often was to others. Once he boldly asked an overweight man what he weighed. Another time when one of his aides brought wealthy Joseph P. Kennedy of Boston to his office to meet him and perhaps unload some of his money in Franklin's behalf, Louis pretended he was sleeping.

Louis Howe's odd behavior at times in no way diminished the high regard Eleanor had for him, nor the warmth she and Franklin felt for their champion. They had many amusing times together. Once a reporter found them laughing and giggling together as they worked on valentines. "Louis Howe, the diabolic impresario of such occasions, has been busy all afternoon with cardboard and scissors and paints." Louis also planned the annual celebration of the Cufflinks Club, whose charter members were those who had traveled with Franklin in the 1920 campaign. One year he fixed up a room in the Sixty-fifth Street house like a Pullman car. Even Romeo, the porter on the original campaign train, was on hand to lend authenticity. Louis had excellent talent for art and poetry. On an occasion when Eleanor expressed worry about Franklin's running for President at the depths of the depression, Louis composed for her a poem in January, 1932, of which the first and last stanzas ran as follows:

> We are the hooded brotherhood of fears
> Barring the pleasant path that lay ahead.
> Who, grim and silent, all these futile years
> Have filled your timid soul with numbing dread.
>
> Fool! Had you dared to speed your pace
> Our masking cowls aside to tear
> And meet us bravely face to face
> We would have vanished into air.

Because Louis Howe's appearance and personality did not lend themselves to the important task of cementing Franklin's support throughout the country, James Farley was brought in as his assistant to perform this duty. Big Jim, who had been a building contractor, had served as state boxing commissioner under Al Smith. In 1928, he caught the eye of Eleanor and it was she who first brought him to the attention of her husband. During the campaign of that year he was placed in charge of the Roosevelt headquarters in New York City. He turned out to have a gift for dealing with people. As Eleanor defined his role, "He told me that if I thought a thing should be done, he would do it, though I would know quite well that he was not really convinced and perhaps had not even bothered to understand what it was all about. . . . He believed in the man for whom he worked, but was not so much concerned with the ideas and ideals for which that man stood."

Jim Farley, tall, bald and an ingratiating gladhander, was well aware

[177]

of the role Eleanor Roosevelt played in his career. With her initial push, he rose to the post of secretary of the Democratic State Committee and later became chairman through Franklin's strenuous efforts when the incumbent, William Bray, proved to be a thorough Al Smith man. Years afterward, Farley told Emma Guffie Miller, Democratic National Committeewoman from Pennsylvania, "It wouldn't matter what Mrs. Roosevelt asked me to do, I would do it. For if it hadn't been for her I would never have gotten where I am for she gave me my first big chance."

It was Louis Howe who conceived the idea of combining Farley's trip to the Elks convention in Seattle in July, 1931 with a wild flurry of meetings with Roosevelt politicians all along the way. And while Louis sat in his office and opened all of Franklin's mail marked "private and confidential," Jim the political drummer dined and talked to politicians in 18 states during 19 days. When he returned he rushed to tell Franklin of his enthusiastic reception in most places. Louis Howe, miffed because he felt that Farley was keeping matters from him, broke off speaking to Farley. Jealous to the core, he believed that Franklin was his private domain and no man was to get too close to Franklin other than he. Into this intolerable state of affairs stepped Eleanor, who sent Farley to Louis to make up. When this was accomplished, the campaign moved ahead on schedule.

The warmth that existed between Franklin and Eleanor and the Hoovers now completely disintegrated as it became apparent that the two men would in most likelihood oppose each other for the Presidency in 1932. Part of this warmth had already cooled by the start of Franklin's second term because of Hoover's ineptness in dealing with the economic crisis. Eleanor's opinion of Hoover was of a piece equal to her remark about Senator James Wadsworth when she said of him, "He has the Marie Antoinette turn of mind—let them eat cake."

In masterminding the Roosevelt campaign for the Presidency, Louis Howe conceived the excellent stratagem of the "Fireside Chat." Franklin began speaking to the people of New York over the radio at frequent intervals, using homey language as one would to a friend sitting with him at his fireside. In addition, Louis insisted that Franklin attend the Governors' Conference each year and play a leading role, in order that the other governors would learn of his leadership merits.

At the Governors' Conference in the spring of 1932, to which Eleanor accompanied Franklin, a fair measure of the leading opponents for the Presidency was readily available. President Hoover came to Richmond, Virginia, to deliver the key address. Unfortunately, this proved to be no contest, for as Hoover started to speak, a strong wind blew his speech off the lectern. Even though his address was being broadcast, Hoover abruptly ended his talk.

Later, as the conference's finale, the governors and their wives were invited to dine with the President in the White House. "I was a little worried about Franklin," said Eleanor, "who had to have somebody's arm and a cane. In addition, he became rather tired if he stood without support for any length of time. We arrived a little ahead of time, since we knew we should have to walk rather slowly down the main hall to get in line, and then we stood and waited."

The dinner was scheduled for eight P.M., but the Hoovers did not appear until eight-thirty. As Franklin waited, clammy sweat broke out over his face and he was in agony. By the time the meal began he had lost all appetite. Ike Hoover, the chief usher at the White House and not related to the President, told Eleanor afterward that "his opponents" plotted to keep her husband standing in hopes he would have to ask for a chair or get too weary." In fact, Franklin was offered a chair twice during the wait, but he sensed the strategy and refused both times.

Eleanor and Louis heard rumors as the presidential campaign for the nomination progressed that the opposition planned a public statement charging that polio was a "progressive disease" which affected the brain eventually. To refute this, Dr. Draper, who had taken care of Franklin after his attack, prepared a counterstatement pointing out that Sir Walter Scott had had polio as a boy yet never lost his faculties.

Additional efforts were made to counterattack the growing whispering campaign about Franklin's state of health. Eleanor said publicly, "If infantile paralysis couldn't kill him, the Presidency certainly couldn't." Franklin went further and submitted himself to a committee of physicians who examined him and issued the following statement: "We believe that his health and power of endurance are such as to allow him to meet any demands of private and public life."

This did not mean, of course, that his legs were not paralyzed. In fact, while making a speech for the nomination in Georgia in early 1932, Franklin was so engrossed that he took his hands off the speaker's table and fell flat on his face. Onlookers rushed to the platform and put him back on his feet behind the protective table. He went on with his talk as though nothing extraordinary had occurred.

Among the other ugly rumors spread by his opposition was one that he and Eleanor would have got a divorce except for the fact that such an action would kill him politically. This was sheer nonsense, as letters between the two during this period testify. When he went abroad in late spring of 1931 to be at his sick mother's bedside in Paris, Eleanor wrote him: "I think I looked so tired chiefly because I hated so to see you go, though I knew it was the best thing for you to do and the sensible thing for me not to go. We are really very dependent on each other though we do see so little of each other. I feel as lost as I did when I went abroad & I will never do that again. . . . Goodnight, dear . . . Dear love to you . . . I miss you and hate to feel you so far away."

The Democratic National Convention was scheduled to begin in Chicago on June 27. Three weeks before, Franklin held a strategy conference at Hyde Park with his advisers. There he and Eleanor, Louis Howe, Jim Farley and the Brain Trust made a final appraisal of his chances and what steps they had to take to get the nomination. The conference was marred somewhat by Sara Roosevelt who interjected herself freely into the discussion. At one point she silenced the entire group with her icy comment, "I don't want my son nominated if he has to be elected on a 'wet' ticket." As best they could, the others proceeded in a gingerly fashion to complete the rehearsal.

Neither Eleanor nor Franklin went to the convention. Louis Howe insisted that he had some last-minute problems to solve, so Jim Farley and Arthur Mullen, a Nebraska lawyer who was to act as floor leader, hurried to Chicago to make last-minute deals. Once the preliminaries of the convention were out of the way, it became readily apparent to Franklin and Eleanor that he was in for a rough time. With nine candidates nominated and the New York delegation in Al Smith's camp, Franklin lost some of his aplomb and Louis Howe raced to Chicago to stem the tide. Renting Room 1702 at the Congress Hotel, Louis immediately ordered a direct telephone line to Albany established in his suite. Shuffling through his file cards on the various delegates, he had key delegates brought to 1702 to talk to Franklin via long distance.

From his thin voice and incessant coughing when she talked to him, Eleanor grew quickly concerned about Louis. The heat and his frenzied activities combined to knock his weight several pounds below his normal 100 pounds. Those who worked with him were certain he would die on the spot. In fact, word came to Albany that he held his conferences while lying stretched out on the floor in his hotel room. All these reports cast a pall over Eleanor's interest in the convention.

Nevertheless, the convention had to go on with its work. Eleanor sat up all night alongside Franklin listening to the radio report of the first three inconclusive ballots. Jim Farley rushed to Louis's room in agitated concern when the third ballot ended at 9:15 A.M. He found Louis "racked by strangling asthma" and "lying on the floor in his shirt sleeves between two blowing electric fans." With a "Stop Roosevelt" movement now in full swing, if they didn't win on the fourth ballot Franklin would be finished. Farley sat down on the floor beside him and they talked in whispers because others were present. "Texas is our only chance," Louis agreed, exhausted.

While Farley and Mullen were trying to swing the Texas delegation to their cause, back in Albany Eleanor was busy mothering the large crowd of newspaper reporters that jammed the mansion grounds. She had put up several in the garage during the night, and in the morning, she supplied hot breakfast to the entire group. As the day wore on slowly, with Franklin in innumerable phone calls, the tension grew almost unbearable. Only a last-minute compromise engineered between Arthur Mullen and Senator Tom Connally of Texas that placed Speaker of the House John Garner on the ticket with her husband put Franklin across on the fourth ballot.

There was good reason now to celebrate. Eleanor rose immediately after Franklin's nomination was assured and took his hand. "I am going to make some bacon and eggs for us." She rolled up her sleeves. He could only smile, for this was the extent of her cooking ability.

They flew to Chicago so Franklin could solidify his victory by making his acceptance speech in person. Eleanor, two of her boys and Sam Rosenman went with him. Twice they had to land—in Buffalo and Cleveland—to refuel. Eleanor sat in the back of the shaky plane and shivered. Her son John's face turned green. Franklin worked over his acceptance speech with Rosenman, and the noise of the plane so great that Franklin had to shout as he rehearsed passages.

At last they arrived in Chicago. In the enormous crowd that greeted them as they came down the stairs, Eleanor spied Louis Howe, frail and pale, his wizened face wreathed in a smile. When the enthusiastic mob surrounded them, Franklin's hat was knocked off and his glasses dropped off his nose.

Louis Howe was angry. He had stayed up all night writing an acceptance speech for Franklin, and he wanted him to use it rather than the speech Franklin had worked up with the Brain Trust. Franklin took Louis's speech, as though he had been waiting for it. And on the way to the convention hall with Eleanor, Franklin grinned and waved at the cheering crowd along the streets while he read Louis's speech.

Arriving at the hall, he insisted that Louis stand on the platform with him and Eleanor while the delegates applauded. At last the time came for his acceptance speech. Was he going to hurt Louis's feelings and deliver his own excellent address? Eleanor wondered. Or was he going to read Louis's speech that he had so hurriedly read on the way to the hall?

Franklin could not hurt the little gnome who had given so many years to him. Yet he believed that his own speech was better. He glanced at Louis and then he began. The first page was Louis's first page without any changes. But after that, he discarded Louis's remaining pages and substituted his own. "I pledge you, I pledge myself, to a new deal for the American people," he said, and the audience went wild.

In the fall campaign against Hoover, Eleanor would not openly campaign for her husband. Behind the scenes she worked again with Molly Dewson, the able director of the Women's Division. She helped prepare the red, yellow and green leaflets about Franklin and the issues involved in the election that were sent out by the thousands and carried from house to house by the "grass trampers," as the volunteer women were called. Her active campaigning was restricted to New York State where she was a chief speaker for Herbert Lehman, who was running that year for governor.

As usual, her branch of the Roosevelt family stood almost solidly behind Hoover. There was one defection—Aunt Corinne, her father's younger sister. When Aunt Corinne was offered the honor of becoming a Republican elector, she refused. "You must understand," she said, "my own beloved niece is the wife of the Democratic candidate. She is the daughter of the brother who was nearer to me in age than Theodore. For her I have the deepest affection and respect. So, much as I would like to pay the highest tribute to President Hoover, I cannot do so in this campaign."

Eleanor joined the train at Williams, Arizona, as Franklin made his big campaign swing to the West. At every whistle stop, Franklin was jovial, though the faces in the crowd disturbed him a great deal. He confided to Eleanor one time, "They have the frightened look of lost children."

He loved the excitement of the campaign, while Eleanor cast a jaundiced eye on the entire procedure. While he stood on back platforms and waved and shook hands, her mind was on his braces and the strain he was undergoing. He loved the blare of the sirens when they left the train and rushed by car to meeting halls. She held on grimly while the motorcycle escorts raced them through the streets. And in the hall while Franklin and local Democrats tried to determine the numbers in the swollen audience, her first thought was whether there were enough fire escapes should the building catch fire. He loved to give the crowds who came to the railroad crossings a good laugh. "And this is my little boy Jimmy," he would announce. And through the doorway to the rear platform would come his six foot, four inch son James, while the crowd doubled up with laughter. For a time he also used the line, "I have more hair than he does." But Eleanor made him drop this good-natured kidding because Jimmy winced every time his father said it.

There were, however, many serious speeches on the issues facing the country. There were also further rumors, many of which concerned Eleanor. One growing whispering campaign was that she was writing a book to justify birth control. The obvious Republican hope here was that this charge would alienate Catholic voters. Actually, Eleanor was writing three books, but not on this subject. One, which she never found a publisher for, was tentatively titled *Thirty Great Americans*. Of the two chapters she had already completed, one was on Alexander Hamilton and the other was on Uncle Ted, whom she called "a wonderful example of the complete partnership of mind and body." Two of her books which were published in 1932 were a children's book, *When You Grow Up to Vote,* and *Hunting Big Game In the Eighties,* containing many of the letters her father wrote during his short life. While this latter book satisfied her own craving to bring her father's worth to light, it also proved another example of her motherliness. A state trooper had injured his spine hopelessly while serving in a motorcycle escort for Franklin. To help his rehabilitation after obtaining for him the best specialist care available, she got him started on a typing course. Later, to help him out, she gave him her father's letters to type, and from the total came her book.

When October arrived and the campaign oratory was at its thickest, Roosevelt strategists insisted that Eleanor would help build up good will for her husband by attending a World Series baseball contest, thus being stamped as a cheering enthusiast for the all-American pastime. Unfortunately, when she did agree to go, she no sooner found her seat than she fell asleep.

It was during the heat of the campaign that Eleanor got the bright idea she would like to fly her own plane. Amelia Earhart, pushing hard for public acceptance of air travel, promised to instruct her after she passed the required physical examination. Elated when she came through the test, she was jolted when Franklin would not let her take the lessons. "Eleanor, what are you trying to do to me?" he yelled at her. "You know I have enough worries on my mind without worrying about your flying around up there somewhere in the sky." She quickly dropped the idea.

[183]

Politicians flocked to Hyde Park to give last-minute advice. Drunk and sober, bombastic and quiet, they spread throughout Sara Roosevelt's house to offer that last word which would defeat Hoover. One drunken western Senator walked into a room where Eleanor was talking to Louie Howe. He bowed deeply to her and paddled over to Louie who lay breathing in asthmatic gasps on the sofa. "You look terrible, Howe," he commiserated. "Take it easy. . . . My shoulders are broad. You can lean on me." Suddenly he wobbled and fell on top of Louie, almost smothering him before Eleanor could drag him off.

On election day, Eleanor and Franklin voted in Hyde Park. Then they dined with friends in their New York City home. Afterward they proceeded to campaign headquarters at the Biltmore Hotel to listen to the voting returns. Louis Howe, who had worked himself into a lather of pessimism, refused to budge from his office across the street from the hotel.

At eleven P.M., when the returns were coming in heavily in Franklin's favor, Eleanor went across the street to get him. She found him hunched over piles of paper on which he had been recording the state-by-state returns, and not too convinced that the election would go to Franklin. Finally she had the telephone operator get Franklin across the street in the small room off the headquarters. "Hello, Franklin," Louis said dourly. "It's not over yet." He talked awhile with only the faintest flicker of a smile crossing his face. When he hung up, he stared silently at Eleanor. Then he pulled open a desk drawer and extracted a bottle of sherry. Carefully he poured some into glasses. "I put that bottle away twenty years ago after the fight over 'Blue-Eyed' Billy Sheehan," he announced with sudden enthusiasm. "And I said then that I wouldn't drink it until Franklin was President."

It was all over now except for Hoover's conceding statement, which the President finally made at two in the morning. When Eleanor returned to Franklin's side, two strangers entered their room. "Who are you?" she asked.

"Secret Service men," they replied. "Our job is to guard the President."

Amid the celebrating at headquarters that night, a reporter named John Boettiger, with the Chicago *Tribune,* came to Eleanor and asked, "I wish I knew what you are really thinking and feeling."

She was startled by the personal question. "I'm happy for my husband," she told him, "because in many ways it makes up for the blow he suffered when he was stricken with infantile paralysis. And I have confidence in his ability to help the country in its crisis."

But she saw the victory as the end of any personal life for herself. "I knew what traditionally should lie before me. The turmoil in my heart and mind was rather great that night."

At the Sixty-fifth Street house, Sara Roosevelt kissed her son resoundingly. "This is the greatest night of my life," she murmured.

Chapter Twenty-One

Aꜰᴛᴇʀ ʜᴇʀ ʜᴜꜱʙᴀɴᴅ'ꜱ ᴇʟᴇᴄᴛɪᴏɴ as President, Eleanor Roosevelt gave serious thought to what might happen to her as First Lady. She viewed the public attention and the general fawning that descended over every President's wife as highly distasteful. The day following the election she returned to her class at Todhunter. When the girls greeted her in awe as "First Lady," she protested, "But I haven't changed any inside."

She considered her teaching and her many other activities as her last fling before settling down to the barrenness of smiling at White House social affairs. Friends watched her take on new projects with a vengeance. She became the editor of Bernarr Macfadden's magazine, *Babies: Just Babies,* a monthly magazine devoted to parents with children under five years of age. Daughter Anna was taken on as her associate editor. She also took to the air with a radio program for a facial cream company. She seemed to be running away from the fate that would soon be upon her.

In the meantime, Franklin struggled with the twin jobs of deciding on his program and on his Cabinet. The only certain assignment was for Louis Howe, who would function as his chief assistant with a desk close by his in the White House. Eleanor insisted that he break with tradition and give women a greater role in the federal government. Ignoring the usual routine of putting a male official of American labor into the Cabinet as Secretary of Labor, Franklin finally gave this post to Eleanor's friend, Frances Perkins, who had served him so well as New York State Labor Commissioner.

With the coming of the Secret Service men to protect Franklin, Eleanor developed strong fears about his safety. These fears were justified when he went south in February, 1933 and an attempt was made on his life in Florida. When she heard about the shooting of Mayor Anton Cermak of Chicago, who was with Franklin at the time, she tried desperately to reach Franklin by phone to find out if he was all right. A woman reporter chanced upon her while she waited for the call to go through. "This is what it is like to be in public life," Eleanor said, concerned.

She made her first start toward moving to Washington in early winter when she visited Mrs. Hoover in the White House. Walking down Connecticut Avenue from the Mayflower Hotel, she thought of the time when Franklin was Assistant Secretary of the Navy and she had agreed with him that it would be wonderful to be the First Lady of the land. Today she found the idea an unhappy one.

It was Eleanor's hope to inspect the White House from top to bottom with Lou Hoover as guide. But Mrs. Hoover rushed her through the place in a single hour. She talked to Eleanor as though she found it an enormous effort. However, Eleanor ignored this poor reception and scribbled furiously on four sheets of legal paper an almost indecipherable outline of the White House routine regarding servants and schedules. Only at the end of the hour when she turned Eleanor over to Ike Hoover to show her the kitchen did Lou Hoover smile. Still another reason for Mrs. Hoover's coolness was her concern that Eleanor did not take her future position seriously. Mrs. Hoover had offered her the use of a White House limousine to bring her to the White House from the Mayflower Hotel. The fact that Eleanor had refused with the light remark that she preferred to walk distressed the First Lady. Franklin's cousin, Warren Delano Robbins, then protocol officer for the State Department, also expressed horror at her behavior. "But, Eleanor," he sputtered, "it just isn't right for you to walk down the street any more like everyone else. You can't do it, and that's all there is to it." But she ignored him.

As for Ike Hoover, he stood openmouthed after her inspection. "Mrs. Roosevelt knew just what she wanted," he said with awe, "and rattled it off as if she had known it her whole life. She had already decided on every last detail of the social plans for Inauguration Day; told me who the house guests would be and what rooms they would occupy, though this was five weeks in the future; gave the menus for the meals, both regular and special; told me what household effects she would bring; what servants should be provided for; what the family liked for meals and when they liked to have them; in fact, everything the Chief Usher could wish to know except what the weather might be on March fourth."

Eleanor's second visit to the White House came on Friday, March third, the day before the inauguration. This was also a tense, unhappy situation, made so by the animosity between Hoover and Franklin. When Eleanor and Franklin came with their son Jimmy to tea on

[187]

March third, the White House atmosphere was supercharged. By then the bank panic was engulfing the nation. No sooner were they seated than Hoover immediately tried to pin Franklin down to joining him in a statement to the country. With his own tenure in office just a day away, however, Franklin smilingly refused. Eleanor, holding a shaky cup of tea in one hand, watched Hoover's face redden. The atmosphere changed to sparking electricity. Franklin tried to pass this off with a broad smile and another pleasantry.

"Mr. President," he told Hoover, "I know it is customary to do so, but you don't have to return our call if you don't want to."

"Mr. Roosevelt," Hoover said between clenched teeth, "when you have been in Washington as long as I have, you will learn that the President of the United States calls on nobody!"

Franklin started to sizzle and Eleanor stood up. "It's been very pleasant," she said, "but we must go now."

They left immediately, with Franklin's face set in cold fury as they drove through the gates. The White House servants told Eleanor a few days later "how difficult it had been for President Hoover even to say good morning or smile at the people of his household."

Inauguration Day, the next morning, was dark, dreary and wet. In the morning Eleanor went with Franklin, his mother, her children and a host of Roosevelt cousins, uncles and aunts from the Mayflower Hotel for prayers at St. John's Episcopal Church. Despite the fact that his old Groton headmaster, Endicott Peabody, was a Hoover enthusiast, Franklin had requested him to conduct services. And Dr. Peabody invoked the blessing of the Lord upon "Thy servant Franklin."

Then they drove to the White House to pick up the Hoovers. Franklin, who drove to the Capitol in a car with Hoover, reported later that conversation had lagged except for Hoover's comments about the "lovely steel" in the new buildings going up along Pennsylvania Avenue. Mrs. Hoover, riding with Eleanor, told her how she would miss the feeling of being waited on hand and foot and never having to make plans.

At the Capitol, Eleanor went to the inaugural stand with her family. It was all so different from her memory of 1905 when she sat in the same place while Uncle Ted was inaugurated. Then it had had so little meaning to her and Uncle Ted's speech had not registered on her, for she hadn't listened to it.

She was concerned now, too, with Franklin's ability to walk to his place alongside Chief Justice Charles Evans Hughes. Actually, great care had been taken to ensure him the shortest walk possible. Two ramps had been erected to the entrance of the platform and he was wheeled out of sight of the crowd to the office of the Senate Sergeant-at-Arms. From there at almost noon, he was wheeled again along a wooden passageway close to the platform outside the Capitol portico. Rising from his seat and tightening his braces, he was supported by his son Jimmy in the final 35-foot walk down the red-carpeted ramp to the oath stand. She saw Louie Howe there beaming and looking like a comic-strip character in his frock coat, striped pants and high silk hat.

The crowd standing and sitting before Franklin as he took his oath and gave his inaugural address made little response. It seemed to Eleanor that the faces of the onlookers were dazed and frightened as they listened to his words. Herbert Hoover had been reported that day as saying, "We are at the end of our rope." The attitude of the crowd seemed to give mute testimony to his remark. The only real enthusiasm came when Franklin said boldly, "Let me assert my firm belief that the only thing we have to fear is fear itself." He had taken the expression from Thoreau, who had written, "Nothing is so much to be feared as fear." Electricity passed through the crowd at Franklin's words about fear and people looked at each other, pleased.

The ride back to the White House where they were to be the proprietors during the next four years was also eerie. Franklin raised his top hat to the crowd every few feet and Eleanor alongside him smiled and waved. But as she noted the scene, "It was very, very solemn, and a little terrifying. The crowds were so tremendous and you felt they would do anything—if someone would tell them what to do."

Once inside the door for the special lunch before the customary parade, they were now officially President and First Lady. However, Franklin looked uneasy. The answer was not hard to find. He had to take his lady's arm and lead the procession to the dining room. The problem was Sara Roosevelt, beaming with joy on this wonderful occasion.

Franklin looked helplessly at Eleanor. Then he took his mother's arm and the two walked first in the procession, with Eleanor walking behind.

Chapter Twenty-Two

FOUR DAYS AFTER her husband started officiating as President, Eleanor Roosevelt accompanied him on a visit to the Nineteenth Street home of Oliver Wendell Holmes. The retired Justice of the Supreme Court excitedly greeted them in the library of the building he called "the house of truth." Clutching a book of Plato in one gnarled hand, the old man—the Great Dissenter—still sharp-brained, talked about the old days of President Wilson when he first had met them.

It was the old gentleman's ninety-second birthday, and Eleanor at forty-eight and Franklin at fifty were mere children to him. What did they have on their minds so he could guide them in a fatherly fashion?

"You are the greatest living American," Franklin told him. "You have lived through half our country's history. You have seen its great men," he went on with emphasis. "This is a dark hour, Justice Holmes. What is your advice?"

The old man's hand quivered as he stared at Eleanor. Then he stared in turn at Franklin. "You are in a war, Mr. President. I was in a war, too. And in a war there is only one rule." His voice rose in volume. "Form your battalions and fight."

With 15,000,000 people unemployed, moaning despair throughout the land, Franklin had stepped into the debris of a nation's economy as no President before him had. Utter chaos faced the nation, revolt perhaps, unless he formed his battalions and fought.

His actions were swift and dramatic. In a hundred days he turned the tide. First he called Congress into special session for March 9, 1933. Then he proclaimed a bank holiday, closing the banks to prevent further ruinous runs on bank deposits by frantic depositors. When Eleanor told him concernedly that she had no cash and felt obligated to pay bills due, he smiled. The first day Congress met, it passed his Emergency Banking Act, which permitted banks considered sound to reopen their doors. A Fireside Chat on March 12 assured the nation person-to-person that deposits were safe. Then the rushing train of government repealed the Volstead Act to permit the sale of wine and beer; passed the Agricultural Adjustment Act for farm aid, the Banking Act and Securities Act to stabilize and reform banks and the stock exchange, the Home Owners Loan Act and the Emergency Farm Mortgage Act, the Emergency Railroad Transportation Act to save free enterprise in railroad management, the Civilian Conservation Corps to give a half-million young men jobs in the nation's forests, the Federal Emergency Relief Administration with a half billion dollars for direct relief, the Tennessee Valley Authority, the National Industrial Recovery Act with its codes of fair practices, labor conditions and wages, and the Public Works Administration with an appropriation of $3,300,000,000 to build airports, schools and other kinds of public works.

The White House was a scene of bedlam during these hundred days. Every night during these weeks there were special conferences continuing apace by the Brain Trusters and the incoming New Dealers. They seldom broke up before two or three A.M. "The men would be working in every room," Eleanor described the scene. "I could not go to bed out of personal curiosity to know what was being done."

The Eleanor Roosevelt who came to Washington as the mistress of the White House made a conscious effort—for a few days—to obliterate the public figure she had been in Albany. In view of her far-flung activities as the governor's wife, she knew she had stirred up a hornet of opposition to herself, and she was determined not to do so again in Washington. Many political opponents of Franklin had called her schoolteaching an indignity, her paid radio broadcasting abhorrent, her editing of a baby magazine a distasteful lending of her name to the publicity-mad health fanatic, Bernarr Macfadden, and her interest in the Val-Kill furniture enterprise a money-grubbing device to capitalize on her husband's position. Of course, none of these charges was true. Yet they rankled her. Shortly before she entrained for Washington, the New York *Post* sneered editorially, "She's certain to wreck the new Administration."

So it was little wonder that she gave up teaching at Todhunter, announced she would do no more radio broadcasting, told Macfadden between his sips of carrot juice that she could not continue as his editor, and turned over her unprofitable Val-Kill enterprise to the workers. When she sadly informed Franklin shortly before they came to Washington that if she could help him with his White House mail she would not feel so useless, he cast an amazed glance at her. "No you can't help on the mail, Eleanor," he said firmly. "That's Missy's job. But you will probably have some other things to keep you busy," he added in the understatement of the century.

Her first big job was to make a home of the spotlighted White House. Then after this was accomplished, she would relegate herself to its rigorous social schedule, some horseback riding through Rock Creek Park, perhaps a course in Spanish and long hours spent in catching up with her reading.

According to H. G. Wells, who visited the White House during Hoover's time, the mansion was "a queer ramshackle place like a nest of waiting rooms with hat stands everywhere and unexpected doors through which hurrying distraught officials appeared and vanished." When he returned to visit the Roosevelts in 1934, he noted, "All the Hoover untidiness had vanished. Everything was large, cool, orderly and unhurried."

She considered the White House her last opportunity to make a home for her remaining children before they were off on their own. It must be as cozy and informal as she could make it, an interpretation of White House living that distressed its chief usher, Ike Hoover, for forty years the major-domo of the establishment. "He was never quite certain," said Eleanor, "that some of the things I did were compatible with the dignity of the President's wife." When she insisted on running the elevator herself, he clutched at his throat and told her emphatically, "That just isn't done, Mrs. Roosevelt."

"It is now," she said just as emphatically, working the controls that closed the door and carried her upstairs.

He found further reason for apoplexy that very first day when he discovered her pushing furniture around. And it was not light furniture either, for she was stocking the living quarters on the second floor with heavy Val-Kill productions to withstand the expected punishment from her energetic sons. When she found her own bedroom too large, she installed her bed in the small adjacent room and converted the bedroom into her sitting room and office. Mrs. Hoover's sitting room became Franklin's oval study and the small adjoining room his bedroom with a four-poster bed that he preferred. Into his oval study she pushed the reproduction of Thomas Jefferson's favorite chair which she had the workmen at Val-Kill fashion for Franklin. On the floor before the fireplace she dropped the lionskin rug sent by Emperor Selassie of Ethiopia, which Franklin prosaically named "Leo." Louis Howe was given the Lincoln Room and Missy LeHand, Franklin's secretary, the housekeeping rooms on the third floor. Also on the third floor Eleanor made room for Franklin, Jr., and John, as well as a nursery for her grandchildren. She nailed pictures and prints all over the living quarters, even on linen closets. Over the door of his oval study, Franklin insisted upon hanging a portrait of her done by Lydia Emmett. "That's just the way Eleanor looks, you know," he told visitors, "lovely hair and pretty eyes."

Even though she worked far into the night and gave the White House a new atmosphere within twenty-four hours after her arrival, there were several minor aspects of change that required intensive effort. One was her insistence on hanging swings for the children from tree branches on the White House lawn. Col. Ulysses S. Grant III, the handsome grandson of Lincoln's top general who was in charge of public buildings and grounds, fought a rugged rear-guard action against Eleanor on this score. "A rope swing will kill a tree eventually," he insisted. "We might let you put up bars and a swing on steel braces, however."

"Really, Colonel," she told him, self-righteously, "I've always had rope swings swung over branches and they never hurt the bark."

Despite her explanation, he refused her permission. Nevertheless, she went ahead and hung one anyhow, with her strong determination to make the White House into a home. And a short time later, passers-by outside the steel picket fence could look in and watch her and her daughter Anna standing up on the swing and pumping double high into the air.

Franklin, however, did not fare as well. Despite the enormity of his pressing duties, he couldn't restrain himself from taking part in the household activities of the White House. Considering himself a master designer, he spent long hours planning much of the upholstery material and drapes. When Eleanor's aunt, Uncle Ted's wife, had been mistress of the White House, she had banned red because the color sickened her. Now when the problem arose of replacing the threadbare drapes for the long windows in the East Room, Franklin chose a bright red color. Unfortunately, his choice met the stubborn opposition of the Fine Arts Commission, and after a long hassle about the exact shade of red to go into the drapes, he admitted final and unhappy defeat.

Even accepting a gift for the White House was a formidable matter, as Eleanor found. When a friend gave her a bust of George Washington as a permanent White House gift, she horrifiedly discovered that hers was not the final decision whether it could be accepted. Not only did the gentlemen who composed the Fine Arts Commission have to approve it, but Congress had to pass a special act to make it legal. Rather than go through this cumbersome procedure, she returned the Washington head.

However, the problem of accepting gifts for the White House was minor compared with her other housekeeping duties. The White House in 1933 still had loathsome cuspidors strewn about the place. Servants still used feather dusters and corn brooms. The nineteenth-century kitchen had a wretched stove, few pots and little work space for the cooks. All over the house, the leaky roof discolored the walls. The plumbing was in such a state of decay that it often failed. To her disgust, she found the sewer pipe to be an open trough. As for the electricity, the White House still operated on direct current. Worst of all, the place was infested with rats.

All these outmoded and unsanitary living ways she changed in the 16-acre estate with the 60-room house. The kitchen she modernized at a cost to the government of $165,000, and the cracked china, which the servants were afraid to handle, she changed with the purchase of a new 1,000-piece set for $9,000. For the servants who had no place to go when they weren't on immediate call except to hideous basement quarters, she had their section redone to lend them dignity. One servant who could not restrain himself from announcing publicly his satisfaction with her concern for his group said, "Oh, Lord, I don't know what we would do here without Mrs. Roosevelt."

The annual expenses involved in running the White House showed a $25,000 out-of-pocket deficit despite Franklin's strenuous efforts to pare costs. Even at formal dinners top-ranking guests walked away with expensive silverware in their pockets. He gave Eleanor a staggering $2,000 each month for food and though meals were plain and guests grumbled about the cooking, there were frequently end-of-month money shortages that required embarrassing calls to butchers and grocers to wait for their payment. With a strange sense of justice, the knowledge that millions of people were unemployed and not eating well produced many an Eleanor Economy Meal for her guests. On one occasion her lunch for Cabinet ladies included soup made from spinach, dandelion greens and bacon fat. After the first spoonful the women looked wretched. "I was only experimenting," she apologized later.

It came as a surprise to Eleanor that although White House servants were paid by the government, she and Franklin had to pay for the food they ate. Ike Hoover could not help her on this score. However, he did have a valuable food tip. "Always include a Republican to a meal in the White House," he told her in confidence. "When you include members of both parties, you thus make the function official and the charge is on the government rather than on you personally."

The White House had its special atmosphere. Knowledge that a host of Presidents had lived in these same rooms before her time had at times an eerie affect on Eleanor. The place was definitely haunted.

"Sometimes when I am working late in my room," she said, "where many Presidents have worked, I get the distinct feeling that there is somebody in the room." Once when she looked up from her desk she was startled to see "Lincoln passing before the window."

It was difficult to make a place homey when millions of people exercised their right each year to tour the first floor of the White House. The second floor was out of bounds to the hordes of visitors, although on occasion Eleanor led various groups on a private tour of the living quarters. Once she showed a large group of grizzly Maine lobstermen through the upstairs rooms. She pointed out the spot where she enjoyed eating her breakfast while gazing out at the magnolia tree planted by Andrew Jackson. "She ain't stuck up, she ain't dressed up and she ain't afeared ter talk," one lobsterman piped up. Pleased, she showed them through her quarters, then through Franklin's, and finally opened the door and led them into daughter Anna's room. "And here is . . ." she started to say only to stop with a gulp. Anna was asleep in the bed. All of them stumbled over each other in a wild exit.

Besides the effect of her friendliness, the informality of the White House was helped by other matters. Baby grandchildren who crawled, cried and cooed on the upper floors could be heard downstairs. Dogs barked and had free run of the place. However, the dogs did not last long, despite the countrified atmosphere they added. Major, a husky muscular police dog, often lay and basked in the light just outside a room where several White House stenographers worked. If he was there at noontime, they skipped lunch rather than walk past his sharp teeth. They had good reason for fearing Major, for one morning he bit visiting Prime Minister Bennett of Canada. Bennett, who had come to Washington to cement close relations between his country and the United States, let out four-letter-word curses on that occasion that were not for the ears of ladies. Eleanor reprimanded Major with a sharp glance. Nor were the gardener's angry oaths at Major shortly afterward any more refined than Bennett's when Major took the seat from his pants with one savage bite. Once when the dog drew blood from another visitor, a White House maid rushed in and told Eleanor the gruesome details. "That settles it," Eleanor said firmly. "From now on we will have to keep iodine in this room!" Eleanor did not banish Major until a later time when he bit Hattie Carraway, the lady Senator from Arkansas.

Her other dogs, while smaller, were also belligerent. Winks, a setter, ate eleven breakfasts off the table one morning. Winks' sad demise occurred one day when another dog reached through the iron bar fence and killed him. Eleanor's favorite dog, an old deaf Scottie named Meggie, was considered harmless until she bit a newspaperwoman on the lip. With the passing of Meggie, Eleanor kept the White House dogless until the coming of Fala.

In the early years the White House was alive with babies. Franklin, whose nature upon arising was several shades below affability, often found his door bursting open with a crash and Eleanor rushing inside to deposit a few babies in bed with him. Occasionally he would be treated to serious fights in his bed between grandchildren claiming sole possession of Grandpa. It was also a common sight for Eleanor to dictate while bouncing a child or two on her knees, and sometimes staid visitors gaped to find her acting the role of bucking bronco with one of her grandchildren holding onto her for dear life.

Still another factor making for informality was the absence of any sticky intrafamily relationship. The White House upper floor heard a great deal of laughter and teasing. The younger boys engaged in whacking pillow-fighting contests and wrestled each other whenever it appeared that quiet had settled in their quarters. Occasionally Franklin joined them in such pursuits. Once when James and Franklin, Jr., came into his bedroom while he sat upright with his useless legs dangling over the side of his bed, he grabbed them suddenly by their shirt fronts and lay back swiftly. His two large boys sailed clear over the bed onto the floor beyond it. Mealtime produced such contests of joking and hectic arguments that servants were often observed with straight faces while their stomachs rolled with inner laughter. High officials who dined with the entire family were often appalled by the conversational give-and-take between the Roosevelts and their children. "Now look here, Pop, you've got it all wrong," one of the boys would explain the facts of political life to Franklin at dinner, or another son would blurt, "That isn't right, Ma," with wild arm-swinging gestures to emphasize her ignorance. At one meal when Franklin failed to get a word in edgewise with his arguing boys, Secretary of the Interior Harold Ickes shook his head and told him with raw sarcasm, "Now I understand how you are able to control Congress." Senator Burton K. Wheeler of Montana, who was also present, corrected Ickes. "Congress is never as bad as that," he averred.

Yet if Eleanor worked hard at maintaining informality in the glare of public attention, it was with the knowledge that the White House was hardly the place for normal family existence. The time this struck home was when one of her boys came home in the middle of the night from a dance and found a strange gatekeeper who did not recognize him. It took almost an hour before someone could be located who would vouch for him. The next morning at breakfast he told his mother angrily, "What kind of a place is this anyway, where you can't get in when you are living here?"

Other guests had different complaints. Amelia Earhart, who was a close friend of Eleanor's, discovered one night when she wanted a midnight snack that the refrigerator was kept locked. General Anastasio Somoza, the President of Nicaragua, carried on like a man denied his birthright when he found that White House protocol put him in a separate room from his wife.

Another tax on informality was the enormous social program decreed by custom for White House residents. The formal entertaining season, which ran from December until Lent, normally included five State dinners and five State receptions. In addition, there were dozens of receptions that Eleanor was required to hold for patriotic organizations and women's groups, at some of which she shook 5,000 hands and served oceans of tea and coffee.

There was little levity at the formal receptions because of the strain her husband was under while standing and shaking hands. On one occasion Franklin was overheard whispering to Eleanor, "I can't stand it another minute. Another minute, I tell you."

"It will be over soon," she said encouragingly. "Just hold on a little longer."

Only when something untoward occurred did Franklin find the receptions amusing. There was one where a sedate, aloof-looking woman lost her petticoat as she came down the line toward him and Eleanor. "What do you think she will do?" he smiled and whispered to Eleanor. The woman's face had turned blank. Hesitating only a moment, she left her undergarment behind her on the floor and proceeded ahead. Succeeding handshakers had to step around the garment, which remained where it had fallen until a servant scooped it up after the last guest had passed by.

Nor were the formal dinner parties much fun, though they were important to the guests. The table was always arranged in horseshoe design with Franklin at the outer center because protocol demanded that no one sit with his back to the President. Eleanor's place at the table was directly opposite her husband. With guests seated according to their official status in political life, problems sometimes arose. Once when Sara Roosevelt was invited to a formal dinner, Eleanor feigned a headache and did not attend. Her reason was a generous one. With her absence, Sara took her place at the table and sat across from her son. Had Eleanor showed up, Sara would have been forced to take a seat far below the salt.

Though he was gregarious, Franklin considered the social season a terrible bore. Once he wrote to Eleanor, "Another year let's cut it out and take a trip to Samoa and Hawaii instead!" Vice President Garner shared his view. Accustomed to going to bed with the birds, he sought out Eleanor and Franklin one time. "I'll tell you what I'll do, Cap'n," he told Franklin. "If it's all right with you, I'll skip that dinner I have to give for you."

"Fine!" Franklin beamed. "I like your idea so much that if it's all right with you, too, I'll cancel my dinner for you."

When they shook hands on their bargain, Garner sighed happily, "That makes two of the eleven eliminated."

Garner had a notorious influence on some of Eleanor's dinner guests. On one occasion she had invited Felix Frankfurter to dinner. Frankfurter, who was still teaching at Harvard at the time, stopped at the Capitol to pay his respects to Garner before going to the White House. Garner was quick to nag him into accepting a drink of his famous white mule likker. "What do you say we strike a blow for liberty?" he exhorted the prim jurist. After some embarrassing coaxing, Frankfurter took a deep breath and replied, "I have heard of your famous blows for liberty, Mr. Vice President, and I would be proud to join you." As it turned out, more than one blow for liberty was struck.

The next morning when Franklin's Cabinet meeting ended, Eleanor was waiting outside the room for Garner. "Oh, Mr. Vice President! What did you do to Felix?" she scolded him.

With thousands of hands to shake at her numerous receptions, it was obvious to Eleanor that unless she learned the proper technique, her hand would swell up like a pumpkin and she would fall in exhaustion. Her successful formula was simple: "Don't let the line stop. Grasp the proffered hand first and draw her past you as you say, 'How do you do.' Stop every thousand hands and have a drink of water." Another important ingredient: "One has to think kindly in order to be able to keep the right attitude toward people who pass by and make them feel welcome."

Yet despite these cautions there were times when the faces before her blurred. One time "I walked into the dining room," she recalled, "after the receiving line was over and saw two old friends. I said, 'Where did you come from?' They told me they had gone through the line and I had shaken hands warmly."

So the White House largely through Eleanor's personality became, as H. G. Wells put it, "cool, orderly and unhurried." But it never became the home of her own that Eleanor had sought since childhood. It was chiefly the harboring point for Franklin, who, as she saw it, spent his days "seeing one long succession of people." To the rest of the family, it was chiefly an intrusion on their privacy and had a devastating effect on their relations with their parents. "We laugh about it a great deal," she wrote for *The New York Times* in April, 1933. "It is rare for us to have an evening alone. We laugh when I formally make an appointment for the children to see their father at given hours when something comes up which really must be discussed and decided. But it is not as much a laughing matter as we make it out to be."

The price of being the son of the nation's leading political figure ran high. On an occasion when one of her boys had a daytime appointment with Franklin, her husband was heavily involved with a vexing political matter. Her son started to explain the problem that he wanted Franklin's guidance on, only to note that his father was reading a document as he spoke. "Did you hear me, Pop?" he asked after a while.

"Why, yes," Franklin assured him absently. Then in the midst of his son's talking, he handed the boy the document and told him, "This is a most important document. I should like to have your opinion on it."

Her son came to her shortly afterward, his face the picture of dejection. "Never again will I try to talk to Father about anything personal."

"Now, now," Eleanor tried to soften his hurt, "you just picked the wrong moment to talk to him. Besides, he was paying you a great compliment in asking your opinion on a matter of importance to the country."

Her son, however, was not assured.

Another time when her son Elliott contemplated a remarriage soon after his second divorce, Franklin was as anxious as she was to prevent him from taking this course without further long thought. "Telephone him and talk him out of it," Franklin told her, late one evening.

"I returned to Franklin's study expecting to find him breathlessly awaiting the results of my conversation," she confessed. "Instead I found him deeply engrossed in going over a letter. . . . When he looked up, I told him that I had been entirely unsuccessful. His face clouded for a moment, and then he said, 'Well, we cannot help it. Do you want to hear my first peace note to the nations?'"

Although Franklin's personal relationship with his children was lost, he was not immune to their problems. "Franklin suffered when things went wrong with the family," Eleanor said, "though these personal things were quickly swallowed up in the much more important things that touched the nation as a whole." As for herself, she once wrote to a cousin, "I have often differed with my children. I have always tried to recognize their motives which lay behind what they said or did."

Franklin, Jr.'s fast driving did not abate when his father became President. According to the White House housekeeper, he delighted in using the mansion's driveway as a raceway. When he went to Spain, a report came back to Eleanor that he had jumped into a bull ring and fought a bull. John, her quiet son, gained international notoriety a few years after his parents became the nation's first family. On a trip abroad, he doused the mayor of Cannes with champagne and hit him with a bouquet of flowers.

Despite the problems with their children, both Eleanor and Franklin tolerated no mention of them by outsiders. Life was too short, and besides, no one was without faults, as the trite expression went. Moreover, most times when the family was together, the central theme was fun and the enjoyment of the moment. "We made it a family practice to look for funny incidents to make Franklin laugh," said Eleanor. Their offspring were considered by them to be children no matter how old they grew. When nineteen-year-old Franklin, Jr., and a friend went down south to visit Franklin on vacation in November, 1933, she wired her husband, "I hope you will see that they go to bed by ten and have plenty of sunshine."

So far as the relationship between Eleanor and Franklin was concerned, it was warm and close. On her wedding anniversary in March, 1933, Franklin sent her a check with the following letter:

Dearest Babs:

After a fruitless week of thinking and lying awake to find whether you need or want undies, dresses, shoes, sheets, towels, rouge, soup plates, candy, flowers, lamps, relaxation pills, whisky, beer, etchings or caviar

I GIVE UP

!

And yet I know you lack some necessity of life—so go to it with my love and many happy returns of the day!

FDR

On her birthday he wrote her:

For Eleanor
One inside of a coat!
I hope it keeps you warm, but it ain't much of a present!
Very much love.

FDR

Chapter Twenty-Three

ONLY TWO DAYS after she moved into the White House Eleanor Roosevelt's avowed intention to remain in the background was swept aside.

Louis Howe was the culprit. Far from recovering from the rigors of his horrendous efforts to get Franklin into the White House, he was already plotting Franklin's re-election in 1936. And as he thought about corralling the winning electoral count four years in advance, the power of women voters loomed large in his mind.

"You must hold regular press conferences for women reporters," he wheezed pitifully to Eleanor, while she hung another of Franklin's favorite sea prints on the wall. "You know that half the people in this country are women and they'd be much interested in your opinions and what you do."

Mrs. Hoover had had an understanding with Washington correspondents that no one was ever to quote her. Other First Ladies before her had steered clear of any public attention, too. But Louie brushed aside such tradition as encrusted and outmoded nonsense. "Besides," he told her, "I heard that all those newspaper ladies are going to lose their jobs because hard-pressed publishers are firing reporters left and right. Those girls are most expendable unless you do something about it."

In the end she agreed.

While the bank holiday gripped the nation during the worrisome morning of March sixth, Eleanor called thirty-five women reporters into the Red Room on the first floor of the White House. Even though she passed out a large box of candy to put them at ease, she herself stood before them "with fear and trembling." It was a pioneering venture for all of them, she quaked. But in no way was it to be a competitor of the President's press conference. "I will answer no political questions," she announced. "Those who ask them will be barred from the press conference."

Hard-bitten Washington newsmen howled with amusement when they found out about her press conference. "Did she tell you what color shoes she is going to wear next Thursday?" they taunted one of the women who covered her conference. "What kind of crackers is she going to serve with soup for lunch?"

However, there was little reason for them to be amused for long. It was true that the first several press conferences did go badly. They were poorly organized. Most of the women were at a loss for decent questions. A few made it their obnoxious duty to protect her whenever a reply of hers made sense. With little show of propriety, they would pop out of their seats with— "Don't you want your reply to be off the record, Mrs. Roosevelt?"

As she gained experience, Eleanor lost her stage fright. She also attended some of Franklin's press conferences to see how he did it. At one of his conferences, newsmen watched her sitting alongside him and knitting a blue sock. At another she came with her dog Meggie and left him outside the door, only to have him spoil the press conference with his lonesome howling.

After a while, she spoke easily at her own press conferences. The reporters in turn grew bolder in their questioning. The mask of pious platitudes dropped away and they began asking about such matters as the divorces in her family and what she thought about various government activities and policies. In reply she spoke with refreshing candor. Sometimes when she did not know the answer, she excused herself momentarily, and called Franklin at his desk for an answer to give to her girls.

The newspaper ladies and Eleanor Roosevelt came in time to form an enthusiastic student-teacher relationship. As a matter of fact, just as she had taken her teen-agers at Todhunter through the local and state political jungles of New York, she did likewise for her press conference girls. On one occasion she led them from the White House to examine a controversial government housing project. Another time they examined together the Agriculture Department's research center at Beltsville, Maryland, only to have some gulp with uneasiness when she had them look into a microscope at the heart of a cockroach.

It was to be expected that an extemporaneous weekly freewheeling press conference would have its share of indirect questions aimed at learning about Franklin's policies and drawing-board programs. As she groped through her early conferences, Louis Howe coached her on how to recognize such questions and how to offer a vague but pleasant reply in return. "Usually I was able to detect the implications of the question and avoid any direct answer," she said with pleasure. "Louis Howe had trained me well."

The press conference was just a starter for Louie, though it brought Eleanor immediate and continuing attention throughout the country. In March, 1933 the second Bonus Army of unemployed veterans marched on Washington. Franklin wanted no recurrence of the brutal army routing of the first Bonus Army from Washington under President Hoover the previous summer.

More than 20,000 had come the first time and about 11,000 the second time. It was true that a vocal minority in both groups were Communists, but the vast majority were ordinary Americans who had lost their jobs and wanted a tiding-over bonus until they found another. When the first Bonus Army came to Washington in 1932, it had settled itself in temporary government buildings on Pennsylvania Avenue and in squalid shacks along the Anacostia River in southeast Washington. Failing to win a money handout from Congress and having nowhere to go, the army stayed on in Washington and frightened President Hoover. On July 28, after he gave them notice to vacate and leave town, they refused to permit a government crew to demolish their makeshift residence on Pennsylvania Avenue. In a tear-gas battle that ensued, one man was killed and several were injured.

It was at this point that President Hoover had ordered his Secretary of War Patrick J. Hurley to evict the Bonus Army. Hurley, with alacrity, ordered the Army's Chief of Staff to "surround the affected area and clear it without delay." What had followed was a weird scene of tanks lumbering down Pennsylvania Avenue and soldiers with machine guns and fixed bayonets coming behind. With soldierly action they cleared the Pennsylvania Avenue section, set the shacks on fire and chased the Bonus Army all the way to Anacostia Flats. Here the cavalry rode roughshod over the routed veterans, burned out their filthy shacks and drove them out with tear gas. Over fifty people were injured and a baby was killed. The nation cried shame.

When the second Bonus Army made its appearance in Washington just as Franklin took office, he told Louis Howe to handle the problem and make sure there was no mistreatment of the World War I veterans. Louie immediately arranged shelter and food for them at Fort Hunt, in nearby Virginia. He also arranged to hold meetings with the bonus leaders in a government auditorium.

However, he made little headway with them until one day when he feigned weariness and asked Eleanor to take him for a ride. As they started out on what she thought was an aimless ride, he directed her casually to the Bonus Army camp just off Potomac Drive. When they came there, he requested her to turn off the ignition.

[204]

"Louis, what is this place and what are we going to do here?" she asked.

"It's the Bonus Army," he told her. "I want you to go into their camp. Talk to the boys. Make a tour of the place. See what they're eating and find out how they are getting along. And above all, be sure to tell them that Franklin sent you."

"But aren't you coming with me?" she stammered.

He gave her a little push out the door. "No," he barked, "I'm going to take a nap. Now get going in there and you're not to miss a thing."

She described what followed. "Very hesitatingly I got out and walked over to where I saw a line-up of men waiting for food. They looked at me curiously and one of them asked me my name and what I wanted." Word spread like wildfire that the President's wife had come to pay them a call and look into their welfare.

She went through the camp, inspected their miserable quarters and ate with them in their big eating hall. She also gave them a friendly speech and the cheers resounded when she led them in singing the old songs of World War I. First it was "Tipperary" and then it was "There's a Long, Long Trail." After she listened to their various complaints, they followed her through the mud to her car, which still contained the sleeping Howe. The noise of their cheering woke him up. "On the way back I answered every question that he put to me."

When she returned to the White House, Secret Service men confronted her in anger. "Don't you realize how dangerous a thing you did? They might have done something harmful to you and we would have been at fault. You should have had protection."

"I did," she told them. "Mr. Howe came along to protect me."

The upshot of her visit was that the leaders of the Bonus Army dropped the annoying threats they had made previously. Docilely they accepted government free fare home. Many took advantage of Louie's offer to put them into CCC camps. The threat of any unpleasantness vanished.

Louis Howe pushed her on to further activities, though by now she needed no great urging. Acting as her literary agent, he obtained several assignments for her to write magazine articles. She also undertook a monthly question-and-answer page for the *Woman's Home Companion,* a weekly column for a news syndicate on life in the White House and a regular assignment as a radio broadcaster for a commercial sponsor. In all these ways, she focused enormous public attention on the activities of her husband's administration. In a gentle motherly fashion, she made Franklin's activities personal and tied a bond between him and the average citizen.

She was also acquiring a reputation as a fighter. Only a week after she was in the White House, she went on a tour of Washington's wretched alley-dwelling slums with octogenarian Mrs. Archibald Hopkins. Mrs. Hopkins, a sprightly and angry lady who had known every President since Lincoln, had spent thirty years in a continual effort to end this blight in the nation's capital. Sixty per cent of the city's crime and an enormous percentage of its contagious diseases centered there. On her deathbed the first Mrs. Wilson, who knew Mrs. Hopkins well, had voiced a last gasping plea for aid to alley dwellers. But nothing came of her request.

During her tour with Mrs. Hopkins, Eleanor grew increasingly angry with the human misery she saw. It became her duty to do something to rectify matters. Without delay she rushed Cabinet wives through the ruins, with the hope that they would join her in the necessary fight. When none did, she invaded the office of Franklin's uncle, Frederic A. Delano, who headed the National Capital Park and Planning Commission. Sweating and fuming simultaneously, he pointed out the difficulties in winning congressional approval for the action she had in mind.

But little did he realize how persistent she could be. Under the glare of national publicity through her press conferences, talks and writings, plus her acquaintance with many key congressmen, her Alley Dwelling Act passed in 1934. Unfortunately, however, she gained little beyond congressional recognition of the problem. When Congress had to appropriate money to put the program into effect, the $3,000,000 revolving fund she wanted turned into a straight appropriation of only a half-million dollars. But she eased some of the blow by talking Franklin into giving the newly created Alley Dwelling Authority $365,000 from his emergency public works funds. This provided far less than half the loaf she wanted. However, it was still sufficient to get the program under way.

When Franklin's Civilian Conservation Corps (CCC) passed Congress in early April, 1933, Eleanor was disappointed that the act provided no aid for unemployed young girls. When she beseeched Franklin with the demand that female CCC camps in the forests be established if only to take the 200,000 wandering homeless girls off the roads and freight trains, he showed no interest. "That isn't the way to handle that problem," he argued.

Nevertheless, she persisted. Finally, in June, 1933, Camp Tera on

Bear Mountain, New York, was established as a test for her optimism. She gave the camp $3,000 cash and the government provided additional funds. The girls at Tera proved listless and uninterested in the gardening activities from the start. When they left at the rate of ten or more a week, she realized that girls in a group lacked the spirit of boys. Eventually Camp Tera was abandoned, though her interest in the plight of unemployed girls never abated. Instead, she reverted to her old practice of personal aid to individual girls. For instance, in 1933, she handed a check for $3,600 to her old friend, Rose Schneiderman, of the Women's Trade Union League. It was the money she had earned from radio broadcasts during the months before she came to Washington.

Rose was flabbergasted at this gift. "Don't tell anyone about it," Eleanor warned her. "But I want you to spend it at the rate of $300 a week for twelve weeks. Give it to girls who need help to tide them over until they get another job." Rose was still speechless when she left.

Now that she was so much in the news and so much involved in government activities, mail for her began pouring into the White House in enormous quantities. She was again a court of last resort, a woman who would understand the problems of women and mothers and a one-woman charity organization and job finder. In nine months in 1933 she received more than 300,000 letters. About 60 per cent asked for money, jobs or her help in interceding for the writers with government agencies. She kept no record of the individuals she helped, but the total ran into several hundred for 1933 alone. She sent a nine-year-old boy a banjo upon receipt of his pathetic letter. At the slightest provocation, she mailed checks all over the country. Tommy, her secretary, often accused her of being too softhearted.

One time she sent a package of food to a woman who said that she and her daughter were starving. The woman would not accept the food when it arrived. "I want money," she scolded Mrs. Roosevelt. An old rich friend asked her to take time from her other activities and send him a general houseman. Preposterous as his request was, she sent one to him. The new houseman had not been on the job long before he quit, and a dozen angry letters peppered the White House— "When do I get a houseman?"

Some of the desperate letters were funny. One read: "I have already wrote the President and I don't hear from you. I will write to Uncle Sam and tell him about you both." Another letter requested her to act as errand girl: "Please send me my wife's form to fill out." Still another requested that she "please find out for certain if my husband is dead, as the man I'm living with won't eat or do anything until he noes for sure."

As time went on, a fairly large share of her mail dealt with praise or condemnation of her activities. Some of the scurrilous mail came from those who shrieked that she was a traitor to her class. This type of class-traitor letter amused her and Franklin, for Franklin believed his job to be a combination of saving basic American traditions while combating the terrible depression.

"If a disagreeing letter rang true I answered it," she said. "I told them I was sorry they felt the way they did, but that I realized perfectly they had a right to their own opinions. But if I did not do what I thought was the right thing to do, I would not be satisfied with myself."

Eleanor made it a practice at breakfast to read the letters rebuking her. This would ordinarily take a strong stomach because so many of these letters were a violent outpouring of spleen. One time she was reading these letters aloud to Ed Flynn, Franklin's political lieutenant in New York. When she came to the postscript of one, she laughed uproariously. For the last scribbled line read: "Where the hell do you buy your hats?"

There was still another phase of her life that began in early 1933. During that spring she went off on a motor trip to Canada and Maine with Lorena Hickok, an Associated Press reporter. She considered the trip a vacation, but when she returned Franklin questioned her closely on what she had seen. It was reminiscent of the inspections she had made for him of New York State institutions. "What did the fishermen eat? How did they live? What were the farms like? What type of education was available?"

All these questions had a purpose. For he wanted many phases of life investigated firsthand around the country, and there was no one else other than Eleanor who he believed would give him a true picture.

He sent her that summer to West Virginia to investigate conditions in the mining area. The Quakers had reported horrible poverty there and he wanted this verified. On that first trip to West Virginia, with Clarence Pickett of the American Friends Service Committee as her guide, the living conditions she saw revolted her. She was still not well known enough to be recognized as the President's wife. Down mine shafts she went in miner's regalia to see how they worked and in miners' homes she looked into the corners to note how poorly they fared. It was not until much later that she was recognized by the miners and was made the subject of a cartoon showing two miners in a shaft who looked up and exclaimed, "Here comes Mrs. Roosevelt!"

"Watch the people's faces," Franklin had ordered her. "Look at the condition of their clothes on the wash lines. You can tell a lot from that."

The worst spot was along Scott's Run, not far from Morgantown. Here in the palmy years, bituminous coal miners earned $25 a day. But with the depression the mines started closing and great unemployment developed. The miners, with no place to move and with no money to move, stayed on with great suffering. "There were children," Eleanor told Franklin upon her return, "who did not know what it was to sit down at a table and eat a proper meal." The children slept on rags on the floor, and the cracker-box company houses were so permeated with coal dust that one felt as though "it would be impossible to get them or the people clean."

She proposed that a model subsistence homestead project be established. "What else?" asked Franklin. She had clinics and schools and small factories in mind. These could be done privately. She could interest socially conscious rich friends in such projects, and she herself could go out on lecture tours and turn over her fees to the Quakers.

She took many of her wealthy friends to the mine fields. With Mrs. Leonard Elmhurst, she established a children's clinic. Bernard Baruch helped her to establish a school. One wealthy New Yorker on going through a house along Scott's Run emerged, pale and sick to his stomach. "I will give you any money you want," he said weakly. "But please do not ask me to go into any more houses. I feel contaminated and it makes me really ill." One time she took a wealthy heiress on a hike along the 12-mile hollow of sulphur-colored Scott's Run. In the blazing heat from eight A.M. until eleven P.M., she led her from shanty to shanty. When they went to bed that night, the girl wanted to move out of her comfortable first-floor room. "I'm afraid someone will come in and kidnap me. I'd like to sleep on the second floor," she begged Eleanor.

"All right, you can," Eleanor told her.

"But I must have a man sleep near where I could call him if anything happened," she went on.

"All right," Eleanor told her. She asked a Quaker gentleman to sleep in a room close by. He was not the sort who could have grappled with a kidnaper. "I wondered what he would do," she laughed, "if someone did come to kidnap her."

There was no stopping Eleanor Roosevelt once she got started on anything. She visualized a model community for the "stranded" West Virginia miners close to Morgantown. A 1,200-acre farm owned by Mr. Richard M. Arthur sixteen miles southeast of Morgantown looked ideal for the purpose. The people could be taken off relief by helping to build their own homes and they would be given enough land so they could grow their own food. Then small industries could be introduced to give the miners regular employment.

Franklin gave her permission to use some of the money appropriated under the NRA. Secretary Ickes of the Department of Interior would buy the land and run the project. Louis Howe, who showed great enthusiasm, would buy the houses and she would be in charge of putting people into the houses. Arthurdale, as the subsistence homestead project was called, would serve as a shining example for all future subsistence projects.

In theory, Arthurdale looked perfect. But in practice it proved a fiasco. Eleanor had a great deal to learn about government mismanagement, duplication and carelessness with taxpayers' money. Louis Howe pulled the first blunder from which Arthurdale never recovered. In his haste to get the project under way, he bought 50 prefabricated summer cottages from a New England factory at what he considered an economic cost of only $50,000. When they arrived, they didn't fit the foundations that had already been laid. All had to be taken apart and then rebuilt.

Eleanor was sickened by this blunder, for the work at Arthurdale was already receiving wide national newspaper coverage. The place was soon overrun with draftsmen, architects and a mass of government employees who had little idea what they were supposed to do except to override each other's orders. Error followed upon error. The wells produced contaminated water. The houses were without storage basements and weren't winterized, and this had to be done as an afterthought. Everything was haste and confusion and waste. Someone got the bright idea of bringing religion to the community, and a church miles away was torn down and later reassembled at Arthurdale.

It was her idea to set the houses on the high land and use the low-lying fertile soil for a community garden. Louie Howe was afraid that the public would consider this too radical. "If you aren't called a Communist before the President leaves the White House," he told her, "we'll all be lucky." Ickes settled the issue by insisting that small separate plots be set up and each house be delivered to its occupants with a cow. Eleanor saw later that her own hope of a co-operative community was the last thought the stranded miners had on their minds. According to her comment to a reporter, "They wanted cows tied to their back fences. They trusted nobody, not even themselves. They had an eye out all the time to see who was going to cheat them next."

It was obvious that the ballyhooed Eden would do her reputation little good, even though little of the fault was hers. Government publicity blurbs announced that the model community would be ready for occupancy by Thanksgiving of 1933. Each family would sit down to its own turkey in its immaculate, cheap house. By the time the first family moved into Arthurdale late in 1934, the individual cost per house ran higher than $12,000. Secretary Ickes, who was the chief culprit along with Louie Howe, tried ungentlemanly to shift the blame over to Eleanor. He claimed that she took to the project "a temperamental architect from New York who spent money lavishly and just about broke down the morale of the staff." He also charged that when he overruled some of the wastrels, they ran to her and she got Franklin to overrule him.

Nor did her troubles end with Ickes. When it came time to think of an industry to support Arthurdale, she went to bat for a congressional appropriation to establish a factory there to produce post-office boxes. Unfortunately, a manufacturer in Indiana had the monopolistic government contract on post-office boxes and he went to his congressman charging that the free-enterprise system was being subverted. Angry speeches from the well of the House of Representatives now denounced her and the appropriation fell through. This was followed by attacks on Arthurdale as a communistically conceived project. This charge was mouthed by Dr. William A. Wirt of Gary, Indiana, who had come to Washington for a short while, and made it his business afterward to label the Roosevelt administration as reddish in hue. Franklin, he said, was a dupe of the Communists, the Kerensky of the coming Red Revolution in America.

Newspapers lapped up everything Wirt had to say about Arthurdale and Eleanor. Little print space was given to her indignant replies. All this was grist for blind Senator Tom Schall of Minnesota, who now took the lead in attacking her. Besides making the usual charges against Arthurdale, within the safety of his senatorial immunity, he claimed on the Senate floor that she was selling autographed suites of Val-Kill furniture to hotels around the country. Blazing angry, she called him up and gave him unshirted hell and asked him to come to the White House for a conference. Schall promised to do so, but he did not show up. Instead, he uttered a further blast at her and charged that she was making a million dollars a year off Val-Kill reproductions. Despite the enormity of his falsehoods, when Eleanor heard that Schall's daughter wanted to get into the entertainment field, she called several of her friends to aid the girl.

Arthurdale made Eleanor the most controversial woman in the country. It spelled attacks of great savagery that were not to abate as long as she was in the White House. Six years afterward, a resettlement expert claimed that Arthurdale was "valuable mostly as showing what not to do." A few dozen other subsistence housing projects went up throughout the country after Arthurdale was in operation. Eleanor played a large part in getting those up, too. She justified all of them, despite their wasteful construction cost. She also continued to give all her earnings from her writing, speaking and broadcasting to the Quakers who had been the first to show her the stranded miners of West Virginia. "I have always felt," she once said, "that many human beings who might have cost us thousands of dollars in tuberculosis sanitariums, insane asylums and jails were restored to usefulness and given confidence in themselves."

The West Virginia mining region was only the first of a long series of places to which Franklin sent his wife. In the spring of 1934, he asked her to investigate conditions in Puerto Rico and the Virgin Islands. She had many things planned for that spring, but he insisted and she went. "People there work for the sugar companies on a season basis in Puerto Rico," he told her. "Between seasons they practically starve. I want them to know that I am interested in their welfare. If you go there, your presence will show the people that I am interested."

Puerto Rico was even more miserable than Scott's Run. Girls from her press conference accompanied her to publicize her findings. Down the slum streets they chased after her on the precarious duckboards flung over piling through which water squirted up at every step. Carrying her chocolate-colored petit-point knitting bag under an arm, she walked through hundreds of foul-smelling hovels and questioned everyone she met along the way. There was no plumbing or electricity. Women sat in the midst of the stench of their filthy surroundings doing embroidery piecework. "I am sure if the women of the United States knew the conditions under which those handkerchiefs, nightgowns and slips were embroidered they would want to boil them before putting them on or using them," she said. When she drove, she made certain her car did not have "telltale license plates" so she could act freely.

Unable to keep up with her running pace, the newsgirls collapsed in a heap one day. Rather than miss seeing some of the horrors that she planned for the afternoon, they got her to agree to go nowhere until they woke up from a short nap. It was several hours later when they woke up, only to find her uneasy and guilty for having missed more investigations that day. On another occasion, inclement weather held her at an airport. No one was there except the owner of the airport and a dog. She immediately took both for a long walk around the field. One of the reporters watched them go off and remarked, "She can't investigate conditions for children right now, so the dog has to do." Another time after a rugged day, they watched unbelievingly as she skipped rope at a bathing beach.

She also went to the Virgin Islands where Governor Paul Pearson, the father of the columnist Drew Pearson, was undergoing serious attack, primarily because he was a Republican. The rum factory there which was the island's chief business was being run inefficiently, and though she found the subject of alcohol revolting, she discussed with him the possibilities of improving the management of the rum industry. Franklin had asked her to investigate whether this would "bring in enough dollars to fight illiteracy, illegitimacy and poverty."

Upon her return, she tried to save Pearson's job, a plum Secretary Ickes wanted for one of his own men. She failed in this effort, though she did well regarding the strengthening of the Puerto Rican economy, then in its third generation of depression. "On my return," she recalled, "I begged my husband to send down some labor people and industrialists to look over the situation." Franklin did as she suggested, but it was many years before the first tangible improvements came in that island's economy.

After this second investigatory trip for Franklin, Eleanor found herself traveling hither and yon for him. He wanted to know about the Dust Bowl, about labor conditions in the Midwest, about minority groups in different parts of the country. Often he interrupted one of his Department heads at Cabinet meetings with— "My Missus told me this." When she got back from one of her trips, he would have her come to his office and he would say, "Well, Ma, what is the story?"

"My eyes," he referred to her proudly, though the Secret Service was enraged by her flying and driving wherever she desired. Driving her own car was one of the issues that riled the Secret Service. When she refused to permit the Secret Service to guard her or have an agent ride with her, Edward Starling, chief of the Secret Service, stormed into Louis Howe's office one morning. Louis was unconcerned with Starling's plea that he talk once more with Eleanor about the necessity of having Secret Service protection. "If she doesn't want the company of your men," Louis told him, "she isn't going to change her mind if I talk to her."

Starling studied him coldly a moment. Finally he pulled a gun from his pocket and threw it on Louie's desk. "Well, all right," he said resignedly, "if Mrs. Roosevelt is going to drive around the country alone, at least ask her to carry this in the car."

[213]

Not only did Eleanor agree to carry the gun, but she also became an expert marksman, to the knee-slapping laughter of Franklin. The revolver frightened her at first, but so had speaking in public. After an enormous amount of practice she finally hit the edge of a target. Once she did this, she improved steadily. On one occasion, the motherly First Lady paid a visit to Clinton Prison at Dannemora, New York. "Where's the pistol range?" she inquired. Later she wrote back to Washington, "I am making as many as four bull's-eyes out of six shots."

The gun did have many handicaps. One time the official of a city where she was going threatened to arrest her when she arrived because the local law forbade firearms. In great agitation, her son James called her and warned her of the consequences. After this the Secret Service provided her with an official-looking tin badge "which entitled me to have a gun as part of my luggage." Another time when her gun needed repair, she had her secretary take it to a shop in New York. Suspicious when the young woman could not produce the gun's license, the shop owner called the police, who came running for the arrest. Only a long explanation by Mrs. Roosevelt saved both her secretary and the gun. On still another occasion, a young man came to Hyde Park for a visit. Late at night as he cut across her lawn, he suddenly remembered that she kept her gun in her room. Hurriedly he beat a retreat lest he waken her and offer her a pot shot at him. "I have never used it on a human being," she laughed the next morning when he told her his experience.

Even though she successfully staved off the Secret Service, she had less success with local police. In Little Rock one time, the mayor gave orders to two burly motorcycle cops to tail her wherever she went. That morning when she had her hair shampooed in a beauty parlor, they sat among the waiting customers and never let their eyes wander off her. Another time in Detroit when she opened her hotel room door to mail some letters, three men popped out of the room next door. "Is anything wrong, Mrs. Roosevelt?" they asked.

Dashing about the country as she did, except for such minor encumbrances, Eleanor gained an enormous measure of freedom from White House officialness. "It is easy in Washington to think that Washington is the country," she said, "and forget that it is a small place." Her trips continually pointed this out to her.

She could forget at times, too, that she was First Lady. She easily fell into her natural role of a woman who pushed steadily for increased political participation of women in politics. Wherever she traveled she exhorted women to take advantage of women's suffrage and make their strong voice felt. Only one of her friends had come to Congress and she believed more should run for office. The one instance was her brides-maid, Isabella Selmes, who had married Bob Ferguson, the young man who had escorted Eleanor attentively during her trying debutante period. After Bob died, Isabella remarried and came to Congress in October, 1933 as Representative Greenway of Arizona. Unfortunately, Isabella, the loveliest member of the House, was a bit of an exhibitionist. She made Washington headlines not by her legislative activities but because she hired a taxicab and a driver for full-time duty. This was not what Eleanor had in mind for a woman legislator. Nor was it very gratifying to read in the Washington *Post* that Isabella had made news again by roller-skating from the House Office Building through the underground tunnel to the Capitol a block away.

Franklin refused to differentiate between women and men voters. On the several occasions that Eleanor asked him to speak to women's groups he turned her down flatly each time. That Congress needed more women he considered of minute significance. Isabella Greenway he regarded highly as a woman and that was that.

But that was not that to Eleanor. When Caroline O'Day, her friend since the early twenties, decided to run for Congress from New York in 1934, Eleanor promised her every assistance. It had been Caroline, the transplanted Southern belle, always in white or gray or black and "chic with fascinating shoe buckles," who had beaten the hard path with Eleanor to talk local Democrats into permitting women to participate in the political backstage. Many a time they had laughed about the man who hid in his house and refused to talk to them until they sat and waited on his porch several hours. Now, wonder upon wonder, at the New York State Democratic Convention in September, 1934, Caroline defeated that very man, Congressman John Fitzgibbons, for the nomination for Representative-at-Large from New York.

Eleanor was to learn firsthand about women in politics. Caroline had two women opponents in that campaign: Natalie Couch, a Republican; and Dorothy Frooks of the Law Preservation party. Instead of concentrating on Mrs. O'Day, Miss Couch spoke as though Eleanor were her opponent and lambasted her and Franklin unmercifully. She called Eleanor's participation in Caroline's campaign a cheap attempt to use White House influence. Louis Howe was aghast at her vituperation. At Buffalo, Eleanor and Miss Couch appeared on the same platform. In a rabid speech, Miss Couch declared to the accompaniment of enormous booing from their female audience that in only a year and a half's time the United States had ceased being a republic. When Eleanor's time to speak came, she spent much of it rebuking the booers.

Then Miss Frooks was heard from. She deluged Eleanor with telegrams and letters demanding that she debate with her. She made sure that copies of each of her epistles reached the newspapers. Among her charges was a bitter one—that Eleanor was speaking for Caroline "to help your friend and the financier of your furniture factory."

Eleanor agreed to debate with her, but she pointed out one significant fact about Miss Frooks. She told her press conference that the previous July Miss Frooks had written her for her help in winning the Democratic nomination.

The debate, which was to take place at the O'Day campaign dinner, never came off because the chairlady would not permit it. Nevertheless, Miss Frooks showed up at the dinner for Caroline. In the hubbub when she was recognized, Miss Frooks was asked not to create a scene and mar the affair. When she demanded that Eleanor answer certain of her questions, Eleanor agreed to do so after she finished speaking.

Yet when Eleanor finished speaking, Miss Frooks did not rise to ask her questions. Afterward, she charged that she had not been given an opportunity to do so, and she told reporters, "Will they be twins in Congress? Perhaps it will be a ventriloquist's act, with Mrs. O'Day sitting as the dummy."

Eleanor was glad when Caroline won handily her seat in the House of Representatives in the November election. But her experience taught her about women in politics. They could be much rougher than men, an unpleasant truth that made her refrain from taking a front-line part in a local political campaign as long as she was in the White House.

Chapter Twenty-Four

FRANKLIN'S LEGISLATIVE PROGRAM roared on. In 1935 came more alphabet agencies: Export-Import Bank (EIB), Securities and Exchange Commission (SEC), National Labor Relations Board (NLRB), Resettlement Administration (RA), Social Security Board (SSB), and the Works Progress Administration (WPA). One critic yelled, "The Roosevelts are everywhere: they are in our food; they are in our hair. The nation is being run to blazes in the name of Roosevelt."

But Franklin and Eleanor were fashioning a new political and moral leadership for the nation to replace the characterless prestige of the fallen rich. It was a team proposition. Where Franklin made available the economic power of government, Eleanor offered her concern for the economic, social and racial underdogs.

For instance, it was Franklin who won far-reaching legislation, such as the National Recovery Act (NRA) with its self-patrolled industrial codes of production, price fixing, and raised labor standards. But it was Eleanor who gave the NRA its heart. She spoke throughout the country on its meaning to the individual. She put over its crucial garment-labeling campaign by heading the advisory committee for this purpose and inserting the first labels in her NRA-made clothes. It was also she who won equal pay for women in industries under NRA when even the most zealous feminists considered the attainment of this status impossible. Perhaps with naïveté, she invited NRA's administrator, General Hugh "Iron Pants" Johnson, to lunch one day. Gruff and overbearing, he came reluctantly. While he smiled at her proposal at first, she talked longer and more passionately than he. "But the NRA codes have set lower minimums for women," he sweated, "because that's always been the American pattern."

"Well, then it's about time you changed it," she told him.

By the time he left, her barrage had hit its mark. Shortly afterward, women workers found themselves on the same pay scale as men.

She was all over Franklin's administration to clarify the details of government action in terms of her underdog principles. When she found that the Department of Agriculture was serious about plowing under cotton and slaughtering pigs in order to raise farm income by eliminating surpluses, she ran to Franklin in high indignation. "With so many people hungry and in rags," she argued, "those surpluses should be given to the poor."

"But don't you realize," he explained, "that what you want will upset Henry Wallace's program?"

"But you have to think about those people, too," she replied.

Shortly afterward, she upset Henry Wallace by telephoning him and pleading that he send some of the pigs to West Virginia miners. He sputtered in vain. Finally, to end her one-woman campaign, Franklin established the Federal Surplus Commodity Corporation. Its task was to purchase farm surpluses and give them to relief agencies for distribution to the poor. From this the Food Stamp Plan, whereby the poor could buy food in regular stores for lower prices, came into existence.

Jim Farley, who was now Postmaster General and chief dispenser of patronage, also suffered from the deluge. The czar of U. S. mail, who was trying to straighten out the airmail mess and modernize mail service, now found himself swamped with urgent letters from her. They came in the morning and they came in the afternoon, in a relentless flow. He was her chief outlet for those who wrote her for jobs. "Many of my letters are heartbreaking," she wrote. "But when I put my mind to it, I can usually think of some agency or friend who will try to help the people who write me, if I can't do so myself." From March, 1933 to September, 1935, she was instrumental in getting Farley to appoint 4,000 women in fourth-class post offices. A typical letter ran: "She seems desperately in need of a job."

However, jobs for others was not her only reason for keeping after Jim. When chain letters swamped the country, she demanded that he investigate. A short time later, the Post Office ruled them illegal. She also kept him informed of hate mongers who were sending their vile literature through the mails. He replied that he was keeping close tab on them. On other occasions, she sent him obscene ads that were being delivered by his mailmen, and he brought court cases against the senders. However, he would not yield to one of her more persistent pleas, which was to issue a stamp honoring women. She and her friend Lillian Wald worked hard on this matter. "Dear Jim," she wrote him to no avail, "can't you give the women a stamp sometime?" If she couldn't get a woman on a stamp, perhaps she could on a memorial. However, Gutzon Borglum rejected her proposal to add the head of a woman to his Black Hills, South Dakota, mountain sculpture of Washington, Jefferson, Lincoln and Uncle Ted.

Eleanor's relationship with the Post Office Department underwent strain one time when Mrs. Florence Kahn, Representative from California and the widow of Rep. Julius Kahn, asked her to help a man. Eleanor talked to him and then sent him over to one of Jim Farley's assistants. A few hours later the Post Office official called in agitation and demanded to know why she had sent him over an insane man. When Tommy, Eleanor's secretary, called Mrs. Kahn for an explanation, Mrs. Kahn laughed. "I thought he was insane, but the only way I could get rid of him was to send him to Mrs. Roosevelt."

While Jim Farley always treated Eleanor with great courtesy despite her deluge of requests, Harold Ickes was one Cabinet member who fumed openly at her calls, letters and memos. When he complained to Franklin about her many ideas for the Interior Department, he claimed that Franklin replied: "My Missus, unlike most women, hasn't any sense about money at all." On several instances, he threatened to resign, a practice Franklin likened to the desk officer who held onto his berth by volunteering incessantly for field duty.

A man who always pounded the table when he talked, Ickes pounded double when he heard from Eleanor Roosevelt. His experience with her over the Arthurdale Subsistence Homestead development convinced him that she wanted to make a laughingstock of him. He disliked her many memos to him about Indian privation, as though he were unconcerned about the welfare of American Indians. He thought her out of bounds when she tried to save the jobs of inherited White House handy men, a domain that belonged to him as administrator of public buildings in Washington. He saw red when she put in a good word for Republican Governor Pearson of the Virgin Islands whom he had marked for removal. He even went so far as to hold against her the fact that the chairs in the Green Room of the White House, where she and Franklin held concerts, were small and uncomfortable.

At times, Eleanor resorted to using Franklin's name to get attention from Ickes. For instance, she wrote him in December, 1933, "My husband asked me to take up with you the following two questions: 1. Status of Missouri River Division Project; 2. Also to see that Assistant Commissioner of Education be a woman and that women get half the jobs under the plan for employing unemployed women."

Undoubtedly the basic source of friction between Secretary Ickes and Eleanor Roosevelt was his deep-seated belief that she was out to get him fired. The truth was that Ickes began his tenure with the Interior Department with the notion that his employees were all villains, and Eleanor was intent on changing this poisonous atmosphere. It was Ickes' conviction that the place was flooded with Teapot Domers and that they must be ferreted out of the Department.

As his administrative assistant, he employed Ebert Burlew, who buttressed this view. An old Republican, Burlew opposed Franklin's New Deal, which rankled Eleanor. In addition, Burlew instigated the program to carry on a continuous investigation of Interior employees. For this purpose, Ickes brought in Louis Glavis, a relentless investigator. In Eleanor's opinion, "Mr. Burlew seemed to have too much power and Mr. Glavis' investigations seemed unusual." The extremes to which this reign of terror went was related to Eleanor by her old friend, Secretary of the Treasury Henry Morgenthau. "When girls in Interior have to go to the bathroom," Morgenthau related to her, "there is always a man on guard outside with a watch in his hand; and when she is in there five minutes, he knocks on the door and says, 'Time's up.'"

Eleanor carried on a crusade to straighten out this weird condition. Even at White House dinners and with Interior people present, Ickes complained, she was outspoken in her charges. At one point he sent Burlew to talk over the situation with her and to deny her charges. Afterward, Ickes wrote in his diary that Eleanor treated Burlew with coldness and didn't give him the opportunity to defend the Department. His anger aroused because he was certain she didn't understand how extensive the problem of old Teapot Domers was, Ickes then asked Franklin to investigate his Department. "It's all Mrs. Roosevelt's fault," he charged. "She's outspoken and has no facts."

Franklin's decision was to retain Ickes but to order him to fire Burlew. Ernest Lindley reported this in the New York *Herald Tribune*. However, by the time Franklin held his next press conference he changed his mind and denied Lindley's story.

The situation remained raw until Ickes finally decided that Interior employees were loyal after all. Nevertheless, he continued to hold Eleanor at fault for his own mistakes. Her tiniest request now became a matter for ridicule. For instance, when she wrote to a man on the engineering staff at Interior and urged him to consider a grade-crossing project in New Jersey, Terrible-Tempered Harold Ickes retorted, "Soon I will expect Sisty and Buzzy to be issuing orders to members of my staff. Fortunately, they can't write yet."

Although Eleanor had little to do with the State Department during her early years in the White House, she maintained a close relationship with Under Secretary of State William Phillips, her old friend of World

War I days. She was also close to the Assistant Secretary, Sumner Welles, Franklin's distant cousin who had attended their wedding. However, Secretary of State Cordell Hull maintained only a distant civility toward her. He viewed her as a radical.

Yet, strangely enough, Hull was a great admirer of her mother-in-law, whom he considered "a warm personal friend" and "in our conversations exhibited at all times a wide intelligence and excellent understanding of international questions and conditions."

Part of Hull's coldness toward Eleanor was occasioned by the fact that Franklin asked her to handle matters that rightly belonged in Hull's bailiwick. For instance, when journalist Louis Fischer was denied the right to bring his Russian-born wife and family out of the Soviet Union by the Stalin government, Franklin requested Eleanor to help him. "Invite the Soviet Ambassador to tea," he told her, "and have him ask Stalin to let them out. You might be able to do what the whole State Department can't."

Constantine Oumansky, the Soviet ambassador, proved noncommittal when he came to her tea. However, by coincidence not long afterward, Eleanor ran into him at the airport. Just before he boarded the plane, he whispered hurriedly to her, "They will be permitted to leave Russia." His word was good and the Fischers came.

Hull's high opinion of Sara Roosevelt's political acumen was not shared by Franklin, who treated her with filial affection but found her a problem. For she neither approved of his and Eleanor's new associates nor did his New Deal please her. She resented the Secret Service men, the reporters and the motley friends of Eleanor's who came frequently to Hyde Park. As a woman used to orchids, expensive furs and a forbidding lorgnette, she found them all beneath contempt. Once when Eleanor brought guests to Hyde Park, she exclaimed in her loudest stage whisper, "Where does Eleanor get all these people?" Another time when Franklin crowded her living room with reporters, bodyguards and government officials she testily announced in a clear voice that carried to all corners of the room: "Franklin should never have gone into politics. Look at these strange people around him all the time. Why they look just like a lot of gangsters." Her special anger she reserved for those occasions when she found cigarette butts in her precious rose garden. If reporters were present when she found one, she snarled, "Newspapermen!" And if Secret Service men were there close to a telltale butt, she yelled, "Secret Service! Bah!"

She was especially concerned about Franklin's political program because her rich friends found it so ghastly. "Franklin, darling," she cross-examined him one time, "why is everyone opposed to so much of your program?"

"Mama," he told her with a smile, "the people who oppose me are those concerned about having to get along with two cars instead of three."

In several instances, she did her best to influence his decisions, as well as those of his associates. When she heard that he planned to recognize the Soviet Union, Sara reproached him with, "Old friends of the family are opposed to recognizing that vile place, Franklin." Another time when Franklin invited Daniel Bell, the director of the Bureau of the Budget, to visit him at Hyde Park, Dowager Mrs. Roosevelt took Bell to task. "So many of my friends ask me when Franklin is going to balance the budget, my dear Mr. Bell," she tried to draw him into a conspiracy. "So tell me, Mr. Bell, when is Franklin going to balance the budget?" Bell changed the subject as fast as he could.

Nevertheless, despite her own opinions on the New Deal, Sara Roosevelt would accept little outside criticism about her son and daughter-in-law. "A chief Delano trait," said Eleanor, "was that you defended your family even though you thought yourself they were behaving terribly."

Franklin and Eleanor were always considerate of the old lady when she came to the White House. One time Eleanor actually made a speech on the subject of mothers-in-law and used Sara as an example of the better kind of mother-in-law. However, newspapers that carried her speech ran a picture of Eleanor, Franklin and Sara with Sara prominently in the center separating the others. Sara's disdain for what went on in the White House was even evidenced by her refusal to drink Eleanor's tea there. Instead, when she planned to visit Washington, she sent her own tea in advance.

On some occasions she brought all fourteen members of her fortnightly club to visit the White House. The timing of these visits was generally inopportune. A typical instance was revealed by a telegram from Eleanor to Franklin, who was out of Washington: "Delighted to get your letter. What time do you get in on Friday? I can't be here until early afternoon. Stop. Is it all right to have friends of Mama's for tea Friday afternoon and also to have members of NYA Advisory Committee for dinner? Much love, Eleanor."

Movies in the White House were shown in the hall outside of Franklin's bedroom on the second floor. Often when Mama and her friends came, he would lay aside his evening work and run a late Hollywood production for them. Knowing how staid and proper the old ladies considered themselves, he played the role of the gay rogue, a source of delight to his visitors. Whenever a pretty actress came into view, from his front-row seat he offered loud and voluble comments about her figure. "Oh, Franklin," Mama would try to restrain him, while her friends gasped.

There was too much going on for Eleanor to pay much attention to Sara Roosevelt. And there were many other Cabinet members and other high government officials who felt the mark of her deep interest in their activities. For one, there was Fanny Perkins, a member of her old *Kaffeeklatsch* in the New York period. Although Franklin told Eleanor and Molly Dewson, who ran women patronage during his first term, that he wanted a symbolic woman in his Cabinet, he was vague when it came to putting Miss Perkins into such select company. He talked vaguely about having her head up a Department of Public Welfare and Education, if he could get Congress to approve such a new department. It was Eleanor who convinced him that he should not wait for this possibility but should appoint Fanny to a place in his first Cabinet. Franklin's original choice for the post of Secretary of Labor was Edward McGrady of the American Federation of Labor. But when Eleanor and Molly kept after him, he appointed Fanny and made McGrady her Under Secretary. She was to please neither labor nor business, and Franklin had to erect labor agency after agency, such as the NRA, NLRB and Social Security, outside of her domain in order to hold the peace and get the job done. A critic described labor's and management's attitude toward her as "a good deal like that of habitués of a water-front saloon toward a visiting lady slummer—grim, polite and unimpressed." Attacked as she was, it was Eleanor who saved Miss Perkins' job a few years later when a wave of strikes broke out and Fanny was accused of being inept. Actually Miss Perkins was quite capable.

Jesse Jones, the cold, conservative banker and real estate operator from Texas who headed the Reconstruction Finance Corporation, was another who resented Eleanor's interest in his domain. "Jesus Jones," as Franklin referred to the tall, heavy-set administrator of government loans to banks and industry, had great disdain for social reforms. So it was little wonder that he gnashed his false teeth whenever Eleanor implored him to hand out some of the money he controlled for human betterment projects. "Because of her many activities," Jones lashed out at her one time, "she might aptly have been termed Assistant President."

Especially did he resent her frequent calls to him to come to the White House to confer with her on philanthropic projects she had in mind. Appeals to his sense of justice for underdogs left him cold. Once, early in Franklin's first term, she called him to a meeting with her and a New York builder. Jones sat stolidly throughout the conversation offering only a few polite grunts from time to time. "Mr. Jones," she told him, "this man wants the RFC to buy some slum property on the lower East Side of New York City. Then with an RFC loan he will tear down the wretched slums and construct a number of large apartment houses to replace them." Jones was noncommittal. Later, back in the sanctity of his office, he rejected the proposal.

However, there were a few proposals of hers that he did approve in order to keep peace with the White House. On one occasion, he backed her great desire to construct a hotel in Washington for single government girls. As a result the Meridan Hotel for women came into being. At other times he did favors for other members of the Roosevelt family under what he considered "Operations Bailout."

Involved were her son Elliott and her brother Hall. Hall had brought Elliott and John Hartford, head of the A&P grocery chain, together. A personal loan of $200,000 soon flowed from Hartford to Elliott. With this and other money, Elliott had begun a far-flung radio network in Texas. When he lost $500,000 in capital—as Jones later made public—he came to his rescue and bailed him out. Later the successors to Elliott made a whopping success of the network. Eleanor took no part in any of the negotiations involved, though Jones said that Franklin had.

Jones was rabid on the subject of Hall Roosevelt. Several times, he claimed, Hall used his relationship to Eleanor to call him about loans. The calls always came from White House phones, said Jones, who admitted to approving two or three loans in which Hall had a personal interest. In one instance, Jones related the story, he approved a "work loan" of $1,250,000 for a gold-mining project in Alaska. It was a "pan-mining" operation, where the gold is found in creek beds. Two days after he had approved the loan, said Jones, one of Franklin's assistants called him.

"The President is very anxious for you to make this loan," Jones said Tom Corcoran informed him. "Because if you do it, Hall will get a job with the company as chief engineer, and FDR wants Hall as far as possible from the White House."

"I've already okayed a loan," Jones told him. "But I'm giving only half of the $2,500,000 he wanted."

Hall flew to Alaska to take the job, Jones said later, but he did not stay long, returning to Washington to call him further about other projects.

But if Jesse Jones took a position on social reforms that she deplored, there were others in the Administration who did not. Chief among these was the pale, painfully thin social worker with deep blue zealous eyes named Harry Hopkins, who headed the Federal Emergency Relief Administration (FERA), then the Civil Works Administration (CWA), and then the highly controversial Works Progress Administration (WPA). He believed as she that the unemployed should work for relief money and not sit in soul-destroying squalor while waiting for a dole.

Eleanor made it a habit to put reports from Hopkins' agency on Franklin's desk with great frequency and to keep her husband posted about events along relief lines. Hopkins' activities interested her most of all among the New Deal programs because he was dealing with human suffering on an individual basis. There was no concern here for general panaceas some of the other administrators toyed with, such as manipulation of interest rates, foreign trade balances, parity and money pump priming. These were people—individuals and families—in great need through no fault of their own. This was something she could understand easily and could work to alleviate.

Hopkins readily adopted this strong ally. In fact, he came in time to wonder which one was really the aide of the other. It was all to his advantage, however, for she constantly defended him from broad sweeping attacks from Secretary Ickes, who had the President's ear. Ickes, who directed the Public Works Administration as part of his authority, considered Hopkins a competitor. In addition, Ickes was aghast at Hopkins' fire-hose method of spending money compared with his own medicine-dropper stinginess. She was also Hopkins' best press agent, for when the WPA came into existence and WPA workers were ridiculed as shovel leaners, she traveled about the country to defend them as being decent people like more fortunate Americans.

The result was that her influence on Hopkins was enormous. For instance, when she got after him to employ more women on the administrative side of WPA, he quickly complied. She was also after him to bring in new blood and not rely on dull old civil servants. Franklin, she said, wanted this, too, in order to "get new blood into the civil service and eliminate people who would be eliminated in ordinary business life." When she got Hopkins to establish the post of director of women workers to look after the welfare of female relief workers, she became the self-appointed adviser to this division. And it was she who made Hopkins drop work relief pay classification by sex, as she had accomplished in the NRA codes. "Why should women librarians and teachers get only thirty cents an hour," she demanded of him, "while unskilled males get a minimum of fifty cents an hour?" He got nowhere trying to defend industry's pay differential, and shortly afterward he removed sex from pay rates.

As a frustrated writer of fiction, Eleanor was also responsible for WPA employment of people in the arts. Eva Le Gallienne, the famed actress, came to lunch one day and excited her by her plea for a national theater under government sponsorship. She hurried to Hopkins with this idea, plus an even broader plan for WPA employment of jobless playwrights and actors. Hopkins succumbed to her proposal and established the Federal Theater Project, which became WPA's most controversial program. But this was only one phase of Eleanor's concern for jobless artistic Americans. She also prodded Hopkins into establishing first a CWA Art Project and then a WPA Arts Project in order to feed artists, muralists and sculptors besides keeping them active at their work. "Hell! They've got to eat just like other people," Hopkins agreed. One further bit of prodding led to the WPA Federal Writers' Project whereby valuable books on the history, customs and geography of each state were written. Incidentally, under the Arts Project, artists gave vent to their futile outlook by drawing thousands of ghoulish paintings of hollow-eyed starving Americans living in mean surroundings. Strung along the walls of many government buildings in Washington, these pictures were enough to destroy appetites.

There was one occasion when Eleanor permitted artistic pessimism to enter the White House by mistake. This occurred when she agreed to let an artist acquaintance make the place cards for a diplomatic dinner. Came the night of the affair and a great stir arose at the table. The cards showed buzzards eating in the street! After that, Eleanor went back to the staid place cards depicting the Great Seal of the United States.

Her crowning achievement came in 1935 when she persuaded cautious Franklin to establish the National Youth Administration. "A stranded generation," she called the youth of the nation. Across the country before a host of audiences she spoke repetitively and earnestly about doing something for the coming generation before it was too late. Youth must be kept busy, shown the benefits of democracy, provided with jobs and encouraged to acquire as much formal education as possible. "First Lady Urges Wider Aid To Youth," front-page stories were captioned.

Speechmaking was not enough. Soon she was discussing various proposals of direct aid with Harry Hopkins and his deputy administrator, Aubrey Williams. What emerged was the plan, eventually known as the NYA. In Hopkins' small office in the dirty, shabby Walker-Johnson

Building a few blocks from the White House, the three went over details: Eleanor, calm but enthusiastic; Williams, unsmiling; Hopkins, nervous, chain-smoking, in shirt sleeves and his collar loose on his neck like Louie Howe's—"like poor people's necks," as a reporter described Hopkins' neck.

After the three agreed on the program, Hopkins and Williams got cold feet, for the next move was to discuss it with Franklin. Hopkins, who in his new prominence could yell at state governors, "You're getting in my hair!" and who could bellow at U. S. Senators, "Quit lousing up my office with protests," got tongue-tied at the thought of sitting down with Franklin and convincing him of the need of the NYA, a program to offer work projects to help high school and college students stay in school.

"We do not feel we should talk to the President about it as yet," Hopkins told her wanly. "There may be many people against the establishment of such an agency in the government and there may be bad political repercussions. We do not know that the country will accept it. We do not even like to ask the President because we don't think he should be put into a position where he has to say officially 'yes' or 'no' now."

"I'll think about what you say," she smiled at the two.

That night, when Franklin was on the verge of falling asleep, Eleanor went into his bedroom. "Well, well," he said, "what new program is hanging fire?"

She described the NYA idea in detail and told him of Hopkins' fear in going ahead with it. He listened sleepily for a while, and then he asked, "Do you think it is right to do this?" knowing full well what her reply would be.

"It will be a great help to the young people, Franklin," she effused, and then changed her expression. "But I don't want you to forget that Harry Hopkins thinks it might be unwise politically. Some people might say it's like the way Hitler is regimenting German youth."

A comparison with Hitler always angered Franklin. "If it's the right thing to do for the young people," he scolded her, "then it should be done. I guess we can stand the criticism, and I doubt if our youth can be regimented in this way or in any other way."

The NYA turned out to be both a political success and a boon to millions of youngsters, enabling them to complete their education on a part-time working basis. "It was not as an answer—but simply as giving hope," Eleanor once said modestly about the program. The NYA was at first part of the WPA, but then became an independent program. It was to know Eleanor Roosevelt, as one observer put it, as "its chief adviser, its chief publicist, its chief investigator." No NYA project at any school was too small and unimportant for her to visit. And on her return, she would barge into the office of Aubrey Williams, pull out page after page of notes on what she had seen and go over them with him. "Gaunt, zealous, wavy-haired, hollow-eyed" Williams listened carefully to everything she had to say, for she was his most enthusiastic supporter. So did his state and regional directors listen when she called them as a group to conferences at her Val-Kill headquarters in Hyde Park. She also put in much time sitting alongside the desk of the Negro educator, Mary McLeod Bethune, who served as director of Negro Affairs for NYA. She, the First Lady, and Mrs. Bethune, who was the youngest of seventeen children and the first in her family to be born out of slavery, concocted many a new NYA project for Negro boys and girls. Aubrey Williams, who gave Eleanor most of the credit for the success of NYA, said of this youth program, "It has done more to create a feeling of self-reliance in Young America than anything since the Alger books."

Chapter Twenty-Five

THERE WAS BAD AS WELL AS GOOD in the wind. The bad was the decay of Louis Howe's strength.

When Louie came to Washington with them, it was obvious to Eleanor that his health was poor. Nevertheless, he continued as Franklin's chief assistant and with as much enthusiasm as before. When he was given a corner office in the working wing of the White House, he protested that it was too large. Besides, it was too far away from Franklin's office. Asked where he would live by newspapermen who treated him with awe because of his known influence with the President, Louie replied, "I don't take up much room. They'll stick me away somewhere in the White House."

Eleanor assigned him the Lincoln Room, which hardly impressed him because, compared with Lincoln, Franklin was much the better man. In fact, he felt this about all the other Presidents. One time when Eleanor took him to Jefferson's home at Monticello, he was cynical about all of Jefferson's possessions. Only once did he offer any admiration for Jefferson, and this was when Eleanor showed him the one-horse gig Jefferson used in riding to the Continental Congress. "Mein Gawd!" Louis slapped his thin cheek. "If he rode to Philly in that gig, I certainly admire his stamina."

In those early hectic days of the New Deal, he looked rather outmoded in his pre-World War I high collar and disreputable bags he called his suits. Amidst all her activities, Eleanor took him to New York with her a few times to buy him a more decent wardrobe. Franklin once said in Louis' presence, "Ludevic just wears his socks until they don't cover his legs any more." (Ludevic was Franklin's nickname for him.) Another time when he and Eleanor were relaxing, Franklin ribbed Louie as he often did. The odor of Louie's cigarette was especially pungent and Franklin exclaimed, "Do you know, Ludevic, there's a rumor going around that the Sweet Caporal factory is closing down because they have only one smoker left in the entire country." "I'll wait till they close down before I change," Louis snapped back.

Eleanor mothered him because he got home to Massachusetts only on weekends, and then only if his desk was halfway cleared of work. She made certain that he ate decent meals and went to bed on time, because he had fallen below his normal 100 pounds. She also knitted several sweaters for him because he complained of drafts.

There was one thing that pleased Louie immensely and that was when the governor of Kentucky made him an honorable colonel. As soon as he heard this news, he had calling cards printed and he handed them straight-faced to visitors. His calling card listed him as "Col. Louis Rasputin Voltaire Talleyrand Simon Legree Howe." Newspapers and letter writers addressed him henceforth as "Colonel," which tickled him. However, on occasion, when his phone rang he would pick up the receiver and bellow into the phone, "This is the medieval gnome speaking."

Some of the joy in acquiring his title was tarnished for him at the outset, though he regained his pride with time. This occurred when the colonel investiture ceremony was completed and he called his long-suffering and lonely wife in Fall River. She believed that he did not spend enough time with his family. And when he called to tell her about the ceremony, she said into the phone, "If you have time for all that foolishness, you've got time to come home."

When he hung up, he turned sadly to the others present and muttered, "Mein Gawd! The family can always cut you down to size."

Louis, of course, considered himself as chief adviser to both Franklin and Eleanor. He was forever presenting grandiose utopian programs to Franklin to help fill in the important chinks in the New Deal panorama. Franklin accepted them graciously and then shelved them. "Louis knows nothing about economics," he told Eleanor. His usefulness to Franklin lay chiefly in his enthusiasm and his ability to make friends for his boss and keep him appraised of public opinion.

His official duties were varied. One of his functions was to fire people for Franklin. He could be quite politic about this. Sometimes he was Franklin's official greeter, as when he went to Union Station to meet British Prime Minister Ramsay MacDonald and his daughter Ishbel. The only trouble in this instance was that he found Ishbel much more attractive a personality than her father and devoted his attention to her. Franklin also shunted government officials to Louis' office when he was pressed for time or didn't want to see them. On the other hand, said Eleanor, Louis "was head of the secretariat and if he felt that someone should see Franklin, they saw him."

Louis also prepared a daily survey of editorial opinion for Franklin.

He believed it was important for him to know what the editors were feeding their readers. In addition, he planned the system for coping with the 6,500 letters that came each day for Franklin. He made sure that Franklin saw a cross-section of the letters and that replies were made swiftly and courteously. Sometimes he brought in funny letters just to give him a lift, as the time he showed him a letter addressed to Franklin Dillinger Roosevelt.

Eleanor realized that Louis was a highly jealous man, and was often motivated by a desire to keep others from getting too close to the President. He had a scathing opinion of most of Franklin's administrators. He called Hopkins' first relief agency, the FERA, which interested Eleanor so much, the worst-run agency in Washington. Hopkins, he exclaimed openly, was an even poorer administrator than General Johnson, whose NRA was a madhouse of confusion. The Department of Agriculture he tossed off with, "Wallace is crazy."

However, his openness in his remarks, according to Eleanor, was highly essential because, outside of her, Louis was the only person who could say what he really believed to Franklin. No one else dared. For that matter, Louie said what he wanted to on every occasion to Eleanor, too. And they were such old friends by now that she could not get angry.

Sometimes, though, she did try to temper his remarks about others. Once when she heard him blast a man who was really quite harmless, she chided him on his language. "What did that man ever do to you, Louis?"

"Don't you remember what he did to Franklin fifteen years ago?" he growled.

"But that was a long time ago."

"That may be," he sneered. "But I remember."

Louis Howe tried to crack the whip over Eleanor as he did over Franklin. Her visit to the Second Bonus Army and her weekly press conferences were just two of his ideas. He still questioned the way she spoke in public, and she acquired a speech instructor. He showed her how a good radio operator broadcasted by going on the air weekly with a fifteen-minute program on the various New Deal programs that Franklin had created. His trouble here was that he got tangled in the details of the programs he discussed. Furthermore, he antagonized Senator Arthur Vandenberg, who attacked him savagely on the Senate floor after each broadcast.

It was Louis who showed great enthusiasm for the trips she took for Franklin. "Often when I was starting a trip," she said, "he'd take a map and point out the places where I planned to visit and say, 'Now in this town you will find the sentiment is thus and so, or in that county you will find that the people think a certain way on a certain subject.' He sensed the feeling of the people better than anyone I have ever known."

When she returned from a trip, he wanted to know all about it, just as he did when Franklin went off somewhere. He was never as cruel in his comments to her as he was to Franklin, for he bragged to Franklin that he was his "devil's advocate." Whenever Franklin mentioned a legislative proposal, Louis would point a gnarled finger at him and rip the proposal to shreds with a burst of cutting comments. Then he would force Franklin to defend himself against his attack. When Franklin did to his satisfaction, he would smile at him as a teacher would at a bright student.

Harsh as he was on the surface, Eleanor knew him as being quite maudlin within. He also liked high jinks. For instance, in 1933 when the all-male Gridiron Club of Washington newsmen held its annual dinner, he suggested to Eleanor that she hold a Gridiron Widows dinner the same night in the White House. She did and made it an annual practice, to the delight of the women reporters who felt left out as a group of practicing reporters. Louis wrote many of the skits and was an expert on make-up. In 1934, when the Gridiron Widows decided on a masquerade party, he made Eleanor up as "Apple Annie." No one recognized Eleanor in her dilapidated shawl and bonnet as she moved about the room moaning, "The Divill, the Divill." The hit of the evening was when she uncovered her face and the girls discovered who she was. The high notes could have been heard blocks away at the Gridiron Club dinner.

Though Eleanor enjoyed the company of her girl reporters, to Louis such association was basically an insurance policy for getting Franklin a better press. It was also, to Louis, a means for attracting American women to Eleanor with the hope that this fondness would shift to Franklin. To prod matters along, he permitted himself to be quoted as saying the time was near when the country would elect a woman as President.

So when Eleanor held her Gridiron Widows parties, it was all to the good. So was the annual informal dance she began holding for newspaper reporters, male and female, in the White House. It was too bad when Franklin showed up at the first of these dances in a wrinkled Palm Beach suit, while all the poor reporters came in formal tails. That Eleanor would dance with the National Press Club fellows was a good democratic stroke, Louis must have chuckled to himself, though he knew she was enjoying herself. She especially liked the Virginia reel, and one year she held a Virginia reel for the reporters. All evening she danced vigorously, starting off with her brother Hall and shifting with little pause to other partners. It was a source of wonder to the newspeople joining her in the dance, for she turned and spun as though she were in her teens instead of in her fifties. One partner with whom she pranced about the long room called it an exhausting evening after their session. When his wife found him, he sat in a limp mess, pale and gasping. "What happened to you?" she asked concerned.

"Holy smoke!" he groaned. "Mrs. Roosevelt almost killed me."

It was in the fall of 1934 that Louis Howe's health began slipping noticeably. Alarmed, Eleanor and Franklin tried to cut down on his activities. When he traveled, which was less frequent now, she made special arrangements with train attendants. His breathing came so hard that he had trouble walking from the train to the street. Conveniently, she arranged for station baggage cars to pass him by "coincidence" and offer him rides on the luggage pullers. The coincidence happened so often that he must have wondered, but he never let on.

She watched him fight to hold on. Daily he grew more hunched and shadowy and his skinny neck resembled a broomstick. Soon he began spending most of his time in the Lincoln Room. He had his bed shifted to the adjoining small dressing room because, he apologized to Eleanor, "I rattle around like a pea in a pod." When she was in town Eleanor came daily to spend hours with her little friend. In one respect this was an ordeal, for his rooms resembled a junkyard caught by a ravaging hurricane. Old newspapers were strewn on the floors and lay in precarious piles on chairs and tables. Sweet Caporal butts were everywhere. Being cooped up in his room, Louis missed most of all not being able to barge into Franklin's office whenever he wanted to. "I've been as close to Franklin as his valet," he admitted, "and he is still a hero to me."

Weak as he was, Louie still demanded a faithful adviser's share in running the show for Franklin and Eleanor. When a boat she was on suffered an accident in the fall of 1934, he was delighted with the newspaper mileage she got, for it meant to him that his carefully nurtured campaign to win the support of women for her was a success. "Franklin trying to live down the disgrace of a Roosevelt running aground, but it comes hard," he wired her. "Suggest you stay ashore or keep out of newspapers."

He pushed her to do more and more writing, though she had a literary agent now who was swamped with requests for articles from magazines.

When she wrote a 90-page child's guide to Washington, *A Trip to Washington with Bobby and Betty,* which appeared in 1935, he considered this another gain in the Roosevelt support department. However, an alligator appeared in this pond to destroy its value. The zealous publisher had concocted what appeared to him to be a master stroke to help sales. He staged a contest for children to write on the back of the book jacket what they would rather see most in Washington. The winner was to get an expense-free trip to Washington and meet Eleanor in the White House.

Trouble came when Eleanor acted as judge, for she had been a dedicated schoolmistress. The essays on the huge pile of book jackets that she read revolted her one and all. They were full of incomplete sentences and bereft of thought and grammar. "They are all impossible," she informed the publisher. "There is not one that deserves to win." Faced with her stern decision, the publisher felt obliged to call off the contest. But this was not the end of the affair. When some parents of contestants cried fraud, the Federal Trade Commission jumped into the fray and investigated both the publisher and Eleanor. In the end the matter was dropped.

By March of 1935, Louis Howe was a ravaged and desiccated man. When he contracted a bad case of bronchitis, on top of all his other ailments, he was rushed into an oxygen tent. Doctors said he could not last out the day. Eleanor broke all her engagements that day and hurried down from New York to be at his side. Franklin ordered a special train put on a siding of the Washington station, to carry Louis' remains to his home in Fall River, Massachusetts. But late in the afternoon, when doctors were having trouble finding a pulse beat, Louis suddenly opened his sunken eyes wide and shouted, "Why in hell doesn't somebody give me a cigarette?"

He managed to stay alive for a year afterward. Eleanor remained in Washington during the next several months in order to nurse him. Louie's wife also came down and read to him all day long. Franklin got him a wheel chair like his own and Louis wheeled himself about the second floor in a circuit covering Eleanor's sitting room and office and Franklin's oval study.

The sicker he got, the greater was his jealousy of all Franklin's associates. He called Cabinet members on the phone from his room and blasted them freely. He also grew more irascible toward Eleanor and Franklin. One time he dispatched a message through Franklin's valet, McDuffie, to the President. "You go back and tell the President I said to go to hell!" Howe barked at the frightened servant.

"I ain't going to tell the President something awful like that," Mc-Duffie told his wife Lizzie, who was a maid at the White House. He prevailed upon her to carry Howe's message for him.

"Mr. President," she told Franklin, "Mr. Howe said for McDuffie to tell you that that was a hell of a message you sent him."

Franklin roared with laughter. "Now, Lizzie," he chided her, "you know very well that Louis said for me to go to hell, didn't he?"

She confessed he had.

In August Louie's condition worsened and Eleanor took him to the naval hospital in Washington. His body was wasted now but his eyes still burned fire. He had every intention of being around to direct the re-election campaign in 1936, and he grew a Vandyke which he thought made him look distinguished. To pass time away, he had several of Franklin's associates come to the hospital to talk over their work and to map out strategy for 1936. The silver-tongued orator from Royal Oak, Michigan, Father Coughlin, once friendly toward Franklin and now in the limelight with an anti-Semitic following, disturbed Louis a great deal. So did the endless Senator Huey Long of Louisiana. Louie collected reports on the two and sent them to Franklin, because he believed that they both presented a dangerous problem for both Franklin and the nation in 1936. On one report on Father Coughlin he sent Franklin, he wrote, "Somebody had better keep an eye on this fanatic and do something about him."

Eleanor and Franklin visited Louie frequently toward the end. Franklin adopted the strategy of being wheeled into Louie's room and calling out, "Louie, you've just got to get back to the White House and get in on the show." Louie smiled wanly.

The tired heart stopped the night of April eighteenth while Franklin was speaking before the Gridiron Dinner. Both he and Eleanor canceled all engagements for the week. They accompanied the body back to Fall River for the funeral. The drooping White House flag at half mast expressed their feelings well. So did the note Franklin sent to Eleanor, "I suggest the following to be put on Louis' tombstone: Devoted friend, adviser and associate of the President."

An important era in the lives of Eleanor and Franklin was at an end.

But despite their great loss, there was no time for mourning. For 1936 was election year and Franklin's New Deal was up for judgment by the electorate.

Franklin's personal popularity within the Democratic Party was at an all-time high, but there were some troublesome matters on the hori-

[235]

zon. The nomination of liberal Governor Alf Landon of Kansas by the Republicans was a bad sign to Franklin that the Republicans were going to try to steal his thunder. Eleanor's friend, Harry Hopkins, was making intemperate remarks about WPA critics around the country, and local scandals in WPA operations were getting bold headlines. To add to the trouble, Al Smith "took a walk" from the Democratic Party and had come out for Landon. Al was also a screaming mouthpiece of the Liberty League, a powwow of entrenched rich, which included the du Pont clan and others as well as old Democratic cohorts such as John W. Davis and John Raskob. "I can't understand it," Franklin complained to Eleanor. "Everything I've done in Washington is like things Al did as governor of New York." Then there were the extremists. Huey Long was dead, slain by an assassin's bullets, but Father Coughlin had entered the political arena with a political party, the Union party, with one-eyed Representative William Lemke of North Dakota as his presidential candidate.

There would always remain in Eleanor's mind the memory of Franklin's acceptance speech at the Philadelphia Democratic National Convention late in June. It was his climactic moment, but also his greatest ordeal.

More than 100,000 cheering Democrats awaited them that Saturday night in Franklin Field of the University of Pennsylvania. When she and Franklin came into view, the Philadelphia Symphony Orchestra struck up "Pomp and Circumstance." The crowd went wild. Franklin was to make his slow, careful walk to the platform and the microphones while he held onto the strong arm of son Jimmy. She waited with usual dread for him to complete his walk.

Everything went well until Franklin caught sight of the old bearded poet, eighty-five-year-old Edwin Markham. The old author of "The Man with the Hoe" had tears in his eyes because he had been asked to read a poem dedicated to Franklin. Twice already he had gone to the microphones for his recitation and both times the orchestra had drowned him out. When Franklin caught the sad face, he nodded to Markham, and the poet pressed in for a handshake. But his effort pushed Jimmy against Franklin, and Eleanor watched with horror as her husband's right leg brace snapped open and he went down on the ground.

Quick action by two Secret Service men brought him upright almost immediately and his brace was resnapped rigidly. But the damage was done. His aplomb was gone. "Clean me up!" he yelled, catching sight of his soiled suit. They brushed him off carefully and retrieved the wrinkled, dirty pages of his speech. He was breathing heavily by now at his disgrace, yet he reached over and shook hands with Markham.

Oddly, only a few persons in the mammoth crowd had any idea what had taken place. When he reached his place, he said to Eleanor, "I hope Garner speaks a long time so I can straighten out the pages of my speech." However, the Vice President, who had been renominated with Franklin, had no intention of making a speech so long after his normal bedtime. Called before the microphones, he spoke only a few sentences before he suddenly announced, "I present to you the President of the United States."

So there was her husband, perfectly miserable after his mishap, delivering what was to be one of the best speeches of his career. "This generation of Americans has a rendezvous with destiny," his words rang out. The crowd broke into a 20-minute ovation that he tried to halt but could not. Afterward he was the picture of the triumphant leader as he circled the crowd four times by car with Eleanor beside him. But on the train back to Hyde Park, it was obvious that he was still brooding over his humiliation at Franklin Field. "I was the damnedest maddest man at that moment you ever saw," he cursed.

With the campaign on, Franklin needed all the help he could muster. He felt the loss of Louis Howe terribly now and he turned to Eleanor for aid in organizing his forces. Word was that the Democratic National Headquarters was a frustrating scene of confusion. "Go there," he told her, "and find out what's wrong and what should be done."

On Tuesday, July 14, she dropped into Democratic headquarters and spent two days in an attic-to-basement checkup. Two days later she sent Franklin a trenchant analysis of the confusion she found. "My feeling is that we have to get going and going quickly," she wrote. Offering her own suggestions, she wanted to know who was responsible for handling the radio campaign; who was making newspaper contacts and sending "feature stories, pictures, mats, boiler plate, etc.?"; who was handling research and what was being done "to check on all inconsistencies in Landon's pronouncements or those of his campaign managers as they relate to his former statements or record?" She insisted that "Mr. Rayburn should come at once to plan the policy and mechanics of the speakers' bureau. Then he could leave for a time." Also, "I think it would be well to start some Negro speakers, like Mrs. Bethune, to speak at church meetings and that type of Negro organization."

Jim Farley, who was nominally in charge of the campaign, was so upset by her report that he made a 20-page reply which he sent to her and Franklin. Yet he called her "the most practical woman I've ever met in politics."

She even established rules of behavior for herself on campaign swings: "Always be on time. Never try to make any personal engagements. Do as little talking as humanly possible. Never let yourself be disturbed by anything. Always do whatever you are told as quickly as possible. Remember to lean back in the parade car so everybody can see the President. Be sure not to get too fat, because you'll have to sit three in the back seat."

To Eleanor, Franklin could not lose the election because he had given new hope and revived the imaginative energy of the nation. As she joyously told the graduating class at the Washington College of Law, "Stevenson's nursery rhyme, I feel, is drawing nearer to the time when it can be justified:

> " 'The world is so full of a number of things,
> I think we should all be as happy as kings.' "

However, Franklin did not share her optimism that he would win. When the *Literary Digest* poll came out with the prediction that Landon would win handily by carrying 32 states and 370 electoral votes, he was smitten with grave pessimism. There was also the Republican campaign that he found highly disturbing.

Landon did not run as the liberal he was but as an arch-conservative. As the campaign progressed, it turned into a dirty contest, with the opposition casting every form of hearsay calumny at Franklin. In making an analysis of its tactics for her husband, Eleanor noted that the opposition was employing "advertising people to do their copy, and the whole spirit is the spirit of a crusade."

The slick whispering campaign against Franklin angered Eleanor. There was one widely spread story about a woman overnight guest at the White House (woman never identified) who had been terrorized by the carryings-on of the President. The utterly false tale, said Eleanor, was that her husband was supposed to have been "shrieking like a maniac in the middle of the night and people rushing to control him." But there was also slander about her, plus an organized campaign by Southern bigots who ran newspaper pictures of her walking with a Negro. However, American campaigns were traditionally a dirty business, part of the price one paid for being in the limelight. Whether she was a political asset or liability to Franklin was summed up well by a Republican who cried, "It isn't fair for the President to cash in on his own popularity and his wife's, too."

Eleanor went along on campaign trips and watched Franklin at his campaigning best from back platforms and at fairgrounds, though inwardly he worried about the outcome. She wrote to Molly Dewson in October, "The President and his gang have the jitters." Only twice did his pessimism rub off on her. Once when he wanted new drapes for the East Room of the White House, she told him, "Let's wait until after the election, so if you lose the new President can select his own." The other occasion was in Philadelphia when she bet Vice President Garner that Franklin would lose Pennsylvania. Garner had told her then: "I got up at six o'clock this morning and walked around the streets. That's about saddling-up time in Texas," he explained to her, "but it's early here. The only people up were policemen, cab drivers and night workers. I talked to them and most of them are going to vote the Democratic ticket and none of them have done that before. We will carry Pennsylvania."

"You are much too enthusiastic, Mr. Vice President," she told him. "The Democrats haven't carried Pennsylvania since the Civil War."

"War Between the States," he corrected her. "So how about betting me a dollar?"

She shook his hand on the bet, cheap insurance for the vote of one of the largest states.

She saw the immense turnout along the campaign trail as sure indication that the country was for Franklin. At least, wrote one reporter, all the nation's disabled were. Curiously, they were at "the front of every crowd like a magnet. Mrs. Roosevelt always knew the disabled would be there, always managed to give them a special welcome."

Even the unpleasantries did not lessen her enthusiasm. In Boston, for instance, a man dashed through the crowd to Franklin's car and called her husband "Son-of-a-bitch!" Once on the train circuit, someone in the crowd threw a dagger that hit a man standing next to Franklin and supporting him while he waved. Fortunately, the dagger proved to be rubber. In another place, a local politician got a bagful of peanuts in his face that was obviously meant for her husband. But such episodes were individual actions and not the feeling of the greeting throngs. Two weeks before the election, Eleanor, in fact, considered further campaigning a waste of time. As she wrote to Molly Dewson, "Even the seasoned newspapermen admit it is all over and want to go home without doing anything more."

It was a great relief to Franklin when Landon conceded on election night and his own self-confidence was restored. Publicly he said that he had known all along he would win. The torchlight parade of Hyde

Park citizens passed up the long driveway that night to honor the village's first citizen. A political sage told Eleanor that her husband had won a colossal victory, having lost only "Maine, Vermont and Hyde Park." As usual, the paraders stopped at the porch where Sara and Franklin sat facing them. Eleanor stood behind them.

Inauguration Day, now moved to January 20 from the customary March 4 by constitutional amendment, was wet and nasty as ever. But the crowds that flooded Washington to see their hero did not mind the dampness. Eleanor ran about the inauguration stand to wrap her family and friends in blankets. Then she took her seat near Franklin as he spoke about the emphasis he intended placing during the next four years on helping the underdogs she loved. "I see one third of a nation ill-housed, ill-clad, ill-nourished." There was still much work to be done.

Though the rain was now a drenching downpour, he insisted that they ride in the parade back to the White House with the car top down. "If they can stand in the rain while we ride by," he told her, "the least we can do is to get wet, too." Eleanor's new blue hat was ruined on that ride and the look of concern she wore the last several blocks was due to her fear that the blue coloring was running down her face.

Chapter Twenty-Six

WHENEVER ELEANOR THOUGHT about Franklin's first term, she got a roseate glow. All the legislation that had poured out of the seemingly endless vat called Congress during those years had electrified the nation. The sense of accomplishment in Franklin, too, was enormous. "He was stimulated," said Eleanor, "by the realization that he was practically accomplishing a revolution. Government had assumed no responsibility for the individual and then suddenly through my husband's efforts that responsibility was accepted by practically everyone."

But a dynamic nation could not remain stationary. It must go on to new adventures. In fact, Franklin's revolution had made only a dent in the depression's hardships. There was more relief to be handed out to the unemployed, industries revitalized and secure employment brought about, labor's rights protected, Negroes emancipated, women brought into politics and moral leadership, religious minorities given safe operation, the aged pensioned, the sick treated, everyone housed properly and youth prepared for leadership.

To a large share of the American public her name became synonymous with all such efforts. "She is a social force all by herself," a reporter noted. Arthur Krock, learned observer for *The New York Times,* wrote that Eleanor and Franklin were "operating as a political team. . . . This is new in American history and many old-fashioned people will criticize it. . . . But many other persons will welcome Mrs. Roosevelt's emergence."

Indeed she formed a team with Franklin, a unique phenomenon in American political life. In many ways she was as good a politician as he. She could handle crowds so that each person felt her special attention. Once when the White House lawn was flooded with 6,000 women who had come to her garden party, an astounded onlooker gasped, "Watching her as she good-naturedly did her best to shake hands with all who could get near her in the crowd, any old-fashioned politician would have recognized a knack for making friends."

In a host of avenues, she augmented his efforts and conserved his strength so he could stick to fundamentals. More than just the chatelaine of the White House, she doubled for him in handling the social duties hoary custom had decreed for American Presidents. She laid a pile of wreaths on enough monuments to dwarf the tall, slender Washington Monument behind the White House. She also attended dedications too numerous to recount, received swarms of delegations and extended her congratulations to worthy organizations in every state.

Besides relieving him of social duties, she assisted him in many other ways. She helped guide his reading by putting "interesting things on the table next to his bed." Some of the things she laid there were books and articles on pressing social problems; others were whimsical tales or straight entertainment. One time she left the thousand-page *Gone With the Wind* with him, only to have him return it the next day with a "You may not believe it but I read it all" look. "He couldn't possibly have read it so quickly, I was sure, and I told him so—but I couldn't catch him on a single point."

Often he used her as his hair shirt. He enjoyed sitting at the dinner table and arguing a line of reasoning or policy which he knew she opposed. Discussions of this sort were generally thrashed out "vociferously and with heat" before they were finished. But they were not just academic arguments to him. For instance, one dinner discussion on American policy toward Great Britain proved to be quite a bitter give-and-take. Eleanor's irritation at Franklin's arguments was monumental. Any onlooker would have expected a family brawl to follow later that evening in the upstairs family rooms. Instead, the next day Franklin asked her to have tea with him and the American ambassador to Britain, Robert Bingham. To her shock, in telling Bingham how to proceed, Franklin ordered him to act in the manner Eleanor had proposed at dinner the previous evening. "Without giving me a glance or the satisfaction of batting an eyelash in my direction, he calmly stated as his own the policies and beliefs he had argued against the night before!"

Franklin could criticize Eleanor in all seriousness, and he sometimes did. But he would not let anyone else say a word against her. One night, listening to the radio, he heard a commentator let go a blast at his wife. With a quick angry motion, he snapped off the dial and sat fuming a long while.

He did not fume, however, when she got on radio broadcasts and made public defenses of his policies. He considered such broadcasts a positive propaganda asset, though members of his own administration cringed when they turned on their radios and found her voice in their rooms. In 1935, for instance, Father Coughlin took to the air exhorting all isolationists to pepper Senators with telegrams demanding the rejection of American participation in the World Court. As President, Franklin could not with due grace to his office engage in a similar lobbying effort in behalf of the World Court.

However, Eleanor could undertake this mission for him and she did, broadcasting the same evening as Coughlin. Unfortunately, with the nation so given to inferiority and isolationism, Eleanor lost to the smooth-tongued priest. The avalanche of anti-World Court telegrams that reached the Senate the next day spelled doom to American participation in the international organization. Secretary of the Interior Ickes, irate at the competitive broadcasting, snarled belligerently, "After all, the people did not elect her President, and I don't think the country likes the thought of the wife of the President engaging prominently in public affairs to the extent she does."

Nor did many members of Franklin's Cabinet view favorably her behind-the-scenes aid to her husband in campaigns. They were aware of the fact that while Jim Farley took the accolades as a political wizard, she was frequently in his office and sat alongside him until he took the action she deemed necessary. However, Franklin considered her activity an important augmentation of his own efforts.

Nor did they consider proper the behind-the-scenes pressure she exerted on her husband and on them to make certain appointments in the government hierarchy. In 1939, for instance, despite pious official denials, she was partly responsible for three controversial nominations. Two were for vacancies then existing on the Interstate Commerce Commission. One of those named to the ICC was her friend, J. Haden Alldredge, and the other was a warm New Deal supporter, Representative Thomas R. Amlie. The third appointment, and one that brought down the roof, was the naming of Mary Winslow, an old worker with the Women's Trade Union League, as U. S. member of the Inter-American Commission of Women. Besides the appalling fact that no American vacancy existed on the commission at the time, Miss Winslow did not meet two basic requirements of the job. She knew no Spanish and she was not a lawyer. After a loud howl from Congress that Amlie had supported radical causes, Amlie begged to have his name withdrawn. Franklin quickly complied and the howls ended.

There were howls, too, from party politicians for her quiet but authoritative role in their affairs. One clear instance took place in 1941 when Senator Morris Sheppard died. According to Texas politicians, she called to the White House the favored candidate to succeed him, Representative Wright Patman, and told him bluntly that he must quit the race. For she insisted that Representative Lyndon Johnson, a former state director of her beloved NYA, should have no liberal opposition in the contest. The result was that Johnson, who was weak politically at the time, was thoroughly trounced by the reactionary Wilbert "Pappy" O'Daniel.

Franklin was willing to have her go off the deep end on occasion because she was so important to him generally. For instance, her travels were highly essential to his popularity, as were the clear investigatory reports she sent him vital for his knowledge of the American countryside. Once he sent her out to investigate the federal prison system. This was to her an unpleasant and depressing assignment compared with checking injustices in farm and urban areas. The sight of caged men and women affronted her. But typically, once she was gone he forgot her errand. "Where's my Missus?" he stopped Eleanor's secretary, Tommy, one morning.

"She's in prison," Tommy told him.

"I'm not surprised," Franklin shot back at her, "but what for?"

When she was away off somewhere grinding out her 40,000 miles a year, he wrote her letters that were often poetic. Once he wrote, "The Lord only knows when this will catch up with my Will o' the Wisp wife." What tickled him about her adventures were stories that she had gone unrecognized, despite the fact that her picture was in the papers almost daily. On one occasion while traveling with Mrs. Helm, her White House social secretary, a puzzled old man approached the two tall women and asked, "Which one of ye be Mrs. Roosevelt?" Another time Eleanor bought some apparel at a Washington department store and asked the clerk to send it to the White House. After close study, the girl asked, "What room number?"

Strange as it may seem, Franklin had similar experiences. Driving his own car, which was specially made with hand controls, in upstate New York one time, he lost his way and asked a farmer for directions. After he was straightened out he thanked the man. "That's all right, bub," the farmer told the President with no sign of recognition.

By her air travels, she did more than any other person in the country to popularize and instill confidence in that mode of transportation. Struggling commercial airlines blessed her existence daily. But danger lurked in the background of her travels. She rode planes in rain and fog in order to keep appointments. Stewardesses knew her as the soothing woman who walked the aisles to comfort passengers on rough air rides. She fed babies for tired mothers and recited poems and told stories to children. Even when she was on solid ground there were dangerous

[244]

moments. For instance, in 1938 she consented to break ground at Treasure Island in California for a new federal building. To play it safe, she insisted to the master of ceremonies that she must not be asked to "pull any levers" or "ride in anything." He dutifully crossed his heart. But no sooner did she climb into the flower-filled seat of an enormous steam shovel than the driver rode off in a fury, plowing up everything in his path. They finally came to a stop in a ditch 300 yards away. She climbed down wobbly-kneed and ashen. "My part in the program is ended," she announced.

There were letters and stories that came across Franklin's desk about her travels that amused him greatly. One cross man wrote him in confidence, "I wonder what you privately think of her yourself. I guess you can't be very happy together, for she would not have so much time for gadding about the country and butting into matters that are of no concern to her." A "Friend, a Democrat" wrote, "Isn't there anything you can do about your wife and our First Lady of the Land talking too much?" There was also the story of the father who was relating the story of Robinson Crusoe to his son. "And there on the sand Crusoe suddenly saw two footprints. Whose do you think they were?"

"Mrs. Roosevelt, Papa."

It took her exhausted women's newspaper corps—those weary souls whose duty it was to follow her on her peregrinations—to cap her travel bottle. At the Gridiron Widows affair in December, 1937, they wanly recited to her:

"Hi diddle diddle, the cat and the fiddle
The cow jumped over the moon.
The moon laughed and laughed and said, 'You're too late!
Eleanor passed here at noon.' "

There were still other ways in which she augmented her husband. On several occasions she stiffened his backbone when he seemed on the verge of faltering on his commitments. Rexford Tugwell, his early Brain Truster who followed them to Washington, observed that sometimes when he grew frightened at attacks on his relief program, she "tended to steady the President's nerve." She also took over one of Louis Howe's functions by making herself available to government officials to talk over programs with her before seeing Franklin.

Another thing she did was to broaden his horizons by inviting guests to the White House whose ideas, she hoped, would stimulate him and make him less of a prisoner of his job. Once, for instance, she invited Anne O'Hare McCormick of *The New York Times* to dinner. "I wonder if you would try to get the President more interested in foreign affairs," she suggested.

She brought him ministers, explorers, social workers, editors, writers, artists, musicians, professors and doctors. Many guests were invited simply to entertain him and lighten his load. Carl Sandburg came one time, strummed his guitar, sang some songs and refreshed Franklin. Others dulled his senses. One morning when he wheeled himself into his office he was out of sorts. "Eleanor had a lot of do-gooders for dinner," he muttered to his secretary, "and you know what that means."

Eleanor on occasion brought to the dinner table government officials whom he had been avoiding and whom she thought he should see. Whenever this happened, he would reproach her sternly with an injured expression during the pre-dinner cocktail ritual in his second-floor study. One time when Aubrey Williams, who ran her favored NYA, could not get an appointment with the President, she invited him to dinner. Williams tried to dissuade her, but when she insisted he came.

Franklin kept eyeing him curiously at the table, but Eleanor controlled the conversation by telling Franklin that he must see a Chinese youth who had just come from the Orient. "This young man will transform your entire point of view on China," she argued.

Franklin winced. "No, I don't want to see him."

But she kept after him, to his repetitively harsh "No!" Finally he yelled in exasperation, "Send your damned Chinaman over to the State Department!"

"But, Franklin," she said, injured, "you know perfectly well that it would be useless to send him there."

"Have him see Harry Hopkins then," he shouted in desperation.

She shook her head. "Hopkins is much too busy to see him."

"Busy!" he said thunderstruck. "What about me?"

"Well, I'll ask him to dinner as my guest," she smiled.

He pushed his food away and shook a finger in the air. "Just remember, I want dinner to be a relaxation, not an excuse for doing business. I have enough of that all day."

Williams, who had sat listening to the conversation, gave out with a burst of laughter. Franklin turned in his direction. "Well, what's on your mind, Aubrey?"

A crimson blush crossed Williams' face. "Business," he told the President. Franklin laughed.

Eleanor had a penchant for writers and many of them trooped to the White House or Hyde Park. Gertrude Stein came once, but she was almost stone-deaf and wouldn't let anyone talk. H. G. Wells came expecting to find a "terrible 'school marm,'" but the only trait of a school-mistress about her was a certain care for precision of statement. There was no pose about either of them. They were not concerned about being what was expected of them, or with the sort of impression they were making." He called them "unlimited people, entirely modern in the openness of their minds and the logic of their actions." He was sur-prised that there was nothing "mystical or pompous or darkly omnis-cient" about them.

She had a strange effect on some writers. Noel Coward wrote her after a visit to Hyde Park that the visit had made him forgetful and he begged her to send him the "battered old Japanese raincoat" he left be-hind. Most amusing was a letter to her from Ernest Hemingway. "I have tried many times to find words to tell you how much I appreciated your letter. It isn't any use. I can't write it. There aren't any words. Or maybe it's that I don't know them." When Clare Boothe Luce came to visit in 1939, Eleanor took her along on a shopping errand to Rhinebeck, about ten miles from Hyde Park. "It would be odd, or rather it wouldn't be the least bit odd," Mrs. Luce wrote her later, "if that paragraph pub-lished posthumously should contribute my only claim to survival as an author. Indeed they might engrave on my tombstone:

"'She once went with Mrs. Roosevelt to buy the President a cake— of such is the Kingdom of God.'"

Certainly the closest relationship Eleanor had with a writer was with rotund, owlish Alexander Woollcott. She had met him casually one time and when *Wine of Choice* played in Washington on tour, she invited him to Sunday supper. For entertainment after dinner, a professional piano player played preludes on the White House Steinway, and Alex sat facing him and leering all the while. Eleanor was certain he would come out with some of his biting sarcasm, but nothing happened except at the close when he let out an injured grunt.

Following that visit he came frequently to the White House and stayed as long as a week at a time. "You know," he once told Ethel Barrymore, "Mrs. Roosevelt runs the best theatrical boarding house in Washington." He considered her at first as of consequence only insofar as she provided him with an entrée to the President. But Franklin ignored him. "He tried too hard to make a hit," an observer noted. There was also the episode at Hyde Park when Franklin watched him devour the large bowlful of strawberries that was meant for all the diners.

Woollcott idolized Franklin, but it seemed that their conversations were always sticky. One time he wrote from the White House to

[247]

Eleanor who was out of town, "As I was going off to the theater last night the President (who, having nothing on his mind these days, has time for such trifles) ventured to predict that we would have a considerably diminished audience. I replied cheerfully that inasmuch as the seats had all been sold I would be undisturbed by the fact that the people did not occupy them. He seemed decently appalled at so commercial a viewpoint."

As time went on he developed an amusing adoration for Eleanor. He wrote her often on White House stationery. "I thought you would get a thrill out of seeing a letter written on this stationery, so here goes," he started one letter. He blurted to Booth Tarkington out of a clear blue sky one day, "Mrs. Roosevelt is the greatest woman alive and if she came into this room, we all ought to get down on our knees before her." Whenever she was attacked by Roosevelt-haters, his rotundity shook with fury. He often wrote her for permission to write articles denouncing her opposition, but each time she prohibited him from doing so.

He considered himself her court jester and she his queen. Eleanor treated him in return with "amusement and friendly tolerance." Once when he tried without success to get past her secretary and go to her room, he drew himself up and cast Tommy a withering look. "What's the matter, Tommy?" he said bitingly, in his best *Man Who Came to Dinner* manner. "Are you afraid I'll compromise her?" Tommy let him pass.

Once after he became a successful radio broadcaster, she came to his room in New York's Gotham Hotel and asked if he would mention one of her underdog causes on his program. "Of course, Mrs. Roosevelt." His voice was syrupy.

Just as they reached the elevator stop, she turned and said, "I don't see how you find time for all the things you do, Mr. Woollcott."

He opened his mouth in shock but for once he was speechless, because he realized how puny the compliment was coming from someone as active as she was. "I nearly pushed her down the elevator shaft," she heard he had told a friend later.

Strangely, for someone who worked hard at bringing guests like Woollcott and others to Franklin's table, on occasion she herself was absent when her presence was essential. When John L. Lewis, the father of the CIO, was omitted from a White House labor luncheon through an unintentional oversight, Eleanor invited him and his wife to come to a private tea with her and Franklin. Unfortunately, on the appointed day one of her boys was sick and she left town to go to him. When

John L. walked in and saw Missy LeHand, Franklin's secretary, pouring the tea his heavy brows formed a deep inverted V. He considered Eleanor's absence a deep slur on himself and his family, and from that point onward animosity was in evidence in his relationship to Franklin.

One of Eleanor's peculiarities was to invite what her mother-in-law would have called "very common people" to spend the night at the White House. "They'll enjoy it so," she once tried to explain her action. "They'll remember it all their lives."

Only a few caused trouble, though many caused anxiety to the Secret Service. Once when she heard a poor man's weary tale of depression woe, she invited him to stay the night in the White House and promised to land him a job the next morning. One look at his disreputable appearance and the Secret Service bosses rushed to her for some sharp talk. "You can't let him sleep under the same roof as the President," they bullied her.

"And why not? He's perfectly harmless."

"Because you can't, that's why. We won't permit it."

But she insisted and he stayed.

The next day when he left, it was noted that some White House silverware had gone out with him. He had repaid her kindness with thievery.

The Secret Service suspected that many of the persons she invited to spend the night in the White House were dangerous radicals. When the first such person showed up, the Secret Service boss paid her a call. "Mrs. Roosevelt," he told her, "So-and-so is not a very nice person. In fact, we have information that he is an out-and-out Communist."

She was affronted by the charge. "I'm not prepared to listen to a lot of idle gossip about my friends," she told him, "and I'll invite anybody here whom I choose to invite."

Following that visit, the Secret Service conducted a security check on all her guests and handed her their findings. With satisfaction they noted that those with unsatisfactory reports were never seen in the White House again.

The differences in the personalities of Eleanor and Franklin Roosevelt showed up clearly during the second term. Franklin didn't think in terms of individuals. His mind ran to broad programs and policy. Eleanor was all individual in approach. For instance when she rode commercial airlines, she talked to other passengers as though they were all on the same level. One person who watched several such amazing scenes said popeyed, "An old-line politician would be dumfounded at her patient attention to discourses on the state of the Union by these passers-by and still more at her serene and sometimes lengthy analyses and defense of government policies."

"They have the same single vote that I have," she said in defense, when criticized for this un-First Ladylike activity. Detractors found it "a cheap desire to ensnare public good will."

Her tree outlook instead of a forest approach permitted her to give things the personal touch Franklin could not. Even at outings at Shangri-la, at Catoctin, Maryland, she busied herself making sure the Secret Service men and marines present ate first before she joined Franklin and the other guests at the table. She maintained an enormous card-index file of persons to whom she sent Thanksgiving, Christmas, birthday, wedding, and anniversary presents. She even went so far as to requisition a White House closet as her "Christmas Closet," into which she began pouring Christmas presents as early as April each year. On birthdays, she not only sent along cakes but also included the candles. At Thanksgiving, hundreds of boxes of "goodies" left the White House for the homes of friends around the country. Very often overnight guests were surprised when handed a box lunch just before they left the White House. And on arriving home, they would frequently find a packaged food delicacy from her. Once a rude male wrote her that he had expected a turkey instead of the capon she sent him! Nearing Christmas, she was up night after night past two A.M. wrapping presents and pouring nearly a ton of candy into her send-away boxes. Never were any presents sent because it was politically expedient to do so. In fact, one recipient was a woman whom she "got to know quite well who had been in the Alderson, West Virginia, prison for having mailed drugs to another drug addict."

If Franklin could not think in terms of individuals, neither was he capable of identifying himself with groups or organizations. On the contrary, Eleanor could and did. Her many efforts on behalf of various groups, interestingly enough, redounded to his credit and gave his administration a more liberal tinge than it would have had otherwise. When she joined the CIO Newspaper Guild, administration opponents charged Franklin with being too pro-labor. However, they did not know what to make of their charge when she refused to cross a picket line of hotel waitresses to attend the annual birthday ball held in Franklin's honor.

Of course, there were her continual efforts with youth and women's groups that added to Franklin's liberal luster. But it was her activities with Negroes that produced the greatest emotions, especially in the South where Democrats closely allied themselves with white supremacy.

It was her pioneering effort that was to lead in time to demands of Negroes for equal rights with whites and for greater participation in local and national affairs. Along the way she made herself available to great personal vilification and profanity by outraged whites. But in the end she gave civil rights for Negroes a big push forward, from which there was no turning the clock back. By her championing of their cause and through her position as First Lady, she gave Negroes an American birthright they had never enjoyed before.

A governor from Georgia once acknowledged the power of her one-woman army in a talk he had with Franklin. "We don't really have any Negro issue in the South, Mr. President," he broached the subject. "It's white agitators from the Nawth who make all the trouble."

Franklin tapped his cigarette ash into an ash tray and turned back to the governor with an impish smile. "You mean Eleanor, don't you?"

The governor nodded.

Yet her championing of Negroes was not a blatant business of fiery speeches or Carrie Nation ax-swinging in a barroom of bigotry. It was done quietly but resolutely and by example to point out the inanities and injustices of anti-Negro mentalities. For instance, down in Birmingham one time where she attended a meeting of the Southern Conference of Human Welfare, whites and Negroes attending were separated by an aisle. Deliberately, she sat among the Negroes. Policemen, waiting for such a move, hurriedly ordered her out of the Negro section, with the admonition that the local ordinance barred integrated seating. Rather than give in, she asked that a chair be placed in the aisle between both sections and occupied it throughout the publicized meeting. Police grumbled when they noted that she had inched her chair closer to the Negro section but they did nothing.

To frighten her from attending further meetings, word was delivered to her that everyone attending would be arrested for violating Birmingham's strong law against any mixed audiences. But she attended and nothing happened.

She was the first First Lady to have photographs taken with colored people, a practice her predecessors barred. She also entertained the National Council of Negro Women several times in the White House. She was instrumental in establishing one of the first Negro vocational schools in the South. This was at Franklin's beloved Warm Springs in Georgia and the school was dedicated to her.

Few of her activities in behalf of Negroes pleased Franklin's press secretary, Stephen Early, who came from the South. Once when she announced that she would hold a garden party on the White House

[251]

lawn for the colored girls of the National Training School for Girls, he went incensed to her with the charge that she was harming her husband. But she held the party on schedule and entertained the sixty girls incarcerated for petty crimes.

The party drew nationwide attention. Later she talked in behalf of improving the living conditions of these young prisoners. They lived in horrible conditions, she said, and had no care or teaching. Her championing of their cause stirred the next Congress to appropriate $100,000 to clean up the place and start an educational program there.

She did a similar job in behalf of the colored Home for the Aged of Washington. White House aides tried to dissuade her from carrying this cause to Congress. However, she insisted upon speaking about the horrors she had seen there. To a congressional committee she pointed out disgustedly, "We should be ashamed. I was sickened. If that is the way we care for people who are not able to care for themselves, we are at a pretty low ebb of civilization."

The congressmen shifted uneasily as she pointed out details of mistreatment of these aged persons. Not long afterward, Congress passed an appropriation to rectify the situation.

She was also a front fighter to expand the facilities of Howard University, the Negro college in Washington. Several times she added the prestige of the White House to the college by addressing the student body. This was not without its problems, however, because of the mobs of people who showed up each time she appeared. In December, 1935, for instance, she addressed the Faculty Women's Club there. So many gate crashers pushed their way into the room that the place was soon a scene of bedlam. With Eleanor hemmed in from all sides, the clubwoman in charge shrilly screamed that she would call the police unless the uninvited left. In the confusion, Eleanor found herself all alone on the street.

Perhaps the most widely publicized blow Eleanor Roosevelt struck in behalf of Negro rights came in 1939 when the great singer, Marian Anderson, was refused permission by the Daughters of the American Revolution to sing in their auditorium, Constitution Hall. In a full outstirring of emotion, Oscar Chapman, Assistant Secretary of the Interior, arranged for her to sing at the foot of Lincoln Memorial, a telling place indeed for such an event. An audience of more than 75,000 came to hear her. While the event was in itself an important occasion for all Negro Americans, its climax came from the White House when Eleanor publicly announced her resignation from the D.A.R.

Another major personality difference between Eleanor and Franklin was that she always spoke her mind while he was not always capable of frankness. Franklin gave those with opposing views the impression he favored each position because, said she, "he disliked being disagreeable." Several claimed later that they were misled by his seeming concurrence with their views. He also led many to believe they were important legislative advisers. One such person was Francis Cardinal Spellman, whom Franklin encouraged to send him letters on vital issues. Harold Laski, the British radical professor, was another. Laski's handwritten letters were difficult to read because his tiny lettering resembled flea droppings in narrow furrows. Whenever one of his epistles arrived, Franklin called out with a strong muttering sigh, "Bring in the magnifying glass."

Eleanor never said anything behind a person's back that she would not say to his face. And on political, social and judicial matters, one always knew where she stood. In fact, her frankness on occasion was disquieting to Franklin. One time, for instance, she caused quite a furore when she got into the Lindbergh kidnaping case and expressed her view that Bruno Hauptmann, the accused murderer, might not have been fairly tried because all the evidence was circumstantial.

Franklin's incapacity for frankness spilled over into other directions. For example, he deplored the shortcomings of his valet McDuffie. McDuffie was often AWOL when he was needed to lift Franklin from one seat to another. As Franklin's barber, he cut the President's hair so short and ragged that Eleanor often gasped at the sight of her husband. Yet Franklin could never bring himself to fire McDuffie. The passing of McDuffie came about indirectly. Once when Eleanor was in Seattle visiting daughter Anna, the phone rang. It was Franklin, one of the most powerful men on earth, calling her. "Eleanor," he pleaded, "I can't take any more of McDuffie's antics. Would you please call him here at the White House and fire him for me?" She did the job for him.

However, in her own activities she was just as tenderhearted as he. When a temperamental White House cook took to screaming as she mixed ingredients and the rest of the kitchen help demanded that she be fired, Eleanor refused to let her go. "We have to treat her like a child," she said soothingly. When White House servants were ill, she visited them in the hospital, to the eye-widening awe of the Negro doctors. Once when a servant was discovered to be a heavy stealer of White House valuables, instead of firing him Eleanor said, "We'll transfer him to a place where he won't be tempted." She found another job for him as a custodial employee in a government building.

In many ways she babied her husband. One time when Franklin finished a fighting speech to a large gathering and started climbing into his car, she hurried to him and pulled down his hiking coat back in front of all watchers. She personally took the time to monogram all his handkerchiefs because he thought no one else could do as well. She also bought all his ties, though he rebelled one year when she gave him gaily colored cravats instead of the somber tones she had previously purchased for him. Once when he was feeling proud because he had just been named as one of the ten best-dressed men in the nation, she told him in her motherly fashion at cocktails one evening before dinner, "Franklin, your trousers are wearing out. I'm going to call in a tailor."

"But I can't afford a new suit," he wailed.

"You will have to get one," she told him flatly. Other guests present laughed in embarrassment.

She had a greater evenness of temperament than he. "He was very slow to anger," she said one time, "but when he was once angry it shook him to the bottom of his soul." On one occasion, she recalled, "an ambitious man through gossip caused an administration official to resign. Later he came and asked Franklin for an appointment. Franklin said, 'You can go straight to hell—which is too good for you.' When I saw Franklin shortly after this episode, he was still white with wrath."

Yet, she could get angry, too. The classic instance came one time during the second term when Secretary of the Treasury Morgenthau advised White House help that he was sending a young couple to visit the White House. By coincidence, another young couple, intent on "crashing" the White House, appeared at the big door at the expected time and were mistakenly permitted to enter. Somehow they found their way upstairs and walked into Franklin's study, where they shook his hand and made themselves comfortable. When Eleanor walked in, she saw immediately that they were strangers. "How dare you do this!" she yelled at them, as she hurried them out. "You have done a dangerous thing, as well as a rude one. You would have been shot on sight if the Secret Service men had seen you." Franklin watched the scene thunderstruck at her fury.

There were other ways in which they differed. Franklin could not take ridicule and he carried grudges. He never forgot that Bernard Baruch, to whom Eleanor kept turning for advice and contributions to her various charities, had supported Al Smith before the 1932 Democratic National Convention. One bystander noted that Franklin could recall every instance in which a person had displeased him and could recite such displeasure in chronological order.

On the other hand, his wife, subject to a press barrage of name-calling, paid no attention to it. Even when the ridicule came close to home, she wasn't affronted. On one occasion, passing through the business end of the White House, she overheard one of the women employees burlesquing the way she sounded on radio. "That was wonderful," she stepped into view and applauded. "You must do that at a party I'm giving." The poor girl tried to apologize, but she would hear none of it. Later when the girl showed up on schedule to perform her mimicry, one glance at Eleanor's beaming face and she lost her voice. Her cousin, Alice Longworth, was another who imitated her well, and several times at parties Eleanor insisted that she do it. Nor did she let politics interfere with personal friendship. When Corinne Alsop, her first cousin and the mother of the young columnists Joseph and Stewart Alsop, came to Washington to attend a meeting of the violently anti-Roosevelt Liberty League, Eleanor put her up at the White House. Long after Japan invaded China Eleanor was still corresponding with the widow of former Ambassador Saito. On receipt of one letter, Madame Saito wrote her, she "jumped with joy."

In his second term Franklin did not approach life as a short-time proposition. Time could be wasted, if he felt like doing so. Once, for instance, when an important official came to discuss business, Franklin frittered away much of the time throwing a ball for a dog to retrieve. When the dog proved to be poorly housebroken, he interrupted the discussion to buzz for a servant to rub the dog's nose into the mess he had made on the presidential rug.

On the other hand, Eleanor watched with horror as the minutes of each day sped past. Her little black appointment book was now crowded with as many as 20 appointments for a single day. One day she visited a homestead project and made 14 speeches. On a blustery November day in New York, she was running down Madison Avenue and turned suddenly into the Lilly Daché hat shop. "I've got ten minutes between appointments," she told the saleslady, "and I want to see some hats." She tried on four that were rushed to her and bought two. Another time when Betsy Cushing Roosevelt was expecting her second child in a New York hospital, Eleanor hurried there. The baby was all day in being born, and Eleanor paced the hospital corridors like a soldier on double time. Finally when granddaughter Kate was born and she determined that mother and daughter were doing fine, she turned to a friend and exclaimed, "Well, I've just got to get into action. I've just got to do something. I can't stand this inaction." With that she was out of the hospital and running down the street to hop aboard a Fifth Avenue bus.

All in all, the political team of Eleanor and Franklin was a powerful

[255]

one. He was the better politician. He took the long view and was practical, while Eleanor's concern with injustices and her overpowering sense of duty made her impatient with delay and maneuvering. When she argued with him to support anti-lynching and anti-poll tax measures in Congress, he demurred. When she persisted, he told her, "First things come first, and I can't alienate certain votes I need for measures that are important at the moment by pushing any measure that would entail a fight."

To her this was not a good answer, but in retrospect she came in time to see that he was right. Franklin's long view also enabled him to use people who might prove of value later on. Eleanor couldn't see this at all. When she found that Franklin had invited Henry Ford and his wife to visit them at Warm Springs, she told Franklin that this would be "a stupid political mistake."

"In what way?" he asked.

"Why Ford did more than any other man to wreck NRA and to have him here would be to encourage NRA opposition and discourage the friends of NRA."

It turned out that Henry Ford was too ill to visit Warm Springs at the proffered time. Nevertheless, Franklin continued writing to him in a friendly vein, calling him his old friend of his Navy days during World War I and exchanging birthday greetings with the automobile manufacturer. When Ford came to lunch finally in 1938, he was more or less sneaked in and out of the White House by Eleanor's brother Hall.

Despite the opposition of 85 per cent of the press to the Roosevelts when Franklin's second term unfolded, their vast popularity with an overwhelming majority of Americans was begrudgingly admitted by their detractors. A case in point occurred in the Mercer County Circuit and Criminal Court in Princeton, West Virginia on August 26, 1937. In a damage suit that day, eleven jurors voted for damages ranging from $12,000 to $50,000. The twelfth juror, a Negro named Joe Cook, voted for Roosevelt. When the astounded judge demanded an explanation for such frivolity, Joe Cook said proudly, "I never overlook an opportunity to vote for Roosevelt."

Chapter Twenty-Seven

ONCE DURING Franklin Roosevelt's second term an observer facetiously noted that Dolly Madison had saved the portrait of George Washington by cutting it from its frame but Eleanor would have lifted the heavy frame from the wall and carried it out of the White House. "Then she would have sat down and written about the fire for the daily newspapers."

The truth was that energetic Eleanor had added a new activity to her daily dozen. She was now a full-fledged daily columnist. Starting with 20 papers in 1936, by 1939, 68 papers with a circulation of 4,500,000 were printing her column, "My Day," and a year later 140 newspapers across the country were running it. The 1936 campaign had brought on a curious spurt in subscribing newspapers, which bothered Franklin because it offset his repeated charge that Republicans controlled American newspapers. His faith in his charge was joyously restored, however, shortly after he defeated Alf Landon, when many Republican papers quietly dropped her column.

Until she got into the swing of things, the column created a real problem at first, for somehow it had to be sandwiched among all her other heavy activities. With a relentless deadline to meet, it had to be written under many strange circumstances. Perforce, she dictated it directly to faithful Tommy, always with great and intense expression, but seldom with any revision. Sometimes she dictated her column with a grandchild on her lap and pulling her hair; sometimes while sitting on a rock atop a mountain or in a speeding limousine, on a hotel bed or on a destroyer. Once when Franklin finished a speech at a CCC camp and was ready to move on, she held him there while she finished her column in a car. Often the problem arose of locating a telegraph office to send her column by deadline time. One time on a wild hunt in Connecticut for Western Union, she drove through a red light and subjected herself to a bawling out from a policeman. But the column had to be delivered in rain, wind and sleet, and only once did Tommy type one and fail to send it in.

Franklin had tried to discourage her from undertaking this chore when she first considered it. "It's too much for you to add to all those other things you're doing," he groaned. There had been enough carping at her bizarre First Lady activities from within his own circle of lieutenants—the haremlike outlook of men who despised women in politics—as well as the sharp attacks on her from Republicans. Besides, he was preparing for his bitter fight to alter the character of the Supreme Court, which was slapping down New Deal legislation left and right. He had enough on his mind, he complained to her, without having to concern himself with further attacks on her. But she had her arguments well prepared. The thousands of dollars she earned each month would go to her charities, which were increasing at a rapid rate. In addition, she would write a sort of diary of her daily activities and would not write about politics. "All right, go ahead," he gave her his weary blessing.

The nature of "My Day" was as she promised him, at first. In fact, it was so banal and so filled with trivia the first year that she underwent a great deal of ridicule. "Do you write your own columns?" she was asked. "Of course," she replied. "If I didn't they would be very much better than they are. That proves it." Especially did she seem to like the words "interesting" and "lovely." As for her grammar, one deprecating soul peppered her with letters about mistakes and beat on her with grammatical rules to follow. "Tell me if you get this, dear," she appendaged to one letter.

Her sharpest critic was Westbrook Pegler, a fellow columnist, once a warm supporter of her husband and a frequent guest at Hyde Park during the 1932 campaign. A professional anti-Roosevelt by the mid-thirties and with an enormous readership, he incensed Franklin one time with a take-off on her column which read as follows: "In the afternoon a group of young people arrived at the Little House and we plunged at once into a very interesting discussion of the duty of the citizen, not only toward his country but towards himself and his fellow man in relation to the past and the future ahead. One gentleman had rather strong ideas on the subject of nail-biting and while, of course, I realize there are two sides to this question, I'm afraid that capital punishment for nail-biters is rather severe. I prefer what seems to me the more democratic way and proposed to approach it as a world problem, since nail-biting is not a matter of race or creed."

The character of her column changed slowly. During 1937, when she began inserting a few controversial items, they were carefully edited out by her syndicate managers. There was still great desire on their part to keep her writing on minutiae, such as the details of the wedding of her son, Franklin, Jr., to Ethel du Pont on June 30, 1937. Even here there was some concern because Ethel's father, Eugene du Pont, was a prominent backer of the violently anti-Roosevelt Liberty League. Because of the great political differences between the two families, there was tension on both sides to ensure that the wedding would come off without mishap.

Everything did come off well. Inundating the area around Christ Church in Christiana Hundred near Wilmington, as well as the du Pont estate, Owl's Nest, five miles away, were special details of Secret Service men, police and 350 soldiers. The affair was almost like a military maneuver with hundreds jamming the church and more than 1,100 guests at the reception held later in the oak-paneled living room at Owl's Nest. Franklin was left to stand for an hour and a half in the receiving line, a matter of great concern to his doctor and the disapproving Secret Service men. Eleanor had to leave in the middle of the affair to hurry to a radio broadcast in Wilmington, where she strangely told the nation, "I don't know whether to be happy or sad. I, for one, always am torn between the realization of the adventure that two young things are starting on and its possibilities for good and bad." Then she rushed back to the reception.

The du Ponts managed to get the last word. The periodically printed du Pont family album, which was supposed to appear next in 1939, was hurriedly rushed to the printers before the wedding. In this way, there was no need to include the name Roosevelt in the family album.

Because it was dictated, the writing in her column never attained real smoothness and grace, though there were poignant descriptions at times. She reported once from a train window, "a little girl, slim and bent over, carrying two pails of water across the field to an unpainted house."

Gradually, as though she were struggling within herself to make her real personality felt, the simple, recorded daily diary gave way to strong opinions on a great variety of controversial subjects. By 1939, and almost unnoticed in its change in emphasis, "My Day" emerged as a vital stump for swaying and influencing public opinion.

"In Washington," journalist Raymond Clapper wrote, "her daily column is read between the lines for tips on policies in the making." Hardly a subject undergoing national attention failed to find its way into her column. Where Franklin had to play it safe because he was bound by his position as President and as leader of a loose-ends political party, no such chains held her. Why not use her column at times for purposes dear to him? No one could hold him responsible. "If I said something which I felt strongly," she admitted, "and Franklin agreed to

[259]

let me say it, it was often a trial balloon. If what I said caused a violent reaction, he could say honestly that he had no responsibility and the thoughts were my own."

Her new-type column writing got a curious reception from Franklin. He was pleased to have this strong propaganda weapon at his disposal. Yet he was intensely concerned with separating Eleanor his wife from Eleanor the columnist. He wanted the benefits of her column without any of its detractions. "I can always say," he told her with a twinkle one time, "that I can't do a thing with you."

Once she started delving into hot national and international problems and coming out with unequivocal opinions and demands for political action, even dinner became a problem. "Are we just talking or are you interviewing me?" he asked her one time at the table. Another time after he had finished explaining his position on a highly important matter, he suddenly gasped at her and exclaimed, "Darling, you can't use this in your column. It really is off the record." On a later occasion, after she was well into a Clarence Darrow-type cross-examination of him, daughter Anna who was present at dinner said poutingly, "Mother, can't you see that you are giving father indigestion?"

Yet when he wanted to express his opinion and could not do so because of his position, he was quick to pass it on to her with a nod. And sometimes to doubly emphasize his stated position, he made sure that his words reached her column. One time, for example, in 1939, her column contained identical phrases and sentences to be found in that day's presidential press conference, a matter that evoked loud wonder whether her opinions had spilled over onto him or whether the reverse had occurred.

As the second term moved along, there were still columns devoted to the Easter egg rolling day on the White House lawn, with statistics, as in 1937, showing an attendance of 53,108 persons, 180 children lost and found, 30 sick and 6 cases of fainting. And there were the usual comments about the gouging practices of the children who charged adults fifty cents each to get them admitted as "parents." There were the stories of her christening the new transatlantic plane, the *Clipper,* and the swift new liner, the *America.* There were also the emotional reports of her visits to slums and California migrant camps and her demands for legislation to aid them. In one Okie camp she found the single water faucet serving the entire tent camp next to the foul privy. When she asked a young work-worn mother if she could enter her tent and look around, she got the reply, "Why certainly, but we haven't had a chance to clean up from last night's flood and a mess of measles." She later told Franklin, trapped as he was as a prisoner in the White House, "I wonder if it strikes you as it does me how remarkable it is that people can keep up their courage and struggle in the face of so many hardships?"

But there was more than concern for the domestic plight of Americans now. There was the world full of injustices to claim her attention also. The day after Franklin's first inauguration in March, 1933, the entire front page of *The New York Times* had been devoted to the inauguration, except for a single item:

VICTORY FOR HITLER
EXPECTED TODAY

It was a strange coincidence that Hitler and her husband should assume power in Germany and the United States at the same time. What troubled Eleanor most about the former Austrian paper hanger was his announced intention to bring the world under his dictatorial control. For she was in spirit a pacifist who spoke out openly even against such innocuous pastimes as the use of toy guns and soldiers by children. As a spirited member of the National Conference on the Cause and Cure of War, along with her close friend Carrie Chapman Catt, founder and chairman of the conference, her international outlook in 1933 was one calling for greater friendship among nations and general disarmament. As an old Navy man, Franklin did not share her view on disarmament and argued often with her that a disarmed United States would be meat for the likes of Hitler. In fact, one time when she prevailed on him to talk to the members of the National Conference on the Cause and Cure of War, he upset the decorum of the gathering by plunging into a strong talk on the need for a strong America. A short time later she showed her divergence from his views further by inducing their close family friend, Admiral Richard Byrd, to help her start a "No Foreign War" crusade.

However, events moved rapidly on her now and strong doubts appeared in her mind. The first shadow appeared in 1935 when Hitler announced he would rearm Germany. The shadow grew the following March when he marched into the Rhineland in violation of the Versailles Treaty. It exploded when Italy's dictator began bombing Ethiopia, and her lip service to pacifism disappeared in mid-1936 when the Spanish Civil War started. "It would be impossible for the United States to remain untouched by the effects of a major war elsewhere in the world," was her new attitude.

The country was politically isolationist now; Congress had passed neutrality legislation barring aid to all belligerents in a war, even aid to nations attacked and invaded. Franklin found himself helpless to change the trend.

However, none of this stopped Eleanor from raising a high moral shield and using her column to fight isolationism. There were attacks on her now from all sides. Speeches of yesteryear were raked up to combat her with her own remarks. "The war idea is obsolete," she had said in 1935. Today she was accused of warmongering.

The Spanish Civil War was a great test case for her. When she raised money for Spanish Loyalist refugee children, she incurred the wrath of the Catholic Church, despite the fact that combatants on both sides were Catholic. To her it was the fight of a democratically elected government against a Fascist uprising with German and Italian backing, despite the muddying of the core with Communist Russia's aid to the Loyalists. Franklin also wanted the Loyalists to defeat Franco in Spain, but he wouldn't come out openly because he believed that Congress would not back him up. To justify his inaction to Eleanor, he argued that the League of Nations had asked the United States to remain neutral. "By trying to convince me that our course was correct," she said, "though he knew I thought we were doing the wrong thing, he was simply trying to salve his own conscience, because he himself was uncertain."

Nevertheless, she never gave up working on him until the Loyalists were finally overwhelmed. By dogged persistence she got him to appoint a committee to raise funds for humanitarian relief work in Spain, with the Red Cross administering the program. On her own, she developed a plan to bring 500 Basque children to the United States until the war was ended. She also adopted some Spanish children, refugees in wretched camps set up in France across the border. And as long as the civil war lasted, she gave him little peace on the issue of aiding the Loyalists. One time she brought up the question with one of Franklin's aides while Franklin was in the room. As though he were not present, she said to her husband's assistant, "We should have pushed him harder." Franklin stared at both but said nothing. Another time when Franco had succeeded in trapping the Loyalist leaders in Madrid, she dispatched an angry telegram to Franklin from Seattle. "Are you or State doing anything?" His reply was a weak: "State Department doing everything possible in Spain."

Franklin would not depart from his ingrained political adage that when a politician advances ideas for which the country is not ready, he can succeed only in losing his following. The process of turning the country from isolationism to responsibility for events outside the nation must be a slow one. Besides, when that did come about, he hoped only to deter Hitler from war. Eleanor could cry out against the injustices she saw overseas as much as she wanted to, but he could not.

The overseas dictators considered Eleanor a real menace. In February, 1939 when she came out for sending military planes to France, Nazi papers screamed headlines at her with demands that she stop making comments. "It is not good for a nation," Joseph Goebbels, propaganda boss of Germany, cried out, "when the wife enters the political china shop." A short time later Goebbels' propaganda line was of a divide-and-conquer nature: "While President Roosevelt is trying to keep the United States out of war, his wife is trying to drag it in." Mussolini also jumped on the anti-Eleanor bandwagon with a call for an "embargo" on her. Eleanor's retort was to label Germany "a sinister power with no scruples" and with a "contempt for those who can't meet her on her own ground."

With the knowledge that time was short before Hitler would bring on a general war, Franklin made his first move to place the power of the United States on the side of the democracies by inviting King George VI of Great Britain and his wife Queen Elizabeth to visit in June, 1939. The visit succeeded admirably in its purpose, though it was attended by a huge comedy of errors. The king and queen came through as gentle symbols of a beleaguered Britain waiting stoically for the Nazi boom to fall.

With her native simplicity, Eleanor treated the visit of the royal couple as an everyday event to be sandwiched among her multitudinous activities. Franklin took it otherwise. Even the invitation itself required evenings of concentration in his upstairs study with several careful re-writes. At the appointed hour for him and Eleanor to go to Union Station to meet the king and queen, who were traveling down from Niagara Falls, he was aghast to find Eleanor in the midst of a probing conversation with some sharecroppers. She had found them stranded on a highway in the Midwest and had brought them to Washington to help them. The result was that when the king and queen stepped off the 12-car gold-and-silver-trimmed train, their only greeter was Mike Reilly, Franklin's personal Secret Service aide. Later, when the Roosevelts had to leave the White House one night to be dined by the royal couple at the British Embassy, Franklin's peevish state revealed itself when Eleanor got out of the White House car to run back for a head covering. "I'm afraid you'd lose your head if it wasn't bound to your neck," he told her petulantly when she returned.

While the king and queen proved to be no bother, the British servants were another matter. Despite Washington's wretched heat, they insisted on obtaining hot water bottles for the royal beds. There were also hysterical outbreaks about getting a proper shower cap for the queen. When the British couple's food problems came up and Eleanor was told to avoid serving suet pudding and capers, she treated it as a joke, because such foods were foreign to her table. Franklin did not like her attitude: "My husband sensed that I was saying something naughty and so I had to become serious and stop playing with words."

The royal servants also got into hassles with White House servants, many of which Eleanor had to settle. To one haughty servant who informed everyone contemptuously, "I am the queen's maid," one of the White House ushers yelled disgustedly, "Oh, you're a big shot, hey?" Eleanor recorded other episodes, all related to the penchant of the British servants for strong drink. "The housekeeper reported that the king's valet was demanding more whiskey. He said he could not drink American beer and he had already had one bottle of whiskey. . . . He did not get any more." Another note: "We learned later that the queen's maid had requisitioned three bottles of gin during a two-day stay and when I told my husband about her he said, 'My, she's a hearty lass, isn't she?'" There were also problems with the entertainers whom Eleanor asked to sing following dinner. Marian Anderson, over whom Eleanor had made a *cause célèbre* with the D.A.R., proved temperamental when asked to sing Negro spirituals. One young man whom Eleanor invited to sing folk songs underwent a complete frisking beforehand by Secret Service and Scotland Yard men because of a rumor that he was a Communist. By the time he was called upon to sing only the faintest trickle of wobbly notes came from his throat.

After the Washington visit which included, at Eleanor's request, a stop in a CCC camp, the king and queen went to New York for a look at the World's Fair and then entrained to Hyde Park where Franklin and Eleanor and Sara Roosevelt awaited them. On the tour of the fairgrounds with Grover Whalen, New York's official greeter, explaining without respite the various sights along the way, the king suddenly leaned over toward the queen and gasped, "I am getting faint." His face had turned a greenish hue, and the tarpaulin was ripped from the car's top to give him air. Also at the fair, the king's gray topper mysteriously disappeared. A ten-year-old urchin was found wearing it in the men's room.

Sara Roosevelt was accustomed to royalty and received her visitors with ease. In 1934, she had visited the king's parents at Buckingham Palace, an event that had pleased her almost as much as the fact that she was able to buy Franklin a tweed suit in England that "cost less than $25." There was her disapproval now when Franklin had a tray of cocktails brought into the library. "My mother does not approve of cocktails and thinks you should have a cup of tea," Franklin winked at the king. "Neither does my mother," the king laughed and picked up a drink.

Eleanor's job as newspaper columnist came into some hard knocks from Sara, who considered it in poor taste to divulge the details of some of the events that took place during the Hyde Park visit. This was especially true of Eleanor's columns devoted to the enormous amount of plate breakage that occurred. "My mother-in-law was very indignant with me for telling the world about it and not keeping it a deep, dark family secret." There was the serving table heavy with dishes that collapsed in the midst of dinner. "Sara's loud comment was, 'I hope none of my dishes were among those broken.'" There was also the butler who misjudged the stairs from the hall to the library after dinner, dropped his heavy tray with a resounding crash and came sliding on his back across the library floor with a look of terror on his face.

On the second day of the visit, Franklin asked George and Elizabeth (familiarity made formal titles ridiculous) to come to a picnic at Hilltop Cottage, the house he had designed and constructed for his own use nearby the Val-Kill furniture factory. Symbolic hot dogs were on the groaning board amidst the lavish layout of turkeys, hams and salads. "I thought I would give them everything American," Eleanor decided, "and for dessert I had strawberry shortcake. I found out later that every place they had been in Canada and in the United States, they were served strawberries in some form!"

Amidst the pleasant day, a further round of mishaps occurred. After Franklin and the king had a swim in the outdoor pool, Franklin backed into a tray of dishes and sent them flying. There was also another entertainment squabble. "I had asked Princess Te-Ata, an American Indian princess, to sing some Indian songs for us," Eleanor noted. "I had known her for many years and I always enjoyed her artistry." Also, on the program, she had scheduled a part-Indian to dance for her guests. "Te-Ata at first was not willing to perform with him because 'he was not an artist and not a true Indian.'" Only after long and patient coaxing was she able to persuade Te-Ata to go on.

At last the royal visit was over. The good will created for England through the "My Day" columns and the news stories by other writers made a deep impression on the nation. Eleanor was at the little Hyde Park station with Franklin for the final farewell. "One thought of the clouds that hung over them and the worries they were going to face, and we turned away and left the scene with a heavy heart."

The muffled storm broke into a beating downpour only a few months later. In August, Franklin angrily noted the final track-clearing for Nazi aggression when Vyacheslav Molotov and Joachim von Ribbentrop, foreign ministers of the Soviet Union and Germany, signed a friendship pact. On September first at five A.M., Franklin called Hyde Park and woke Eleanor. "Babs," he said huskily. "It's happened. Germany has invaded Poland."

World War II was on. War—and she had four eligible sons, in case the fighting should spread to the United States. "I hope we can avoid it," Franklin said.

Chapter Twenty-Eight

THERE WAS precious little time to lose now. In order to help England and France against Germany and the Soviet Union, Franklin called a special session of Congress for September 21 to repeal the Arms Embargo provisions of the Neutrality Acts. One of Eleanor's tasks became that of going out on the hustings to drum up support for the repeal. Colonel Charles Lindbergh had come flying upon the scene to spread the gospel of isolationism and the opinion that Hitler's Germany was riding the crest of the wave of the future. He found himself back in the limelight he had known after his flight to Paris in 1927.

The Administration's answer to Lindbergh was Eleanor. When the colonel and Senator Burton K. Wheeler of Montana began a cross-country stint to instill in audiences the fear of taking an affirmative stand on aid to Britain, she followed in their wake. In the rabidly isolationist Midwest, this was a fairly thankless job. In St. Paul, for instance, she found herself drowned out by catcalls. But she was used to such treatment. Her cause was more important than herself. *Time* Magazine, which often had expressed Republican distaste for her and Franklin, took note of her persistent solitary effort and noted that in the end she "did much to wean the country away from isolationism."

Her sights were farther ahead than the repeal of the Arms Embargo. Less than two weeks after the start of World War II, even though the United States was not at war, she suggested to Franklin and some of his advisers that there be officially established "an international group continuously to plan for future peace." Sumner Welles, who was brought into the discussion of her proposal, later said she wanted to set up a body "similar in composition to the Security Council of the United Nations." She proposed that all the anti-Axis countries meet "without delay to study the future structure of the world . . . to iron out differences among member nations and be prepared at the end of the war to present for final approval of the peace conference postwar policies already agreed upon in principle."

Franklin rejected her proposal, said Welles, on the advice of Harry

Hopkins, who was "instinctively inclined toward isolationism." Other advisers called her plan "political dynamite." The sad part about it, Welles noted, was that the alternative to her proposal was to wait until a peace conference met after the war to do this job.

Strangely, all the while Eleanor worked on public opinion to end the blight of isolationism and give thought to the postwar world, she carried on an activity that was diametrically opposed to these goals. This was her odd role as patroness of the American Youth Congress, a "loud, sloganeering, chip-on-shoulder, treat-'em-rough mob" of radical youngsters.

She had been of vast importance to American youth through her work in bringing the National Youth Administration into existence in Franklin's first term. NYA meant an opportunity for millions of young people to continue their schooling. But there were other aspects of the youth problem, she felt, that also demanded her aid. They needed jobs and they needed guidance, for they were the coming generation.

When the American Youth Congress was formed in the mid-thirties as the top body for 60 organizations, she was quick to take on the function of sponsoring it. She invited AYC leaders to the White House to add to the organization's prestige, gave them advice and money, got speakers for them and spoke often herself. "It seemed a good way to find out what young people were thinking," she said.

Unfortunately, there was little about the AYC that was not to prove of great embarrassment to her. For its membership was not representative of American youth but was instead a down-the-line pro-Soviet clambake. Those who opposed this line found themselves squelched at meetings or given the bum's rush. In 1937 they staged a sit-down strike outside the White House because they claimed the President was not taking their advice for a monumental handout program for youth. When Franklin invited them in for a talk, they were coarse and rude. Several squashed cigarettes out on his expensive rug.

Eleanor continued working with the AYC because no other large groups of American youth were organized. In addition, because they were such mixed-up creatures that they called out the mother in her, she felt she couldn't desert them. Once she ordered the AYC leaders to come to her sitting room in the White House to ask them point-blank if they were Communists. "In every case," she said, "they said they had no connection with the Communists, had never belonged to any Communist organizations and had no interest in Communist ideas." She accepted their word, "realizing that sooner or later the truth would come out."

[268]

On one occasion she went to a congressional hearing with AYC leaders who conducted themselves with little dignity. This was a two-day session with the House Un-American Activities Committee starting on November 30, 1939, where the AYC underwent investigation. While Eleanor sat as a spectator, the young people cavorted by running about the room to distribute pamphlets and talking out loud. One of the AYC leaders, Joseph Lash, even went so far in his testimony as to sing a song for the committee. It went: "If you see an un-American lurking far and near, just alkalize with Martin Dies and he will disappear."

She had decided by now that the organization was pro-Communist, for when the Russians wantonly attacked Finland in November, 1939, the AYC justified the attack. Only a small minority decried the attack. Nevertheless, she did not break with the AYC at that time. Lash stayed with the organization with her blessing to combat the Communists there. She would give the AYC one more chance.

In February, 1940, when the AYC came to Washington for its meeting, she spent two hours on the White House phone arranging sleeping space for delegates at the Fort Myer riding hall and in the guardhouse there, and she paid for their transportation. Some of the key delegates she installed in the White House. She even induced Franklin to address them on February 10.

More than five thousand obstreperous youths appeared on the south lawn of the White House that rainy day. When Franklin looked down, he grimaced at the sight of their blatant banners: *The Yanks Are NOT Coming* and *Keep America Out Of War*. So far as they were concerned, he noted, he was a warmonger and not doing right by their hero Russia. The result was a harsh lecture. He called their stand against loans to Finland "unadulterated twaddle," and to a crescendo of boos and hisses he charged, "The Soviet Union, as everyone who has the courage to face the facts knows, is run by a dictatorship as absolute as any other dictatorship in the world. . . . It has been said that some of you are Communists. That is a very unpopular term these days. As Americans you have a legal and constitutional right to call yourselves Communists, those of you who do. You have a right peacefully and openly to advocate certain ideas of theoretical Communism; but as Americans you have not only a right but a sacred duty to confine your advocacy of changes in law by the methods prescribed by the Constitution of the United States—and you have no American right," he said sternly, "by act or deed of any kind, to subvert the government and the Constitution of the nation."

This was hardly the way to treat invited guests, but the words were long overdue. Later when the AYC met in the Departmental Auditorium, Eleanor sat in the second row and listened to John L. Lewis, head of labor's C.I.O., as he denounced Franklin's talk. Then she stood up to answer all questions. Her patience was at an end and she cautioned the congress "not to boo or hiss until I have finished, then you may do whichever you please." She called their pro-Russian approach "claptrap."

There was one important lesson Eleanor learned from her sad experience with the Communists of the AYC that was to come in handy years later in dealing with the Russians at the United Nations. "They are a disciplined group," she filed away in the back of her mind. "They take orders and they carry them out."

With the outbreak of war in Europe, the chief topic of conversation in the United States was whether Franklin would run for an unprecedented third term. Eleanor was frankly opposed to his continuation in office. When a good friend of hers, Mrs. William Brown Meloney, the organizer of the New York *Herald Tribune* Forum, wrote and told her that she wanted a discussion on a possible third term, Eleanor sent Franklin a note in August, 1938: "She wants you for a third term and I thought this most unwise. You know I do not believe in it, however I think you should say if Murphy is the man."

Her further feeling on the subject was revealed the next year in a memo Harry Hopkins wrote on May 29. "I had lunch today with Mrs. Roosevelt at the White House," he said. "After luncheon we went out in the garden—Mrs. Roosevelt had her knitting—and discussed for three hours the State of the Union.

"Mrs. Roosevelt was greatly disturbed about 1940. She is personally anxious not to have the President run again, but I gathered the distinct impression that she has no more information on that point than the rest of us. She feels that the President has done his part entirely. That he has not the same zest for administrative detail that he had and is probably quite bored. She thinks that the causes for which he fought are far greater than any individual person, but that if the New Deal is entirely dependent upon him, it indicates that it hasn't been as strong in foundation as she believes it has with the great masses of people. Mrs. Roosevelt is convinced that a great majority of the voters are not only with the President, but with the things he stands for. . . ."

There was ample evidence to her that Franklin did not intend to run for a third term. One indication was that he had quietly signed a contract with *Collier's* Magazine to write articles for an annual salary of $75,000. Another was his effort to give Harry Hopkins a build-up of prestige to pave the way for his candidacy. The build-up included moving Hopkins out of the WPA into the Cabinet post as Secretary of Commerce, surrounding him with associates from the world of big business and making frequent statements about his ability. Eleanor also entered into this effort to give Hopkins a sound build-up by using "My Day" for this purpose. For instance, she wrote in a 1938 column: "It was good to see Mr. Hopkins yesterday and to have him spend the night with us. He is one of the few people in the world who gives me the feeling of being absorbed in doing his job well. . . . He seems to work because he has an inner conviction that the job needs to be done and that he must do it. I think he would be that way about any job he undertook."

But the Hopkins bubble burst when he developed a cancer of the stomach. Even after a successful operation, he still lacked energy and his body was unable to make use of fats and proteins. Half in jest and half in disappointment, he wrote Eleanor in August 1939 that the doctors were pushing long tubes down his throat. He could become a professional sword-swallower, he told her. "I am sure I have found a way to earn my livelihood," he said, "if and when the New Deal should be thrown out of Washington."

By September Franklin crossed him off his list of possible successors. He told Eleanor sadly, "The doctors have given Harry up for dead."

In vain did Franklin look for other possible successors who could win in 1940. Not one seemed to have enough public stature to ensure a victory after a short campaign. Of course, Eleanor finally had to admit, there was none because Franklin had been the whole show. He was like the upas tree of ancient lore that killed off everything that came beneath it for shelter. But she still hoped someone would be found in time so Franklin could retire gracefully. In fact, a few years before she had rented a third-floor five-room apartment in New York and they talked frequently about making their home in New York City after January 20, 1941.

Why not Eleanor for President? many asked, but she laughed off this suggestion. A Gallop poll early in 1939 revealed that 67 per cent of Americans approved of her conduct, while only 58 per cent approved of Franklin. William Allen White, the sage of Emporia, Kansas, whom Franklin laughingly accused of being on his side three and a half years out of every four—and the remaining half year falling during the election period—wrote Franklin a letter on December 22, 1939: "If you will agree to let her serve your third term, I shall be for you against all comers. Every time she does anything, she reminds me of T.R. She is his reincarnation."

[271]

Sara was also wishing that Franklin would not run again. She was concerned about what her friends would say if he should. She was tired of the crowds that descended on her estate and of the photographers whose appetite was endless. Asked one time for repeated poses from one cameraman, she said to him scathingly before turning on her heels, "Oh, there's always one more." She was also moved by the change in Franklin's appearance during his second term. "He does seem decidedly older," she said in 1939. "I have noted quite a little change in the past four or five years." And then, raising her handkerchief to her eyes, she added, "I am getting old and I will have to die sometime; but I hope it won't be while Franklin is in office." She wanted her boy home again.

As 1939 went out and the so-called "phony war" in Europe changed the next year with startling speed with the Nazi invasion in April of Denmark and Norway and the May blitzkrieg in Holland, Belgium and Luxemburg, the mystery about Franklin's intentions deepened. The newsgirls of Eleanor's press conferences did their best to pry from her by indirection whether Franklin would run again. "Will the social season next winter be the same as usual?" or: "Where would you hang all these prints in Hyde Park?" or: "Are you doing much thinking about the weather for January 20, 1941?" To all these questions she merely smiled.

It was probably when the Nazi army sliced through France in June 1940 that Franklin finally determined he would run for a third term. Eleanor's attitude was that she would have nothing to do with the July Democratic National Convention in Chicago. She told Franklin with finality: "You have made up your mind you will not go to the convention even if you are nominated but that you will speak over the radio, and that means, I hope, I do not have to go?"

"No, you don't have to go there," he told her firmly.

"Then I'll go up to Hyde Park and stay at my cottage," she told him.

However, the 1940 convention turned into a mess. Harry Hopkins had gone to Chicago to re-enact Louis Howe's role of 1932. But he was green to politics and many of the delegates whom he invited to his third-floor suite in the Blackstone Hotel resented his claim to be Franklin's manager. Jim Farley was also out there, grousing now because he felt that Franklin should have given him his backing for the nomination. One delegate who didn't know which way to turn for leadership slapped his own cheek disgustedly and complained, "The boys know they have rings in their noses, but they don't know who holds the leading strings."

There was little chance to prevent Franklin's nomination, though there was much backbiting. For instance, Vice President Garner informed Farley, "Jim, the two of us can pull together to stop Roosevelt." Other Cabinet members with a presidential bug also harbored a secret hope that the convention might reject Franklin and nominate them. Added to the ineffectual managing of Hopkins, all this was rapidly bringing the convention to a chaotic state.

Following Franklin's nomination, the convention went to pieces. When word was passed around that Franklin wanted Secretary of Agriculture Henry A. Wallace as his running mate, the stadium was in an uproar. Boos echoed and re-echoed as the delegates voiced their strong disapproval.

The convention was out of hand when Jim Farley called Eleanor at Hyde Park. "You've got to come," he harangued her. "We need you —badly!"

"I'll fly out tomorrow," she told him reluctantly. "Meet me at the airport alone. I don't want a delegation."

She arrived in Chicago during the afternoon of the eighteenth. Farley was there and so were several newspaperwomen. He insisted that she submit to an interview, though she tried to beg off. Meanwhile, back at the convention stadium, Chairman Alben Barkley rendered his opinion that the voting for Vice President be put off until the evening. "No —No," the delegates roared. But he banged his gavel and called a recess until the evening.

As Eleanor drove into Chicago with Farley, he told her that Franklin had never informed him whom he wanted for a running mate. "It should be Jesse Jones or William B. Bankhead or Paul McNutt," he offered his opinion. "Do you know," he smiled at her, "your son Elliott is planning to second Jesse Jones' nomination?"

Once in the hotel, she called Franklin and repeated what Farley had told her. "Let me talk to Jim," he said. She handed the phone to Jim, who immediately launched into a halfhearted argument with Franklin about Wallace. Finally Jim blurted, "You're the boss. If you say so I will do all I can to nominate Wallace, but I will have to work fast. The delegates are ugly."

By the time she reached the convention hall, the booing was equally divided between Franklin and Wallace. The delegates were running about and all was confusion and turmoil. The pandemonium was ear-splitting, as she made her way to the platform next to her son Franklin, Jr. Her old friend Frank Walker, who was shortly to replace Jim Farley as Postmaster General, hurried to her side, his face broken out with sweat. "This is the time for you to speak," he pleaded with her.

Tall and erect, she walked to the speaker's stand. Spotlights blinded her and the stench of cigar smoke hung in the air. Suddenly, as the delegates caught sight of her standing there, they lapsed into complete silence. It was awesome and eerie. Not a cough or a chair-shake was heard during her short extemporaneous talk. With her simple heart-to-heart talk she gathered the clan back into Franklin's corner. It was her great dignity more than the words themselves that brought the delegates to their senses. What she gave them was a talk about the burdens of the Presidency: that they must all forget their political differences and work together for the greatest good of the nation as a whole and to do "what this country can to bring this world to a safer and happier condition."

At her conclusion there was no applause. "I felt as though I was in church," one delegate said. She waited until the organist finished playing "God Bless America" before taking her seat, and as she sat down the delegates finally applauded. When the roll call began now, she remained in her place until Wallace was nominated for Vice President. Farley acknowledged that her speech had saved the day for Franklin.

As soon as Wallace was nominated, she drove back to the airport and caught a plane. Down the runway it went only to be waved to a halt. There was a phone call for her, someone shouted frantically. It was the President of the United States. "I want to thank you, Babs," Franklin expressed his gratitude. "You did a very good job."

Senator George Norris of Nebraska, who had worked so hard for the TVA, paid her the ultimate compliment in a letter he wrote her. "When it seemed the battle . . . about to be lost, you came on the scene and what you said in that short speech caused men of sense and honor to stop and think before they plunged. Like Sheridan in the Shenandoah, you stopped the fleeing warriors. The country owes you a debt of gratitude it can never repay and which it does not now fully comprehend."

The campaign that fall against the Republican nominee, Wendell Willkie, was anticlamactic, in comparison with the hectic convention. As usual, Eleanor became a strong campaign subject. Millions of large campaign buttons were distributed among Republicans which announced, "We don't want Eleanor either." But she laughed when questioned about this form of attack. "If I could be worried about mud-slinging," she said, "I would have been dead long ago." But she was concerned when Elliott was injected into the campaign. He had been commissioned as a captain in the Army Air Force and it disturbed her to catch sight of the buttons proclaiming, "Make me a captain, too."

[274]

As for Wendell Willkie, she couldn't work up any personal animosity toward him. In fact, she said, "I met him at a dinner given in honor of Walter White [head of the National Association for the Advancement of Colored People] and thought he was courageous and sincere."

This was one election Franklin was confident he would win. Because of the war situation he intended to restrict himself to a few radio speeches. However, he did do some campaigning rather late in the fall. It was at Madison Square Garden on October 28 that he hit upon the euphonious names of "Martin, Barton and Fish," while quoting the voting records of these Republicans. Wherever he spoke after that, Eleanor waited for the crowds to take up the chant "Martin, Barton and Fish." There came one serious blunder that was to dog Franklin's reputation; that was during his October 29 speech in Boston when he told his enthusiastic audience, "Your boys are not going to be sent into any foreign wars." Through carelessness or through design, he omitted the words "except in case of attack" from the end of that sentence.

Election night, 1940, Eleanor had a buffet supper for Franklin and their friends at her Val-Kill cottage in Hyde Park. Afterward all went to Sara's big residence to listen to the returns. Sara and her friends occupied a small room off the front hall where they talked and listened to the radio. "Tully," Sara confided sadly to Franklin's secretary that night, "a lot of my friends and some of my relatives are not going to like this at all tomorrow."

Franklin sat over news tickers and charts in the dining room surrounded by his sons, staff aides and Uncle Frederic Delano. Eleanor kept walking from one room to the next to bring more food to the listeners. Asked in one room how the election was coming out she replied vaguely, "I heard someone say that Willkie was doing quite well in Michigan." A visitor from another era would have guessed that politics was not her forte.

Chapter Twenty-Nine

ELEANOR FOUND few things to laugh about in the term beginning January 20, 1941. One time she and Franklin chuckled over the woman who called up in an overbearing yet frantic voice and demanded, "My kitchen is afloat. Will you please send over the White House plumber right away!" There was also the incident at St. James Church at Hyde Park, where Franklin was senior warden. When the minister hung up a sign, *Church of the President,* a wag chalked in underneath: *Formerly God's!* And of course there was a Cousin Alice who had filled the air with expletives against Franklin during the third-term campaign. After the third term started, Eleanor nevertheless invited her to attend the diplomatic reception. Franklin's aide, General Edwin "Pa" Watson, bet the President that she wouldn't dare to come. At the evening reception when Alice was announced, Franklin nudged Eleanor and shouted, "Pa, you lose!"

Eleanor saw plainly that Franklin sorely missed Louis Howe. At Franklin's request she had performed many of the duties Louie would have. However, she was constitutionally unable to be selfless like Louie and as devoted to a single purpose: Franklin's political status. She had grown so much since 1932 that she had developed a personality too strong to subject itself to anyone else's. There was no "good soldier" in her, as there was in Jim Farley, for instance, who had done things solely because a superior had asked him to. She had to determine her own views and was often at loggerheads with those of Franklin. For example, on one occasion, a United States Senator got letters from her and Franklin, each expressing the opposite view on the same subject. Throwing both aside, he exclaimed with exasperation, "Can't those two ever get together?" In addition, she spread herself about in so many different activities that she was seldom on hand when a crisis arose and Franklin needed her. Who else was there to prod others continually about the injustices being perpetrated against women, youth, Negroes, sharecroppers, slum dwellers, the aged and' suffering humanity overseas? For all these causes she had to raise money through books, lectures, columns, radio broadcasts and even movie shorts. Over a half-million dollars she gave away during her first eight years in the White House, despite the sniping of congressmen and editors who treated her, *The New Yorker* deplored, "as if she were a crooked wrestling promoter." When she donned grease paint and made movie shorts on her family's hobbies in 1940, the outcry was enormous. Yet the activity was harmless itself. Her only revealing remark concerned her son, Franklin, Jr., about whom she said, "I think his hobby is arguing. He loves it. He could argue forever."

Because of her whirling activities, Franklin had to look elsewhere for his latter-day Louis Howe. He found him in Harry Hopkins, the gaunt relief administrator whom he first tried to establish as his successor in 1940 and then, when Hopkins' health failed, invited to live in the White House. Here, said Eleanor, Franklin "shaped Harry; he widened his horizons and taught him many things about domestic politics and foreign affairs."

But Hopkins could never be another Howe. Louie had been with Franklin from the outset and had a community of experiences that produced a warmth and even a glow that no newcomer could attain. For another thing, Louie was older than Franklin, which gave him a maturity in Franklin's eyes no younger man could have. Because of these factors, Eleanor noted, Louie could be independent while Harry could not. Where Louie could tell off Franklin, Harry did not dare. Where Louie "gave his opinions honestly," Harry in dealing with Franklin "frequently agreed with him regardless of his own opinion," Eleanor said.

However, if Franklin wanted Hopkins as his closest assistant, Eleanor was not one to disagree. Just as she had been motherly toward Louie Howe, she now proceeded to act in a similar manner toward Hopkins. And, like Howe, Harry was sick most of the time and often irritable. Once he apologized to her by note, "Terribly sorry I made such a spectacle of myself the other day, but I was feeling pretty miserable." His second wife had died of cancer at the age of thirty-seven and left him with a six-year-old daughter to look after. To lighten his burden, Eleanor legally became young Diana's guardian until Hopkins remarried again during World War II. She also kept watch on his clothes. One time when she found out that he had only three shirts, and all a bit frayed, she went shopping and bought him six more. A serious problem she had with him in the White House was that he smoked in bed. On one occasion a servant found a smoldering cigarette among his sheets and a raw wind blowing through the open window. But this was not as repugnant to her as the fact that "people who could give him luxuries and the kind of party in which he probably never before had the slightest interest became important to him." To her it was shady and not in keeping with his position to relish the company of night-club regulars and race-track buffs. Once when she chided him about such activities and told him about the loneliness of Diana, he said, injured, "That's totally unimportant. The only thing that is important is to win the war."

When Franklin won his third term and the emphasis of his administration turned toward foreign affairs, Eleanor's role seemed momentarily cloudy. In fact, at the Gridiron Widows' party in December 1940, when the newsladies asked how she planned to conduct herself during the third term, she said, "I will not tell you. I will show you instead." With that she hurried behind the black curtain at the rear of the stage. Then she quickly changed to a black silk dress and a grandmother's white cap. When the curtain parted slightly and she appeared as though framed, everyone gasped, "Whistler's mother!"

However, she was no Whistler's mother, for Franklin had her real role very much in mind. Harry Hopkins would serve as his personal emissary with foreign governments while Eleanor would be his liaison with the domestic scene. The chief problem here was that the two areas of action were soon to be so intertwined as to be almost inseparable.

The year 1941 saw the big build-up in defense industries and the armed forces, as well as direct aid to those opposing the Berlin-Rome-Tokyo Axis. Harry Hopkins rushed to England to build a solid foundation for Franklin with Prime Minister Winston Churchill and then later to meet with Joseph Stalin, when Hitler turned on his ally in June and invaded the Soviet Union. He also directed the vast Lend-Lease program and in his spare time kept tabs on the vital war industries.

Eleanor, in turn, was soon immersed in domestic and foreign matters. Early in 1941, the *Wall Street Journal* told the business world: "Mrs. Roosevelt is increasingly active; watch her for tips on policies. . . . She talks to officials . . . has been calling on bigwigs . . . gave the first hint of the Lend-Lease bill." Actually little escaped her attention, sometimes to Franklin's annoyance. When she tried to coax him into giving his blessing to a refugee resettlement program in the British, French and Dutch Guianas, he quickly turned thumbs down because of the climate there and added the caution, "I think it is not best to discuss this out loud, however." Another time when she wanted to know why he did not halt oil shipments to Japan, as editors throughout the country were demanding, he replied with a memo stating that if he did this Japan would "increase her purchases of Mexican oil and furthermore, may be driven by actual necessity to a descent on the Dutch East Indies."

On her own she investigated alleged discrimination in the budding war industries. "I wanted to see the fight for the rights of minorities go on during the war period. I also thought that the groundwork should be laid for a wide health program after the war." Oddly, Hopkins proved her major opponent in this endeavor. "If it doesn't bear directly on the war, we can't be bothered with it," he told her. However, she thought that the postwar goals of the fight were as important as the fight itself and continued throughout this period to prickle Franklin as the conscience of the Administration. One result of her agitation for non-discrimination was the widespread rumor throughout the South that she was organizing Negro kitchen and scrubbing-board help into "Eleanor Clubs." The purpose of the "Eleanor Clubs," the wild stories went, was to bring about the organization of labor unions for maids to strike for higher wages and shorter hours. Another purpose, the rumors said, was to reduce Southern matrons to the position of doing their own housework by offering enticing jobs in the growing war plants. "Out of the kitchen by Christmas" was supposed to have been the slogan of the bogus "Eleanor Clubs."

Other aspects of the broad new economic sweep occupied her attention. When the Office of Production Management was established in 1941, she descended on its co-director, William Knudsen, former head of General Motors, with the demand that he do something to help the people thrown out of work in the conversion of the auto industry. Knudsen, used to bossing a business and thinking in terms of profits, stared openmouthed as she lit into him. "Mr. Knudsen looked at me like a great big benevolent bear," she said, "as if to say, 'Now Mrs. Roosevelt, don't let's get excited.'"

When she returned to his office a month later, he tried to brush her off with: "Something is being worked out, Mrs. Roosevelt." However, she knew nothing was. "I wonder if you know what hunger is?" she told him caustically. "Has any member of your family ever gone hungry?" He gulped at her bread-and-butter approach to life.

Later, back in the White House, she said, "The slowness of our officials in seeing ahead, in seeing the very obvious things that are developing, is responsible for the whole mess." Knudsen did not last long after that.

She didn't fare so well in her activities regarding the immense ballooning in the numbers of women workers who rushed to get jobs in defense plants. In a long memo to Harry Hopkins, she wrote prophetically, "If great numbers of women are going to be used undoubtedly many married women will be needed. This is going to have an effect on the way of life and on the homes in the United States. . . . We would want to preserve as far as possible, because of the preference of our people, a sense of home life." She laid out a complex program which included the "possibility of chain restaurants near plants, day nurseries and play schools adjacent . . . the providing of transportation to both grade and high schools . . . and community laundries."

She also plunged into the problems of service people and their dependents. Often Franklin backed her up in this area. On one of her requests he wrote to Under Secretary of War Robert Patterson, "What shall I tell Mrs. Roosevelt about this?" Once on the question of service dependents, she sent Franklin a short memo: "If a mother is wholly dependent shouldn't she get the same as the wife?" Franklin scrawled his waggish reply on her memo: "It depends on the mother." When the WAVES came into existence later, Franklin asked her to help prepare a list of eligible women for commissioned officers. When the name of one young woman was suggested to her, she shook her head. "She won't do. You have to be a college graduate to be a naval officer." Then, realizing the incongruity of her position in making out her list, she smiled wanly. "I wouldn't be eligible myself."

1941 also saw the determined pitch of the isolationists to fight against Franklin's defense efforts. Eleanor had long since passed the point of considering them with anything other than ill humor. When Franklin read his "Aid to Britain" message to Congress in January, she expressed great shock when his message was not applauded by Republicans. "I really felt that it was something that went very deep," she said on-the-record. Senator Vandenberg, then a die-hard isolationist, lambasted her for what he called an un-First Ladylike utterance and Franklin's speech, too, as a "war by proxy" message. When she attacked him at her next press conference for playing "with words when the world is on fire," he noted gleefully in his diary, "Those who heard her said she showed more raw anger than ever before."

Nor did her anger abate when the American Youth Congress leaders, to whom she had given so much of her time and money, now came to picket the White House for the American Peace Mobilization. "The Communists have been taught what to say and how to say it," she rejoined when they now attacked her. In April 1941, she backed the anti-AYC International Student Service which had hired as its secretary her former AYC protégé, Joseph Lash, and she traveled from college to college to talk on democracy to student forums.

[280]

In June when the Nazis attacked the Soviet Union and Franklin joined Winston Churchill in offering aid to Russia, the anti-Communist isolationist wing went after Franklin and Eleanor. Dredged up were her activities with the AYC and his action in paroling from prison the head of the American Communists, Earl Browder. In November 1941, Franklin sent her a facetious note:

"I think I will send Browder as Ambassador to Berlin. The place is vacant!"

Eleanor replied in the same vein, "Please do!"

1941 was also a year of great sorrow for Eleanor and Franklin. In the same month both Franklin's mother and Eleanor's brother died. Sara died of a circulatory collapse at eighty-six on September 7, at her beloved matriarchal home in Hyde Park. Franklin was terribly shaken by her death. Workmen on her estate were startled when, as an omen of her power, the biggest tree on her property toppled over with a thunderous crash at the same time that she died.

Eleanor considered her brother's death the greater tragedy, because Hall was a lost soul who never fulfilled the high expectations she had held for him. He was a wanderer and a roamer, this six foot, three inch, 240-pound blond man whom she had raised and watched over from early childhood. His good qualities required more than the ten fingers on her two hands to enumerate. He had great charm, energy, strength and brilliance. But "whenever his responsibilities became irksome he tended to thrust them aside." He was undisciplined and he would not adjust himself to other people's demands or needs, factors that offset his assets. But more than this, he had developed a penchant for gin, a thirst that he could not and in the end did not care to drop.

On the day that Sara was buried next to Franklin's father, Hall, who was then in Vassar Hospital in Poughkeepsie, insisted that Eleanor take him to Walter Reed Hospital in Washington. His liver was no longer in functioning order and he lasted less than three weeks beyond Sara. Every day his tearful sister came from the White House to visit him, and in his last week she spent entire nights with him. Only his strong heart kept him alive so long. There were thoughts about the little boy who played "Friday" to her "Crusoe" in the woods close by Grandmother Hall's place at Tivoli. There were thoughts about his son Danny, who had fought in the Spanish Civil War, only to come home and lose his life in a plane crash. He needed his liquor more than ever toward the end, and though she knew it had been his ruination, he must have it, and so she brought him his ration of gin each day to the hospital. He finally died at age fifty on September 25.

After his funeral, Eleanor plunged into her first and only official government job under Franklin in order to drown her sorrow. Franklin had requested her to become the deputy director of the Office of Civilian Defense under New York's Mayor Fiorello La Guardia, or, as *Time* put it, she was to be "OCDiva to La Guardia's OCDemon." OCD under La Guardia was floundering and Franklin wanted civilian defense preparations speeded up in case the country went to war and was bombed. The "Little Flower" from New York was dragging his feet, said Franklin, because he considered the agency unimportant and far below the Cabinet post or directorship of the entire defense economy that he thought he deserved. In addition, he had not resigned his job as mayor and proposed to run OCD with his left hand.

Eleanor had known La Guardia a long time. In fact, she had taken a great personal interest in the internal affairs of New York City, sometimes to the displeasure of La Guardia, who disliked outside interference and criticism. Always excitable, he was not above pounding his desk and roaring when another of her letters came across his desk. As a friend described his political philosophy, "Fiorello was ready to fight 'Them' to the death, constantly on the alert lest 'They' get him first."

She did not belong in the "They" category, though her letters did tempt him. There were pleas to his City Hall desk to find jobs and housing for young people, gypsies, etc.; relief and medical care for the poor and sick; and paroles for worthy individuals. She also protested when things were removed from the city's budget. One letter she sent him asked him to look into a woman's complaint that a Negro woman had pushed her son's wife in the face on a subway train. She complained that the height of a new building would block necessary sunlight for the little children on the other side. Once she quizzed him about the small number of Negro policemen in the city. "Do you know why we haven't more colored policemen?" he fairly shouted his written reply. "Because we can't get them."

He always talked to her with startling frankness. On one occasion she had him to lunch in her small apartment in New York City. As he was leaving he paused at the door and told her in the fashion of a farewell: "My wife never asks me where I have been, nor whom I saw, nor what I did, but she always asks me what I had to eat. Today I can truthfully say I did not have too much!"

So the new team of La Guardia and Roosevelt went into close action on the ninth floor of the Dupont Circle Apartments in Washington. La Guardia had been reluctant to take her on, despite the fact that she worked without pay and paid her own expenses. "She is too controversial a person," he worriedly told friends. Besides, he realized that she opposed his narrow outlook on civilian defense. "He was more interested in whether there were good fire engines, but he was not interested in the other side of OCD—morale building," Eleanor soon discovered. The result was a continuing rear-guard action on her part to change his outlook. "Frequently heads of divisions, including myself," she reported, "were unable to discuss with him some of the things we hoped to get settled."

The office hours she put in at OCD—many to take her mind off her brother's tragic end—were staggering. One morning Franklin stormed at her with great annoyance, "What's this I hear? You didn't go to bed at all last night?"

"I have to work on my mail sometime," she tried to explain to him before she left for another day at OCD.

He let out a low whistle as she picked up an armful of papers and rushed out the door.

Pearl Harbor Day came with a savagery on December 7. Only the day before Franklin had sent a personal message to Emperor Hirohito asking him to remember his "sacred duty to restore traditional amity and prevent further death and destruction in the world." And at the very moment of the attack, Admiral Nomura, Japan's special envoy who had been Franklin and Eleanor's old friend from their Woodrow Wilson days, was conferring with Secretary of State Hull on steps for maintaining the peace. "For months now," Eleanor said over the radio that evening at 6:45, "the knowledge that something of this kind might happen has been hanging over our heads and yet it seemed impossible to believe."

When reports came the next evening that the Japanese air force was bombing San Francisco, she and La Guardia flew out there. The West Coast she found to be suffering from hysterical fear, for the reports were false. Up and down the coast she traveled for a week holding meetings and talking on the radio to soothe the hysterical population.

She returned to grateful thanks from Franklin for her work there. However, she also returned to battle with him verbally about the fate of more than 100,000 Japanese Americans living on the West Coast. Franklin tended to agree with his military advisers that their continued presence in Western states only added to the hysteria of the area. West Coast-stationed generals went further and called them spies. "But they are good Americans," she argued, "and have as much right to live there as anyone else." When she expressed herself publicly on this score, Western editors berated her roundly. Typical was the editorial in a Los

[283]

Angeles paper: "When she starts bemoaning the plight of the treacherous snakes we call Japanese (with apologies to all snakes) she has reached the point where she should be forced to retire from public life." Hers was a losing fight, for Franklin signed the order to ship the Japanese Americans to inland prison camps. As it turned out, this was the greatest injustice of the war period: the FBI found not a single pro-Japanese spy in their midst. Franklin, however, though admitting his error, believed that under the circumstances then prevailing he could not have followed another course.

Her stand in championing the Japanese Americans had brought her many new enemies. Though the nation was unified as never before by the coming of war, personal attacks on her continued without abatement. At the moment she was most vulnerable as an official of OCD and charges against her were soon to reach fever pitch.

Certainly the OCD was the most disorganized of the wartime agencies. Established by a loosely worded executive order, its top officials were never certain as to its functions or its authority. La Guardia had retained control over the protective side of OCD. A fire buff of three-alarm dimensions, he visualized horrendous bombing attacks by the Axis to be combated by a heroic fleet of OCD fire fighters. As for Eleanor's job as his deputy, he scratched a cheek and brushed her off with a "Why don't you handle the mobilization of civilians for civilian defense?" Even so he demanded that all plans and programs come to him for decision and made them off the cuff as he hurried back and forth between Washington and New York.

The total operation was soon a madhouse, or, as *Time* described it, "bustling nonsense." The vast overstaffing and the quaint programs put into force were all blamed on Eleanor. A "Know Your Government" division employed 200 clerks to "handle inquiries developed by radio programs." No one present could explain what that meant. In addition, there came into being a Physical Fitness Section with a Director of Industrial Recreation who toured factories and lectured workers on how to breathe and why Sunday picnics were necessary. There were also co-ordinators for 61 sports including archery, badminton, horseshoe pitching and eurythmic dancing for children in air-raid shelters.

Eleanor was not entirely blameless for the mess. She had brought in a movie actor, Melvyn Douglas, to head the Arts Council, and Mayris Chaney, a protégée of hers, to head children's activities in the Physical Fitness Division. Miss Chaney's chief claim to fame was a dance step she invented and which she called the "Eleanor Glide." Miss Chaney called Eleanor "Lady" and was called "Tiny" in return.

[284]

With all her political experience she should have known better. Immediately she found herself subject to ridicule from all sides. It was a trying short period. Congressman Hoffman of Michigan, who made a career out of attacking her, asked for a "Bundles for Eleanor" campaign in tribute to her ability to get jobs for her friends. Daily the antics of OCD made the headlines until finally both she and La Guardia resigned. After she helped select James Landis as La Guardia's successor and walked out of the Dupont Circle Apartments for good on February 20, she told the press, "I realize how unwise it is for a vulnerable person like myself to try a government job. To know me," she added, "is a terrible thing." There were no "real tangible accomplishments in the OCD," she admitted later.

Never again would she consider an official role in Franklin's administration. In March, 1942 when the rumor spread that she would head the WAACs, she scotched this story quickly with: "I can't take a government position because of my being the President's wife—I found that out."

Chapter Thirty

THE WAR YEARS were long and hard. Franklin was engaged in frenzied activities. Unlike the old days, Eleanor had trouble seeing him now during the day. Gone were the old years when she would burst into his press conferences to whisper to him about extraneous matters or "float" into his office when he held important meetings with Cabinet officers and use up the time in general talk. She was now generally limited by circumstances to discussing things with him in his upstairs study during cocktail time before dinner or to sending him memos. Considering that they were man and wife and living in the same house, the latter means of communication was especially ironic.

There were occasions when a talk with Franklin might have saved her grief. Early in 1942, for instance, she spoke on the radio and exhorted housewives to cut down on sugar consumption if they wanted to avoid sugar rationing. Early the next morning across the entire nation a wild stampede of housewives cleaned out grocery stores of sugar and made rationing a necessity.

Another opportunity for her to be with Franklin was to join him on the war production factory inspections he made on occasion. With the outbreak of war, these had to be secret with a maximum of security. Workers were most often shocked to look up from their assembly lines and find the presidential jeep coasting by. "By God, if it ain't old Frank and Eleanor!" one once shouted. But security was difficult to maintain. For Franklin had acquired the black Scottie Fala from Cousin Margaret Suckley and Fala had to be walked in train stations along the travel route. "The Informer," the Secret Service men dubbed Fala because he was so easily recognized. Fala's original name was Big Boy, but Franklin changed it in honor of a Scottish ancestor, "Murray the Outlaw of Fala Hill."

With the war came a steady stream of foreign visitors to the White House. As a model for the rest of the country, Eleanor followed all rationing regulations no matter who was coming to dinner. At Franklin's behest, Congress increased income taxes steeply in 1942, and to cut his own home expenses he slashed Eleanor's White House food allowance from $2,000 to $1,500 a month. From then on he watched like a hawk the amounts of food put on the table. In October 1942, he wrote her caustically, "For instance, for my luncheons I have pleaded—when it is an egg dish—for only one egg apiece; yet four eggs for two people constantly appear." She agreed with him when he suggested that they curtail purchases of linens and clothes. One time at dinner his cigarette burned a hole in the tablecloth. He glanced swiftly at Eleanor; then furtively covered the hole with a salt shaker.

One of the first foreign visitors to arrive after Pearl Harbor was Prime Minister Winston Churchill, who came shortly before Christmas. Eleanor put him up at the east end of the second floor in the Rose Suite, across the hall from Harry Hopkins. Already that day, Eleanor had put in time at OCD, written her column and gone to the Salvation Army Christmas party, the Catholic Charities Christmas party and the Alley Dwellings Christmas tree programs. The result was that at dinner while Churchill waxed eloquent about the Allied cause she fell asleep in her chair. Nor did matters improve the next day when at lunch Eleanor asked him about his wife's activities in the war. "Mrs. Churchill and the wives of my Ministers deserve the highest praise," he told her. "They don't engage in any public activities and make no public appearances. They always stay at home," he added with satisfaction. When all eyes at the table turned to stare at Eleanor, Churchill paled. "Have I said anything wrong?" he asked.

One of the chief problems Franklin faced with the British Prime Minister was that Churchill slept away the afternoons and worked far into the night. Franklin, who put in full days in the West Wing office, found their night sessions a real burden. In January, Franklin's weariness was evident. However, Churchill strained his heart opening a window when the air conditioning failed and had to go to Palm Beach, Florida to recuperate. Even so Franklin's needed rest was interrupted one time when Churchill called Wendell Willkie and the telephone operator rang Franklin by mistake.

Under the security pseudonym of "Naval Person," Churchill made several other visits to the United States. He and Franklin generally got along well. "They used to argue on military tactics all the time," said Eleanor. "His friendship with Churchill, with whom he sometimes disagreed, was real and they had a good time talking nonsense rhymes and talking of things of a variety of interests." One time when the discussion turned on continuing American aid to Britain after the war, Churchill exclaimed, annoyed, "What do you want me to do? Get on my hind legs and beg like Fala?"

Eleanor and Churchill treated each other as family members without false formalities and meaningless social talk. In May, 1943, for instance, when she, Franklin and Harry Hopkins took him to Shangri-La, the President's retreat 4,000 feet high in Maryland's Catoctin Hills near Thurmond, she and the Prime Minister got into an enormous hassle. Eleanor wanted to ride in the front seat of the car, but Churchill insisted that she ride in the back with Franklin. "The British Empire went into action," Churchill said of this momentous argument. "After about three minutes' conflict of wills, I won, and Mrs. Roosevelt took her proper seat by her husband's side. Harry Hopkins filled the fourth seat, and we whirled off amid our cyclist escort."

Churchill's victorious air ballooned further two hours later when they passed Barbara Frietchie's house in Frederick. "This moved Harry Hopkins," said Churchill, to quote the famous lines: " 'Shoot if you must this old grey head, But spare your country's flag,' she said." When Churchill asked Eleanor and Franklin if they could add to the rest of Whittier's poem and got a negative reply, a broad smile crossed his face and he "sailed steadily on" through it to the end, with Eleanor, Franklin and Harry offering only a weak chorus of ". . . she said" at appropriate points. And at Thurmond, Churchill showed his satisfaction further by dropping in at a beer parlor to drink beer with the local citizens and drop nickels in the jukebox.

Churchill's empire and power approach to world peace also troubled her. At still another visit during September, 1944, Churchill came to lunch at Eleanor's Val-Kill place in Hyde Park. No sooner was food set on the table than the two leaped into a long argument on how to reorganize the world in the postwar period. "The best way to maintain peace," Eleanor insisted with deep conviction, "is to improve the living conditions of the people in all countries." Churchill, who ate as much as two men and drank large draughts of brandy and scotch, bit his long black cigar in anger. "That's not the way to do it," he cut through her. "The best means for achieving a durable peace is an agreement between England and the United States to prevent international war by combining their forces. Of course, we might take Russia in, too," he added, "but not China." "But that approach doesn't take into consideration all the poor people in the world," she said with feeling, "whose misery only brings unrest and trouble." The argument ended in a stalemate when neither would admit to any equity in the other's position.

Eleanor found nothing democratic about another White House visitor,

Madame Chiang Kai-shek, who came for aid to her beleaguered China. "She can talk beautifully about democracy, but she does not know how to live democracy."

Madame Chiang was in a New York hospital before coming to the White House. Eleanor, who wanted everything just right for the visit, wished to talk to her before she came to Washington. She was told by Madame Chiang's aides that she could telephone her only on the Saturday before the visit, and then at 6:30 P.M. precisely, not earlier or later. Winston Churchill was at the White House that same February, 1943, and Eleanor and Franklin wanted her to lunch with him "to meet me at the White House," said Churchill. "The invitation was refused with some hauteur. Madame was of the opinion that I should make the pilgrimage to New York. The President was somewhat vexed that she had not adopted his plan. It was my strong desire to preserve unity in the Grand Alliance, and I offered to go halfway if she would do the same. This plan was however considered facetious, so I never had the pleasure of meeting this lady until the Cairo Conference."

No sooner did Madame Chiang make her appearance at the White House than stories were afloat about her bad manners. She had brought her own crepe de chine sheets with her. Every time she got out of bed two sheets and two pillowcases had to be changed and a fresh blanket spread had to be sewn on the blanket before she climbed back in. This did not irk Eleanor so much as her handclapping to bring Franklin's business aides running, as though they were houseboys.

Madame Chiang had brought along her young niece, Miss Kung, who wore men's pants and shoes and let it be known that she was the 76th direct descendant of Confucius. Young Miss Kung's attire did not fool Eleanor but it did Franklin. At the first meal, Franklin tried to be sociable and told her, "Well, my boy, I understand you went sight-seeing today." Harry Hopkins quickly passed him a note that made his face redden: "This is Miss Kung." Franklin laughed embarrassedly and told Miss Kung, "You know I call everybody 'My boy,' whether they are boys or girls."

In addition, there were several other embarrassing moments for Eleanor during that visit. Madame Chiang's aides were forever barging into her room at odd times to inform her of Madame's eating desires. The problem of getting her to pose for pictures with Eleanor on the south lawn proved almost as formidable as the decision of when to start the second front in Europe. Once, at dinner, Eleanor remarked when everyone was seated, "All business talk will now be adjourned." Madame Chiang, who had been buzzing into Franklin's ear in the Southern drawl she had picked up while going to school in Macon, Georgia, looked up sharply for a moment, then continued her business conversation. At another dinner, on a day when labor leader John L. Lewis had filled the front page with threats of labor unrest, Franklin asked Madame, "What would you do in China with a labor leader like John Lewis?" She quickly passed the side of her hand across her throat. "Well, how about your gentle and sweet character?" Franklin asked Eleanor later.

The façade of friendliness ebbed the day Eleanor took her to Franklin's press conference. Madame Chiang sat between them with Eleanor holding a protective hand on her visitor's dainty arm. No sooner did the conference begin than Madame tried to turn it into a personal forum to pressure Franklin to step up aid to China. When a newsman finally asked Franklin about it, he said, "We will send more ammunition as the Lord is willing."

"The Lord helps those who help themselves," Madame Chiang told him sternly. Eleanor dropped her arm.

Another visitor to disrupt White House life was lanky, austere General Charles de Gaulle, leader of the Free French movement. He came in 1944 at the urging of General Eisenhower, who believed that good relations with de Gaulle was essential to military success in France. The visit was a flop. Franklin summarized to Eleanor the strain that the French general produced: "That fellow is so damned rude. One morning when he comes down the stairs he thinks he is Joan of Arc, and the next day he thinks he is Clemenceau. I wish he'd make up his mind."

A funny visitor proved to be Foreign Minister Molotov of the Soviet Union. "Mr. Brown," as his security name read, was found by the White House valet, whom Eleanor had assigned to him, to be carrying strange items in his suitcase. These included a loaf of dark rye bread, a salami and a loaded pistol. "I heard that the White House food was considered poor," Eleanor was reported to have told a friend, "but I didn't realize our food was that bad." One night he wandered out of the White House gate and bought a bag of peanuts from the Greek vendor in front whose place of business Eleanor had saved when city authorities chased him away. Another evening he was located on F Street where he was staring at the clothing in shop windows. Franklin enjoyed chiding Molotov for having taken part in the negotiations for the Russo-German Non-Aggression Pact of 1939. As for Eleanor, Molotov sought her out for long talks on social reforms. "I liked him very much," she said.

Eleanor and Franklin enjoyed an especially close relationship with Norway's Crown Princess Martha and her children and with the royal womenfolk of Holland. Martha had the run of the White House and the Hyde Park residence. One time when Queen Wilhelmina of Holland came to the White House, Eleanor brought her along to her press conference. The queen, who possessed extraordinary talent for simple yet straightforward talk, painted a dark picture to the newsgirls about the appalling increase in tuberculosis in Occupied Holland. When the conference ended and the girls walked out the door, she suffered great remorse concerning her talk. "When the Nazis read what I have said," she gasped at Eleanor, "they are bound to retaliate against my people." With a dash, Eleanor raced down the hall to stop the girls and insist that Wilhelmina's talk had been off the record.

Franklin liked the old queen who dressed like a housewife in her kitchen. He also enjoyed having her daughter, Crown Princess Juliana, and her two granddaughters, Beatrice and Irene. Irene was two then and made him roar with laughter because her only English word was "No." The girls played so hard with Fala that he jumped into Franklin's lap to keep them away. When Margriet, Juliana's next child was born, Eleanor became her godmother.

One thing about Eleanor that disconcerted Franklin during the war was her habit of mixing the VIPs with unknowns at the dinner table. He did not mind this at the informal Sunday night suppers, a practice they had inaugurated at Albany, with Eleanor's using a battered chafing dish to scramble eggs at the table. However, a melting pot of dinner companions at regular meals suited him not at all. He could be caustic at times. There was one meal in 1942 when a "sweet young thing" interrupted talk to ask him questions. "How did General MacArthur get to Australia?" he repeated. "Why, he rowed his family all the way from Corregidor to Australia." "What is my Shangri-La used for? It's the take-off place for Tokyo bombers."

She had Queen Wilhelmina and Joseph Lash at the same table, Juliana and some boys and girls from West Virginia, and Churchill and her dancing protégée, Mayris Chaney. One time she created an international incident when she invited the writer Louis Adamic and his wife to dinner while Churchill was at the White House. Adamic's invitation had come because he had written a book that pleased her, *Two Way Passage,* in which he proposed that foreign-born Americans return to rebuild their homelands and take over the governments after the war. Dinner conversation was short and inconsequential because she was taking the Adamics to Constitution Hall for the Philadelphia

[291]

Orchestra concert. Later Adamic wrote a book called *Dinner at the White House* in which he magnified the words and facial expressions of those at dinner into an anti-British farce. Eleanor was appalled when he "seemed to think every smallest detail of the evening had some particular significance or meaning behind it." Angered by all this insipid nonsense, Churchill sued Adamic for libel and collected several thousand dollars.

She didn't have to worry about what was said when Alexander Woollcott came to dinner during the war. One time when he was in Washington as part of the cast of *The Man Who Came to Dinner,* he invited himself to dinner at the White House and stayed two weeks. "Welcome, Mrs. Roosevelt," he greeted her one afternoon as she entered the White House. "Come right in. I am delighted to see you. Make yourself at home."

One time Woollcott dined in a Washington restaurant with Thornton Wilder and a young marine. Because of the late hour he brought the marine back to the White House and graciously offered him Winston Churchill's bedroom. Churchill was not there that night. "I wish to deny in advance," Woollcott wrote Eleanor at Hyde Park, "the rumor which eventually must come to you, that I quartered a whole regiment of marines in the White House during your absence. It was only one marine."

Although entertaining foreign visitors became big business during the war years, Eleanor did not let this interfere with her many other activities. Nor did she mind taking on new jobs. Harry Hopkins suggested to Franklin that a visit by her to England would do much to bolster morale both of the British people and American soldiers stationed there. She was quick to agree to go when Franklin broached the subject to her. "We are going to invade North Africa soon," he told her early in October, 1942, "so I think it would be good timing if you had a chance to talk to our troops before they leave England."

Hers was one of the first nonstop flights across the Atlantic. As the plane got out to sea she saw several ships zigzagging below and "wondered whether my son, Franklin, Jr., might not be on one of the destroyers." Along with her had come her secretary Tommy, Colonel Oveta Culp Hobby, head of the WACs, a State Department courier and a few others not officially part of her entourage. When the plane landed in Ireland, Mrs. Hobby had to don civilian clothes, for Ireland was neutral, and in uniform she would have been liable to internment. In Dublin, Eleanor's uncle David Gray, who was American ambassador to Ireland, pointed out, there was great fear of lurking enemy agents.

The servants in the house where he sent her before she flew to London were not informed who she was and were told in cloak and dagger style to refer to her as "the lady"—"which seemed a little evasive to me," she complained, especially since she had been recognized when she landed by people exclaiming, "Why, there's Mrs. Roosevelt!"

The king and queen of England came to London's Paddington Station to greet her on Friday, October 23. No announcement had been made of her arrival, yet an enormous crowd was on hand to cheer and applaud her. Also at the station were Admiral Stark, General Eisenhower, Foreign Secretary Anthony Eden and Lady Stella Reading who was to handle part of her visit. Not far from the end of the red carpet, *Daily Mirror* headlines screamed, "We're sure glad to have you, ma'am!" The *Spectator* wrote, "The woman who, in American history, has played the greatest role in public affairs."

She stayed with the king and queen at Buckingham Palace for two days and then was off in a three-week mad whirl of army camps, factories and bomb-scarred homes. She almost froze at the palace because the heat was not turned on until November first. Dinner turned out to be a skimpy three-course affair with no trimmings. Her talks with the royal couple were intimate. Franklin had written King George on October 17, "I want you and the queen to tell Eleanor anything in regard to the problems of our troops in England which she might not get from the Government or military authorities." Her son Elliott, who was then stationed in England, came to London and had dinner with her and the king and queen one evening. Afterward, they sat up half the night talking in her freezing room, their teeth chattering all the while. Each knew of the impending North African invasion, yet neither would mention it to the other.

Little of her time was spent in formal ceremonies. After her stay at the palace and a tour of London rubble with the king and queen, she delivered two dozen oranges she had brought from the United States for the son of the Duchess of Kent, who was Franklin's godson. She had a bad cold now, but she had no intention of altering her schedule which included, among other things, inspection of 26 camps in 19 days. Bill Phillips, her old friend who was now an adviser to General Eisenhower, insisted that she cancel this nonsense. "You'll never make it, Eleanor," he scolded.

He was wrong. Franklin hadn't given her the security name of "Rover" for naught. She was a blur of activity rushing from one camp to another and pausing in between for long talks with individual soldiers. The boys needed thicker socks. Their chief gripe was that the folks back home were writing them despairing letters of their hardships under rationing. Everywhere she collected family addresses back in the States. One time when she set out to visit Elliott's unit at Steeple Morden, her driver lost his way. The security call went back to the American Embassy in London: "Rover has lost her pup." Back came directions. She made one inspection of the Auxiliary Territorial Airforce women in a heavy downpour without rubbers or a raincoat. Mrs. Churchill in traveling with her one day collapsed on a staircase from exhaustion and Colonel Hobby went into hiding to avoid Eleanor.

Besides the camps, she also visited ordnance plants, airplane factories, and even inspected Liberty ships. When she visited London's depressing East End, her car was surrounded by so many thousands of cheering people that she was late to her other appointments that day. It was a great welcome for the indefatigable Eleanor. One fire warden in the East End wiped his eyes after she spoke to him and sobbed, "She tried to make a blinkin' 'ero out of me."

She also spent a weekend with the Churchills at Chequers, the Government's country estate for the prime minister. Churchill, who disliked the austere life to which wartime Britain was being subjected in order to survive, expressed great displeasure at breakfast one morning with the ragged-looking food placed before him. Later she also had dinner with the Churchills and other officials back in London. Though she hadn't wanted any unpleasantness, dinner was marred when she and Churchill developed a bitter argument about the merits of Loyalist Spain and the winning Franco government. Talk flew fast across the table as she defended the Loyalists and he, Franco. "I think perhaps Mrs. Roosevelt is right," Mrs. Churchill censured him when his eyes blazed. "I have held certain beliefs for sixty years," Churchill said loudly to her, "and I'm not going to change now!" With that, his wife stood up and dinner was over.

Nevertheless, Churchill was well pleased with her visit to England. He wrote her later, "Your visit has given great pleasure and comfort throughout this island and yr presence and speeches have been an inspiration to the many places you have visited in yr indefatigable tour. . . . You certainly have left golden footprints behind you."

After three weeks in England, Franklin wanted her home. When a delay arose over the question of how she would return, he wired the American Embassy, "I don't care how you send her home, just send her." He was at the Washington airport to greet her on November 17 when her plane landed. He was concerned about her bad cold, which brought back the story of her farewell visit with the king and queen at

Windsor Castle. The king was also suffering from a deep cold and the two spent much of the time in a chorus of nose blowing. Aunt Maude Gray, who had accompanied Eleanor to the castle, was fit to be chained afterward. "My word, Eleanor!" she scolded her with obvious distaste. "I never was so humiliated in all my life! The way you used those nasty little tissues and wadded them up in your hand while the king used such lovely sheer linen handkerchiefs. What could they possibly have thought of you!"

Franklin laughed. "And there is one thing I never want to eat again," Eleanor told him. "After three weeks of Brussels sprouts, I'm through with them."

"Torch," the American invasion of North Africa, had already begun. The great Soviet victory against the Nazis at Stalingrad was already in the making. For the first time in the war the Allied outlook seemed bright. It was a time to start planning ahead. There were arguments at dinner early in December, 1942 when Eleanor condemned American use of Admiral Darlan in North Africa. Darlan had been deputy to aged and senile Marshal Pétain, whom the Nazis had permitted to establish the subservient French Government at Vichy in Southern France. Darlan had gone to Africa to visit his sick son when the invasion was under way. Immediately he had assumed the duties of High Commissioner in French North Africa and declared himself on the Allied side.

Eleanor believed that the meaning of the war was being undermined by collaborating with Darlan. Admiral William Leahy, who had served Franklin as his representative to Vichy, opposed her view. It was not a matter of living up to so-called ideals, he argued, but a matter of expedience in saving lives. Franklin was caught in the middle. "It's only a temporary expedient," he said, "justified solely by the stress of battle. I am opposed to Frenchmen who support Hitler and the Axis." The matter settled itself on December 24 when Darlan was assassinated and Franklin flew to Casablanca early in January to meet with Churchill and straighten out the mess.

Because of her crowning success in raising morale in England through her visit, Franklin decided after his return from Casablanca that Eleanor should take a good-will trip to the South Pacific. "The boys out there haven't had many visitors," he told her, "and you'll do them a lot of good."

"If I go," she said, "I want to be allowed to see our men on Guadalcanal and other islands."

"No, you can't go to Guadalcanal," he insisted. "It's too dangerous a place and I won't agree."

"But I'll never be able to face these men again if I'm going to be so near an island they've given so much to take and I don't actually go there."

He finally "broke down" and gave her a letter to Admiral William "Bull" Halsey which said he was willing to have her visit Guadalcanal "if it did not interfere with the conduct of the war." Later he wrote to Halsey that "no matter what he wrote or what he said, I was not to be allowed to go to Guadalcanal."

Because she promised Norman Davis, chairman of the Red Cross, that she would inspect South Pacific Red Cross installations, he asked her to wear a Red Cross uniform on her trip. This she purchased at her own expense and set off by plane in August. In addition, she promised to turn over all her writing earnings from the trip to the Red Cross.

This trip was another amazing exhibition of energy and endurance. She flew 23,145 miles, made 17 island stops and spent eight days in New Zealand and eleven in Australia. In New Zealand she covered 1,000 miles in old trains, and on the islands she bumped along jungle roads in jeeps and command cars. On Christmas Island a young lieutenant colonel couldn't take his eyes off her. "You're the first white woman I've seen in ten months," he apologized. There were hospitals filled with wounded to visit, camps to inspect and outposts filled with lonely boys to go to for chats. Plumbing was almost nonexistent in many places. In one place, when she turned on the light in her room she found the floor crawling with red bugs—"I nearly disgraced myself with screaming." Everywhere, as in England, the boys complained about the mail from home, crying notes about food shortages and bad transportation.

When she got to Noumea she gave Admiral Halsey Franklin's letter. Halsey was displeased that she had come at all, let alone permitting her to visit Guadalcanal. He delayed giving her a green light, but he had never met up with a personality as strong as hers. In the end, he gave her his blessing and she flew there.

There were few amusing incidents in a whirlwind swoop that permitted her only three or four hours of sleep a night and exhausted the trailing admirals and generals. One morning at 9:30 she appeared unannounced at a Red Cross club with her retinue of red-eyed, heavy-breathing, top-ranking officers. They dragged themselves after her when she opened a door and went into a room. There stood two undersized privates in their underwear in front of an electric heater. Their mouths flew open when she approached the boys, shook their hands and began an earnest conversation as though there were nothing wrong. The facial expressions of the two privates could best be described as paralyzed shock. When it was over and she started out the door, both boys rubbed their scorched legs in agony.

All was not an unmitigated blessing. She found in some places that the officers had been making fun of her. A story Admiral Halsey said had been originated by Tokyo Rose, propaganda broadcaster for Japan, followed her from island to island. The false and vicious tale was that she had said, "The marines are a bunch of animals who should be locked up for a good while after they return from overseas." In her talks with the boys, she made it a point to mention this rumor and thus was able to undo much of the damage. At one island, she wrote in her diary, the colonel in charge was a regular army man and a Massachusetts Republican who "was snobby and not pleased to see me." He decided one day to make her squeal with fright. "The Colonel took us up to his radar station and I have never seen a steeper road. But since I was sure he took me to see if I would be afraid, I summoned all of my experiences of driving with Hall (my brother) and tried to behave as though I usually drove over such roads."

Toward the end of her five-week trip, news reached Franklin that she was ill. However, she wouldn't quit even though "I had been walking around with pneumonia." Josephus Daniels reported in his North Carolina paper: "When Eleanor Roosevelt was flying over the islands in the Far East and telling soldiers she would bring home messages to their families, Franklin Roosevelt made his prayer, 'Oh Lord, make Eleanor tired.' "

When she finally returned to Washington, she had lost 30 pounds. Yet she considered the trip highly successful. Typical was the letter one soldier wrote home: "I have always been 'agin' her until now, but she has the faculty of seeming as though she is not in the slightest hurry, that she came all the way out here just to talk to you and you and you."

Upon her return, Franklin tried to get her to rest, but she had too much to do. In addition, she bent his ear about what she thought he should do for the boys in the Pacific. Asked at his press conference whether she had told him about her trip, he replied ruefully, "Yes, she's been talking about it ever since she got back."

She had promised hundreds of boys in the South Pacific that she would contact their families upon her return. Once she called a girl to inform her that she had seen her husband. "Perhaps you will have a bite with me tomorrow so I can tell you all about him." She hadn't given her name and the girl asked, "How will I recognize you?"

[297]

"Just look for a tall, gray-haired lady in the hotel lobby," she said quickly.

"Oh, no! It can't be!" the girl cried out in shock the next day when she discovered she was lunching with the First Lady.

On another occasion she called a girl and said, "I have a message from your fiancé. This is Mrs. Roosevelt."

"Don't be funny," the girl yelled into the phone. "Who do you think you're kidding?" And with that she hung up.

Besides these calls and her regular duties, Eleanor also helped edit the film of her trip, which was released to 9,000 theaters. When it was shown it was to evoke fuming protests from Republicans because in it she told Franklin's favorite war story. This was about the private in the Pacific who was depressed because he hadn't shot any Japanese. "I'll give you a chance," said his commanding officer. "Go hide in a foxhole and yell, 'To hell with Hirohito!'"

He did this, but when he returned he was even more depressed. "Did you carry out my orders?" his officer demanded.

"Yes," was his reply. "But when I yelled, 'To hell with Hirohito,' a Jap jumped up and said, 'To hell with Roosevelt,' and I couldn't shoot a fellow Republican, could I?"

She took one more trip for Franklin, this time a 13,000-mile inspection and good-will tour of the Caribbean area in March, 1944. He personally mapped out her entire itinerary. Franklin told her that the men stationed there "felt they were in a backwater and chafed to be where they could do what they considered a more important job." He wanted Eleanor to tell them "that they were not forgotten, even though they were not on the front line."

Chapter Thirty-One

1944 saw the unfolding of Eleanor Roosevelt's great tragedy. Franklin was slowly wearing out and circumstances prevented her from easing his burden. When she welcomed him home from his Teheran conference with Stalin and Churchill, she noted that he suffered from a low-grade fever and a cough that he could not shake off. "Cold weather bothered him," she said, "because his circulation was bad and his feet got cold so that rubbing was necessary."

She had many other indications of a growing change in Franklin, though at the time they seemed minor. One was the numerous complaints that came to her from him about his food. There was an early note to her registering his disgust with having chicken so often. "I am getting to the point where my stomach positively rebels and this does not help my relations with foreign powers. I bit two of them yesterday." With his loss of appetite his temper sometimes failed. Once she asked him what he wanted for dinner that night, "Dammit! I don't want beef," he exploded.

"Then what do you want?"

"I want a steak." Yet when he had his steak he merely toyed with it.

There were still other telltale signs. The long illness and death of Missy LeHand, Franklin's secretary, was a blow to Eleanor but not as much as it was to Franklin. Missy had treated him with idolatrous worship for more than two decades and had been considered part of the family. One of Franklin's lifelong attributes, said Eleanor, was his "ability to pull down a shade after receiving bad news and then go back to work." He had been a "completely controlled person." He was less so now.

She also found that a strange loneliness overtook him at times. Even though it was he who had insisted that she make the Caribbean inspection tour, upon her return she learned he had written a sad letter about his temporary, solitary batching— "My Missus is in Recife, Brazil; Anna is in Boston; Jimmy is in Hawaii; Elliott is in a camp near London;

Franklin, Jr., is at the Miami camp and Johnny is on an aircraft carrier headed out."

With the snowballing problems of the war, the domestic economy and postwar planning, she found he sometimes had trouble concentrating. Yet she watched his hours of toil grow steadily longer instead of shorter. Nor was he able to laugh off with her as in the past the pounding criticism from opposition editors. On his way to Africa in November, 1943, he had written her: "It is a relief to have no papers. I am going to start a one-page paper." She also noticed that while he gave his annual reading of Dickens' *Christmas Carol* to the growing number of grandchildren, he was skipping more pages each year. The only parts he still read with relish were the story of Fezziwig and the Christmas party "and the waking up of Old Scrooge and his calling out the window to get the turkey for Bob Cratchett's family," said Eleanor.

In the past she had made it a practice to leave marked passages from letters, memos and articles at his bedside for him to incorporate into his speeches and messages. She did less of this now. Nor did she engage him in the give-and-take discussions that had been such an essential part of their political partnership. He could not "bear to listen to a real discussion, such as we had always had," she discovered. This became clear one evening when she, Franklin and their old friend, Harry Hooker, were arguing hectically about the merits and demerits of compulsory military service. Eleanor stopped talking at once when she glanced at Franklin's face and saw he was greatly upset. Hooker told her afterward, as though she were the sole culprit, "Don't ever argue with Franklin again."

When her husband's fever and cough persisted in the spring of 1944, she tried to curtail his daily list of visitors to a minimum. This proved a difficult task because so many government officials insisted that a meeting was essential. "Don't press him and wear him out," she pleaded. "Go easy on him."

In April she was pleased when Franklin accepted an invitation from Bernard Baruch to visit Hobcaw, his plantation in Georgetown, South Carolina. The two weeks he told her he intended to stay there seemed too short to her and she gave her blessing when he remained at Hobcaw a month. Once she flew down to see how he was getting along. Jesting and joking, he looked much improved to her and when he finally returned to the White House he was like the Franklin of old.

By D-Day on June sixth, she noticed that he seemed full of vitality, though highly nervous and concerned with the momentous Normandy Invasion. "What are you thinking of?" she asked him.

"I wonder how Linaka will come out," he said vaguely. Russel Linaka had worked on tree plantings for Franklin at Hyde Park and was now in the Navy.

D-Day brought up the question of a fourth term. "All that is within me cries to go back to my home on the Hudson," he informed the nation. She knew how much he meant it. Yet he would not quit, and though she had opposed his seeking a third term, she voiced no opposition to a fourth. The old Roosevelt bounce was sure to return, given time and proper care.

"I have as little right to withdraw as the soldier has to leave his post in the line," he told her bluntly. She did not protest because she was aware that he had set his heart on establishing a new international organization to maintain the peace and improve the world's economy. There was still no agreement among the Allies. Besides, she knew that even when the organization came into existence, he would want to be present to oversee it off to a good start. "There's still another reason," he facetiously told Eleanor. "I really want to be re-elected to a fourth term so I can fire your housekeeper. She's been giving me oatmeal every morning for months now." During this period when his intention to run was not yet made public, Eleanor visited Alex Woollcott, who was dying after suffering a heart attack. In comparison Franklin was in blooming health. "Tell your husband to run again," Woollcott urged her. "He'll win because he will be fighting not for himself but for all humanity, and because in the last analysis," her friend beamed, "America has always been happily predisposed toward a safe and sane Fourth."

As the time for the Democratic National Convention in Chicago approached that July, Eleanor talked with Franklin about keeping Henry Wallace on the ticket. Franklin growled at her suggestion. "He never was a politician and is not a very good one now, but he has long been a thinker," she tried to convince him. Besides, in the public's mind he was closely identified with Franklin's programs.

"He is too idealistic and that makes him a bad politician." Franklin shook his head. "Furthermore," he concluded sternly, "Wallace had his chance to make his mark and if he could not convince the party leaders that he was the right person, I cannot dictate to them twice."

Franklin planned to go by train through Chicago to the West Coast and from there fly to the Pacific Theater of Operations to meet with General MacArthur. Eleanor rode along with the intention of leaving him in California. The entire train buzzed with talk about vice-presidential prospects. Once Wallace had been rejected, Eleanor wanted Supreme Court Associate Justice William O. Douglas as Franklin's running mate.

Franklin was partial to Douglas, too, but unfortunately Douglas was off fishing somewhere and not on the train to plead his cause with the politicians.

It was in the newspapers that Eleanor read that Senator Harry Truman of Missouri had been selected to run with Franklin.

She was concerned about Franklin after she left his train. Press photos that ran of him in the newspapers just before he took off for the MacArthur talk were like a death mask. In fact, even before his departure, he wrote her from San Diego on July 21 that he visited Camp Pendleton and "then I got the collywobbles and stayed in the train in the P. M. Better today," he assured her. "Lots of love, devotedly. F."

It was her hope that Franklin would do as little campaigning as possible in order that his body have an opportunity to replenish itself. Friends had told her of a speech he made at the Bremerton Navy Yard upon his return from the Pacific. His leg braces had hurt him so much that any pressure on them made him gasp with pain. Every time he turned a page or gestured during that talk, he winced and almost broke out in moans. Finally, aching so badly, he supported himself off the ground by flexing his powerful arm muscles against the speaker's stand. To Eleanor it was as though she were back in the twenties again with Franklin making those first painful speeches after his polio.

The campaign that fall was the dirtiest Eleanor ever experienced. Emboldened by the rare opportunity to practice for four campaigns, the opposition's treatment of her reached an all-time low. Even her friend, Clare Boothe Luce, running for Congress in Connecticut, joined in the below-the-belt name-calling of Franklin.

In the White House she watched Franklin's aides walking worriedly about as Dewey's campaign swung into action. When the opposition's name-calling and ridicule were set methodically in daily motion, Eleanor showed no concern, though Franklin's advisers, especially his speech-writing assistants, Sam Rosenman and Robert Sherwood, impatiently waited for Franklin to begin his campaign. One morning she scolded them for having worked half the previous night. "I saw your lights burning at three A.M.," she reproved them. "You shouldn't stay up so late."

"But what were you doing up so late yourself?" they chorused.

"Working," she said, as though that were a different matter.

She had watched her husband's progress from local to national politician and now to international politician, and no campaign was to interfere with the settlement of postwar problems. Early in September, while Dewey was running hard against Franklin, she went with Franklin to Quebec to discuss with Churchill the problem of what to do with postwar Germany. Half the month disappeared in discussing this problem. Afterward she invited Clementine and Winston Churchill to visit them in Hyde Park so Franklin could get some relaxation with old friends. On a quiet evening while Eleanor sat knitting, she burst into laughter when Franklin leaned over and took Churchill's arm. "My dear Winston,"—he waved his other hand—"the British Empire doesn't exist any longer. It's just a figment of your imagination."

She watched Churchill rise slowly, a puckish expression on his face. He pretended to be carrying a heavy load in his arms and dropped it on Franklin. "Do you want India? Here it is."

She knew that this respite was just what Franklin needed, and a few days later when Franklin's aides were tearing their hair with anguish over the Dewey head start, she felt no qualms about his beginning his campaign. That first speech—on September 23 at Dan Tobin's Teamsters' Union dinner in Washington—was one she would always recall with pleasure. It was masterful and put the opposition on the defense for the rest of the campaign. "The Republican leaders have not been content to make personal attacks upon me—or my wife—or my sons— they now include my little dog, Fala," she heard him say with sham severity. "Unlike members of my family, Fala resents this. When he learned that the Republican fiction writers had concocted a story that I had left him behind on an Aleutian island and had sent a destroyer back to find him—at a cost to the taxpayers of two or three or twenty million dollars—his Scotch soul was furious. He has not been the same dog since. I am accustomed to hearing malicious falsehoods about myself, but I think I have a right to object to libelous statements about my dog."

Begrudgingly, even Republican leaders admitted that the speech was the best of her husband's career. Afterward, he admitted quietly to her, "I think the people prefer the big man with the little dog to the little man with the big dog."

Eleanor did some campaigning that October. "You can't live in the White House for eleven years and not make friends and foes," she admitted. "But if because you have certain convictions you have made foes, would those people on election day let their feelings toward you influence their vote? I doubt it very much." The opposition attacks on her followed closely the line of her old foe Westbrook Pegler, who called her ultimate goal "some scheme containing the most binding elements of Communism and Hitlerism" and said her "innocent, wholehearted, humane enthusiasms" were "only a disguise."

She passed her sixtieth milestone that month, but she objected to her birthday solely on the score that the Red Cross would no longer accept her blood. "I'm getting old," she told her press conference, "but I don't feel old. I feel that I have a great deal of vitality left—at least five more years of active working life." This was an underestimation of vast proportions.

During that last month of the campaign the Republicans concentrated their attack on the state of Franklin's health. To dispel the doubts, because she believed he was in no danger of dying, Eleanor joined him in an open-car ride through New York City on October 21. Unfortunately, the rain that fell that day was one of the heaviest downpours in the city's long history. They were both thoroughly drenched by the time she took him to the Washington Square West apartment she had rented in April, 1942.

Here she now ordered him to change his clothes. He had a bourbon and took a nap. When he complained to her upon awakening that he still felt a chill, he drank more bourbon. That evening she went with him to the Waldorf-Astoria where he was to make an address on foreign affairs. At the reception he had some martinis, and later in the ballroom he enjoyed the excellent wines. Later when he finally started to speak it was embarrassing the way he suddenly stared at her—as though he were surprised to find her there.

To one side went his prepared speech as he went into long reminiscences about "My Missus," and her importance to him. Sitting before him and looking from Eleanor to him, his speech writers were aghast. On and on he went about "My Missus." Then after what seemed an interminable time, he returned to his prepared speech. It was a touching scene, though the papers next day made no mention of his ad-libbed remarks.

Toward the end of the election contest, she watched his appearance grow haggard. When he insisted that she join him in a last-day campaign in the original stamping ground of his 1910 election contest for the State Senate, she agreed. It was obvious that he wanted to relive and savor that first political fight.

The weather was raw in Dutchess County and she dressed warmly. Franklin was attired in a greatcoat with a beaver collar and his old brown campaign fedora sat on his head. Memories poured out for her as they made the rounds of the district. Missing from the scene was their old friend Louis Howe. At Bank Square in Beacon, a crowd of more than 1,000 persons crushed against their car. Louie would have been in the mob sizing up sentiment for Franklin. Franklin insisted that he could not speak to the Beacon crowd without an introduction by Morg Hoyt, "who has been introducing me for at least the last hundred and fifty years." Morg, who, Eleanor knew, had introduced that beginning politician back in 1910, stepped forward and repeated his talk.

Election night was cold, too. A large crowd had come to the Hyde Park place and Eleanor had secluded Franklin and Admiral Leahy in the dining room with two news tickers beating out the election returns. A radio also blared. At the torchlight parade in front of the house, Franklin wore his great cape and pushed his hat back at a rakish angle. She stood behind him with Anna and he looked ill as he gave a short talk before returning inside.

As usual Eleanor kept busy feeding the horde of guests. From time to time she looked into the dining room to keep close watch on Franklin. As the evening wore on, Franklin looked gravely anxious about the outcome of the election. He was jittery and expressed concern that Dewey would beat him. Henry Morgenthau kept popping in and out to express his concern, too. Rattled by the ticker news, Franklin finally asked a Secret Service man to stand outside the dining room and bar all guests except Eleanor. When Morgenthau reappeared and couldn't gain admission, he wailed, "But I'm his friend." Indeed he was, but the tired President wanted to worry without him. It was not until 3:45 A.M. that Dewey conceded and Eleanor was able to get Franklin to bed.

After the election Eleanor was happy when Franklin hurried to his beloved Warm Springs for a three-week vacation and an effort to regain his energy. But it was obvious to her upon his return that he had made little headway. When he insisted that all thirteen grandchildren be delivered to the White House to visit with him at the time of his fourth inauguration on January 20, 1945, it was, said Eleanor later in retrospect, as though he were "having a premonition that he would not be with us very long." Ironically, Harry Hooker, who was so concerned about Franklin's health that he no longer argued with him at the table on the proper way to carve a duck, had suffered a heart attack and Eleanor put him to bed in the White House. For two months, as 1945 came in, she nursed him.

With the enormous demands on her own time, it was a relief to Eleanor to have daughter Anna living at the White House to help look after "Pop." When Eleanor had to leave the White House for speeches, inspections and conferences, it was good to know that Anna would be having lunch with Franklin and watching over his visitors. There was also Fala to bring him relaxation and he enjoyed having Cousin Margaret Suckley, always calm and ladylike, sit in his room and knit while he worked.

Both Eleanor and Franklin missed their boys dreadfully. A President's wife was no more immune from concern for sons on war fronts than was any other mother. Nor was Franklin different from any other father. However, there was exciting pride in their war records. There was the letter from Colonel Evans Carlson to Eleanor that was full of praise about her Jimmy, second in command of the famed Carlson's Raiders before the Makin Island foray. "We are on the eve of the Great Adventure," Carlson had written dramatically. Elliott had flown in dangerously unprotected planes in Africa, while Franklin, Jr., was in a host of spectacular adventures as commander of a small naval vessel. Elliott's eyesight was so poor that he never should have been accepted by the military in the first place. "Franklin (Jr.) had been such a gay young man about town," Eleanor laughed, "that when the young boys under him were on shore leave, he knew exactly where to look for them in the morning."

However, along with the concern, pride and humor, both Eleanor and Franklin were appalled by the continual attacks on the boys during the war. On one occasion, with anger Franklin showed her a letter from one of the boys which ended, "Pops, sometimes I really hope that one of us gets killed so that maybe they'll stop picking on the rest of the family."

By 1945 Franklin had grown even more thin-skinned about attacks on his boys. Unknown to Elliott, his dog Blaze had displaced three servicemen on a plane. When Franklin submitted the routine nomination to raise Elliott to a brigadier general, congressional opposition centered on Blaze. It was disquieting to Eleanor to watch Franklin's mounting anger under this sort of attack.

The world could not stop because Franklin was hurt by the attacks on their boys or because he was not well, Eleanor realized. In fact, she told him, "The next four years will probably be the most difficult years the world has ever seen." The Germans were on their last legs now despite their impressive victories in the Battle of the Bulge. The Russians were moving swiftly toward the west in what appeared to be a headlong rout of Hitler's best armies. The postwar period gave evidence of coming on with unexpected haste and Franklin had better be prepared for it.

Harry Hopkins had made note of her concern with domestic matters which Franklin had cast aside as unimportant. Hopkins wrote for his own records: "Mrs. Roosevelt urged the President very strongly to keep in the forefront of his mind the domestic situation because she felt there was a real danger of his losing American public opinion in his foreign policy if he failed to follow through on the domestic implications of his campaign promises. . . . She impressed on both of us that we must not be satisfied with merely making campaign pledges: the President being under moral obligation to see his domestic reforms through, particularly the organization of our economic life in such a way as to give everybody a job. She emphasized that this was an overwhelming task and she hoped neither the President nor I thought it was settled in any way by making speeches."

After the inauguration, a bleak little affair performed at the White House instead of on the Capitol stands, Eleanor insisted that Franklin take her along to the Yalta Conference where the last thorny problems involved in establishing the United Nations were to be tackled. "If you go," he told her negatively, "they will all feel they have to make a big fuss over you. No other wives will be there." He preferred having her stay behind to keep an eye on the boiling home front for him. "I'll take Anna," he said when he read her face. "It will be simpler if I do."

It was true, she knew, that the home front was in a state of disquiet. The papers were full of Blaze's airplane ride. More important, a place had to be found for Henry Wallace now that he was no longer Vice President. Franklin's solution shortly before leaving the country was to nominate Wallace as Secretary of Commerce and head of the Federal Loan Agency. Eleanor realized the horror of this situation because Jesse Jones, who would have to be dispossessed to make room for Wallace, held the support of conservative congressmen. Though Franklin was already at sea, she sent him an urgent message on January 29 telling him to separate the Commerce Department and the FLA nomination by executive order so that Wallace might have a chance to be confirmed. Two days later she sent him another message to come out with a strong statement for Wallace. In the end her strategy worked and Wallace was confirmed as Secretary of Commerce.

When Franklin returned from Yalta, he brought her a harem costume, compliments of Ibn Saud of Saudi Arabia. But there were no jests on his lips, for he felt rotten. "Pa" Watson, his aide and close friend, had died on the trip and Harry Hopkins was so ill that he was confined to his bed. A pervading tiredness had settled upon Franklin. At Malta, on the way home on February second, he wrote Eleanor, "Dearest Babs: Got in safely. Lots of sleep but need still more!" He was still concerned about Elliott's raise in military grade— "I hope for news of the Senate confirmation of Elliott."

[307]

She learned later how frightened Churchill had been by Franklin's appearance at Yalta. "I noticed that the President was ailing," he said about their departure from Alexandria. "His captivating smile, his gay and charming manner, had not deserted him, but his face had a transparency, an air of purification and often there was a far-away look in his eyes."

These were what Eleanor noticed when she first saw him on his return. Yet now that he was back and once more in charge of the nation from Washington, where was he to find time to rest? With a heavy heart, she went with him on March first on his ride up Capitol Hill to report to Congress on his trip. He made a great point of explaining that he had to sit down because he could not wear his leg braces.

She was fighting time now with him. Their fortieth wedding anniversary dinner on March 17 was a pleasant and carefree occasion. "Well, the war is almost over in Europe," he told her, "and it shouldn't last too long in Asia. After the war," he confided, "you and I will go to the Near East and settle the difficulties there. There are lots of difficulties there."

"I thought we were going to Hyde Park?" she queried.

He ignored her interruption. "And then we'll go to the Far East." His eyes grew wide. "We'll go to China and fix things there."

"Let's go to Hyde Park," she repeated.

He stared at her and smiled broadly.

He was going to Warm Springs again for a needed rest. It was settled between them that she would accompany him to San Francisco later in the month to inaugurate the United Nations. In London, Winston Churchill had announced that she and Franklin would visit England afterward and would be accorded "the biggest reception since Lord Nelson made his triumphant return to London."

She wanted Anna to accompany Franklin to Warm Springs, for her own schedule during the next few weeks was crowded, and Franklin would not want her to cancel her long-scheduled talks. Besides, he would have thought something was wrong had she done so. However, Anna's son, Johnny Boettiger, was ill in the Washington Naval Hospital, and Anna could not go with him.

Those last days before departure for Warm Springs were irksome to her fading Franklin. Newspapers were making big copy over Franklin's agreement at Yalta to give the USSR three United Nations delegates. More important, he complained to her that Stalin was not living up to his promises regarding free elections for Eastern Europe. Before he left Washington he wrote several stern letters to Stalin.

Another indication to her of his mounting feebleness was that he wanted the familiar with him at Warm Springs. Cousins Laura Delano and Margaret Suckley accompanied him. Eleanor's World War I part-time secretary, Nancy Mercer, now Mrs. Winthrop Rutherfurd, also went to Warm Springs at his request. And Eleanor telephoned him daily.

April twelfth arrived. Eleanor's appointment book for the day showed seven appointments, including a press conference at eleven A.M., a two-thirty meeting with a Mr. Ross, a four o'clock benefit at the exclusive Sulgrave Club for the Thrift Shop and a seven P.M. dinner with the Quaker Friends. A glance at her April sixteenth appointments would have revealed: "8:30 A.M. FDR return?" and a notation that he was scheduled to arrive at the Forest Glen station stop near Silver Spring, Maryland.

At her press conference that morning she was both a political personage and a wife. Questions were varied and she answered them all in good humor. She told the girls that we should withhold judgment on what should be done in postwar Germany without a Hitler. She also said she was preparing for her trip to San Francisco's United Nations Charter Conference, and that she had talked to Franklin and he had said he felt fine.

It was early in the afternoon when the blow fell. Laura Delano called up in great distress. While he sat signing letters and having a portrait drawn, Franklin had fainted. He had been carried to bed and doctors summoned. In great agitation, Eleanor called Franklin's personal physician, Dr. Ross McIntire, who was in Washington. "There isn't any cause for alarm," McIntire assured her. "Let's plan on going to Warm Springs tonight. In the meantime, why don't you keep your afternoon engagements? If you don't it will cause great comment."

With full misgivings, Eleanor set out for the Sulgrave Club. Her mind was elsewhere as she sat next to Mrs. Woodrow Wilson. Not long after her arrival, she was told she was wanted on the phone. As if in a bad dream she picked up the receiver. "Steve Early, very much upset, asked me to come home at once. I did not even ask why." Franklin was gone, she told herself. "The load grew too great for one man to carry." Always the proper lady, she returned to the tea to apologize for leaving so soon "in this way."

All the way back to the White House she sat with her hands clenched. In her second-floor sitting room, Steve Early and Dr. McIntire walked, both the color of paste. "The President has died," Early blurted. "I am more sorry for the people of the country and the world," he went on heavily, "than I am for us."

Her mind went blank and she froze. "I'll call Vice President Truman," he told her.

It was the worst moment of her life. Yet by the time Truman arrived she tried to pull herself together. All she could think of was how sorry she felt for Truman. "The President has passed away," she told him. "He died like a soldier."

Truman choked, startled. "What can I do?" he asked her.

"Tell us what we can do," was her reply. "Is there any way we can help you?"

She cabled her sons who were far away: "Father slept away. He would expect you to carry on and finish your jobs."

In a daze she changed to a black dress, and shortly after seven-fifteen she boarded a plane with Steve Early and Dr. McIntire for Georgia. Before daylight broke she walked into Franklin's little white cottage on Pine Mountain. Without a word, she went in alone to be with him.

By ten A.M. the funeral party was ready to leave for Washington. She insisted that the hearse stop briefly in front of Georgia Hall where the patients were lined up in front to say good-by to Franklin. From their eyes, she saw that they had cried all night. As the hearse passed by, Franklin's favorite musician, Negro Coast Guardsman Graham Jackson, softly played "Going Home" on his accordion. A voice from the crowd cried out, "Please Gawd, take care of him." On the train back to Washington, said Eleanor, "I lay in my berth all night with the window shade up, looking out at the countryside he had loved and watching the faces of the people at stations, and even at the crossroads, who came to pay their last tribute all through the night."

After the funeral services in the East Room, Franklin's body was taken to Hyde Park for burial in his rose garden. Of her four sons only Elliott was able to attend. When the cannon volleys had fired the presidential salute and the crowd had left, she stood alone at his grave. Her hand touched the small pearl fleur-de-lis pin Franklin had given her before they were married in 1905.

By the time she returned to the White House to remove her accumulations of twelve years, more than 25,000 letters of condolence awaited her. In a week she was packed and ready to move out. Toward the end of the week she invited her press-conference girls to a last farewell. By habit they came with notebooks. "I only want to say good-by," she told them. "This is not a social gathering. Not a press conference." All eyes were wet. When she raised her hand during her short farewell talk, it was shaking badly. By the time she finished everyone was crying.

At night, she asked the Secret Service men, who had never been able to keep up with her whereabouts, to come to her upstairs sitting room and bade them good-by. She also asked the White House office workers and all the servants whom she had got to know so well. Old staunch friends like Bernard Baruch and Admiral Leahy dropped in for chats, but did not stay long because her face was strained.

On the last evening, she rose, put on her hat and coat and walked out the front door. In a drizzling rain she rode to Union Station, where she and Franklin had gone to meet the king and queen of England. Later that evening when she arrived in New York, she was surprised to find reporters crowding the station. She shook her head and walked swiftly through them. "The story is over," she told them bluntly.

Chapter Thirty-Two

THE DEATH OF FRANKLIN left an immense gap in Eleanor's existence. Widowhood, after more than forty years of marriage, produced a raw feeling that the rest of her days would be a sad epilogue to a story that was over. Had she not been able to carry on her far-flung activities solely because of Franklin's prestige and his willingness and helpfulness? Would her fate now be any different from that of other Presidents' widows—the sad ladies dressed in black with mournful expressions frozen on their suffering faces and invited now and then to presidential receptions to be stared at?

Nor was Franklin's death just a personal calamity for her. All over the world peoples and heads of states and governments took his loss personally, as though someone who was steering them through troubled waters had left them in mid-passage. In Asia and in Europe, in Africa and in the Americas, men and women cried openly. The young especially, including almost all in the nation's armed forces, who could hardly recall having lived under another President during their short years, felt the loss most deeply.

Though she had maintained a brave ladylike front following Franklin's death and throughout the torturous funeral ceremonies that followed, those about her felt her pervading sadness and bewilderment. Her son Franklin, Jr., observed, "When Father died, she was worried at first about having to make decisions on her own, and about assuming responsibilities, because, before, he had always been there to advise her and, if she flew off now and then on a tangent, to check her." In the cold weeks after Franklin's death she had trouble even on the minor problem of determining oil purchases for the Hyde Park house. One of Franklin's decisions before he died was that if anything happened to him, Fala was to be returned to Cousin Margaret Suckley. "Please let Mummy keep Fala," her son Jimmy persuaded Miss Suckley. "She has no one living whom she is personally responsible for." But even though the little Scottie came to live with her, Fala was as sad as Eleanor for a long while. Whenever a car approached he would be off like lightning to greet his old master only to return sadly, his head drooping in disappointment. He also had the misfortune of being almost chewed up by the huge Blaze, Elliott's dog.

The 25,000 letters of condolence that came pouring in during the first week after Franklin's death reached the deluge of 100,000 in the next few weeks. Almost all were heart-stirring tales of gratitude for what Franklin's existence had meant to the writers. "When your husband became President," a typical letter went, "I had no job and no savings and nowhere to turn for help to keep my family from starving. . . . He changed our whole lives." One of the most significant notes came from Dr. George Draper, who had stood alongside Eleanor and Louis Howe against Sara Roosevelt back in 1921 when Franklin contracted polio. "Wasn't it lucky," Draper wrote, "that you, Louis Howe and I urged Franklin to keep going on the main track of his career rather than to permit himself to be switched off on a permanent siding?" "Certainly Franklin justified our confidence that he could go on and should go on and he met the challenge gallantly," she replied. "Up to the last I never heard him complain."

"The work here is endless and the mail still pours in," she wrote in May to Harry Hopkins, who had looked the picture of death himself at Franklin's funeral. There was no way possible for her to thank each letter writer personally. President Truman graciously relayed her gratitude to the American public at one of his press conferences. Some of the White House stenographers were also put to work temporarily to help out on her correspondence. One of the new President's administrative assistants discovered this activity one day and snarled at the girls, "Mrs. Roosevelt is no longer riding the gravy train! Stop it!" But Mr. Truman remanded his assistant's order when he got wind of it and the man departed from the White House for good shortly afterward.

There was also a big decision to make about her residence. The Hyde Park home was designated a national historic site by the Secretary of Interior in 1944. However, Eleanor and the immediate family retained life interests in the home and the 33.23 acres included in the site. Her decision was aided by a memo from Franklin she found after his death. "It informed us," she said, "that we had a right to live here if we wished, but that we would be happier if we did not try to live in this big house. He knew that my tastes were not for the formal living which this big house would entail." There was even an amusing warning. "He warned us that the people might want to come here afterward and we would not feel justified in keeping them out, so he pictured us as looking for privacy in the attic or in the woods!" The result was that she decided to live in the remodeled two-story Val-Kill furniture factory, now defunct, and she took it over for her own use in 1947 when her two associates in that venture, Nancy Cook and Marian Dickerman, moved out and went to Connecticut.

At Val-Kill she was two highways and two miles away from the big house. Yet her proximity to Franklin's grave in his mother's rose garden brought her further moments of woe. Foreign dignitaries and friends, such as Churchill, Baruch, Josephus Daniels, came in a steady outpouring to pay their respects and it was her duty to escort each to the grave. Aged Josephus Daniels, Franklin's boss at the Navy Department during World War I, wrote her after his visit, "It seemed like the spirit of Franklin was with us." Another time General Eisenhower provided contrast when he came to lay a wreath on her husband's grave. "He was anxious to see Fala," Eleanor noted, "since he had a Scottie of his own and was devoted to this breed and especially to his own dog." Few who came to Franklin's grave could treat it as other than a personal loss. Even four years later, when India's Prime Minister, Jawaharlal Nehru, came to call, there were disconcerting moments when he was overcome in talking about Franklin. His voice broke and the welling tears that bubbled in his eyes cast a pall over the gathering. When Winston Churchill stood before Franklin's grave, he wiped the tears from his eyes and his sincerity touched Eleanor. His had been a relationship with Franklin no two other heads of government had ever enjoyed. Later, puffing his giant black cigar, he repeated to Eleanor the overpowering fears that had descended upon him at Yalta. "If the combined brains of the Allies had spent ten years on research to find the unhealthiest and worst place for the meeting, they would in the end have agreed on Yalta. When I took leave of him in Alexandria Harbor, I must confess that I had an indefinable sense of fear that his health and strength were on the ebb."

Fortunately, there was her apartment in Washington Square West in New York City to which she could go for refuge from the oppressive Hyde Park atmosphere of those first few months. It was in this apartment Franklin had planned to finish his first post-presidential book, one on American history. Their joint house with Sara on East Sixty-fifth Street had been sold during the war. The Washington Square apartment was soon a cluttered place with the heavy furniture that had followed her and Franklin on his political career. The same Huntington portrait of her father, painted in the seventies and a dining-room fixture at the Sixty-fifth Street house, now watched her from its gilded frame

[314]

on a dining-room wall. "It seems good to have the old pieces back again," she said.

However, it was not the old her mind was groping for but the new. It was inevitable, despite her sadness, that she cast aside her mourning and live in the world again. In the first place, a woman of her class and breeding did not wear her emotions on her sleeve. The code was to carry on. True, one needed an iron will to maintain a stoical expression on one's face, but she possessed that iron will. On April 29, less than three weeks after Franklin's death, she made her first public appearance. She came unexpectedly to the dedication of the new 45,000-ton, $90,-000,000 aircraft carrier, *Franklin D. Roosevelt,* whose name President Truman had ordered changed from its original U.S.S. *Coral Sea.* Not only did she refuse the solicitudes of Navy Secretary James Forrestal, but she insisted that she make a brief address at the dedication rites.

In the second place, a woman with her tremendous energies could not remain long on any side line. To live was to function. "That damned Roosevelt extra gland!" her young cousin, Joseph Alsop, called it. Only a week after Franklin's passing, she had resumed her daily newspaper column. Readers, accustomed to the column's reading as though it had been written on the run, found it even worse now and without a shred of self-confidence. But she wouldn't give it up or take a rest. In fact, she planned to add to this newspaper writing a monthly magazine column and the second volume of her autobiography.

However, the third and most compelling magnet for bringing her out of her shell at an early time was her overwhelming sense of duty and concern with underdogs. Her own personal tragedy was minor compared with what others were undergoing. This would be so until her last breath. "I sometimes remember when I was young and could just sit down to read or sew and I think, 'Goodness, that would be nice.' But," her face clouded, "I could not possibly stop any of the things I'm doing." William L. White, editor of the *Reader's Digest* and son of her old admirer from Emporia, Kansas, venerable William Allen White, wrote with admiration, "All the feeble folk—the lame, the halt, the blind, the persecuted and despised of men, the various minorities laboring under discrimination—all of these come to her with their troubles as children to a mother, knowing that they will get not soft soap, but real compassion and a truly helpful wisdom that comes only from the deep earnestness of her tender heart."

The war in Europe had ended on May eighth and there were millions upon millions of new underdogs for her to champion now. Mussolini and Hitler were gone. The United Nations Charter Conference was busily at work in San Francisco. "If only Franklin had just a month of grace—only that," she said wretchedly.

However, there was too much to do to dwell on such thoughts. She felt a great need for making the lot of the new President easier. Franklin had paid as little attention to Harry Truman as he had to his predecessors, Vice Presidents John Garner and Henry Wallace. Unschooled in foreign affairs, Truman was beset with the enormous task of making the peace. "You are the instrument chosen as a guide in this terribly serious situation," she wrote him, "and if there is anything which any of us can do to help you, you have a right to call upon us all." She offered him the advice that "during the war my husband had a map room and there were experts who daily briefed him on what was happening in every part of the world. It seems to me now we are engaged in the war for peace in which there enter questions of world economy, food, religion, education, health and social conditions as well as military and power considerations. I have a feeling that it would be helpful if you could build a small group of very eminent non-political experts in all these fields whose duty it would be to watch the world scene and keep you briefed day by day in a map room."

Before the San Francisco conference on the United Nations Charter began on April 25, Truman had written her and asked her if she cared to join the American delegation. It was a gallant gesture, she told him, but she could not accept. On May 10, when it appeared that the Russians were intent upon preventing the United Nations from coming into existence, he sat down that evening and wrote her a longhand letter of eight pages pouring out his vexation against the Communists. In her soft and soothing reply, she told him to type his letters henceforth and not waste time sending her longhand letters. She also advised him to get on a personal basis with Churchill. "If you talk to him about books and let him quote to you from his marvelous memory everything on earth from Barbara Frietchie to the Nonsense Rhymes and Greek Tragedy, you will find him easier to deal with on political subjects. He is a gentleman to whom the personal element means a great deal."

As time went on Truman took to writing her often to find out how Franklin would have approached various problems. "I never think of anyone as the President but Mr. Roosevelt," he told her frankly. When political opponents got wind of his attitude, the gag line spread around Washington, "I wonder what President Truman would do if he were alive?"

With her first independent steps, she was implored from all sides to run for office. Thousands of letters came to her imploring her to run for President or Vice President in 1948. She rejected the pleas and added, "I do not think we have yet reached a point where the electorate is ready for a woman Vice President who might possibly become President." When New York's Democratic boss, Edward J. Flynn, begged her to run for the United States Senate in 1946, she shook her head: "I want to be able to say exactly what I please and to feel free." Even Harold Ickes, the old curmudgeon who had done so much screaming during the Roosevelt era about her attentiveness to his Department, demanded that she run for the Senate. He pointed out that the last talk he had with Franklin was on the crucial New York political situation. Franklin had wanted Fiorello La Guardia to run against Governor Tom Dewey. Now if she got on the ticket for the Senate seat, Ickes urged, her following would sweep Dewey out of the Albany mansion and into the political ash can so far as the 1948 presidential election was concerned.

But with all these cogent arguments, she could not be swayed. "I feel very strongly that running for office is not the way in which I can be most useful," she wrote him in May, 1945. "My children have labored for many years under the baffling necessity of considering their business of living as it affected their father's position and I want them to feel in the future that any running for political office will be done by them.

"That does not mean, however, that I do not feel my responsibility as a citizen, but the minute I accept a position from the party and am a new hand, I would have to be willing to follow the party line pretty consistently. I hope to continue to work with the Democrats and for them, but I think the knowledge that I will be free of any obligation may at times be very healthy."

The next month she was already after Robert Hannegan, Democratic National Chairman, with letters about the political situation in the country and the policies the Democrats would have to follow in order to win in 1946. One thing she insisted upon was the appointment of women to important government posts. "Many men are made a little uncomfortable by having women in these positions," she told him, "but I think the time has come to face the fact that you have to win as many women's votes as you do men's votes and that the Democratic Party probably has more strength among women if it stands as the liberal party and the party of human rights than it has among the men."

With the end of the fighting against Germany, American-Soviet relations had undergone a serious deterioration. President Truman had ended Lend-Lease to Russia and a Stalin request for a six-billion-dollar loan had mysteriously been lost in the State Department files. Meanwhile in Europe the Soviets had jumped into country after country along its borders and installed Communist governments. American Ambassador to the USSR Averell Harriman was reputed to have formed President Truman's "get tough" policy within days after Truman became President. She wrote to Harriman, "Since we always have to sit down together when war comes to an end, I think before we have a Third World War, we should sit down together." On one occasion she came to Washington to see Harriman and scolded him roundly for causing this swift schism that could lead only to a new state of war nerves.

Weak as he was, wasted Harry Hopkins had gone to Moscow at Mr. Truman's request in May for talks with Stalin. Out of this venture came a softening Soviet attitude at the San Francisco United Nations Charter Conference and an agreement to meet with Truman at Potsdam in July. When Hopkins returned he wrote Eleanor, "We are doing almost everything we can to break with Russia, which seems so unnecessary to me." He had taken a job as $25,000-a-year impartial chairman of the suit and cloak industry in New York, as successor to former Mayor Jimmy Walker. Sensing his own end to be near, he urged Eleanor in July to go to Russia and talk with Stalin. She would go, she replied, solely as a correspondent for the syndicate handling her newspaper column and not as an official. "The Russian Government and the Russian people would receive you as the widow of the President and there is just no way out of that one," he told her frankly. In that case, she said, she would not go.

By August she was back again in general circulation, a black-garbed figure speaking now and then at colleges and before organizations and taking part in the New York City mayoralty contest between William O'Dwyer and Jonah Goldstein. Her comments were as sharp and frank as ever. A strong O'Dwyer supporter, she wrote to a labor leader, "You believe Judge Goldstein will be beholden to you and therefore a good mayor."

All of her activities were however a thrashing about without real focus. Was there not a single activity upon which she could hinge her energy and experience? Was she destined to spend her years as the grand old faultfinding lady of the Democratic Party?

The answer came with great suddenness. Following his "honeymoon" with Congress after he became President, Mr. Truman was swiftly losing public support. Those who visited his White House complained that it lacked the prestige and dignity of his predecessors'. Typical was the reaction of Cousin Joe Alsop who, in a letter to Eleanor, likened

Truman's White House to "the lounge of the Lion's club of Independence, Missouri, where one is conscious chiefly of the odor of ten cent cigars and the easy laughter evoked by the new smoking room story."

In addition, there was great public concern about the prestige of the United Nations upon which the peoples of the world were centering their hopes for a peaceful existence. The United Nations Charter Conference in San Francisco, after two months of doubts, had come off well. However, the deterioration of relations between the United States and the Soviet Union might nip in the bud this new international agency before it got into operation.

What was needed, Truman reasoned, if the United Nations was to get off on a flying start, was a first-rate American delegation and the prestige of the Roosevelt name. How better to get this than to ask the widow of Franklin Roosevelt to serve as a member of the American delegation to the London organizational meeting of the United Nations General Assembly in January 1946?

So in December, only a few weeks before the meeting, he pleaded with Eleanor to go to London. Her first reaction was to think about her horrible experience in the only other official government post she had held, with the Office of Civilian Defense under Franklin. Her later reaction was that this might not have been so bad had she not been the wife of the President at the time. "I want to thank you very much," she wrote Truman, "for the opportunity you have given me of being part of this Delegation. It is a great privilege and my only fear is that I shall not be able to make enough of a contribution. I do feel, however, that you were very wise in thinking that anyone connected with my husband could, perhaps by their presence, keep the level of his ideals."

On New Year's Eve amid a great deal of hoopla, members of the American delegation arrived at the pier to board the *Queen Elizabeth*. Newsreel cameramen were grinding out the record of the approaching polished limousines and the farewell remarks of the delegates. Senator Tom Connally, picturesque chairman of the Senate Foreign Relations Committee, spoke earnestly of the importance of the occasion. Senator Arthur Vandenberg, ranking Republican on the Foreign Relations Committee and sporting his big denicotinized—or as he put it—"de-sexed"—cigar, did likewise. The chairman of the delegation, former Secretary of State Edward R. Stettinius who had succeeded Cordell Hull as Secretary only to be ousted by Truman to make way for James F. Byrnes, gave the crowd a flashing grin. While all this was going on, a taxicab lumbered unnoticed onto the pier and a tall woman dressed in mourning black climbed out and hurried toward the gangplank. No one noticed her until she was almost on board, when a Custom's man spied her and shouted, "But, Mrs. Roosevelt! Can't I help you on board?"

Almost to a man the American delegation had voiced strong opposition to her appointment when it was first announced. In fact, in the Senate where confirmation was necessary, Senator Theodore Bilbo of Mississippi in a typically prejudiced speech denounced her for her pro-Negro views, while Senator William Fulbright of Arkansas argued that the choice of delegates showed that the United States didn't take the United Nations seriously. John Foster Dulles, dour New York lawyer and an alternate delegate, expressed great indignation. "He felt the world was coming to an end when he heard I was joining the delegation," said Eleanor. On hearing all these negative opinions, she momentarily lost her self-confidence. This showed up in a column she wrote on her departure: "The day is here at last when I am to sail, apparently with quite a number of others, for London Town! I am told we will be 'briefed,' whatever this may mean during the trip. . . . I need it in the worst possible way."

She wanted desperately to get the United Nations off on the right foot, for it was Franklin's legacy to the world. He had given his last energies to this dream, and it was the culmination of all those fretful years since she and Franklin had watched Woodrow Wilson collapse in the midst of his unsuccessful fight for the League of Nations. But what could she—a mere woman with little formal education—hope to accomplish? "I am an old woman deeply interested in human problems and eager to help her country in any way she can," she told James Reston of *The New York Times* aboard ship. But she was more than that, President Truman had insisted. She was a force all by herself and a leader—a world leader. "Your country needs you—indeed, this troubled world needs you," he had written her imploringly.

At the beginning of the five-day voyage, the other delegates raised their eyebrows in disbelief when she announced she would take part in all their work. This meant reading the long reports of the Preparatory Commission and joining in the daily discussions. But when she did all of her "homework" each night in her cabin and did as much talking as any of them in the give-and-take sessions, their skepticism faded. In addition, she served as chief pep-talker and goader. "I hope the United Nations will discuss and act on problems and not bury them," she warned the delegation, "as some committees of the League of Nations did." By the time the ship docked at Southampton and the mayor

[320]

greeted them in his quaint fore-and-aft hat and fur-trimmed coat, there was general enthusiasm about her. "I want to say that I take back everything I ever said about her, and believe me it's been plenty!" Senator Vandenberg chortled. Dulles, who could not forget that it had been Franklin's victory over Dewey in 1944 that had deprived him of fulfilling his lifelong ambition to be Secretary of State, was still not convinced.

London was intensely curious about her. Her brave wartime visit had only served to whet the city's appetite. Great crowds blocked traffic about the entrance to Claridge's Hotel on Brook Street. They cheered themselves hoarse every time she showed her face. Men raised their hats when she walked by and women applauded. Inside the hotel she complained because her suite was too elegant, and when the king and queen invited her to come to lunch, she told them matter-of-factly, "I'd be delighted to come but I couldn't stay long because I have to get back to work."

The spirit of Franklin hovered over the conference at the outset. When she walked to her front-row seat next to a Russian delegate at conference headquarters in Central Hall on January tenth, all eyes were on her. She had hoped to remain inconspicuous, but when Belgium's Prime Minister, Paul Henry Spaak, was elected General Assembly President, the first thing he did was to point a finger at her. "I want to give a special welcome to one of the delegates," he beamed, while she squirmed uneasily. "I refer to the lady who bears the most illustrious and respected of all names. I do not think it would be possible to open this assembly without mentioning her and the late President Roosevelt and expressing our conviction that his death was a great grief to us and an irreparable loss." She did not dare acknowledge the greeting, for her eyes were filled with tears.

The Assembly soon plunged into men's work. Billowing stale cigar smoke surrounded her as the representatives of the fifty-one member nations set themselves to the task of breathing life into Franklin's ideal. To get the show on the road, the Assembly had to establish the controversial Security Council, Economic and Social Council (ECOSOC), International Court of Justice, Trusteeship Council and an Atomic Energy Commission to control atomic energy production and establish an international inspection system. Of the regular American delegates, Tom Connally became a member of the Political and Security Committee, Vandenberg sat with the Administrative and Budget Committee and Eleanor with the Social, Humanitarian and Cultural Committee. Senior adviser to the American delegation was Adlai Stevenson, who had been an assistant to Franklin's Secretary of the Navy Frank Knox.

The days turned into weeks of debate. The shine of the initial gathering vanished and bitter and unseemly squabbles heaped one on top another. It was a patchwork force at best, with Soviet delegates bursting out with angry charges against the West and posing as the injured party. Members who had initially considered her as one would a statue slowly turned to her for advice and guidance; for obviously she was above personal ambition and represented no political faction. "She simply moved in as a super-mother," said one observer, "presiding over a large family of often noisy, sometimes unruly, but basically good-hearted boys who now and then need firmly to be put in their places." It was a role that came naturally to her.

Andrei Vishinsky, the chief Soviet delegate who was best known for his prosecutor's role in the Soviet purge trials of the mid-thirties, was the main disruptive force. He nagged and bullied the Assembly with a boundless venom. Simple issues turned into mammoth diatribes against non-Communist nations.

The explosive hour came near the end of the Assembly's work. The question had arisen regarding the million or more refugees from Poland, the Baltic States and Yugoslavia. Vishinsky demanded that they be returned to their countries of origin regardless of their desires. In addition, he wanted a resolution passed forbidding freedom of speech in the miserable refugee and displaced persons camps, or, as he put it, "propaganda against returning to their native lands."

"The meeting was in chaos," said Tom Connally. "The whole Assembly threatened to disintegrate." Delegates were confused. The hour was late for someone to demolish Vishinsky. But who could do it? If no one came forward, Vishinsky's belligerence could well stampede the Assembly into appeasing him and thus dooming the refugees to slave labor camps or death behind Russia's borders.

Throughout Vishinsky's wild jabbering and threats, Eleanor sat staring sternly at him, her anger kindling. Suddenly she rose and the bedlam subsided. "It was her presence that saved the day," said Connally. "She was the only person with enough stature in everyone's eyes to squelch him."

She was the mother again faced with a misbehaving boy whose stentorian voice in threshing rebuttal to her patient firmness made him look all the more ridiculous. Her words came out softly but firmly. "One of the most dramatic episodes of the Conference," John Foster Dulles called it later, "a debate where Mrs. Roosevelt, with moving simplicity, pleaded for tolerance and where Mr. Vishinsky, with the explosive power of a great prosecutor, denounced tolerance as a dangerous weakness." She gave the delegates a basic philosophy in her exchange with Vishinsky. "We here in the United Nations," she said with great feeling, "are trying to frame things which will consider first the rights of man and what makes men more free—not governments, but man!" When she finished the spontaneous debate, Vishinsky was demolished. Her words were destined to affect the lives of more than a million persons.

After the delegates voted down his proposal, Vishinsky sought her out. "Mrs. Roosevelt, I admire your fighting qualities," he expressed himself with a mixture of awe and condescension.

"Why, thank you." She grinned and her eyes shone. "You're a real fighter, too. Perhaps next time you might try using your fighting abilities on the right side." He glanced at her, surprised, then hurried away.

Before she left Europe, she was back in her old stride. But even more, she had emerged as an independent personality whose assuredness commanded respect. No longer was she just the widow of Franklin Roosevelt.

Her ability to stand on her own legs exhilarated her. As of old, she ignored the influenza she contracted now in England and carried on as though it were a minor nuisance. The other Conference delegates, who were worn out from the activities involved in getting the United Nations into operation, were flabbergasted to discover that not only had she done everything they did and more, but she was also busy on many other fronts. She had made herself available for personal talks with English brides of American soldiers, lectured here and there, inspected bomb-ripped Germany, and corresponded with Truman. In one long letter she wrote him that she had been in touch with General Eisenhower after talking to groups of American soldiers who were grumbling about sitting around in England and doing nothing. "They are good boys," she told Eisenhower, "but if they don't have enough to do they will get into trouble. That is the nature of boys, I am afraid, in any situation."

Chapter Thirty-Three

I N 1946, President Truman insisted that she serve again on the U. S. delegation to the United Nations. It was to be her chief career until he went out of office.

Harry Hopkins had lobbied with her to make Hyde Park the permanent home for the United Nations. It would be a fitting tribute to Franklin, he said, for the memorable fight he had made to bring the UN into existence. But when Hopkins died in January 1946, she was left without an ally. The final decision went elsewhere: temporary headquarters would be at Lake Success in Flushing, Long Island, with permanent headquarters erected later in New York City.

Her first day at Lake Success was auspicious. The opening session of the United Nations General Assembly began on October twenty-third. As she came striding into the building on her way to the meeting hall, a woman attendant with a dustcloth in her hand intercepted her. "Excuse me, Mrs. Roosevelt," she greeted her. "I just wanted to say welcome and to tell you how glad I am to see you here. We women have a real stake in working for peace."

In all her seven years with the United Nations, Mrs. Roosevelt was its chief tourist attraction and most popular and effective member. Visitors queued up in long lines hoping to catch a glimpse of her. Outside the meeting halls, she could be seen loping along with a heavy briefcase in one hand and a fur scarf over the other arm. Though she had no office at Lake Success, she put in a strenuous nine A.M. to seven-thirty P.M. day six days a week. Besides the formal sessions there were daily meetings of the U. S. delegation plus her committee meetings. At lunch time, on these crowded days, she asked for no special favors but stood her turn with other lunchers in the cafeteria line. After lunch, she made it a point to discuss problems with representatives of various organizations. "A mature Edith Wharton hero capable of meeting modern problems," an observer described her.

Though she had tangled with Vishinsky at the first United Nations General Assembly in London, she was determined to meet the Russians

[324]

part way in the future. Churchill's "Iron Curtain" speech had come in the spring of 1946 and the separation between East and West had widened. "Since Harry Hopkins I do not believe that anyone has talked 'frankly' to Mr. Stalin personally," she wrote to Joe Alsop. "And certainly most of us haven't talked honestly with people like Mr. Gromyko, Mr. Vishinsky, etc. I am going to make a great effort to get to know Mr. Gromyko and tell him a few of the things I feel."

Young Gromyko saw "red" when she asked him one day to supply her with figures on the number of slave laborers there were in the Soviet Union. As for Vishinsky, he considered her the chief thorn in his side as long as he represented the Communists at the United Nations.

Their fights were among the chief debates at the General Assembly meetings. In the fall of 1946 they rowed about the establishment of the International Refugee Organization and the IRO budget of $160 million. *The New York Times* called the debate and her victory over Vishinsky "the most dramatic event of the session." While he talked and she sat listening to him, her face was a study of deep disagreement. And often before he finished what he wanted to say, she would be waving the triangular sign, "United States," as a signal that she wanted to be heard.

Among his maddening tactics was the technique of arguing against a proposal and when he lost in the Assembly vote, reopening the fight. She never let this pass. On the IRO battle, she told him bluntly, "Representatives of the USSR have taken part in drafting the report now under consideration. They have won many concessions to obtain their cooperation. They evidently are ignoring all former discussions and beginning again." When he pooh-poohed the need of the IRO, she demolished his arguments with: "As long as a million people continue to be refugees, they delay the restoration of peace. While they remain in a solid mass in assembly centers, they deteriorate individually, and collectively they represent a sore on the body of mankind which is not safe to ignore." She heard after her successful duel that the Russian delegates were calling her "Fascist."

Few delegates from neutral nations were not swayed by her talk. There was one, however, from a southeast Asia country who, throughout the entire IRO debate, stared from Mrs. Roosevelt to Mr. Vishinsky in great bewilderment. He knew not a word of the French, Russian, English or Chinese into which each speech was translated and transmitted over telephones to the seats of all delegates. "There he sat"—she watched him with pity—"through the entire session with great faithfulness while understanding not a word."

Vishinsky was not the only member of the Soviet bloc to tangle with

[325]

her. As in a bad dream, others harangued the meetings with long lists of inane charges against the West. Once when a Yugoslavian delegate shouted himself almost into apoplexy with snide and false statements that the United States engaged in political trickery and posed as a humanitarian power while permitting great unemployment, starvation and racial discrimination, her patience vanished. "The longer I listen," she jumped on him, "the more I think the time has come for some very straight thinking among us all. The ultimate objective that we have is to create better understanding among us, and I will acknowledge that this is going to be difficult. And I will give you the reasons why. I have never heard a representative of any of the USSR bloc acknowledge that in any way their government can be wrong. They may say it at home—I do not know—and they may think it is wrong to do it outside. They are very young and the young rarely do acknowledge anything which they may have done that may not be quite right. With maturity we grow much more humble, and we know that we have to acknowledge very often that things are not quite perfect. Because we acknowledge it does not mean that we love our country any less, that we do not basically believe in the rightness of the things that exist in our country. What it does mean is that we know that human nature is not perfect and that we hope that all of us can contribute to something better. Now I don't expect the millennium immediately, but I do expect and hope and pray that we are going to see a gradual increase in good will rather than a continual backwards and forwards of telling us what *dogs* we are and how bad we are. I see no sense in that at all. I am weary of it all, and I say to all my colleagues that I hope we can work with good will."

When she finished her chastisement, the room was filled with complete silence for several minutes.

The pity of her forthright stand against the Communists was that shortly afterward her son, Elliott, on a visit to Russia, muddied the water. At an American Embassy affair in Moscow, Elliott was quoted by an Embassy official as saying that the Russians never broke their pledges but that the United States and Britain had violated the Tehran, Yalta and Potsdam agreements. He also was quoted as saying that the United States was supporting the United Nations for imperialistic reasons. American newspapers as well as Soviet papers were quick to spread his thoughts. For fear that he would be spreading more nonsense that would harm the United States, she dispatched a quick telegram to Moscow. He was being quoted, she told him, "and the Republicans were going to bait him on everything that an inconspicuous person could say."

At the same time, his book *As He Saw It,* with its innuendoes of opposition to Churchill and Britain, appeared in bookstores. To Joe Alsop, who had taken Elliott apart in a newspaper column, she wrote, perplexed and angry: "I am old and it makes no difference to me what anybody says or thinks either in praise or in blame. But when you are young, I think it makes a difference. I have often differed with my children. I have always tried to recognize their motives which lay behind what they said or did. I make no comparison between any of my children. . . . As you grow older you will realize that there are always two sides to every story and that sometimes people sin but they rarely sin alone." She wanted Joe to meet with Elliott in her presence for a talk. But he refused. The pity was that she could not divorce herself from her children when their public views did harm to her own.

She had a similar muddying experience with Vishinsky in 1947. President Truman had asked her to answer Vishinsky's wild tirade charging the United States with warmongering. General George C. Marshall, then Secretary of State, informed the Truman Cabinet on October 20 that her reply on this occasion plus her other work made her the outstanding delegate from the West: "The most intelligent, cooperative and effective assistance came from Mrs. Eleanor Roosevelt."

Yet during this same period Republicans in control of the House Un-American Activities Committee were charging her with aiding notorious Communists to enter the United States during the thirties. The committee's action was a thinly veiled effort to befoul the Roosevelt administration. "I see red every time they start a ghoulish attack on the President," Truman wrote her. The case in point involved a Communist musician, Hans Eisler, whom she did not know personally and who had written to her in 1939 from Mexico about his desire to enter the United States. On that occasion she had sent two routine notes to the State Department, as was her practice regarding matters pertaining to the Departments. As Sumner Welles wrote her after the committee released her two notes to favored reporters before holding a hearing, "The proven facts in the case establish beyond the shadow of a doubt that the entrance of Eisler into this country as a non-quota immigrant had not the slightest connection with the notes you had sent me."

Temporary damage was done her by the committee's widespread publicity. But despite it she went on with her work. She continued to argue frequently with Vishinsky and other Soviet delegates. In total she made hundreds of speeches answering Communist slander. "One

Communist is just like another," she told them. "They all think, talk and act the same. Why Mr. Vishinsky really isn't any different from any of the Communists I used to meet in the American Youth Congress." Once when an Iron Curtain delegate asked her to be reasonable, she told him, "Try as you may you can't understand why they [the Russians] act as they do even when you project yourself into the position their country occupies." It was hard for them to join in a fair debate, she said, because "the Russians have always liquidated their opposition."

The Communist charges knew no bounds. "No, gentlemen, wife beating is not legal in Alabama," she rebutted one charge. "Please see Page 507, Volume 194, *Southern Reporter, Williams* versus *Williams.*" On another occasion Vishinsky launched into a fiery description of what he called "American concentration camps." For documentary proof he read off a list of their locations. "You didn't do your homework," she told him. "All those places you listed were prisoner-of-war camps during the last war." He subsided quickly.

The repetition they engaged in was appalling to Eleanor, who viewed it as a dodge to prevent any action. Once after a lengthy repetitive debate a weary delegate sought her out. "Well, Mrs. Roosevelt," he said, wiping his brow, "at least we got that point out of the way." She laughed. "That's what you think. It will be brought up again tomorrow as a new topic," she replied. On another occasion, she led a Soviet delegate to one side and scolded him roundly. "Why you could have boiled all that down into ten minutes and not taken a couple of hours. Next time try doing that."

He looked at her wryly. "Why are you in such a big hurry, Mrs. Roosevelt?"

She was of course in a hurry to settle the problems of the world as they came up and to plan ahead for progress. Yet it was often a matter of tilting at windmills to speed up the Russians. She could answer their charges, and she always did. Truman wrote her one time, "When necessary you have without fear faced the Russian bear with an admirable defense of democratic institutions and objectives. Who can tell— you may ultimately break down Russian resistance?"

On occasion when the Soviet delegates droned on with endless boring speeches, she would cat-nap before them. This was especially galling to them because they wanted her to suffer. A problem arose when television cameras were permitted to record the meetings. Adlai Stevenson, who was on the American delegation until he ran for governor of Illinois, was given the task of waking her whenever the cameras were to focus on her. A nudge was often sufficient. Once when the TV cameramen were turning their cameras toward her, he quickly scribbled a note and put it in her hand. She yawned and scribbled back, "I know it and am wide awake!"

With her firm championing of the American view against all Communist comers, it was not long before she became an object of derision to Soviet papers and magazines. *Izvestia* called her "a hypercritical servant of capitalism . . . a fly darkening the Soviet sun." The *Literary Gazette* pointed up her effectiveness with such name-calling as "a garrulous feeble, old woman, consumed with an anti-Soviet fever and playing an ugly role." Such extreme attempts to discredit her were important matters to the Communists because they realized that her words had enormous influence with their own peoples. There were other names, too. The Soviet press nicknamed her "schoolteacher." Self-righteously they wrote open letters to her with sarcastic appeals to her in Franklin Roosevelt's name and memory to quit advocating "imperialism." "Meddling old woman," they baited her when she wouldn't call a halt. But she was used to being called names. For had she not had a good training ground under Westbrook Pegler's roundhouse attacks? Franklin should have "punched her in the snoot," Pegler had once choked in wrath. And his own collection of nicknames included such dandies as "Eleanor the Great," "Little Nell," "the old girl," and "the gab." So there was some good in Pegler's mean activity after all.

Though the Russians bore the brunt of her attacks because of the vicious game they played, there were times when she found herself in disagreement with American foreign policy. One such occasion occurred in the spring of 1947 when the unilateral "Truman Doctrine" went into effect to help Greece and Turkey "against aggressive movements that seek to impose upon them totalitarian regimes." Her reaction was to pepper Secretary of State Marshall and Under Secretary Acheson with letters charging that the doctrine weakened the United Nations. "I hope never again," she wrote Marshall on March 26, "that this type of action will be taken without at least consulting with the Secretary-General." Truman's reply in May was that the action was necessary because "the Russians have failed to carry out a single commitment they made either with him [FDR] or with me."

Despite the heckling she got from Yugoslavian delegates to the United Nations, she went to bat for Yugoslavia when mass starvation appeared imminent in the spring of 1947. With the UN not prepared to handle food relief, she bombarded the White House and the State Department with demands that American generosity be displayed despite ideo-

[329]

logical differences. Not even Truman, who was firmly committed to his "containment" policy regarding the Communists, could withstand her moral onslaught. Finally Under Secretary of State Dean Acheson announced the success of her campaign by a letter on May 7 in which he wrote her, "This country will never sacrifice humanity in order to carry out any policy."

There was also the subject of the new nation of Israel that brought her into opposition with the Administration. In March 1948, when she opposed niggardly American aid to Israel while other nations were arming the Arabs, she sent a blistering note to Truman. When Secretary of State George Marshall called for a new mandate over Palestine, she sent in a letter of resignation from the UN delegation on the ground that she would continue speaking out and this would prove an embarrassment to the Administration. In his reply Truman wrote that Marshall had tossed her letter of resignation aside on the ground that she was too valuable where she was. Though she stayed on, she continued to speak out, as she said she would, and also kept after Truman to recognize Israel. Finally in May when the United States recognized Israel, Truman sent her a letter of explanation: "Since there was a vacuum in Palestine and since the Russians were anxious to be the first to do the recognizing, Gen. Marshall, Sec. Lovett, Dr. Rusk and myself worked the matter out and decided the proper thing to do was to recognize the Jewish Government." Until the actual recognition, the U. S. United Nations delegation had not been told about it and Warren Austin, the chief United States delegate, had talked in opposition to recognition as part of the Administration's policy. "I am sorry that it caused any disturbance," Truman apologized to her.

The single activity into which she poured most of her energy during her United Nations career was the writing and passing of the document known as the Declaration of Human Rights. In the spring of 1946 she served on a UN commission of nine persons to outline a program for drafting an International Bill of Rights. Not only did she take on the job as chairman but she also doubled as French translator, a language in which she was almost as fully conversant as she was in English. The following January, when the Commission on Human Rights was established, she was again elected chairman by acclamation.

The task she laid out for herself was enormous. With so many different ideologies represented among the UN member nations, coaxing delegations to accept a single and meaningful document was no small matter. First there would be the problem of writing the Declaration. Then after the Declaration was accepted by the United Nations, the job would be to get all member nations to sign a covenant or treaty giving it the force of law.

The struggle to get the Declaration written and approved by the United Nations required two long years. She worked with little respite during that entire time, often attending as many as three committee meetings in a single day. Many members complained that their remaining youth and middle age were giving way to her hard regime. If she could squeeze in lunchtime sessions and late evening meetings, she did so. When one member expressed concern for his health on the ground that he was almost fifty, she commiserated though she was herself nearing sixty-five at the time. Sir Benegal Rau, India's permanent delegate to the United Nations Security Council, referred to her as "a U. S. phenomenon comparable to Niagara Falls."

As chairman she had her problems at first because she was not familiar with parliamentary procedures. It took her a long time to realize that Robert's "Rules of Order" were more than just an academic exercise. But when she did, she became such an expert that she could have recited any section from rote. From disorderly sessions, the meetings began in time to take on the appearance of stringent business.

As in the General Assembly, the Communist bloc proved to be her chief scourge. On her committee, she admitted, "Soviet delegates don't speak as free people at all. They just say what they have been ordered to say and that is all. If they ever did give any signs of acknowledging a point, they wouldn't last long. Take Pavlov," she cited an example. Alexei Pavlov, sporting an old-world beard, was her opposite number on the Human Rights Commission. "Why one time Pavlov made a speech saying that workers were dying by starvation in California by the thousands! Now Mr. Pavlov had been in the United States for a long time. He didn't believe what he said. He knew better. But they know the line, they are told what to say and they say it."

Bombastic and slanderous as they were most of the time, the Communist delegates sometimes sat in surprised and stunning silence. "Many was the time Professor Pavlov came to me," she said, "and asked, 'Mrs. Roosevelt, would you mind postponing the meeting? I haven't received my orders from Moscow yet.'"

Everything was good for a wrangle with the Russians. On one occasion she found herself in a two-hour hassle with Indian and Soviet delegates who had teamed up against her in a battle over the words "caste" and "class." Both were trying to make it appear that she was in favor of a social order including these categories and insisted on strong language in the proposed Declaration in opposition. However, she real-

[331]

ized that this would only serve to play hob with any general acceptance of the Declaration. It would also open up whole new avenues of further controversy. She finally squelched them with, "Gentlemen, we admit class and caste do exist but we don't try to emphasize them." There were fights on defining marriage rights of men and women that produced great tittering from neutral delegates, fights on the meaning of the word "democracy," and fights just for the sake of fighting.

Aware of Communist tactics from her AYC experience, she could beat them at their own game. A common Communist technique was to keep a meeting in session until others got tired and left before proposed action could be taken. Once when Communist members tried that in committee, she cornered other members and won a *sub rosa* agreement to outlast the Communists. After talking fast all day to prevent a vote, the Reds were appalled to find all members still sitting in their places when evening came. The hours wore on with the Communists growing hoarser by the minute. Patiently she smiled and nodded to them to continue even after midnight passed. Their fury was boundless but they continued speaking. It was not until daybreak that their voices failed them. "Now we will take the vote," she told them, smiling. Dead on their feet, they could no longer protest and the vote went her way.

Only one time did she lose control of herself. This occurred when a Soviet delegate objected to the presence of the delegate from Nationalist China. "Mr. Chairman," as he persisted in calling her, "Dr. Chang has absolutely no right to his seat. He must be thrown out, Mr. Chairman."

She informed him that Chang was seated properly, but that according to parliamentary procedures, he could appeal to the committee to overrule her. When the vote went against him, he immediately buzz-sawed his way into a screaming speech. The Nationalist Chinese were criminals; the United States was helping them; and Mr. Chairman was using her lofty post for nefarious political purposes.

Generally calm, her eyes widened wrathfully and down came her gavel with an angry bang. Her face was crimson and her breathing was heavy. "I am sorry, sir," she snapped at him in fury. "This is no place for propaganda speeches and I must ask you to draw your remarks to a close."

However, when she saw that he was enjoying himself immensely, she told him calmly that he could finish his speech. His heart was no longer in his work, and after a few more wild charges he stomped from the room.

She had tried at first to be friendly with the Russian delegates but it was no use. "The most intimate thing Alexei Pavlov ever said to me," she once confided, "was in Paris at my apartment at the Crillon. He brought Mr. Borosilov, another delegate, along with him. As they were leaving, Mr. Borosilov lost his hat behind a chair. We walked to the door as he was searching for it and Mr. Pavlov whispered quickly to me, 'Do you like Tchaikovsky? I do!'"

President Truman, who was kept informed by others of what she was going through, wrote her, "I have marveled at the poise and patience that you have maintained in the face of the maddening technique of the Russians. Not only have they been deliberately non-cooperative but they have conducted themselves with a boorishness worthy of stable boys. I have observed with great satisfaction that you have put them in their place more than once."

However, her task had to go on and she wanted to succeed. She utilized various techniques of her own to speed the work. She brought the delegates to Hyde Park for informal picnics and entertainment to lessen the stiffness with which they treated each other at meetings. She also used a disarming method to move things along. One ruse was to cut into vague flights of pedantry with, "I am probably the least learned person around this table, so I have thought of this article in terms of what the ordinary person could understand." Other times she said, "Of course I am a woman and don't understand all these things. But don't you think it would be a good idea if . . . ?" Her high hurdles, she realized, were the Russians who wanted no declaration and the talkative members of other delegations who enjoyed hearing their own voices. In the sessions around the long oval table in the center of the meeting room, she sometimes tried to stare down long-winded orators. She wrote in her newspaper column, "No one can tell me that women like to talk longer than men." To the dawdlers, she would utter an urgent "yes-yes," as though their points were already made. Once she told a speaker whose tongue had galloped on for almost an hour, "Have you ever noticed about when it is that people begin to remove their headphones? After about ten minutes," she frowned.

Her big challenge came in December, 1947, almost a year after the Human Rights Commission was established, at the commission meeting in Geneva, Switzerland. After she was held up by several days of foggy weather in Shannon, this was a meeting she almost missed when the plane narrowly averted crashing and then slid drunkenly in the snow before coming to a stop. As usual, she had walked back and forth in the aisle soothing other passengers.

She was past the point of hearing endless talk. "You all know that we have very little time before most of us wish to return home for Christmas," she informed commission members bluntly. It was news to them. "I certainly intend to get back to see my sixteen grandchildren at Hyde Park." She shook a stern finger of warning. "What I propose is that only a single person be permitted to defend any point, amendment or article. Besides, speeches must be short." A heart-rending cry came up from several delegates, but she was insistent and the vote went her way in the end. "Dictator!" a Soviet delegate was overheard charging her.

The sessions started on December third and were over on the seventeenth. "A miracle," one of her colleagues hailed her finesse. "It was simple," she said. "I just made them work from the beginning exactly as people at conferences work at the end." When the Russians ingeniously proposed lumping together the Declaration and the treaty covenants because this would take forever, she batted them down with one of her motherly talks. "A declaration involves only a moral obligation, yet it expresses what everyone believes to be true," she told the delegates. "This is the first step and I think it should be taken separately."

"Nyet! Nyet!" shouted the Communists. But she pushed her proposal through. There was no dillying and dallying with her. She could turn her slightly deaf ear to short tirades and she could whip off her glasses and gavel complainants down. All attention had to be given to the Declaration. And word by word and line by line the basketful of proposed articles for the Declaration were read, argued over and altered in morning, noon and night meetings.

When the meetings finally ended, a Russian delegate with red-rimmed eyes and drawn expression tottered over to her. He had made himself obnoxious throughout the session with his frequently magpie screeching of "decadent democracies." His tired breathing came hard as he now shook her hand and said, "Mrs. Roosevelt, you must be exhausted. I know I am and so is my wife, even though she was not a member of the Commission." Whereupon she remarked with a twinkling smile, "I never felt better. Perhaps it's because I belong to one of those 'decadent democracies.'"

The work was not over yet. In May, 1948, at the same time that she was feuding with the Truman administration over Israel, she held meetings with her drafting committee to write a new draft in line with comments on the Geneva draft received from member governments. Then there was the task of getting the new draft through her full commission where the barking Communists yelped at every word. Final

[334]

action was to get it through Committee Three—the Humanitarian, Social and Cultural Committee—of the Economic and Social Council, and then to win the approval of the General Assembly.

The Declaration she set in motion reached its climactic moment in Paris in December, 1948. After eleven weeks of feverish debate in Committee Three—a single line of the Declaration brought on a five-day fight—the Declaration passed on December 7. Two days later the Palais de Chaillot, where the General Assembly met, was jammed to capacity with excited onlookers. Nor were they disappointed when she and her old antagonist Vishinsky had it out in a sharp running debate. Cunning Vishinsky fought the Declaration to the end, arguing that day and most of the next. On the tenth he submitted a long series of amendments, in case he couldn't get the year's postponement on a final vote. He was in fine fettle with confusing arguments, such as, "The ideas of hate, fascism and war must not have complete freedom of expression." Eleanor in turn was simple, direct and inspiring. "The Declaration of Human Rights might become the Magna Charta of all mankind."

Dr. Herbert V. Evatt, the General Assembly President, called for the vote late that night. The air was electric as the first nation was named. Vishinsky sat slumped in his seat. It had become apparent to him that he had lost. When the final vote was tallied, the Soviet bloc to save face abstained from voting. So did Saudi Arabia and the Union of South Africa. "Forty-eight to nothing," Evatt announced.

All eyes turned in her direction. "It is particularly fitting," Evatt said happily, "that there should be present on this occasion the person who, with the assistance of many others, has played a leading role in the work, a person who has raised to greater heights even so great a name— Mrs. Roosevelt, the representative of the United States of America." Pandemonium broke out.

"It was after midnight when I left the Palais de Chaillot," she said. "I was tired. I wondered whether a mere statement of rights, without legal obligation, would inspire governments to see that these rights were observed."

She was to spend the next four years working on the Covenant by which all member nations would legally obligate themselves to carrying out the thirty articles in the Declaration. Though this work was still unfinished when she left the United Nations at the end of 1952, the Declaration itself had made its own mark. Not only did it figure in the preamble of the Japanese Peace Treaty, but it also influenced the constitutions of Costa Rica, Indonesia, India and Libya, and has been referred to in federal court decisions in the United States.

When she made her last speech to the United Nations on December 20, 1952, members accorded her a standing ovation. *Reader's Digest* hailed her as the "champion of human rights throughout the world." The only sour note in her leaving the United Nations after General Eisenhower was elected President came from John Foster Dulles, slated as next Secretary of State. He wrote her a curt note informing her that her services would no longer be needed on the next delegation. She replied that she was fully aware "that all ambassadors submit their resignations on December 31, and mine will be in."

President Truman was furious when he learned that Dulles had written his harsh letter almost two months before the Eisenhower administration was to take office. On January 19, 1953, the day before he quit the White House, Truman found time to write to her: "Since that evening in 1945 when you responded to my offer of assistance with 'What can we do for you?' you have done many things for me. In your work on the Human Rights Commission, you brought honor to all of us. Your poise and patience and good will have been valuable in sessions of the UN General Assembly as well. The reports you have brought to me have been stimulating and useful. You have been a good ambassador for America."

Chapter Thirty-Four

ELEANOR'S LIGHT BROWN HAIR was now completely gray. A grand-mother many times over in Franklin's time, in 1949 she became a great-grandmother. It was time, many in her family argued, for her to slow down and take things easy. But as Admiral Dicky Byrd, her close friend for decades, wrote her more in earnestness than in jest, "I don't believe you would be happy if your life were not hectic."

"You see," she explained, "I have nothing to do but work. I have no family responsibilities. I can take on anything that comes along that seems worth while."

And what work it was! Her most intensive effort during the postwar years was to help the United Nations survive and grow. Yet the history of Eleanor Roosevelt as she moved swiftly through her sixties and into her seventies was jam-packed with dozens of other activities. The Lady of the UN, as she was familiarly referred to by colleagues in the United Nations, was also taking an active part in domestic politics, writing a daily newspaper and monthly magazine column, writing or co-authoring a half-dozen books, making personal appearances and reciting "Peter and the Wolf" with symphony orchestras, conducting her multitudinous charities, appearing on her own daily radio show and weekly half-hour television program, lecturing at colleges and before a variety of organizations, and traveling to the ends of the earth to investigate conditions firsthand and counsel foreign governments. "A jet plane with a fringe on top," a friend aptly characterized her.

Her life resembled a crowded cupboard, each drawer filled to the brim with a variety of articles. One top drawer held her political interest in domestic matters. There was of course Harry Truman with whom she must discuss burning national and international matters. She realized that others might have gone about the awesome task of advising a President with great care and humility, but she was always frank . . . franker as time went on. Her power even in absentia was evidenced one day in 1948 when Secretary of Defense James Forrestal pugnaciously occupied almost an entire Cabinet meeting decrying her opposition to universal military training. He spoke as though the opinion of this elderly woman without any political backing wielded sufficient power to offset that of the entire Administration.

In person she was even more formidable, though she lost as often as she won. During this period of Cold War turbulence, for instance, she served as a prickly reminder to Truman that to break off relations with Russia would only worsen international relations and not improve them, as so many of his advisers counseled him. The sharp increase in his use of military men on the civilian side of government, she cautioned him, was not in keeping with the nation's traditions. "There are two things that I wish to avoid above all else," she told him in her true partisan style, "one, war; two, a Republican victory." Her efforts, however, to have Truman sit down with Stalin were without success. Stung by his unsatisfactory meeting with Stalin at Potsdam in 1945, he refused to see him again. Nevertheless, she carried on a rear-guard fight all the way through his two terms in the White House to get him to change his mind. When he refused to alter his view, she went to work on Secretary of State Dean Acheson. Not even her concerned opinion that Churchill wanted to be the mediator with the Russians and "show himself as the 'reasonable one' and the U. S. as 'unreasonable and bad children' " dented Acheson's stiff Cold War stand.

Despite her failure on this major matter, she did serve as Truman's conscience on other foreign problems. There was Palestine, of course, and there was Franco's Spain. When the Administration's policy toward Spain turned in the direction of recognition in 1948, following a bombardment by pro-Franco Senators, her blast at the State Department brought an immediate stiffening and reversal of direction by Truman. Again when the Administration did not show much interest in fighting for an appropriation for the U.N. Children's Emergency Fund (UNICEF) to provide food for undernourished children abroad, her direct intervention with Truman hastened the desired action. "Sometimes I despair of grown people," she chided him, "but if there is any point in saving civilization, certainly it is the children we want to keep alive."

There were also her long memos to Truman, which he encouraged, on American foreign policy and how it might be improved. These covered such things as analyses of the economic and political situations in foreign countries and areas, as well as psychological appraisals. For instance, in one memo she wrote him in December 1948, she revealed her deep grasp of the world situation: "France is the greatest headache still. Many of the young men who fought in the Resistance Movement, or who were taken

[338]

to camps and forced labor out of the country, returned or finished their period of the war depleted physically and mentally. . . . The French are not naturally Communists but they find it hard to be staunch in the sense that the British are and so they have accepted many Communist things. This does not frighten me for the future but it creates great difficulties for the present. . . . Our relations with the British must I think be put on a different basis. We are without question the leading democracy in the world today, but so far Great Britain still takes the attitude that she makes the policies on all world questions and we accept them. This has got to be remedied." (Truman wrote her, "Disraeli might just as well be Prime Minister these days.") Elsewhere in her lengthy memo she went on, "The Arabs have to be handled with strength. One of the troubles has been that we have been so impressed with the feeling that we must have a united front in Europe that it has affected our stand in the Near East. . . . I still feel it is hard for the State Department to accept policies without certain individuals trying to inject their own points of view and I do not think all of them have the knowledge and experience to take a world point of view." Near the close she reminded him not to concentrate on Europe and the Near East: "Our real battlefield today is Asia and our real battle is the one between democracy and communism. . . . Never was there an era in history in which the responsibilities were greater for the United States and never was a President called upon to meet such extraordinary responsibilities for civilization as a whole."

Nor did her role with Truman begin and end solely on international matters. When the President attempted to cloak himself in Franklin's mantle, she believed he should earn his way. She got after him when he dropped Frances Perkins from his Cabinet and needled him until he found another place for her on the Civil Service Commission. She also pestered Oscar Ewing, Federal Security Administrator, to appoint more women to his agency. When she thought that Truman was ignoring the plight of mistreated American Indians, she wrote him on their behalf. One detailed letter was concerned with the problems of the Indians of Port Berthold Reservation in North Dakota. Any cases of injustices to veterans and widows by the Veterans Administration that came to her attention she swiftly relayed to him. When he inaugurated the government's security program and loyalty tests which led on inexorably to McCarthyism and the bedevilment of Truman himself, she forecast what would result in an angry letter. "I feel we have capitulated to our fear of Communism, and instead of fighting to improve democracy, we are doing what the Soviets would do in trying to repress anything we are afraid might not command public support, in order to ensure acceptance of our own actions."

She also goaded him on steadily to do more work in the field of social welfare. When Henry Wallace began to emerge as a threat, she told him bluntly in January, 1948, "The great trouble is that Mr. Wallace will cut in on us because he can say we have given lip service to these things by having produced very little in the last few years."

The election in 1948 posed a special problem for both Eleanor and Truman. Two of her boys—James and Elliott—were pushing for the nomination of General Eisenhower on the Democratic ticket. While she would have no part of Eisenhower, neither would she come out for Truman. Although she took no direct part in the convention that year, she did try to influence the choice for Vice President by promoting Supreme Court Justice William O. Douglas. "Your acceptance," she wrote Douglas, "would give hope to many for the future of a liberal Democratic Party." But, as in 1944, when with a little effort he could have been Franklin's running mate for the fourth term, Douglas did nothing.

After Truman was nominated, he sought Eleanor's support eagerly. As the months went by he increased his efforts to win a public statement from her because he realized the potency in the Roosevelt name. Her choice was not a happy one. It was she who had made Henry Wallace Vice President in 1940, yet the election of Wallace on the Progressive ticket in 1948 with its serious anti-American and pro-Soviet overtones was unthinkable to her. "Mr. Wallace thinks sweetness and light can achieve peace," she wrote to a friend. "This is less realistic than I am."

But whether opposition to Wallace was enough to reason to support Truman was another matter. However, as the election drew close and Truman persisted in asking for her help, she finally made a statement in his behalf. The reaction in the White House, one observer noted, was that large tears of gratitude welled in Mr. Truman's eyes. The President later acknowledged that her support tipped the scales in his favor in the close November election.

After Mr. Truman's narrow but impressive victory, she continued to serve as presidential conscience, though his new self-confidence lessened her influence. But there were other ways in which she could make her voice heard on public affairs. There was her column, and it could be a potent voice at times. When she gave space, for instance, to a speech on housing made by Helen Gahagan Douglas, the congresswoman from California wrote her excitedly, "Letters are already beginning to pour in plus telephone calls as a result of your two columns reporting my speech." She was writing with more force now. "My husband never told me what to write and what not to write," she explained the change, "but of course I was always conscious that whatever I wrote might have repercussions. So I censored myself. Nowadays, however, I don't feel any such inhibitions. I write as I please."

However, writing as she pleased brought on occasional controversy. She found this out when she wrote a column on June 23, 1949 on the Barden Bill to provide Federal aid to education. In that column she proposed limiting treasury money to public schools and not letting any go to private or parochial schools. The previous year when she had opposed the banning of the *Nation* Magazine by New York schools, she had incurred the smoldering wrath of Francis Cardinal Spellman, who had been a warm supporter of her husband. The deceptive calm between the Cardinal and her was now shattered over her June column on school aid.

On July 22, Cardinal Spellman released to the press a wrathful letter he had written her. "Misinformation, ignorance or prejudice," he denounced her column and sizzled on, "Your record of anti-Catholicism stands for all to see . . . documents of discrimination unworthy of an American mother." No matter what she had further to say, he warned her, "I shall not again publicly acknowledge you."

It was an unfortunate move on Spellman's part to attempt to paint her with an anti-Catholic brush, but it was a bombshell that made headlines from coast to coast. Yet if he thought she would fall into a cringing state because of his attack, he knew little about her. Had she not worked hard for Al Smith in 1928? She posed the question in a subsequent column. When she sent her boys to Groton, a private Episcopal school, should she have demanded, as he was doing now for Catholics, that the Federal Government should have helped pay part of her expenses?

The controversy raged for two weeks and boomeranged on the Cardinal. Almost all the letters that came to her on the issue favored her position. Friends like former New York Governor Herbert Lehman spoke out immediately in public for her, and several prominent Catholics, such as New York Mayor O'Dwyer, labeled the Cardinal's charge of anti-Catholicism pure poppycock.

Edward J. Flynn, County Chairman of the Democratic Party in the Bronx, approached the Cardinal to meet with Mrs. Roosevelt. In the end the Cardinal sent a monseigneur to her to patch up the affair. He had a statement from Cardinal Spellman that he wanted to read to her. The page of paper that he handed her said in part: "We are not asking for general public support of religious schools. . . . There are, however, other incidental expenses involved in education, expenses for such purposes as the transportation of children to and from schools, the purchase of non-religious textbooks and the provision of health aids."

She sent a letter to Cardinal Spellman's office in Manhattan which said that she found it reassuring to learn the Cardinal was requesting only "auxiliary services." At the Vatican where the controversy had vexed high church authorities, Pope Pius XII announced on August 13 his pleasure that Cardinal Spellman's second statement had "resolved the dispute." But Eleanor still insisted on the last word. "I again wish to reiterate that I have no anti-Catholic bias," she said. "I am firm in my belief . . . that there shall be recognition of the fact that all citizens may express their views freely on questions of public interest."

Some weeks after the controversy ended, Eleanor was going through her mail at her Val-Kill cottage in Hyde Park when her secretary, Tommy, rushed into her room to say that Cardinal Spellman was downstairs. "Well, well," she replied. When she came downstairs, Spellman smilingly informed her that he was on his way from New York City to Fishkill and thought he would make a call on her. The fact that he had to ride miles past Fishkill to get to Hyde Park did not enter the conversation at tea. Nor was their controversy ever brought up. The purpose of the call showed up a few days later when a monseigneur dropped in and got her agreement to mention the Cardinal's visit in her column.

Throughout the post-Franklin years, though she had emerged as an independent being, Eleanor Roosevelt nevertheless found herself considered the symbol of her husband's political period. Democratic conventions clamored for her to appear and lend dignity to their activities. On September 3, 1946, for instance, shortly before her hectic debates with Vishinsky at the United Nations, she pounded the gavel as temporary chairman of the New York Democratic Convention at the Albany armory. Later she made a stirring keynote address. She also made the keynote address at a California Democratic convention. She went further than keynoting in 1950 when she sat up all night on a plane from New York to Los Angeles and then spent the next 33½ hours launching the campaigns of her son Jimmy and Helen Gahagan Douglas against Governor Earl Warren and Richard Nixon, then running for U. S. Senator. After a steady round of conferences, luncheons, banquets, press conferences and talks, she flew back to New York.

Democratic national conventions were her dish both in 1952 and 1956. At the 1952 convention, as soon as she rose she received the greatest ovation ever given a speaker. For twenty minutes the cheering continued while she embarrassedly asked that it be halted. Her speech was a vigorous attack on the critics of the United Nations, which she made at Truman's request. In 1956, however, at the Chicago convention, she and Truman were opponents. At a press conference on August 12, she rebuked Truman for his attack on Adlai Stevenson and questioned Truman's support of Averell Harriman as a subterfuge to bring on a deadlock between Stevenson and Harriman so that he could swing the nomination to Senator Stuart Symington of Missouri. Then she crossed the street to Truman's hotel to have lunch with him. When she arrived at the International Amphitheatre all delegates stood in silent tribute as she walked to her seat. Then came thunderous greeting as she rose to speak. Fingering the white Adlai button pinned below her right shoulder, she gave an impromptu speech on how it was time to let the young people run the country. This was her answer to Mr. Truman, who was still trying to dominate the Democrats.

Candidates for the vice-presidential nomination in 1956 carried on a wild scramble to win her support. One who came to her suite in the Blackstone Hotel was young Senator John Kennedy, who had written a book on political courage. Her room was a madhouse with children, grandchildren and friends sitting on the two beds and all talking at the same time. Phones rang and she politely interrupted Kennedy's request for her support to take a call. Finally she turned to him and said, "I am concerned about your failure to have taken a position on McCarthy."

"It was a political necessity in my Senate race not to speak out against him," he apologized.

She looked at him coldly. "It's been some time since you were elected."

He told her he had been ill at the time of the Senate proceedings against McCarthy, but that from what he had read he would have agreed with the censure vote. "Besides, it is a dead issue," he argued.

She drew up tall and shook her head. "The greatest Senators are not those who are most effective in getting bills passed, but those who have great convictions—like Herbert Lehman."

Kennedy did not win her support.

Not all of her activities during the period since Franklin's death were political, in the strict meaning of the word. In hard-to-find spare time, she also managed to do enough lecturing, writing and broadcasting to qualify as a full-time professional in each of these fields. She gave as many as 100 lectures in some years, more than many in this field who devoted all their time to this occupation could give without collapsing. Her writings were also voluminous. In 1949 she proved to be one of the more successful writers in the country when the second volume of her autobiography ran serially in *McCall's* for a fee of $150,000. Additional thousands of dollars poured forth from extensive Book of the Month Club sales and foreign rights. She also got $3,000 a month for a question-and-answer page of facts and advice from *McCall's* plus $30,-000 for her daily column from United Features Syndicate.

Friends were amazed when she added to her crammed schedule late in 1948 by going on radio in a daily program of interviews with her daughter Anna. The show, called "Eleanor and Anna," was carried by 200 stations and, despite her calm soothing voice and manner, produced an almost daily crisis because she was so busy at the time with her Declaration of Human Rights. By the time the show went on the air, she was the only unruffled member of the production cast. *Variety* said of her show: "Mrs. Roosevelt ranks with the standout commentators on the air. She displays more courage and is more positive than most of the others put together."

She was also busy with her son Elliott in various ventures. In 1947 she was in the Christmas tree business with him and the next year he opened the Val-Kill Inn on the highway close to her cottage. He had big plans for converting part of her remaining property into a farming and pig operation. "All a part of our five-year plan," he told reporters. When the venture failed, Elliott formed the Roosevelt Enterprises which was devoted to selling Eleanor's services on radio and television.

In 1950 the Roosevelt Enterprises included a daily radio show and a weekly half-hour television interview program. Both appalled her friends in their commercial aspects. On the radio program, Elliott handled the commercials. Listeners were stunned when he reminded them that "Mother uses" a certain kind of bobby pin. Between her comments, he would cut in with a long spiel about a soap, with a punch line that further information about the soap could be obtained by "dropping a card to the Roosevelts."

Billboard wrote in anger at Elliott's poor taste, "The show proves that a boy's best friend is his mother." Neither show continued for long. With the end of this episode she went back to her other activities.

Eleanor Roosevelt was an enormous personality and symbol. Various honors were pressed on her for her deserving work. Though she never went to college, she amassed some Phi Beta Kappa pins. A host of colleges conferred degrees upon her, including the University of Utrecht in Holland and renowned Oxford in England. She lectured at the Sorbonne, France's oldest university, and gave a thoughtful course on the United Nations at Brandeis College in Massachusetts, on whose board of trustees she served. On one occasion the Roosevelts of Holland

[344]

invited her to spend a day with them, a treat she especially enjoyed.

One of the honors she truly treasured was the first award of the Nansen Medal to her in 1954. Named after Dr. Fridjof Nansen, the great Norwegian explorer and heroic High Commissioner for Refugees of the League of Nations, the medal was awarded her for her outstanding work "in behalf of refugees." In addition to her efforts in the United Nations to bar the forced repatriation of refugees, she had intervened personally on innumerable individual cases and had even adopted a score of refugee children. Still another award to please her was the Philip Murray Award from the CIO Community Services Committee in 1955 for "inspiring the American people to act in community affairs." The $5,000 that came with the award she sent to the Warm Springs Foundation. Attached to the check was her note that she would like $2,500 to go to Dr. Jonas Salk, the discoverer of the anti-polio vaccine. He looked tired, she said, and she wanted him to have the money to take a needed vacation.

Chapter Thirty-Five

A s A PLAIN CITIZEN, she discovered while traveling abroad during this period, her position was extraordinary. Everywhere she was treated with almost hysterical deference. The Roosevelt name had almost an hypnotic power overseas. This never changed no matter how many return trips she made to the same place. When she attended the Geneva, Switzerland meeting of her UN Human Rights Commission in December, 1947, it seemed as though the entire city turned out to greet her. Everywhere she stopped traffic. Whenever she emerged outdoors from her hotel, the cheering was reminiscent of the adulation paid a football hero in the United States.

It was the same when she journeyed to London in April, 1948 as the guest of the Pilgrim Society to unveil the ten-foot-high standing statue of Franklin in Grosvenor Square. The king and queen were at her side and Attlee and Churchill spoke. Every speaker tried to outdo the others. Attlee sent her a note the next day: "I wish I could have done more justice to the President in my speech, but I shall never be an orator." Greatly perplexed by her treatment, she wrote to Grace Tully, "I hadn't fully realized how much love and gratitude there was for Franklin in England and in the other countries I visited."

However, the tribute at the London unveiling of Franklin's statue was not for him alone. At her London hotel every man removed his hat whenever she entered or left. And one night as she entered the royal box at the theater, mountainous applause greeted her. The London *News Chronicle* aptly described her charm: "She has walked with kings, but never lost the common touch."

When she showed up at the unveiling of another Franklin Roosevelt statue in Oslo in June, 1950, a crowd of 40,000 persons greeted her. Her simplicity and modesty was moving. She traveled with only two small suitcases and objected to all shows of fuss. "A great man's great wife," an Oslo paper hailed her.

There were other statues and other plaques that many nations and cities heaped upon Franklin's memory. One action that pleased her a great deal was what the people of Nottingham, England did in his honor. Rather than erect another statue, the people there subscribed to a living memorial known as the "Roosevelt Scholars." These are awards to English scientists, businessmen, newsmen, social workers and teachers who are sent to the United States to learn through travel and contact about the ways of Americans and improve British-American understanding. The Roosevelt Scholars program was inaugurated by General Eisenhower in 1945. Mrs. Roosevelt made it a point to receive each Roosevelt Scholar and prepare him with door-opening letters to prominent Americans. In addition, she made sojourns to Nottingham. On a visit in 1957, she gave a magnificent speech on the close relationship between the United States and Britain, although she expressed her opinion that the United Nations did the right thing in upsetting the British-French-Israel Suez adventure. However, she placed the blame for the episode on the United States for having failed to maintain a close relationship with France and England, our oldest allies. She also laughingly warned her listeners that speaking so close to Sherwood Forest was a dangerous undertaking since a midwestern American state had condemned the saga of Robin Hood as "un-American."

Sometimes governments have altered national policy at her entreaty. In 1957 when Morocco held Jews in wretched internment camps and would not permit them to migrate to Israel, she wrote to the Sultan to halt this situation. Two weeks later the Jews were permitted to go to Israel.

Her numerous trips around the globe were more than a mere satisfaction of a basic restlessness that came over her after Franklin's death. Heads of governments clamored for her to come, to get her firsthand advice on their activities and programs. For instance, Juliana of Holland wrote her in 1951, "I wish I could have a talk sometime with you at these most important moments in history." The present Queen Elizabeth of England once sent her a message that was read aloud by the excited master of ceremonies in an English city in the midst of a speech Eleanor was making. "Queen Elizabeth wants to see Mrs. Roosevelt at six P.M." he fairly screamed. The house came down with roars of approval. Because the hour was late, guests at the affair were concerned that she wouldn't get to the palace on time. A committee rushed her to the train station and the engineer was urged to proceed to London posthaste. When the train arrived only minutes late after a mad dash through the countryside, one of the party delivering her to the queen climbed into the engineer's cab and gave the driver a large tip. "What's it for?" the engineer demanded. "No one ever tipped me before in my life."

"It's for bringing Mrs. Roosevelt safely to London," was the hushed reply.

"Mrs. Roosevelt! Why, I would have brought her for nothing," said the engineer, pocketing the money.

Many of her trips were made to raise morale. This was especially true in Holland and France where she lent optimism to a war-weary people. In Paris, for instance, where she went to attend the UN General Assembly's sixth session in the fall of 1951, the French Government pleaded with her to hold regular broadcasts in French to the people of that nation. With Europe then seething with war jitters, she quickly complied.

All of France listened to her broadcasts. In a quiet and simple manner she made complicated issues clear and her reassuring tone did much to dispel the national gloom. All these broadcasts, of course, were sandwiched among the United Nations meetings she attended, as were the many broadcasts she made in German, Spanish and Italian to dispel jitters there, too. A French politician said of her broadcasts, "Her voice has done more to create good will for the United States in Western Europe than that of any other American."

Her most ambitious venture was a round-the-world trip she took in early 1952 after the UN General Assembly finished its sixth session. This was a trip occasioned by a visit of India's Prime Minister Nehru to Hyde Park in October, 1949. Sitting on her floor while he talked with her, he invited her to visit his country. Because of her other responsibilities she could not take him up until 1952, when on a ten-week sweep she explored Lebanon, Jordan, Israel, Syria, Pakistan, Siam, Indonesia and the Philippine Islands as well as his nation.

No sooner had she departed on this earth-girdling trip than Radio Moscow denounced her as "a sworn enemy of peace and democracy" and charged that Dean Acheson had sent her to India and Pakistan "to promote the formation of a police force for combating the people's struggle for freedom." After stopping at Beirut, Damascus, Amman, Jerusalem and Tel Aviv where she held conferences with government leaders until they were talked out, held press interviews and made swift forages into the countryside for heart-to-heart conversations with the local citizens about their problems, she flew to Pakistan for a hectic week and then moved on for a month in India.

At Karachi the Government staged her entry with a dash of color. She climbed into a cart and rode off, pulled by a camel in a procession yanked along by 127 camels. It was a fast week filled with incidentals such as reviewing troops at Karachi, Lahore and Peshawar and carefully staged dinners at the mansions of potentates. However, most of her time was taken reconnoitering the gruesome slums of the country and talking to women's organizations. In a country where women in general were considered little more than chattels, her visit did much to give women a morale boost. In the teeming countryside, though she did not speak the language, Pakistani poor felt she had penetrated into the depths and details of their lives. Although treated everywhere like a visiting head of state, she was always herself and no one thought it incongruous that after a serious discussion with government leaders about their problems, she demonstrated the Virginia reel and the Roger de Coverley dance to Pakistani teen-agers.

There was an early flaw in her visit to Pakistan which she was unaware of at the time, but which she quickly corrected. The Begum Liaquat Ali Khan, widow of Pakistan's late Prime Minister, had invited her to the country. This possessiveness toward Eleanor Roosevelt on the part of her chief rival rankled Pakistan's other female spokesman, Miss Fatima Jinnah, sister of Pakistan's founder. Miss Jinnah immediately announced a boycott of Eleanor and instructed the Girl Scouts whom she headed to do likewise. There were to be only frowns when she came by and no talking to her. However, when Eleanor arrived and was apprised of the sour situation, she called Fatima Jinnah. When her call was refused she persisted with other calls, and finally Miss Jinnah grudgingly permitted her to come visit. Five minutes with Eleanor and Miss Jinnah became a great admirer and the incident was smoothed over.

In India Nehru doted on her like a brother. He had her address the Indian Parliament and opened all doors in India to her. One thing about visitor Eleanor Roosevelt was that in all countries she tried to adapt herself to local customs. In India one of the local ways she picked up was the Hindu posture known as *namaskar*. Memsahibs of the old school ties were always outraged when foreigners bowed their heads and folded their hands, as *namaskar* called for, because they looked upon such actions by outsiders as a condescending sacrilege. However, in Eleanor Roosevelt's case, her *namaskar* pleased them immensely except for those few instances when she dined with fabulously wealthy hosts and *namaskar*ed to low-caste footmen at the dinners.

On one occasion *namaskar* almost proved her undoing. An enormous crowd of Hindus jammed the streets before the Taj Mahal Hotel in Bombay with the hope of catching a glimpse of her. Many lay down in front of her car to halt its getaway. When she emerged from the hotel and climbed into her open car, the cheering was earsplitting. Without a word she solemnly bowed her head and folded her hands. At the sight of her *namaskar*, the crowd went wild and yelled, "Eleanor Roosevelt *zindabad!*" ("Long live Eleanor Roosevelt"). People pressed forward, clawing on each other, to get near her. After a while she lowered her hands, but when she saw that the yelling was continuing without abatement, she returned to her *namaskar*. Every time she lowered her arms, the crowd's roar grew loud in disappointment, and in respect she resumed the Hindu posture. After more than ten minutes of this show of endurance, however, she suddenly swayed in dizziness and her knees buckled. Just as she began falling headlong out of the car, an aide caught her arm and pulled her down into the car seat. "There won't be any *zindabad*," he informed her worriedly, "if you continue to *namaskar*."

What impressed Indians most about her were two things: her unlimited energy at the age of sixty-seven, and the reverence with which everyone treated her. On the subject of her vigor, one of her Indian aides reported a few years later that he still hadn't made up for the exhaustion her almost round-the-clock sprinting had brought on him. In Bombay an Indian textile worker spread more than 100 yards of silk along the path she was walking into a tenement. She could do no wrong. No eyebrows raised when she came to a Bombay reception wearing the same cotton dress and tennis shoes she had worn that day in making the rounds of the city's worst slums. Everywhere the comment on her was that if she were a typical American, then the United States was a wonderful place. "Don't read *Uncle Tom's Cabin* and think it is the United States," she cautioned every audience. "Her visit offset years of Communist propaganda," a reporter observed.

There was not a year since Franklin's death when she did not make a "visiting statesman" trip abroad. In 1953, for instance, her big trip was to Japan, arranged by the Japanese Committee for Intellectual Inter-Exchange. The name Roosevelt, which had been so detested during the war, was now, she found, revered. "Symbol of human rights and the brotherhood of man," one Japanese paper hailed her. Besides a visit with the emperor and empress and a recitation she gave with the Tokyo Symphony Orchestra, both of which endeared her to the Japanese, she went on her usual cross-country spree. A series about her in a Japanese paper noted that in appearance she dressed "as a Japanese midwife does" with her low black shoes and the black leather bag she carried.

"Mrs. Roosevelt represents the conscience of America," the paper went on. Each day in Japan, she held a 30-minute press conference, dictated "My Day," held meetings with various organizations, did some field investigating, and tried to help individuals with personal problems. To her hotel came thousands of letters from Japanese who besought her to spare a few moments to help straighten out their lives. She made a special trip to Hiroshima to talk to the people who had undergone the frightful atomic bombing. In the midst of the outpouring of the miserable personal tales, her interpreter started to cry. She quickly took his hand. "I can understand well without further interpretation," she told him.

One unpleasant experience in Tokyo helped clear up a two-year mystery. Leaving the Labor Ministry Building, she found twenty screaming women who said they were members of the "Women's Democratic Society" and demanded an interview. "I'm sorry," she told them, "I have too tight a schedule today." As she made her way through them to her car, they went wild. "Go home, Yankee! No more Hiroshimas! We women don't want war!" She realized by then that they were Communists. When she got inside her car, they surrounded it and prevented it from moving. One little woman, who didn't look Japanese, pulled and yanked on her clothes in a bold attempt to drag her out of the car. When the guard on duty at the entrance of the building came running, he got hit in the face by this furious woman and a general melee broke out. Finally other guards hurried to the wild scene and helped restore order. "It was insignificant," Eleanor calmly brushed off the entire incident.

However, the scene was not insignificant in one respect. The leader of the Communist women turned out to be Anna Rosenberg Fujikawa, the American-born wife of a Japanese official of the Electrical Workers Union. Two years before when Eleanor's friend, Anna Rosenberg, had been named Assistant Secretary of Defense, witnesses had contested her confirmation in the Senate with the charge that they had known an Anna Rosenberg as a Communist. It had been an embarrassing time, but now the mystery of the Communist Anna Rosenberg had been cleared up with this mauling scene thousands of miles away in Tokyo.

Well into her seventy-third year, she made two important trips in 1957. One was to Salzburg, Austria, the other to Russia. The Salzburg trip brought back memories of her visit to the angry Bonus Army outside of Washington with Louis Howe in 1933. After encouraging the Hungarian uprising against the Communists in 1956, the Government of the United States had promised to accept the 35,000 Hungarian refugees who escaped Marshal Zhukov's tanks. However, while many were awaiting processing, the total was cut to 32,000. While in Glasgow, Scotland, she was informed that the 3,000 stranded refugees of Camp

[351]

Roeder along the highway on the outskirts of Salzburg had gone on a hunger strike.

It was during the afternoon of May 14 that she drove into Camp Roeder with Abba P. Schwartz, a friend. No one was outdoors and an ominous silence hung over the camp. She was well into the camp grounds when she discovered she was being watched from windows. Suddenly a few windows popped open, some heads appeared, then came the surprised call of "Roosevelt" when she was recognized.

They met with her in the large hall used for a dining room. Some came on stretchers. A dignified white-haired man who was their leader had drawn up a hasty petition which he proceeded to read in Hungarian. A woman who translated it into German did such a wretched job that Eleanor corrected her poor German along the way. The touching petition began: "We beg your honor as one of the most respected political personalities of the free world to accept our plea and help in solving our difficult case and please support the request of the mentally and bodily tortured Hungarian refugees. . . ."

"I deeply sympathize with you," she told them, "but I am a private citizen with no way or means of doing things for you in the Government of the United States. Furthermore, I belong to the opposition party. The only medium I have for helping you is through my writing.

"But I do have some advice for you," she told them frankly. "By your strike you have highlighted your problem and brought your plight to the attention of officials. However," she warned them as an understanding but stern mother, "if you want to emigrate to the United States you must get back on a normal diet so you will be able to pass physical requirements."

There was no immediate agreement to end the hunger strike, but it was obvious to accompanying aides that the Hungarians were much impressed with her. When she made a tour of the camp, they followed after her in a body and crowded about staring at her.

Her talk broke the hunger strike, which was called off a few hours after she bade farewell to the Hungarians. Due to her intervention, the camp leader wrote her, they would start eating again. Austrian officials in charge of the camp expressed their gratitude to her for having prevented the tragedy of 3,000 self-starved Hungarians. It threatened to be a half-loaf victory, for when she pleaded by letter with President Eisenhower to take the 3,000 into the United States, he replied that unfortunately Congress had jurisdiction over the problem and not he. However, the next day Mr. Eisenhower ordered the Hungarians in the camp to be paroled into the United States.

As for her trip to the Soviet Union in September, 1957, it was several years overdue. She had first considered such a trip in 1945 as a reporter, but when Harry Hopkins told her she would be treated as an official, she had called the trip off. In 1946 when Elliott met Stalin in Moscow, the first words of the Communist dictator were, "When is your mother coming?" It was not until 1954, when she was out of the United Nations and no longer the subject of vile Soviet slander, that she again contemplated a visit. However, in July when the Soviet Government barred visas to journalists who planned to accompany her, she refused to go. More than a year later Foreign Minister Molotov happened to be on the same ocean flight as she. "You are invited to come to the USSR any time and bring anyone with you," he told her en route.

A desire to combine the trip to Russia with one to Communist China —which the State Department would not approve—delayed her trip for two years after her conversation with Molotov. In her usual feverish activity she barely got away. Shortly before she was to leave she received a letter from a farmer in Pennsylvania who wrote her despairingly of his problem and invited her to come see things for herself. In typical Eleanor Roosevelt fashion, she dropped everything and hurried to spend a weekend with this stranger's family. It was a weekend amid fairly primitive living conditions, including early-day outhouses.

From this, she crossed the Atlantic soon after for Moscow, arriving on September third. Years of bitter Soviet propaganda against her had left no mark on the Russians, for everywhere she was treated with great respect and courtesy. Because of her age, then almost seventy-three, additional irksome courtesies were paid her. This started at the airport when the driver of her car proceeded into the city at a turtle's pace. It turned out that he was driving so slowly "because of my age." "Speed it up," she ordered, and he did, though he didn't like it a bit.

Together with her desire to do a great deal of traveling in the Soviet Union and talk with the people, her chief interest in making the trip was to talk directly with Nikita Khrushchev, the Soviet leader. Unfortunately, Khrushchev was at his vacation home at Yalta and wouldn't set a time for the interview. Pinned down to Moscow while she waited for word from him, she dared take only a quick three-and-a-half-hour jet ride to Tashkent in Central Asia, 2,000 miles away, another swift sortie into the ancient city of Samarkand, close by Tashkent, and a dash to and from Sochi on the Black Sea not far from Yalta. The rest of the time, and against her intentions, she spent her weeks in and about Moscow. Finally, on the twenty-third, after she sent him a wire telling him that she had to leave the Soviet Union in a few days, Khrushchev said he would see her on the twenty-sixth. Later when she was back home, visiting Soviet medical men came to Hyde Park for lunch. "But why didn't you visit our clinics in Siberia and in other places?" they asked her. She told them off in no uncertain words. "Your Mr. Khrushchev saw to that," she snapped at them.

As for her talk with Khrushchev, it was his first talk on a give-and-take basis with someone from the West. On her way to his villa, she stopped first at the Yalta conference palace to see where Franklin had met with Churchill and Stalin and to walk through the dining room, bedroom and study Franklin had used at the Yalta Conference, more than a decade earlier. The setting brought back memories of Franklin's desire to live peacefully and without any loss of honor with the Russian bear.

The short, stocky Khrushchev had asked her to submit questions in advance. He also agreed to permit her to use a tape recorder during their talk. After a two-hour recording, they continued informally. The conversation was serious but friendly. Khrushchev was on the defensive most of the time as she hammered away at the Soviet policy to disrupt and endanger the peace of the world. Chief point of their conversation dealt with the crying need for disarmament. But there was no meeting of minds. "What can I tell you, Mrs. Roosevelt?" he argued. "When we increase our arms, it means that we are afraid of each other."

She whipped off her glasses. "The Soviet Union wishes to spread throughout the world not only through the use of soldiers but through other agents," she charged.

He laughed. "Am I also an agent?"

"You may have been for all I know," she told him caustically.

"You hate Communists," he said to her, as though to put her in the wrong.

At the close of the recorded session, she told him grimly, "You can say we had a friendly conversation, but we differ."

"We didn't shoot at each other," he corrected her.

There was little question that she had made a deep impression on him. She was the mother again and he the errant boy—the bully boy to whom all others had deferred because they feared him. For the first time he had met someone on his home territory who would not accept his pat answers. But only time would tell whether she had made a personal dent in the Iron Curtain.

Chapter Thirty-Six

O N THE SECOND FLOOR of her two-story apartment in a remodeled brownstone house on New York City's East Sixty-second Street, Eleanor Roosevelt bounces out of bed these days at seven A.M. to begin her 18-hour day. With an ability to sleep like a hibernating grizzly bear—without doubts about her past or worries about the future—six hours under light covers refresh her thoroughly. "Besides," she admits matter-of-factly, "it's hard to keep Roosevelts down."

Once up she proceeds enthusiastically through a regime of calisthenics. Outside, the narrow street is early-morning quiet, for the pawnshop, delicatessen and hardware store near her place are still closed. A septuagenarian, she no longer maintains the strenuous exercise routine she once did, nor does she enjoy postdawn horseback riding, a former "must" on her stay-healthy program. Today when pressed for time, she gets her daily dozen out of the way by turning the hard mattress on her bed. So neat is she that a friend observed, "Mrs. R. finds herself unconsciously starting to take the bedclothes off the bed in the morning regardless of where she spent the night." Another indication of increasing years, she no longer takes the ice-cold shower she formerly subjected herself to after exercising. She is also a vitamin hound, plus a firm believer in the value of garlic pills for improving one's memory. Besides all these health measures, once each month she religiously pays calls on her osteopath and chiropodist. Her shoes are low, large and roomy and offer no strain for the inordinate amount of walking she does each day. Though in excellent health, she has most times taken along a physician, Dr. Gurewitsch, on her overseas jaunts to such places as Europe, the Far East and into burly Comrade Khrushchev's resort residence on the Black Sea.

As the day progresses there are other health rules she follows. She neither smokes nor drinks, the latter well understandable because of the ruinous drinking of some members of her family. During prohibition, she refused to serve cocktails to dinner guests. However, Franklin side-stepped her early outrage against liquor by stocking a small room and inviting guests to join him there behind closed doors. Today she maintains a variety of liquor bottles for thirsty guests. Smoking, like bridge playing or gum chewing, she finds repulsive. However, in the White House, she had to steel herself to take an after-dinner puff on a cigarette, for the rule was that women guests could not smoke if the First Lady did not. Despite the impression she makes of being relaxed, she works hard at it. At least twice a day she lies outstretched with her back on the floor, her feet crossed and her arms at her sides. Forcing her mind to go blank, she remains thus for fifteen minutes "sinking" into the floor. This is one of the things she picked up during Franklin's fight to the death against "Blue-Eyed Billy" Sheehan in 1911 when she joined a class in relaxation in Albany.

Unlike her late husband, who growled and barked until he was well into the day's tasks, she is invariably in good humor in the early morning hours. Once dressed, she reads *The New York Times* and the *Herald Tribune* for newsworthy subjects she can philosophize upon in her daily column. With the training Louis Howe gave her in reading only lead paragraphs, she skims through both papers in minutes. Despite her knowledge of several foreign languages, newspapers abroad pose special problems. Even the excellent London *Times* carries only a fraction of the news coverage of the New York papers. And in the Soviet Union with its strict censorship and serious omission of news from other places, she felt she was living on the moon. When she talked with Khrushchev she chided him for this special form of isolation: "When you read a paper in the Soviet Union, you find very little news about the outside world." "Do you say anything good about the Soviet Union in your newspapers?" he snarled back.

Breakfast time is usually at eight-thirty. Not an impressive trencher-woman, she dabbles with her food and eats sparingly. She weighs in at slightly over 140 pounds, which is thin for her tall frame. "I have lost an inch in height in recent years," she admits, "and am only five feet ten inches tall today." Her thinness, which resulted from an unrecouped 30-pound loss during her ten-week trip around the globe in 1952, has had a decidedly aging effect.

Yet with her excellent coloring, clear blue expressive eyes and soft gray hair, she is more than conventionally pretty. In fact, those who meet her for the first time are impressed by the wide dissimilarity between reality and the horrifying photographs that have been one of her trademarks. One relatively important change in her appearance resulted from an automobile accident she had on New York's Saw Mill River

[356]

Parkway in August, 1946. "I went to sleep. It was the sound of the motor. Those poor people!" she explained anxiously to witnesses at the scene when she crossed the center strip while driving and crashed into two cars. As a result of smashing her face against the steering wheel, she damaged two prominent front buckteeth. On their remains, a dentist set straight porcelain caps, which give her face in repose a warm gentle smile instead of the previous seriousness. "Mrs. Roosevelt is becoming beautiful!" a French ambassador said, kissing his fingers when he saw her afterward.

Young in heart and mind, her youthful spirit belies her years. Even college students, to whom she often lectures and joins in discussions, think of her as a contemporary rather than as a relic of a bygone era. In addition, she stands upon her womanly prerogative to fight against mistaken notions that she is older than her years. On one occasion when a television interviewer mistakenly added a year to her age, she was quick to set the record straight in a cold denial rather than let the slip pass.

Despite her own opinion that her birthdays should go unnoticed, friends do not hold the same view. Each birthday has become a gala occasion, the most festive so far coming on her seventieth birthday in October, 1954. To her embarrassment, a thousand guests came to the party in her honor at the Roosevelt Hotel in New York. President Eisenhower sent the gathering the following wire: "Since 1933, when she came upon the national scene as the wife of the President, she has carved out for herself, by her own multitudinous activities, a prominent place in our country's life." Among the guests were Trygve Lie, former United Nations Director General, Bernard Baruch, Dag Hammerskjold, current United Nations chief, Henry Morgenthau and Ralph Bunche. *The New York Times* reported that the dozens of speakers shepherded to microphones by master of ceremonies Edward R. Murrow got a "maximum of adjective mileage into each brief tribute." Most touching was one from Clare Boothe Luce: "Mrs. Roosevelt has done more good deeds on a bigger scale for a longer time than any woman who ever appeared on our public scene. No woman has ever so comforted the distressed, or so distressed the comfortable." Even Eleanor's old opponent, Andrei Vishinsky, came to the party. However, after listening to the solid cannoneering of tributes, Vishinsky rubbed his head wearily and took his eyes off Eleanor. "If I were an American," he remarked to a young man at his table, "I would be a Republican!"

By nine o'clock, Mrs. Roosevelt is ready to begin her day. Several mornings a week she hurries down the avenue to her office in the Carnegie Endowment Building on East Forty-sixth Street which houses the American Association of the United Nations. For the AAUN, Mrs. Roosevelt occupies the seat of chairman of the board of governors. The chief function of the AAUN is to serve as the American branch of an organization now operating in more than forty countries with the purpose of spreading the word about the value of the United Nations and building up public support for it. Mrs. Roosevelt's main responsibility is to organize state and local AAUN chapters. Not only does she receive no pay for her work, but she is also a heavy cash contributor in meeting the AAUN's expenses. So far, from coast to coast almost 175 chapters have come into existence, and she has played a part in organizing almost all of them.

This requires a great deal of traveling and speaking along the circuit to get the new chapters organized and to spur them on to greater activity. In a single year she clocked more than 50,000 miles at this endeavor. She is profoundly earnest about her work with the AAUN and has a prodigious capacity for sustained work in its behalf. As the stellar attraction of this organization, enormous crowds come to hear her make her pitch for the United Nations. When she spoke for the AAUN at Fargo, North Dakota, 6,000 persons showed up for the meeting. At an open-air gathering in Florida, she attracted 11,000 persons, with people coming from places 50 miles away to hear her. She does her speaking off the cuff, except for writing down the first and last lines of each talk, as Louis Howe so carefully trained her. Like a traveling salesman, when she finishes her business in one city, she moves on to the next and makes repeat visits at intervals. Sometimes she flies all night without sleep to be on hand at special ceremonies. Once when her son Franklin, Jr., heard she had sat up all night, he scolded her. "Take it easy, Mummie," he scowled.

She patted his cheek. "Sweetie, I have no aches and pains. I'm not tired. And I'm perfectly happy."

When she doesn't go to her AAUN office, she works out of her apartment, which she rented sight unseen for $425 a month while she was in Japan in 1953. The two floors are cluttered with pictures that more or less tell the story of her life. Covering the walls are pictures of Franklin, her five children, nineteen grandchildren, seven great-grandchildren, and various friends, including Nehru, Madame Chiang, Churchill, Bernard Baruch, the Indonesian leader Sukarno and the man she admires most today in American politics, Adlai Stevenson. Also hanging on a wall are four paintings by Louis Howe.

[358]

There are other tenants in the building on the floors above her two stories, as she is well aware. On one occasion when Adlai Stevenson returned from a trip abroad where he had discussed the continuing international crisis with heads of governments, he called her excitedly. "I must see you immediately and tell you about my trip," he told her. "You are the first person I must talk to."

"Do come, Adlai," she urged.

Shortly before his expected arrival, a rumpus occurred in the outer hall. When she went out to investigate she found a young man who occupied the floor above her. There he stood in a bathrobe pounding and yanking on the locked door that opened on the stairway leading to his apartment. In great agitation he explained that he had come out to see a friend for a moment and the door had slammed locked behind him. "And my bathtub is filling up with water!"

Balding and chubby and wearing a neat but wrinkled business suit, Stevenson arrived on the scene. "Ah! Mrs. Roosevelt," he greeted her.

"Adlai, we must do something," she told him quickly, and explained the mumbling youth's predicament. "We must turn the water off in the basement! Go down and find the pipe and turn the thing on the top."

Adlai rushed down the stairs. Soon came shouts of desperation: "Is it off? Is it off?"

"No, Adlai, the water is still coming!" she yelled back at him.

"Is it off yet?" came a wailing call minutes later from the basement. "I've turned every movable object down here."

Finally, he wearily climbed the stairs, his suit smudged and his hands dirty. The bath water by then was leaking through her ceiling. "I'll go get the locksmith down the avenue," she volunteered and dashed out of the building. Stevenson threw up his hands and left without telling her about his trip.

Her present apartment is her fourth personal place in the city. Her first, which was a three-floor walkup on East Eleventh Street, was her hideaway when detained in the city during Franklin's first two terms. Her brother Hall had an apartment across the hall. The second place, on Washington Square, was the one Franklin planned to use as a writing studio following his long White House stay. After his death she moved to the Park Sheraton Hotel, and from there to her present abode because she wanted a private garden where dogs could romp.

The small bricked-in garden in her rear yard is today the private domain of Duffy, a Scottie sent to her as a present by two Toledo, Ohio youngsters. "I call him 'Mister Duffy,'" she says, "because he is so dignified." Mister Duffy is her third postwar Scottie. The renowned Fala died in his sleep in April, 1952, a few days before his twelfth birthday, and is buried close to the sun dial in the ancestral rose garden in Hyde Park. It was for Fala that she once canceled a hotel reservation in Portland, Maine, when the manager did not seem enthusiastic about having a dog as guest, and moved to a motel. During Fala's last years he enjoyed the companionship of his grandson, Tamas McFala, a large Scottie whose mother, Buttons, and Fala, according to concerned bystanders, "fought like cats and dogs." Tamas lived only a year longer than Fala.

When she works at home, Mrs. Roosevelt operates from a second-floor room filled with books and two desks for herself and her secretary, an Irish colleen named Maureen Corr. While Miss Corr is her chief secretary, Mrs. Roosevelt has another secretary at the AAUN. Miss Corr replaced Tommy, her secretary of a quarter century, who died on the anniversary of Franklin's death in April, 1953. It was Tommy, she admits, who taught her what few rules of punctuation she knows. Inseparable though the two were, Mrs. Roosevelt could never get Tommy to call her Eleanor, even though Tommy could be highly critical of her on occasion. Their standard conversation of many years running went like this:

MRS. ROOSEVELT: "From now on I want you to call me Eleanor."
TOMMY: "Sure, I'll call you that, Mrs. Roosevelt."

The hiring of Miss Corr was in typical Eleanor fashion. Sent over by an employment agency, she did not learn who her prospective employer was until she came face to face with Mrs. Roosevelt. As Tommy before her found the case to be, Miss Corr has learned to her weariness at times how full Mrs. Roosevelt's days are. For instance, what she dictates in three hours takes two full days to transcribe. It is characteristic of Mrs. Roosevelt that she works others as hard as she works herself.

At home, even though her phone number is unlisted in the telephone directory, the telephone jangles all day. Thousands of letters pour in each week, the overwhelming majority coming from strangers who want her help. Often when she herself cannot help she turns to friends to lend aid. Once she wrote to Bernard Baruch to help find a job for a boy who lost both his legs in a train accident while AWOL. If she exhausts all avenues of aid, she writes a sympathetic reply. Not long ago she got a letter from a stateless person to whom she had written a comforting letter a few years earlier when she was unable to help him. Her letter had filled him with new courage, he wrote her. "From then on a great change within myself took place." He had gone on to financial and mental success.

She also maintains a large correspondence with friends she has made over the years. These letters show a real intimacy. For instance, Britain's Queen Mother wrote her when the king died, "It is almost impossible to believe that the king is no longer with us. He was so full of plans and ideas for the future, and a zest for life, and it is hard to think of life without him." Clementine Churchill also writes to keep her informed of her husband's health. After his stroke, she wrote Eleanor, "He is getting stronger every day, but it has been an anxious and sad experience."

Her biggest avalanche of letters in the recent past was on her opposition to the late Senator Joseph R. McCarthy of Wisconsin. Much of this correspondence was unprintable as well as ungrammatical. McCarthy himself never attacked her personally. "This business of acting frightened, that is one thing I hate," she said of his methods and goal. One McCarthy fan, the head of a large American corporation, wrote her every few weeks over a period of months a steady stream of vile letters, in one of which he told her how the sight of her "mug" in the morning paper made him feel like throwing up.

Many of her telephone calls and letters are requests for her to speak or appear at benefits. She culls through them carefully and takes on from 50 to 100 such engagements a year. She records the dates in her little black book and knows in July where she will be the following February. When paid for these talks, as has always been her custom, she turns over the receipts to charity, a sum running on an average of $30,000 a year. Almost as though on a magic carpet she can speak in three such widely separated cities as Baltimore, Chicago and Detroit on the same day and be back in New York that evening. She manages this by careful planning and by not tarrying beyond a set time in any place. Once when her son Jimmy learned that she was to speak at a Washington luncheon, he called her in New York and said he wanted to see her while she was in the capital. Since this would have raised havoc with her tight schedule, she told him it would have to be another time.

Her popularity is so great that political opponents in the cities she visits plead with news photographers to take pictures of them with her. In this way they hope to acquire some of the aura of her liberalism. Vice President Richard Nixon was one who benefited from having his picture taken with her when she came to Washington in 1957 to help dedicate the new B'Nai Brith Building. Her animosity toward Nixon dates back to 1950 when he loosely bandied about Communist charges to defeat Eleanor's friend, Helen Gahagan Douglas, who was opposing him for a U. S. Senate seat. Even later when Nixon reportedly apologized for that campaign by saying he was young then and wanted to win, she said coldly and has said so since, "I don't believe he really has any convictions of his own."

On short trips she rides railroad coaches. She goes air coach across the Atlantic, sitting up all night and reading or talking. She claims that she rides air coach across the Atlantic instead of taking a berth because she is too tall to dress herself in a small cubicle. Friends know her as a woman who stints on herself in order to have more money to spend on others. In the White House she prided herself on keeping five separate sets of books, but actually money management has always bewildered her. Her income tax statements are always in the government's favor because the poor records she keeps do not show all the legitimate deductible expenditures to which she is entitled. Franklin, on the other hand, spent late hours when he was President working over his income tax statement to save himself five dollars. "Members of her family are always coming to her to be bailed out of tight financial pickles," says a friend. "Besides, she keeps several acquaintances—and some strangers—alive with regular money handouts."

In addition, she needs money for the hundreds of gifts she showers on various individuals each year. All of her children, grandchildren (who call her "grandmère"), great-grandchildren, cousins, uncles, aunts and friends benefit from her largesse. Once she gave her son Jimmy a $12,500 bauble that figured prominently in the divorce proceedings against him by his second wife. She still sends flowers to Jimmy's first wife, Betsy, now the wife of the American Ambassador to England. Generally she sends presents in inverse ratio to the recipient's financial status. A case in point was her wedding present to the royal Elizabeth and Philip in 1948. Princess Elizabeth wrote her from Windsor Castle in March, "Dear Mrs. Roosevelt, I feel I would like to write and tell you how delighted I am to receive your wonderful wedding present of twelve bath towels, and also dusters and cloths."

In the city she averages about 15 to 20 appointments a day, all of them coming off as though she had waited all day for each visitor. When she has callers at her apartment, she generally discusses their business with them in her first-floor living room. She sits in an armchair that faces the pillow-strewn sofa each visitor occupies. She wears a hearing aid for her right ear in her glasses, though she can hear a private whisper across the room whenever she wishes. Her expressive eyes she has willed to the Eye Bank. Normally during a business conversation she wears an expression of deep concern and concen-

[362]

tration. Her nervous system is unusually steady and she may sit without stirring except to cross and uncross her long fingers.

When the business is settled she does not prolong a conversation. She will offer a calm summation, flash a friendly smile and walk her visitor to the door for a quick good-by handshake. Anything she promises to do she puts into motion the same day.

This hectic schedule has been going on for so long that it has become her way of life. In 1954 when she planned to go to the Soviet Union, she kept her little black engagement book empty for the time she expected to be away. When the trip fell through, she was suddenly faced with the prospect of an empty month. Another person might have jumped at the chance to get a rest, but not Eleanor. Friends observed that within a few days she had grown jumpy. The inaction gnawed at her innards. With a burst of energy she took on many of the requests she had turned down and was happily booked solidly again within the week.

Generally the lunch hour in New York City finds her behind a microphone and looking out into a sea of women members of one organization or another. Her short talks on national or international issues, peace, disarmament, refugee problems, slum clearance, women and youth problems, education and matters of morals have been the high point of hundreds of conventions. She maneuvers about the city to these luncheons by subway, bus or taxi, and is embarrassed when people recognize her, which occurs almost all the time. When a girl on a bus jumped up breathlessly and offered Mrs. Roosevelt her seat, Eleanor's reaction was that this courtesy was shown her because she is old. New York taxi drivers, notoriously hard-bitten individuals, drive her about as though she were a case of eggs.

From two to four P.M. each day she closets herself with her secretary back in her apartment to dictate her "My Day" column and any other writing chore she is currently engaged with. Her dictation is still a dramatic recitation replete with gestures and changing facial expressions. Her concentration while dictating is complete. On one occasion she spoke out her "My Day" column while taking a bath. Unnoticed by her, the water overflowed the top of the tub and flooded the room.

The nature of her column has undergone a further change in recent years. Today she writes almost entirely on issues rather than on her personal doings. Hard-hitting and controversial, she seldom lapses into the Eleanor of old who wrote one time, "I think spring and autumn are my favorite seasons," and then added, for fear she might offend some readers, "There's beauty, of course, in every season." She still has trouble with punctuation and admits to a terrible time when it comes to avoiding split infinitives. "There are two things in life I would like to do," she confesses, "—to write a novel and a play. The things that happen in life are not so important as what they do to people and that is what makes them of such extraordinary interest."

After her column is finished, she often has a tea to attend. She can still shake a thousand hands without suffering any discomfort. Once when she spoke at a university, the college president asked her to shake hands with her audience before and after her talk. When she told him that she would not have time for all this, he replied in all seriousness, "If you cancel anything, I'd rather you shook hands and didn't give the lecture."

Sometimes there are radio and television shows in which she participates. She prefers making extemporaneous talks. "I find that if I do not think about what I am saying, I become bored with my own conversation." She is always relaxed for her appearances on the air and her friendly easy manner has moved technician after technician to say, "Mrs. Roosevelt is a doll." She has also made some recordings and is sometimes referred to by phonograph record moguls as the "Peter and the Wolf" lady. All this started in August, 1950 when Serge Koussevitsky asked her to narrate "Peter and the Wolf" with the Boston Symphony Orchestra at Tanglewood. "But I don't know any music and I am unfamiliar with the score," she protested.

However, he would not accept a refusal and she went on. In preparation she spent hours working out the musical cues and rehearsing with the orchestra. Not only did she make a recording in private with Koussevitsky's orchestra but she also recited Prokofiev's piece before 9,000 listeners one night on the lawn at Tanglewood. The fee she earned went quickly to the Berkshire Music Association and to another of her charities. A critic who caught her Tanglewood performance said, "She sounded like grandmother reading a pleasant little story to her grandchildren." In 1953 she delighted the Japanese with a repeat performance with the Tokyo Symphony Orchestra, and in March, 1956, despite a heavy cold, she did "Peter and the Wolf" with the local Dutchess County Philharmonic Orchestra, once for children and a few days later for Hyde Park and Poughkeepsie adults.

Frequently she squeezes out spare minutes from her afternoon time tube to drop in on people who need comforting. The range of people who do is startling. Once she visited a boy in a mental hospital when his mother, a stranger to her, wrote, "I know a visit from you would do him so much good." Another time when she was in England, in the spring of 1957, she comforted sad Queen Elizabeth whose son Charles had had his tonsils and adenoids removed the preceding day.

In the city she may have guests in for dinner or she may go out to a formal dinner where she is expected to speak again. Sometimes she varies this routine with an evening at the theater or at a concert. When she started coming frequently to affairs at the Waldorf, the manager began calling her insistently to find out which entrance she planned to use. "Nonsense," she told him, "I know my way around the Waldorf as well as my own home." As a result of her unco-operative nature, an assistant manager is stationed at each door on those nights to make sure she gets a royal welcome.

Her apartment has no dining room, a matter of deep concern to her children because of the inappropriateness of serving world-famous guests by setting plates on their laps. Today, thanks to her offspring, guests have aluminum folding tables to balance their coffee cups on instead of wobbly knees. She is an excellent hostess and tells amusing stories, generally of embarrassing experiences that have happened to her in her past. She has also memorized an extraordinary amount of poetry and on short notice recites Milton's sonnet "On His Blindness" without flaw.

Though she is difficult to know intimately, many consider themselves to be her close friends. Actually, despite her continual stance in the public limelight, she is essentially the same shy person she was in her childhood. She admits today that her greatest fault is still the one she had as a girl—"my desire for approbation from those I love." She is in essence a lonely person who takes refuge in crowds.

Of those who feel especially close to Eleanor Roosevelt today, are Mary Lasker, Anna Rosenberg, Trude Lash and Adele Levy, an active worker on world health problems and a member of the Julius Rosenwald clan that built the Sears, Roebuck mail order business to financial prominence. Another was Sumner Welles, of whom she said fondly, "My mother and his mother were good friends." Due to their long association when she was in the White House and he in the State Department, Mr. Welles helped her out in many ways. For instance, she got him to keep an eye on her aged Cousin Susie, Mrs. Henry Parrish, with whom Eleanor lived during her debutante period shortly after the turn of the century. In one of his private-eye letters he told Eleanor that "she [Cousin Susie] rarely sees any of the old friends who are left." He told of an old friend who got her on the phone only to have her bellow, "I thought you were dead!" When Cousin Susie finally died, she left Eleanor $90,000 plus her exquisite jewelry. The Dowager Marchioness Lady Reading, who was her guide on her 1942 trip in wartime England, is also a close friend.

"The Sergeant," as The Dowager Marchioness is called behind her back, heads the Women's Voluntary Services today in England and still takes protective charge of Eleanor whenever she is in the British Isles, to the disgruntlement of Sir Campbell Stuart, head of the Pilgrim Society. Adlai Stevenson is often in her company, and though she insists that the country needs him as President, she does not believe he could be elected if he ran for a third time.

Then there is Bernard Baruch, well into his eighties, who drops in often. At public affairs he holds her hand and busses her cheek. One time when he thought she would be there, he sent her flowers in care of the French Embassy in Washington. The accompanying card read: "My affectionate thoughts always with you and him." "When I arrived at the Embassy," he wrote Eleanor later in embarrassment, "Madame Bonnet thanked me for the flowers I had sent her. I wonder what she is going to think when she reads the card." Baruch helps bail out many of her shaky charities. He is also the person she turns to most often for advice. One crisis that he helped her resolve was how to dispose of the $25,000 Vargas aquamarine given her and Franklin by President Vargas of Brazil in 1936. In 1947 when Drew Pearson claimed that she had no right to cut up the stone and sell its pieces to raise money for charity, the Vargas aquamarine was featured on front pages from coast to coast. Upon Baruch's advice, to avoid unfavorable publicity she turned the stone over to the Franklin D. Roosevelt Library in Hyde Park. Here it is now featured in a case for the visiting millions who come to the library. Nevertheless, she and Baruch do have minor misunderstandings. Once when she told a group that he had said, "Each family has a problem child," he was quick to write her a note denying he had ever said it.

On weekends, summer days and holidays Eleanor leaves the city for her Val-Kill cottage in Hyde Park. Here she is a different person, emerging into a personality that is difficult to relate to the woman with whom the entire world is acquainted. She doesn't need an alarm clock, but gets up instead with the postdawn barking of the dogs. She does her own shopping, driving to the local stores in an open convertible. Back home she puts away the ironed linens. She knows everyone in the village, stops to talk to one man about his new son and to a worried woman about her sick child. The daughter of the woman who runs the local fruit stand was suffering from a blood disease, so she quietly took her to New York for examination and bore all the expenses herself.

Val-Kill is the place for the long walks she can't take in the city. Through the groves that Franklin planted, she lopes along with a long stride, her body angled forward like a skier. No one can keep up with her. One morning two gentlemen visitors offered to hike with her. A half hour later they were back. "We lost sight of her," one puffed. During a blizzard on one occasion she was scheduled to make a radio address in Poughkeepsie five miles away. Unable to get her car out, she cut across the heavy snow in the field to the highway where she hitchhiked her way into the city. After the show she returned the same way, utilizing the holes in the deep snow she had made on her way out to get back to the house.

Val-Kill is also the place for swimming. She is still a good swimmer and a graceful diver. Even though her pool is spring-fed, it has a special filtering apparatus installed on orders from the Secret Service when Franklin was President. Her pond at Val-Kill was dredged as a birthday present from FDR in 1938. "I will take you cruising on it," he wrote her endearingly. The next year he sent her a torn piece of wrapping paper on which he wrote his birthday greeting, and attached to it was a check to seed the lawn by the swimming pool.

There are no elegant appurtenances at Val-Kill. Its architecture is mongrel, though it is not cramped like her city apartment. Old heavy furniture is scattered through its twelve rooms and the rugs are worn. There is, however, a cheery porch which she uses for a dining room. Pictures are everywhere here, too. She points proudly at a picture in one cluster and says, "That's Uncle Ted." His fiery eyes still flash. In the same cluster she acknowledges another picture with, "That is Johnny Boettiger. He was one of my favorite persons." Boettiger's ending was sad. Shortly after he and daughter Anna were divorced, he remarried. Later, he suffered a nervous breakdown and leaped to his death from a New York hotel window.

Franklin's "dream" cottage over the hill from Val-Kill, known as "Top Cottage," is no longer in the family. Elliott, who lived there when he was married to actress Faye Emerson, sold it. Nor does Mrs. Roosevelt own her own place, for she has willed it to Elliott. "My son Elliott owns all the land there, and at my death my house and ground immediately adjoining revert to him."

Mrs. Roosevelt maintains loose contacts with her brood. She never interferes with their family life or activities except when they are in trouble and come to her for aid. Daughter Anna, now past fifty and a grandmother, lives in Syracuse with her third husband, Dr. James Halstead. James, who is now a congressman from California, lives with his third wife. On the big Rolling R. Ranch in Meeker, Colorado that is owned by Minnewa, his fourth wife, lives Elliott. Mrs. Roosevelt's

[367]

two youngest sons, Franklin, Jr., and John, live close by her. After a short political career and a noisy session of lobbying for the Trujillo government in the Dominican Republic, Franklin, Jr., has settled down with his second wife to the life of a gentleman farmer in Dutchess County. He is also a wholesaler of foreign-make cars. John, who at six feet six inches is the tallest of her children, is his mother's neighbor at Val-Kill. Although he is the only Roosevelt who has not been divorced, he has not endeared himself to the political Roosevelts because he is a Republican.

At Val-Kill, Mrs. Roosevelt's overflowing guests generally constitute an odd assortment. She thinks nothing of mixing prime ministers, ambassadors, United Nations officials, and successful business people and writers with college students, teen-age children of friends, and unemployed actors. When they arrive, she usually rushes outdoors to help carry their luggage in. If they want to see the sights, she chauffeurs them about. As a hostess she caters to their every whim, an activity that infuriates some of her friends who think this beneath her. The summer before she went to interview Khrushchev she spent her days at Val-Kill chauffeuring a teen-ager back and forth from the local summer theater. "Someone had to do it," Mrs. Roosevelt explained.

Whenever she is at Val-Kill, Mrs. Roosevelt always looks in at the Franklin D. Roosevelt Library and Museum near Sara Roosevelt's house. She comes hurrying over in her convertible and walks through the rooms where mementos of her life with Franklin are on exhibition. It is already so far behind her that it all seems to belong to a long-ago past. Yet it has an immediacy to her when friends and relatives come there with her. One sad visit came when Franklin's favorite uncle, Frederic Delano, arrived at the library a short time before his passing in 1953. The library meant nothing to his tired mind. "Come," he said, "let's go over to the house and talk with Franklin." To him Franklin was still alive. Another individual, an uncle of Eleanor's, tells her each time he comes that he has been in spiritual contact with Franklin.

Heads of state still trek to Hyde Park to see where Franklin lived and where he is buried. When the Shah of Iran came to the United States a few years ago, he visited the FDR museum to see the fine Persian rug his government had given Franklin. Franklin had installed the rug on the floor of the President's Room at the museum, a room where he held many war conferences and wartime Fireside Chats. "If you will notice," the Shah remarked to Mrs. Roosevelt proudly, "the thousands of tiny knots in the rug were tied by the hands of seven- and eight-year-olds."

[368]

"Seven- or eight-year-old children!" she said, outraged.

An aide quickly whispered to the Shah. "Oh, we have child labor laws *now*," the Shah assured her hastily.

Tourists who spy her at the library and museum can hardly believe their eyes. Once while she was talking to a group of her guests under the big tree outside the library, an old heavy colored woman ambled past on the sidewalk. Catching sight of Mrs. Roosevelt, her eyes widened and she circled the group, coming up behind her idol. Then with a swoop she fell forward, throwing her arms around Mrs. Roosevelt's shoulders. Without faltering in her talk, Eleanor disentangled herself and gave the woman a friendly smile. Another time a poor-looking couple from the Midwest drove up in a jalopy and spotted her outside the library building. "Mrs. Roosevelt!" they shouted. "You must take a picture with us." She agreed when she saw their faces. A ten-minute scramble followed while they hunted for their box camera. Finally when they came back to report sadly that they couldn't find it, she joined them in hunting through all their belongings in their car. She found it eventually and the picture was taken, though she was certain it would be another poor likeness of her.

When it is cold in Hyde Park, she sometimes takes her cross-country hikes and comes to the library in the tweed coat Franklin bought her in Scotland on their honeymoon. The coat has a Sherlock Holmes-type hood and makes her look quite young. The cloth is not the least worn even though it has been put to heavy use for more than half a century. Its hemline has been raised and lowered a dozen times in keeping with changing styles.

There is another tweed coat, orange-red in color, that she wears when the weather is bitterly cold. This coat also has a long story. When Franklin was governor of New York, a woman whom he did not know occupied herself sending him love letters. For weeks on end she posted herself on the stairs of the capitol to catch a glimpse of him. Finally she wrote him a letter telling him that she would kill herself if he didn't make her acquaintance. Perturbed, he asked Eleanor to do something about the woman. Eleanor sought her out and took her in hand and won the assurance from her that she would not commit suicide. Though Franklin never met the woman, she later sent him a bolt of cloth as a present. From this he made a suit and Eleanor fashioned the orange-red tweed coat.

At Hyde Park Eleanor also engages in the charity that is dearest to her heart. This is the Wiltwyck School located on 350 acres just across the Hudson River at Esopus. Wiltwyck, a nonsectarian, interracial and non-punitive institution, was founded originally in 1937 under the auspices of the Protestant Episcopal City Mission. Boys aged eight to twelve are committed to Wiltwyck as neglected or delinquent children, either by New York City's Department of Welfare or the Children's Court. They represent New York's "most deprived and damaged children for whom there is no other institutional care available." Nor does care for these boys stop with treatment at Wiltwyck. While the boys are at the school, caseworkers in the city work with their families to modify their attitudes and change the families' existence so that the boys won't revert once they leave Wiltwyck and return home.

These are "lost" little souls, almost all of them Negro boys coming from squalid Harlem homes, and as such they are dear to Eleanor's big heart. She leads the band in raising money to meet the school's expenses. Soon after she starts a conversation with anyone, she is bound to solicit a contribution for Wiltwyck. She is herself one of the school's largest contributors, turning over a large share of her lecture earnings each year to her boys.

In a quiet way the school has worked wonders with its boys. Its most famous graduate is Floyd Patterson, currently the world's heavyweight boxing champion, who came originally to Wiltwyck lost, bewildered and out of touch with reality. That he found himself while at Wiltwyck is a matter of inspiration to the hundreds of other youngsters who have passed through the school.

In the summers she has the boys of Wiltwyck at her Val-Kill place for picnics. Often she invites internationally known persons to come and help entertain the hundred youngsters. At those gatherings she is a whirlwind of service, rushing about to prepare the food and wait on the boys. Under the glare of the hot sun, her hair is soon falling over her wet face and her white tennis shoes are scuffed green by her long swift strides through the grass. All the hotdog rolls are buttered with her loving care. Once when the embarrassed director of Wiltwyck tried to dissuade her from this menial task, she looked up from her work with a challenging expression and said, "When the King and Queen of England were here I buttered the rolls. Why should I do less for the boys from Wiltwyck?" He had no answer.

So Mrs. Roosevelt goes seriously on her charming and highly useful path through life. Certainly she has been wrong on occasion when she depended on her emotions instead of her capable head. She still is more apt to say "I feel" instead of "I think." This has led her to accept some among her vast collection of underdogs who have been unworthy of her time and effort, and who have brought her more criticism than has been heaped on the head of any other American woman in history. There have been smug professors who have scoffed at her for not having read as much as they. There are still politicians who turn blue with rage at the mention of her name because she wielded influence without going through the pain of an election.

Despite these pinpricks, her unique position as the most renowned and admired woman in American history is assured. The like of Eleanor Roosevelt is not apt to appear again.

Up her long climb to the summit, the prophetic words written sixty-five years ago by Uncle Ted's wife still echo: "The ugly duckling may turn out to be a swan."

Bibliography

THE CHIEF SOURCE of material for this book came from the personal papers, record books and voluminous correspondence of Mrs. Roosevelt, which she so graciously permitted me to examine. Another basic reference source was the enormous collection of Franklin D. Roosevelt papers and letters maintained by the F.D.R. Library at Hyde Park, New York. For extending me every courtesy and for their learned aid, I must acknowledge a great debt to Mr. Herman Kahn, director of the F.D.R. Library, and his excellent staff. Still another vital source resulted from conversations with a host of individuals too numerous to detail.

Secondary sources I utilized ran into the thousands of publications. Below are listed some of the books examined. However, this is only a small part of the literature. Special reference should be made to Mrs. Roosevelt's "My Day" columns, which have been running since the end of 1935; her monthly columns for the *Woman's Home Companion, Ladies' Home Journal* and *McCall's;* her radio addresses and talks before various organizations; her weekly press conferences while in the White House; her many magazine articles. Use was also made of the *New York Times,* London *Times,* translations of Norwegian and Japanese newspapers, UN and U. S. State Department materials, hundreds of excellent magazine articles and, of course, the columns of Mrs. Roosevelt's implacable derider, the irrepressible Westbrook Pegler. Some of the useful books are:

Black, Ruby, *Eleanor Roosevelt,* 1940.
Burns, James M., *Lion and the Fox,* 1956.
Carmichael, Donald S., *F.D.R., Columnist,* 1947.
Carter, John F., *The New Dealers,* 1934.
Churchill, Sir Winston, *Second World War,* 6 vols., 1948–1953.
Connally, Tom, and Steinberg, Alfred, *My Name Is Tom Connally,* 1954.
Creel, George, *Rebel at Large,* 1947.
Daniels, Jonathan, *End of Innocence,* 1954.
Daniels, Josephus, *Tar Heel Editor,* 1939.
Dows, Olin, *Franklin Roosevelt at Hyde Park,* 1949.
Farley, James A., *Jim Farley's Story,* 1948.
Flynn, Edward J., *You're the Boss,* 1947.
Flynn, John T., *Roosevelt Myth,* 1956.

Forrestal, James, and Millis, Walter, *Forrestal Diaries*, 1951.
Freidel, Frank, *Franklin D. Roosevelt*, 3 vols., 1952–1956.
Furman, Bess, *Washington By-Line*, 1949.
Gunther, John, *Roosevelt in Retrospect*, 1950.
Hagedorn, Hermann, *Roosevelt Family of Sagamore Hill*, 1954.
Hatch, Alden, *Citizen of the World*, 1948.
Helm, Edith, *Captains and Kings*, 1954.
Hoover, Herbert C., *Memoirs*, 3 vols., 1951–1952.
Hoover, Irwin (Ike), *Forty-Two Years in the White House*, 1934.
Hull, Cordell, *Memoirs*, 2 vols., 1948.
Ickes, Harold, *Secret Diary*, 3 vols., 1953–1954.
Jones, Jesse, *Fifty Billion Dollars*, 1951.
Kilpatrick, Carroll, *Roosevelt and Daniels*, 1952.
Kiplinger, W. M., *Washington Is Like That*, 1942.
Leahy, William D., *I Was There*, 1950.
Lindley, Ernest, *Franklin D. Roosevelt*, 1931.
Longworth, Alice R., *Crowded Hours*, 1933.
McIntyre, Ross T., *White House Physician*, 1946.
Moley, Raymond, *After Seven Years*, 1939.
Nesbitt, Henrietta, *White House Diary*, 1948.
Partridge, Bellamy, *Roosevelt Family in America*, 1931.
Perkins, Frances, *The Roosevelt I Knew*, 1946.
Pollard, James, *Presidents and the Press*, 1947.
Reilly, Michael F., *Reilly of the White House*, 1947.
Robinson, Corinne R., *My Brother Theodore Roosevelt*, 1932.
Robinson, Edgar, *The Roosevelt Leadership*, 1955.
Roosevelt, Eleanor, *This Is My Story*, 1939.
—— *If You Ask Me*, 1946.
—— *Personal Recollections, Franklin D. Roosevelt and Hyde Park*, 1949.
—— *This I Remember*, 1949.
—— *India and the Awakening East*, 1953.
—— *It Seems to Me*, 1954.
—— and De Witt, William, *UN: Today and Tomorrow*, 1953.
—— and Hickok, Lorena, *Ladies of Courage*, 1954.
Roosevelt, Elliott, and Roosevelt, Eleanor, *Hunting Big Game in the Eighties*, 1933.
Roosevelt, Elliott, *FDR: His Personal Letters*, 4 vols., 1947–1950.
Roosevelt, Franklin D., and Rosenman, Samuel I., *Public Papers and Addresses of Franklin D. Roosevelt*, 1938–1950.
Roosevelt, G. Hall, *Odyssey of an American Family*, 1939.
Roosevelt, Mrs. James, *My Boy Franklin*, 1933.
Roosevelt, Theodore, *Autobiography*, 1913.
Rosenman, Samuel I., *Working with Roosevelt*, 1952.
Schlesinger, Arthur, Jr., *Age of Roosevelt*, 1957.

Schriftgiesser, Karl, *Amazing Roosevelt Family*, 1942.
Sherwood, Robert E., *Roosevelt and Hopkins*, 1948.
Starling, Edmund, *Starling of the White House*, 1946.
Steeholm, Clara, *House at Hyde Park*, 1950.
Stiles, Lela, *Man Behind Roosevelt*, 1954.
Timmons, Bascom, *Garner of Texas*, 1948.
Tugwell, Rexford G., *Democratic Roosevelt*, 1957.
Tully, Grace, *FDR, My Boss*, 1949.
Vandenberg, Arthur, and Vandenberg, Arthur, Jr., *Private Papers of Senator Vandenberg*, 1952.
Warner, Emily Smith, *Happy Warrior*, 1956.
Whittelsey, C. B., *Roosevelt Genealogy, 1649–1902*, 1902.

Index

[377]

[380]

DATE DUE

APR 15 '84			
DEC 18 '84			
MAR 22 '88			
4-5-88			
SEP 25 '89			
OCT 1 0 '89			
FEB 20 '90			
MAR 22 '90			
APR 22 '92			
JUL 23 '93			

HIGHSMITH 45-220